David Michalek

ALEX ROSS has been the music critic for *The New Yorker* since 1996. He is the author of the international bestseller *The Rest Is Noise: Listening to the Twentieth Century*, which was a finalist for the 2008 Pulitzer Prize and won a 2007 National Book Critics Circle Award. In 2008, he was named a MacArthur Fellow.

ALSO BY ALEX ROSS

The Rest Is Noise: Listening to the Twentieth Century

Additional Praise for *Listen to This*

"Running through every piece is a spirit of adventure, common sense, joy, and, ultimately, engagement." —Alan Moores, *The Seattle Times*

"An impressive but never showy blend of historical reportage and thoughtful analysis . . . The triumph of *Listen to This* is that Ross dusts off music that's centuries old to reveal the passion and brilliance that's too often hidden from a contemporary audience. It's a joy for a pop fan or a classical aficionado."
—Alan Light, *The New York Times Book Review*

"Hugely enjoyable . . . offers fresh and unexpected stimulation at every turn." —Charles Hazlewood, *The Guardian* (London)

"Such a pleasure to read . . . a critic with an unusually wide frame of reference." —*The Economist*

"It is rare to find a music critic who can write as authoritatively about Mozart and Schubert as he can about Radiohead and Björk. . . . [*Listen to This*] is a reminder that a love of music need not—nay, should not—be bound by category." —*Toronto Star*'s "Ten Best Books of the Year"

"Lively and fascinating . . . Ross has a wonderful knack for catching the human gesture embedded in a musical phrase."
—Ivan Hewett, *The Daily Telegraph* (London)

"*Listen to This* reveals . . . [Ross] to be the exact kind of critic his era needs . . . In other words, he's a thinker with style and a stylist who thinks. . . . Alex Ross is one of the great civilized pleasures anywhere on any subject." —Jeff Simon, *The Buffalo News* (Editor's Choice)

LISTEN TO THIS

ALEX ROSS

PICADOR

FARRAR, STRAUS AND GIROUX
NEW YORK

www.picadorusa.com
www.twitter.com/picadorusa • www.facebook.com/picadorusa

Picador® is a U.S. registered trademark and is used by Farrar, Straus and Giroux
under license from Pan Books Limited.

For book club information, please visit
www.facebook.com/picadorbookclub or e-mail marketing@picadorusa.com.

The following essays were originally published, in slightly different form, in *The New Yorker*: "Listen to This" (February 16, 2004); "Infernal Machines," which incorporates portions of two *New Yorker* articles, "The Record Effect" (June 6, 2005) and "The Well-Tempered Web" (October 22, 2007); "The Storm of Style" (July 24, 2006); "Orbiting" (August 20, 2001), originally as "The Searchers"; "The Anti-Maestro" (April 30, 2007); "Great Soul" (February 3, 1997); "Emotional Landscapes" (August 23, 2004), originally as "Björk's Saga"; "Symphony of Millions" (July 7, 2008); "Song of the Earth" (May 12, 2008); "Verdi's Grip" (September 24, 2001); "Almost Famous" (May 21, 2001); "Edges of Pop," which incorporates four *New Yorker* articles, "Grand Illusions" (May 19, 2003), "The Art of Noise" (July 13, 1998), "Eighty-two Very Good Years" (May 25, 1998), and "Generation Exit" (April 25, 1994); "Learning the Score" (September 4, 2006); "Voice of the Century" (April 13, 2009); "The Music Mountain" (July 29, 2009); "The End of Silence" (October 4, 2010), originally as "Searching for Silence"; "I Saw the Light" (May 10, 1999), originally as "The Wanderer"; and "Fervor" (September 25, 2006).

Portions of "Blessed Are the Sad" originally appeared in *The New Republic* as "Why Is Light Given" (March 23, 1998).

Owing to limitations of space, all illustration credits and acknowledgments for permission to reprint lyrics can be found on pages 379–380.

Designed by Jonathan D. Lippincott

The Library of Congress has cataloged the Farrar, Straus and Giroux edition as follows:

Ross, Alex, 1968–
    Listen to this / Alex Ross.— 1st ed.
        p. cm.
    Includes bibliographical references and index.
    ISBN 978-0-374-18774-3
    1. Musical criticism.   2. Popular music and art music.   3. Music—History and criticism.   I. Title.
    ML3785 .R67 2010
    780—dc22

                                                                2010010283

Picador ISBN 978-0-312-61068-5

First published in the United States by Farrar, Straus and Giroux

First Picador Edition: November 2011

FOR DANIEL ZALEWSKI

AND

DAVID REMNICK

. . . I follow with my eyes the proud and futile wake. Which, as it bears me from no fatherland away, bears me onward to no shipwreck.

—Samuel Beckett, *Molloy*

CONTENTS

PART III

PREFACE

Writing about music isn't especially difficult. Whoever coined the epigram "Writing about music is like dancing about architecture"—the statement has been attributed variously to Martin Mull, Steve Martin, and Elvis Costello—was muddying the waters. Certainly, music criticism is a curious and dubious science, its jargon ranging from the wooden ("Beethoven's Fifth begins with three Gs and an E-flat") to the purple ("Beethoven's Fifth begins with fate knocking at the door"). But it is no more dubious than any other kind of criticism. Every art form fights the noose of verbal description. Writing about dance is like singing about architecture; writing about writing is like making buildings about ballet. There is a fog-enshrouded border past which language cannot go. An art critic can say of Mark Rothko's *Orange and Yellow* that it consists of an area of yellow paint floating above an area of orange paint, but what good does that do for someone who has never seen a Rothko? The literary critic can copy out a few lines from Wallace Stevens's "Esthétique du Mal"—

> And out of what sees and hears and out
> Of what one feels, who could have thought to make
> So many selves, so many sensuous worlds . . .

—but when you try to spell out the meaning of those lines, when you try to voice their silent music, another hopeless dance begins.

So why has the idea taken hold that there is something peculiarly inexpressible about music? The explanation may lie not in music but in ourselves. Since the mid-nineteenth century, audiences have routinely adopted music as a sort of secular religion or spiritual politics, investing it with messages as urgent as they are vague. Beethoven's symphonies promise political and personal freedom; Wagner's operas inflame the imaginations of poets and demagogues; Stravinsky's ballets release primal energies; the Beatles incite an uprising against ancient social mores. At any time in history there are a few composers and creative musicians who seem to hold the secrets of the age. Music cannot easily bear such burdens, and when we speak of its ineffability we are perhaps protecting it from our own inordinate demands. For even as we worship our musical idols we also force them to produce particular emotions on cue: a teenager blasts hip-hop to psych himself up; a middle-aged executive puts on a Bach CD to calm her nerves. Musicians find themselves, in a strange way, both enshrined and enslaved. In my writing on music, I try to demystify the art to some extent, dispel the hocus-pocus, while still respecting the boundless human complexity that gives it life.

Since 1996, I've had the huge good fortune to serve as the music critic of *The New Yorker*. I was twenty-eight when I got the job, too young by any measure, but I strove to make the most of my luck. From the start, my editors encouraged me to take a wide view of the musical world: not simply to cover star performers at Carnegie Hall and the Metropolitan Opera but also to lurk in smaller spaces and listen for younger voices. Following my distinguished predecessors Andrew Porter and Paul Griffiths, I've maintained that modern composers deserve the same lavish treatment that is given to canonical masters—a conviction that led to my first book, *The Rest Is Noise: Listening to the Twentieth Century*. I've also periodically detoured into pop and rock, although, having grown up in classical music, I feel unsure of my footing outside it. In all, I approach music not as a self-sufficient sphere but as a way of knowing the world.

Listen to This combines various *New Yorker* articles, several of them substantially revised, with one long piece written for the occasion. The book begins with three aerial surveys of the musical landscape, encompassing both classical and pop terrain. The first chapter, from which the title comes, began as a preface to *The Rest Is Noise*, although I soon realized that it had to be a freestanding essay. It is a kind of memoir turned manifesto, and when it was published it elicited an unexpectedly strong response from readers, with hundreds of letters and e-mails arriving over several months. Many of these messages came from music students and recent conservatory graduates who were struggling to reconcile the grand tradition in which they had been schooled with the pop culture in which they had come of age. The intense frustration that they and I feel in the face of the pince-nez stereotype of classical music runs throughout the book. The second chapter, "Chacona, Lamento, Walking Blues," is the new thing—a whirlwind history of music told through two or three recurring bass lines. "Infernal Machines" brings together various thoughts on the intersection of music and technology.

With a rough map in place, I follow the traces of a dozen or so musicians living and dead: composers, conductors, pianists, string quartets, rock bands, singer-songwriters, high-school band teachers. In the final section, I try in a more personal way to describe three radically different figures—Bob Dylan, Lorraine Hunt Lieberson, and Johannes Brahms—who touch on things almost too deep for words. My last book unfolded on a big historical canvas, with political forces constantly threatening to overwhelm the solitary voice; this book is more intimate, more local, revisiting many times the abiding question of what music means to its creators and its listeners on the most elemental level. Above all, I want to know how a powerful personality can imprint itself on an inherently abstract medium—how a brief sequence of notes or chords can take on the recognizable quirks of a person close at hand.

Maybe the only trait these musically possessed men and women have in common is that they are unlike one another or anyone else. Many are exiles, wanderers, restless searchers. A shy avant-garde Finn becomes a Los Angeles celebrity. An Icelandic singer dances her way through the streets of Salvador, Brazil. A Japanese pianist interprets the German repertory in the foothills of Vermont. An elder of rock and roll meanders across the land, deconstructing his hits. A great German composer traverses an inner landscape ravaged by sadness. One way or another, they unsettle whatever genre they inhabit, making the familiar strange.

The *Great Soviet Encyclopedia*, in one of its saner moments, defined music as "a specific variant of the sound made by people." The difficult thing about music writing, in the end, is not to describe a sound but to describe a human being. It's tricky work, presumptuous in the case of the living and speculative in the case of the dead. Still, I hope to give a few lingering glimpses of all those sensuous selves.

WHERE TO LISTEN

If you would like to hear some of the music discussed in these pages, a free audio companion is available at www.therestisnoise.com/listentothis. There you will find streaming samples arranged by chapter, along with links to audio-rich websites and other channels of direct access to the music. An iTunes playlist of twenty representative excerpts can be found at www.therestisnoise.com/playlist. For a glossary of musical terms, go to www.therestisnoise.com/glossary.

PART I

PART 1

LISTEN TO THIS

CROSSING THE BORDER FROM CLASSICAL TO POP

I hate "classical music": not the thing but the name. It traps a tenaciously living art in a theme park of the past. It cancels out the possibility that music in the spirit of Beethoven could still be created today. It banishes into limbo the work of thousands of active composers who have to explain to otherwise well-informed people what it is they do for a living. The phrase is a masterpiece of negative publicity, a tour de force of anti-hype. I wish there were another name. I envy jazz people who speak simply of "the music." Some jazz aficionados also call their art "America's classical music," and I propose a trade: they can have "classical," I'll take "the music."

For at least a century, the music has been captive to a cult of mediocre elitism that tries to manufacture self-esteem by clutching at empty formulas of intellectual superiority. Consider other names in circulation: "art" music, "serious" music, "great" music, "good" music. Yes, the music can be great and serious, but greatness and seriousness are not its defining characteristics. It can also be stupid, vulgar, and insane. Composers are artists, not etiquette columnists; they have the right to express any emotion, any state of mind. They have been betrayed by well-meaning acolytes who believe that the music should be marketed as a luxury good, one that replaces an inferior popular product. These guardians say, in effect, "The music you love is trash. Listen instead to our great, arty music." They are making little headway with the unconverted because they have forgotten to define the music as something worth loving. Music is too personal a medium to support an absolute hierarchy of values. The best music is the music that persuades us that there is no other music in the world.

When people hear "classical," they think "dead." The music is described in terms of its distance from the present, its difference from the mass. No wonder that stories of its imminent demise are commonplace. Newspapers recite a familiar litany of problems: record companies are curtailing their classical divisions; orchestras are facing deficits; the music is barely taught in public schools, almost invisible in the media, ignored or mocked by Hollywood. Yet the same story was told forty, sixty, eighty years ago. *Stereo Review* wrote in 1969, "Fewer classical records are being sold because people are dying . . . Today's dying classical market is what it is because fifteen years ago no one attempted to instill a love for classical music in the then impressionable children who have today become the market." The conductor Alfred Wallenstein wrote in 1950, "The economic crisis confronting the American symphony orchestra is becoming increasingly acute." The German critic Hans Heinz Stuckenschmidt wrote in 1926, "Concerts are poorly attended and budget deficits grow from year to year." Laments over the decline or death of the art appear as far back as the fourteenth century, when the sensuous melodies of Ars Nova were thought to signal the end of civilization. The pianist Charles Rosen has sagely observed, "The death of classical music is perhaps its oldest continuing tradition."

The American classical audience is assumed to be a moribund crowd of the old, the white, the rich, and the bored. Statistics provided by the National Endowment for the Arts suggest that the situation is not quite so dire. Yes, the audience is older than that for any other art—the median age is forty-nine—but it is not the wealthiest. Musicals, plays, ballet, and museums all get larger slices of the $50,000-or-more income pie (as does the ESPN channel, for that matter). The parterre section at the Metropolitan Opera plays host to CEOs and socialites, but the less expensive parts of the house—as of this writing, most seats in the Family Circle go for twenty-five dollars—are well populated by schoolteachers, proofreaders, students, retirees, and others with no entry in the Social Register. If you want to see an in-your-face, Swiss-bank-account display of wealth, go look at the millionaires sitting in the skyboxes at a Billy Joel show, if security lets you. As for the graying of the audience, there is no denying the general trend, although with any luck it may begin to level off. Paradoxically, even as the audience ages, the performers keep getting younger. The musicians of the Berlin Philharmonic are, on average, a generation younger than the Rolling Stones.

The music is always dying, ever-ending. It is like an ageless diva on a nonstop farewell tour, coming around for one absolutely final appearance. It is hard to name because it never really existed to begin with—not in the sense that it stemmed from a single time or place. It has no genealogy, no ethnicity: leading composers of today hail from China, Estonia, Argentina, Queens. The music is simply whatever composers create—a long string of written-down works to which various performing traditions have become attached. It encompasses the high, the low, empire, underground, dance, prayer, silence, noise. Composers are genius parasites; they feed voraciously on the song matter of their time in order to engender something new. They have gone through a rough stretch in the past hundred years, facing external obstacles (Hitler and Stalin were amateur music critics) as well as problems of their own invention ("Why doesn't anyone like our beautiful twelve-tone music?"). But they may be on the verge of an improbable renaissance, and the music may take a form that no one today would recognize.

The critic Greg Sandow has written that the classical community needs to speak more from the heart about what the music means. He admits that it's easier to analyze his ardor than to express it. The music does not lend itself to the same kind of generational identification as, say, *Sgt. Pepper*. There may be kids out there who lost their virginity during Brahms's D-Minor Piano Concerto, but they don't want to tell the story and you don't want to hear it. The music attracts the reticent fraction of the population. It is an art of grand gestures and vast dimensions that plays to mobs of the quiet and the shy.

I am a white American male who listened to nothing but classical music until the age of twenty. In retrospect, this seems bizarre; perhaps "freakish" is not too strong a word. Yet it felt natural at the time. I feel as though I grew up not during the seventies and eighties but during the thirties and forties, the decades of my parents' youth. Neither my mother nor my father had musical training—both worked as research mineralogists—but they were devoted concertgoers and record collectors. They came of age in the great American middlebrow era, when the music had a rather different place in the culture than it does today. In those years, in what now seems like a dream world, millions listened as Toscanini conducted the NBC

Symphony on national radio. Walter Damrosch explained the classics to schoolchildren, singing ditties to help them remember the themes. (My mother remembers one of them: "This is / The sym-pho-nee / That Schubert wrote but never / Fi-nished . . .") NBC would broadcast Ohio State vs. Indiana one afternoon, a recital by Lotte Lehmann the next. In my house, it was the Boston Symphony followed by the Washington Redskins. I was unaware of a yawning gap between the two.

Early on, I delved into my parents' record collection, which was well stocked with artifacts of the golden age: Serge Koussevitzky's Sibelius, Charles Munch's Berlioz, the Thibaud-Casals-Cortot trio, the Budapest Quartet. The look and feel of the records were inseparable from the sound they made. There was Otto Klemperer's Zeppelin-like, slow-motion account of the *St. Matthew Passion*, with nightmare-spawning art by the Master of Delft. Toscanini's fierce renditions of Beethoven and Brahms were decorated with Robert Hupka's snapshots of the Maestro in motion, his face registering every emotion between ecstasy and disgust. Mozart's Divertimento in E-flat featured the famous portrait in which the composer looks down in sorrow, like a general surveying a hopeless battle. While listening, I read along in the liner notes, which were generally written in the over-the-top everyman-orator style that the media favored in the mid-twentieth century. Tchaikovsky, for example, was said to exhibit "melancholy, sometimes progressing to abysmal depths." None of this made sense at the time; I had no acquaintance with melancholy, let alone abysmal depths. What mattered was the exaggerated swoop of the thought, which matched my response to the music.

The first work that I loved to the point of distraction was Beethoven's *Eroica* Symphony. At a garage sale my mother found a disc of Leonard Bernstein conducting the New York Philharmonic—one of a series of Music-Appreciation Records put out by the Book-of-the-Month Club. A companion record provided Bernstein's analysis of the symphony, a road map to its forty-five-minute sprawl. I now had names for the shapes that I perceived. (The conductor's *Joy of Music* and *Infinite Variety of Music* remain the best introductory books of their kind.) Bernstein drew attention to something that happens about ten seconds in: the fanfarelike main theme, in the key of E-flat, is waylaid by the note C-sharp. "There has been a stab of intrusive otherness," Bernstein said, cryptically but seductively, in his nicotine baritone. Over and over, I listened to this note of otherness. I bought a score and deciphered the notation. I learned some time-beating gestures from Max Rudolf's conducting manual. I held my family hostage in the living room as I led the record player in a searing performance of the *Eroica*.

Did Lenny get a little carried away when he called that soft C-sharp in the cellos a "shock," a "wrench," a "stab"? If you were to play the *Eroica* for a fourteen-year-old hip-hop scholar versed in Eminem and 50 Cent, he might find it shockingly boring at best. No one is slicing up his wife or getting shot nine times. But your young gangsta friend will eventually have to admit that those artists are relatively shocking—relative to the social norms of their day. Although the *Eroica* ceased to be controversial in the these-crazy-kids-today sense around 1830, within the "classical" frame it has continued to deliver its surprises right on cue. Seven bars of E-flat major, then the C-sharp that hovers for a moment before disappearing: it is like a speaker stepping up to a microphone, launching into the first words of a solemn oration, and then faltering, as if he had just remembered something from childhood or seen a sinister face in the crowd.

I don't identify with the listener who responds to the *Eroica* by saying, "Ah, civilization." I don't listen to music to be civilized; sometimes, I listen precisely to escape the ordered world. What I love about the *Eroica* is the way it manages to have it all, uniting Romanticism and Enlightenment, civilization and revolution, brain and body, order and chaos. It knows which way you think the music is going and veers triumphantly in the wrong direction. The Danish composer Carl Nielsen once wrote a monologue for the spirit of Music, in which he or she or it says, "I love the vast surface of silence; and it is my chief delight to break it."

Around the time I got stabbed by Beethoven's C-sharp, I began trying to write music myself. My career as a composer lasted from the age of eight to the age of twenty. I lacked both genius and talent. My spiral-bound manuscript book includes an ambitious program of future compositions: thirty piano sonatas, twelve violin sonatas, various symphonies, concertos, fantasias, and funeral marches, most of them in the key of D minor. Scattered ideas for these works appear in the following pages, but they don't go anywhere, which was the story of my life as a composer. Still, I treasure the observation of one of my college teachers, the composer Peter Lieberson, who wrote on the final page of my end-of-term submission that I had created a "most interesting and slightly peculiar sonatina." I put down my pen and withdrew into silence, like Sibelius in Järvenpää.

My inability to finish anything, much less anything good, left me with a profound respect for this impossible mode of making a living. Composers are in rebellion against reality. They manufacture a product that is universally deemed superfluous—at least until their music enters public consciousness, at which point people begin to say that they could not live without it. Half of those on the League of American Orchestras' list of the twenty composers most frequently performed during the 2007–2008 season—Mahler, Strauss, Sibelius, Debussy, Ravel, Rachmaninov, Stravinsky, Shostakovich, Prokofiev, and Copland—hadn't been born when the first draft of the repertory got written.

Throughout my teens, I took piano lessons from a man named Denning Barnes. He also taught me composition, music history, and the art of listening. He was a wiry man with tangled hair, whose tweed jackets emitted an odd smell that was neither pleasant nor unpleasant, just odd. He was intimate with Beethoven, Schubert, and Chopin, and he also loved twentieth-century music. Béla Bartók and Alban Berg were two of his favorites. He opened another door for me, in a wall that I never knew existed. His own music, as far as I can remember, was rambunctious, jazzy, a little nuts. One day he pounded out one of the variations in Beethoven's final piano sonata and said that it was an anticipation of boogie-woogie. I had no idea what boogie-woogie was, but I was excited by the idea that Beethoven had anticipated it. The marble-bust Beethoven of my childhood suddenly became an eagle-eyed sentinel on the ramparts of sound.

"Boogie-woogie" was a creature out of Bernstein's serious-fun world, and Mr. Barnes was my private Bernstein. There was not a snobbish bone in his body; he was a skeleton of enthusiasm, a fifteen-dollar-an-hour guerrilla fighter for the music he loved. He died of a brain tumor in 1989. The last time I saw him, we played a hair-raising version of Schubert's Fantasia in F Minor for piano four hands. It was full of wrong notes, most of them at my end of the keyboard, but it felt great and made a mighty noise, and to this day I have never been entirely satisfied with any other performance of the work.

By high school, a terrible truth had dawned: I was the only person my age who liked this stuff. Actually, there were other classical nerds at my school, but we were too diffident to form a posse. Several "normal" friends dragged me to a showing of *Pink Floyd The Wall*, after which I conceded that one passage sounded Mahlerian.

Only in college did my musical fortress finally crumble. I spent most of my time at the campus radio station, where I had a show and helped organize the classical contingent. I fanatically patrolled the boundaries of the classical broadcasting day, refusing to surrender even fifteen minutes of *Chamber Music Masterworks* and the like. At 10:00 p.m., the schedule switched from classical to punk, and only punk of the most recondite kind. Once a record sold more than a few hundred copies, it was kicked off the playlist. The DJs liked to start their sets with the shrillest, crudest songs in order to scandalize the classical crowd. I tried to one-up them with squalls of Xenakis. They hit back with Sinatra singing "Only the Lonely." Once, they followed up my heartfelt tribute to Herbert von Karajan with Skrewdriver's rousing neo-Nazi anthem "Prisoner of Peace": "Free Rudolf Hess / How long can they keep him there? We can only guess." Touché.

The thing about these cerebral punk rockers is that they were easily the most interesting people I'd ever met. Between painstakingly researched tributes to Mission of Burma and the Butthole Surfers, they composed undergraduate theses on fourth-century Roman fortifications and the liberal thought of Lionel Trilling. I began hanging around in the studio after my show was over, suppressing an instinctive fear of their sticker-covered leather jackets and multicolored hair. I informed them, as Mr. Barnes would have done, that the atonal music of Arnold Schoenberg had prefigured all this. And I began listening to new things. The first two rock records I bought were Pere Ubu's *Terminal Tower* compilation and Sonic Youth's *Daydream Nation*. I crept from underground rock to alternative rock and finally to the full-out commercial kind. Soon I was astounding my friends with pronouncements like "*Highway 61 Revisited* is a pretty good album," or "*The White Album* is a masterpiece." I abandoned the notion of classical superiority, which led to a crisis of faith: If the music wasn't great and serious and high and mighty, what was it?

For a little while, living in Northern California after college, I thought of giving up on the music altogether. I sold off a lot of my CDs, including all my copies of the symphonies of Arnold Bax, in order to pay for more Pere Ubu and Sonic Youth. I cut my hair short, wore angry T-shirts, and started hanging out at the Berkeley punk club 924 Gilman Street. I became a fan of a band called Blatz, which was about as far from Bax as I could get. (Their big hit was "Fuk Shit Up.") Fortunately, no one needed to point out to my face that I was in the wrong place. It is a peculiar American dream, this notion that music can give you a new personality, a new class, even a new race. The out-of-body experience is thrilling as long as it lasts, but most people are eventually deposited back at the point where they started, and they may begin to hate the music for lying to them.

When I went back to the classical ghetto, I chose to accept its limitations. I realized that, despite the outward decrepitude of the culture, there was still a bright flame within. It occurred to me that if I could get from Brahms to Blatz, others could go the same route in the opposite direction. I have always wanted to talk about classical music as if it were popular music and popular music as if it were classical.

For many, pop music is the soundtrack of raging adolescence, while the other kind chimes in during the long twilight of maturity. For me, it's the reverse. Listening to the *Eroica* reconnects me with a kind of childlike energy, a happy ferocity about the world. Since I came late to pop, I invest it with more adult feeling. To me, it's penetrating, knowing, full of microscopic shades of truth about the way things really are. Bob Dylan's *Blood on the Tracks* anatomizes a doomed relationship with a saturnine clarity that a canonical work such as *Die schöne Müllerin* can't match. (When Ian Bostridge sang Schubert's cycle at Lincoln Center a few years ago, I had the thought that the protagonist might never have spoken to the miller girl for whose sake he drowns himself. How classical of him.) If I were in a perverse mood, I'd say that the *Eroica* is the raw, thuggish thing—a blast of ego and id—whereas a song like Radiohead's "Everything in Its Right Place" is all cool adult irony. The idea that life is flowing along with unsettling smoothness, the dark C-sharpness of the world sensed but not confirmed, is a resigned sort of sentiment that Beethoven probably never even felt, much less communicated. What I refuse to accept is that one kind of music soothes the mind and another kind soothes the soul. It depends on whose mind, whose soul.

The fatal phrase came into circulation late in the game. From Machaut to Beethoven, modern music was essentially the only music, bartered about in a marketplace that resembled pop culture. Music of the past was either quickly forgotten or studied mainly in academic settings. Even in the churches there was incessant demand for new work. In 1687, in the German town of Flensburg, dismissal proceedings were initiated against a local cantor who kept recycling old pieces and neglected to play anything contemporary. When, in 1730, Johann Sebastian Bach remonstrated with the town council of Leipzig for failing to hire an adequate complement of singers and musicians, he stated that "the former style of music no longer seems to please our ears" and that expert performers were needed to "master the new kinds of music."

Well into the nineteenth century, concerts were eclectic hootenannies in which opera arias collided with chunks of sonatas and concertos. Barrel-organ grinders carried the best-known classical melodies out into the streets, where they were blended with folk tunes. Audiences regularly made their feelings known by applauding or calling out while the music was playing. Mozart, recounting the premiere of his "Paris" Symphony in 1778, described how he milked the crowd: "Right in the middle of the First Allegro came a Passage that I knew would please, and the entire audience was sent into raptures—there was a big applaudißement;—and as I knew, when I wrote the passage, what good effect it would make, I brought it once more at the end of the movement—and sure enough there they were: the shouts of Da capo." James Johnson, in his book *Listening in Paris*, evokes a night at the Paris Opéra in the same period:

> While most were in their places by the end of the first act, the continuous movement and low din of conversation never really stopped. Lackeys and young bachelors milled about in the crowded and often boisterous parterre, the floor-level pit to which only men were admitted. Princes of the blood and dukes visited among themselves in the highly visible first-row boxes. Worldly abbés chatted happily with ladies in jewels on the second level, occasionally earning indecent shouts from the parterre when their conversation turned too cordial. And lovers sought the dim heights of the third balcony—the paradise—away from the probing lorgnettes.

In America, musical events were a stylistic free-for-all, a mirror of the country's mixed-up nature. Walt Whitman mobilized opera as a metaphor for democracy; the voices of his favorite singers were integral to the swelling sound of his "barbaric yawp."

In Europe, the past began to encroach on the present just after 1800. Johann Nikolaus Forkel's 1802 biography of Bach, one of the first major books devoted to a dead composer, may be the founding document of the classical mentality. All the earmarks are there: the longing for lost worlds, the adulation of a single godlike entity, the horror of the present. Bach was "the first classic that ever was, or perhaps ever will be," Forkel proclaimed. He also said, "If the art is to remain an art and not to be degraded into a mere idle amusement, more use must be made of classical works than has been done for some time." By "idle amusement" Forkel probably had in mind the prattling of Italian opera; his biography is addressed to "patriotic admirers of true musical art," namely the German. The notion that the music of Forkel's time was teetering toward extinction is, of course, amusing in retrospect; in the summer of 1802, Beethoven began work on the *Eroica*.

Classical concerts began to take on cultlike aspects. The written score became a sacred object; improvisation was gradually phased out. Concert halls grew quiet and reserved, habits and attire formal. Patrons of the Wagner festival in Bayreuth, which opened in 1876, were particularly militant in their suppression of applause. At the premiere of *Parsifal*, in 1882, Wagner requested that there be no curtain calls for the performers, in order to preserve the rapt atmosphere of his "sacred festival play." The audience interpreted this instruction as a general ban on applause. Cosima Wagner, the composer's wife, described in her diary what happened at the second performance: "After the first act there is a reverent silence, which has a pleasant effect. But when, after the second, the applauders are again hissed, it becomes embarrassing." Two weeks later, listeners rebuked a man who yelled out "Bravo!" after the Flower Maidens scene. They did not realize that they were hissing the composer. The Wagnerians were taking Wagner more seriously than he took himself—an alarming development.

The sacralization of music, to take a term from the scholar Lawrence Levine, had its advantages. Many composers liked the fact that the public was quieting down; the subtle shock of a C-sharp wouldn't register if noise and chatter filled the hall. They began to write with a silent, well-schooled crowd in mind. Even so, the emergence of a self-styled elite audience had limited appeal for the likes of Beethoven and Verdi. The nineteenth-century masters were, most of them, egomaniacs, but they were not snobs. Wagner, surrounded by luxury, royalty, and pretension, nonetheless railed against the idea of a "classical" repertory, for which he blamed the Jews. His nauseating anti-Semitism went hand in hand with a sometimes charming populism. In a letter to Franz Liszt, he raged against the "monumental character" of the music of his time, the "clinging firmly to the past." Another letter demanded, *"Kinder! macht Neues! Neues!, und abermals Neues!"* Or, as Ezra Pound later put it, "Make it new."

Unfortunately, the European bourgeoisie, having made a demigod of Beethoven, began losing interest in even the most vital living composers. In 1859, a critic wrote, "New works do not succeed in Leipzig. Again at the fourteenth Gewandhaus concert a composition was borne to its grave." The music in question was Brahms's First Piano Concerto. (Brahms knew that things were going badly when he heard no applause after the first movement.) At around the same time, organizers of a Paris series observed that their subscribers "get upset when they see the name of a single contemporary composer on the programs." The scholar William Weber has shown how historical repertory came to dominate concerts across Europe. In 1782, in Leipzig, the proportion of music by living composers was as high as 89 percent. By 1845, it had declined to around 50 percent, and later in the nineteenth century, it hovered around 25 percent.

The fetishizing of the past had a degrading effect on composers' morale. They started to doubt their ability to please this implacable audience, which seemed prepared to reject their wares no matter what style they wrote in. If no one cares, composers reasoned, we might as well write for one another. This was the attitude that led to the intransigent, sometimes antisocial mentality of the twentieth-century avant-garde. A critic who attended the premiere of the *Eroica* saw the impasse coming: "Music could quickly come to such a point, that everyone who is not precisely familiar with the rules and difficulties of the art would find absolutely no enjoyment in it."

In America, the middle classes carried the worship of the classics to a necrophiliac extreme. Lawrence Levine, in his book *Highbrow/Lowbrow*, gives a devastating portrait of the country's musical culture at the end of the nineteenth century. It was a world that abhorred virtuosity, extravagance, anything that smacked of entertainment. Orchestras dedicated themselves to "the great works of the great composers greatly performed, the best and profoundest art, these and these alone," in the redundant words of the conductor Theodore Thomas, who more or less founded the modern American orchestra.

In some ways, Levine's sharp critique of Gilded Age culture goes too far; while much of the audience unquestionably appropriated European music as a status symbol, many leaders of the orchestral world—among them

Henry Lee Higginson, the founder of the Boston Symphony—saw their mission in altruistic terms, welcoming listeners of all classes, nationalities, and races. The cheaper seats at the big urban concert halls didn't cost much more than tickets for the vaudeville, usually starting at twenty-five cents. All the same, paternalism stalked the scene; classical music began to define itself as a mode of spiritual uplift, of collective self-improvement, rather than as a sphere of uninhibited artistic expression.

Within a decade or two, the American symphony orchestra seemed so ossified that progressive spirits were calling for change. "America is sad-dled, hag-ridden, with culture," the critic-composer Arthur Farwell wrote in 1912. "There is a conventionalism, a cynicism, a self-consciousness, in symphony concert, recital, and opera." Daniel Gregory Mason, a maverick Columbia professor, similarly attacked the "prestige-hypnotized" pluto-crats who ran the New York Philharmonic; he found more excitement at open-air concerts at Lewisohn Stadium, in Harlem, where the audi-ence expressed itself freely. Mason delightedly quoted a notice that read, "We would respectfully request that the audience refrain from throwing mats."

In the concert halls, a stricter etiquette took hold. Applause was rationed once again; listeners were admonished to control themselves not only dur-ing the music but between movements of a large-scale composition—even after those noisy first-movement codas that practically beg for a round of clapping and shouting. German musicians and critics concocted this rule in the first years of the twentieth century. Leopold Stokowski, when he led the Philadelphia Orchestra, was instrumental in bringing the prac-tice to America. Mason wrote in his book: "After the Funeral March of the *Eroica*, someone suggested, Mr. Stokowski might at least have pressed a button to inform the audience by (noiseless) illuminated sign: 'You may now cross the other leg.'"

In the 1930s, a new generation of composers, conductors, and broad-casters embraced Farwell's idea of "music for all." The storied middlebrow age began. David Sarnoff, the head of NBC, had a vision of Toscanini con-ducting for a mass public, and the public duly materialized, in the millions. Hollywood studios hired composers such as Erich Wolfgang Korngold, Aaron Copland, and Bernard Herrmann, and even pursued the modernist giants Schoenberg and Stravinsky (both of whom asked for too much money). The Roosevelt administration funded the Federal Music Project, which in two and a half years entertained ninety-five million people; there were concerts in delinquent-boys' homes and rural Oklahoma towns. Never before had classical music reached such vast and diverse audiences. Those who consider the art form inherently elitist might ponder an irony: at a time of sustained economic crisis, when America moved more to the left than at any time in its history, when socialistic ideas threatened the national religion of free enterprise, classical music attained maximum popularity. Toscanini's Beethoven performances symbolized a spirit of selflessness and togetherness, both during the Great Depression and in the war years that followed.

Yet many young sophisticates of the twenties and thirties didn't look at it that way. They saw the opera and the symphony as cobwebbed fortresses of high society, and seized on popular culture as an avenue of escape. In 1925, a young socialite named Ellin Mackay, the daughter of the chairman of the board of the New York Philharmonic, caused a stir by abandoning the usual round of debutante balls for the cabaret and nightclub circuit. She justified her proclivities in a witty article titled "Why We Go to Cabarets: A Post-Debutante Explains," which appeared in a fledgling magazine called *The New Yorker*; the ensuing publicity enabled that publication to get on its feet. Opening night at the Metropolitan Opera was one of the dreaded rituals from which the Jazz Age debutante felt liberated. Mackay caused an even greater scandal when she became engaged to Irving Berlin, the composer of "Alexander's Ragtime Band." Her father publicly announced that he would disinherit his daughter if she went through with her plans. Ellin and Irving married anyway, and Clarence Mackay became a buffoonish figure in the popular press, the very image of the high-culture snob.

The defections were legion. Carl Van Vechten, the notorious author of *Nigger Heaven*, started out as a classical critic for *The New York Times*; he witnessed Stravinsky's *Rite of Spring* and hailed the composer as a savior. Then his attention began to wander, and he found more life and truth in ragtime, Tin Pan Alley, blues, and jazz. Gilbert Seldes, in his 1924 book *The Seven Lively Arts*, declared that "'Alexander's Ragtime Band' and 'I Love a Piano' are musically and emotionally sounder pieces of work than *Indian Love Lyrics* and 'The Rosary'"—Gilded Age parlor songs—and that "the circus can be and often is more artistic than the Metropolitan Opera House in New York." For young African-American music mavens, the disenchantment was more bitter and more personal. In 1893, Antonín Dvořák, the director of the National Conservatory in New York, had prophesied a great age of Negro music, and his words raised hopes that classical music would assist in the advancement of the race. The likes of James Weldon Johnson awaited the black Beethoven who would write the music of God's trombones. Soon enough, aspiring young singers, violinists, pianists, and composers ran up against a wall of racism. Only in popular music could they make a decent living.

There had been a major change in music's social function. In the Gilded Age, classical music had given the white middle-class aristocratic airs; in the Jazz Age, popular music helped the same class to feel down and dirty. A silly 1934 movie titled *Murder at the Vanities* sums up the genre wars of the era. It is set behind the scenes of a Ziegfeld-style variety show, one of whose numbers features a performer, dressed vaguely as Liszt, who plays the Second Hungarian Rhapsody. Duke Ellington and his band keep popping up in the background, throwing in insolent riffs. Eventually, they drive away the effete classical musicians and play a take-off called *Ebony Rhapsody*: "It's got those licks, it's got those tricks / That Mr. Liszt would never recognize." Liszt comes back with a submachine gun and mows down the band. The metaphor wasn't so far off the mark. Although many in the classical world spoke in praise of jazz—Ernest Ansermet lobbed the word "genius" at Sidney Bechet—others fired verbal machine guns in an effort to slay the upstart. Daniel Gregory Mason, the man who wanted more throwing of mats, was one of the worst offenders, calling jazz a "sick moment in the progress of the human soul."

The contempt flowed both ways. The culture of jazz, at least in its white precincts, was much affected by that inverse snobbery which endlessly congratulates itself on escaping the elite. (The singer in *Murder at the Vanities* brags of finding a rhythm that Liszt, of all people, could never comprehend: what a snob.) Classical music became a foil against which popular musicians could assert their cool. Composers, in turn, were irritated by the implication that they constituted some sort of moneyed behemoth. They were the ones who were feeling bulldozed by the power of cash. Such was the complaint made by Lawrence Gilman, of *The New York Tribune*, after Paul Whiteman and his Palais Royal Orchestra played Gershwin's *Rhapsody in Blue* at Aeolian Hall. Gilman didn't like the *Rhapsody*, but what really incensed him was Whiteman's suggestion that jazz was an underdog fighting against symphony bigwigs. "It is the Palais Royalists who represent the conservative, reactionary, respectable elements in the music of today," Gilman wrote. "They are the aristocrats, the Top Dogs, of contemporary music. They are the Shining Ones, the commanders of huge salaries, the friends of Royalty." The facts back Gilman up. By the late twenties, Gershwin was making at least a hundred thousand dollars a year. In 1938, Copland, one of the best-regarded composers of American concert music, had $6.93 in his checking account.

Despite the ever-cresting surge of jazz and pop, classical music retained a high profile in America as the era of depression and war gave way to the Cold War and its attendant boom economy. Money was poured into the performing arts, partly in an effort to out-culture the Russians. Grants from the Ford Foundation led to a proliferation of musical ensembles, orchestras in particular; where there had been dozens of professional orchestras, now there were hundreds. Multipurpose performing-arts centers went up in New York, Los Angeles, and Washington, D.C., their façades evoking sleek secular cathedrals. In the early years of the LP era, classical music made quite a bit of money for the major record labels; Decca ended up selling eighteen million copies of its pioneering studio recording of Wagner's *Ring of the Nibelung*.

The real reckoning arrived in the 1960s, when classical music made a decisive and seemingly permanent move to the cultural margin. The advent of Dylan and the Beatles again jeopardized classical music's claim on "high art," and this time an entire generation seemed to come of age without identifying strongly with the classical repertory. The audience grayed, attendance declined. According to one report, the classical share of total record sales dropped from 20 percent to 5 percent in the course of the decade. The music now occupies somewhere around 2 percent of the market. In an ironic twist of fate, jazz now has about the same slice of the mass audience, leaving Duke Ellington in the same league as Mr. Liszt.

All music becomes classical music in the end. Reading the histories of other genres, I often get a funny sense of déjà vu. The story of jazz, for example, seems to recapitulate classical history at high speed. First, the youth-rebellion period: Satchmo and the Duke and Bix and Jelly Roll teach a generation to lose itself in the music. Second, the era of bourgeois pomp: the high-class swing band parallels the Romantic orchestra. Stage 3: artists rebel against the bourgeois image, echoing the classical modernist revolution, sometimes by direct citation (Charlie Parker works the opening notes of *The Rite of Spring* into "Salt Peanuts"). Stage 4: free jazz marks the point at which the vanguard loses touch with the masses and becomes a self-contained avant-garde. Stage 5: a period of retrenchment. Wynton Marsalis's attempt to launch a traditionalist jazz revival parallels the neo-Romantic music of many late-twentieth-century composers. But this effort comes too late to restore the art to the popular mainstream.

The same progression worms its way through rock and roll. What were my hyper-educated punk-rock friends but Stage 3 high modernists, rebelling against the bloated Romanticism of Stage 2 stadium rock? In the first years of the new century there was a lot of Stage 5 neoclassicism going on in what remained of rock. The Strokes, the Hives, the Vines, the Stills, the Thrills, the White Stripes, and various other bands harked back to some lost pure moment of the sixties or seventies. Many used old instruments, old amplifiers, old soundboards. One rocker was quoted as saying, "I intentionally won't use something I haven't heard before." A White Stripes record carried this Luddite notice: "No computers were used during the recording, mixing, or mastering of this record."

The original classical music is left in an interesting limbo. It has a chance to be liberated from the social clichés that currently pin it down. It is no longer the one form carrying the burden of the past. Moreover, it has the advantage of being able to sustain constant reinterpretation, to renew itself with each repetition. The best kind of classical performance is not a retreat into the past but an intensification of the present. The mistake that apostles of the classical have always made is to have joined their love of the past to a dislike of the present. The music has other ideas: it hates the past and wants to escape.

In 2003, I bought an iPod and began filling it with music from my CD collection. The device, fairly new at the time, had a setting called Shuffle, which skipped randomly from one track to another. There was something seductive about surrendering control and letting the iPod decide what to play next. The little machine went crashing through barriers of style in ways that changed how I listened. One day it jumped from the furious crescendo of "Dance of the Earth," ending Part I of *The Rite of Spring*, into the hot jam of Louis Armstrong's "West End Blues." The first became a gigantic upbeat to the second. On the iPod, music is freed from all fatuous self-definitions and delusions of significance. There are no record jackets depicting bombastic Alpine scenes or celebrity conductors with a family resemblance to Rudolf Hess. Instead, as Berg once remarked to Gershwin, music is music.

A lot of younger listeners seem to think the way the iPod thinks. They are no longer so invested in a single genre, one that promises to mold their being or save the world. This gives the lifestyle disaster called "classical music" an interesting new opportunity. The playlists of smart rock fans often include a few twentieth-century classical pieces. Mavens of electronic dance music mention among their heroes Karlheinz Stockhausen, Terry Riley, and Steve Reich. Likewise, younger composers are writing music heavily influenced by minimalism and its electronic spawn, even as they hold on to the European tradition. And new generations of musicians are dropping the mask of Olympian detachment (silent, stone-faced musician walks onstage and begins to play). They've started mothballing the tuxedo, explaining the music from the stage, using lighting and backdrops to produce a mildly theatrical happening. They are finding allies in the "popular" world, some of whom care less about sales and fees than the average star violinist. The borders between "popular" and "classical" are becoming creatively blurred, and only the Johann Forkels in each camp see a problem.

The strange thing about classical music in America today is that large numbers of people seem aware of it, curious about it, even knowledgeable about it, but they do not go to concerts. The people who try to market orchestras have a name for these annoying phantoms: they are "culturally aware non-attenders," to quote an article in the magazine *Symphony*. I know the type; most of my friends are case studies. They know the principal names and periods of musical history: they have read what Nietzsche wrote about Wagner, they can pick Stravinsky out of a lineup, they own Glenn Gould's *Goldberg Variations* and some Mahler and maybe a CD of Arvo Pärt. They follow all the other arts—they go to gallery shows, read new novels, see art films. Yet they have never paid money for a classical concert. They almost make a point of their ignorance. "I don't know a thing about Beethoven," they announce, which is not what they would say if the subject were Henry James or Stanley Kubrick. This is one area where even sophisticates wrap themselves in the all-American anti-intellectual flag. It's not all their fault: centuries of classical intolerance have gone into the creation of the culturally aware non-attender. When I tell people what I do for a living, I see the same look again and again—a flinching sideways glance, as if they were about to be reprimanded for not knowing about C-sharps. After this comes the serene declaration of ignorance. The old culture war is fought and lost before I say a word.

I'm imagining myself on the other side—as a forty-something pop fan who wants to try something different. On a lark, I buy a record of Otto Klemperer conducting the *Eroica*, picking this one because Klemperer is the father of Colonel Klink, on *Hogan's Heroes*. I hear two impressive loud chords, then what the liner notes allege is a "truly heroic" theme. It sounds kind of feeble, lopsided, waltzlike. My mind drifts. A few days later, I try again. This time, I hear some attractive adolescent grandiosity, barbaric yawps here and there. The rest is mechanical, remote. But each time I go back I map out a little more of the imaginary world. I invent stories for each thing as it happens. Big chords, hero standing backstage, a troubling thought, hero orating over loudspeakers, some ideas for songs that don't catch on, a man or woman pleading, hero shouts back, tension, anger, conspiracies—assassination attempt? The nervous splendor of it all gets under my skin. I go to a bookstore and look at the classical shelf, which seems to have more books for Idiots and Dummies than any other section. I read Bernstein's essay in *The Infinite Variety of Music*, coordinate some of the examples with the music, enjoy stories of the composer screaming about Napoleon, and go back and listen again. Sometime after the tenth listen, the music becomes my own; I know what's around almost every corner and I exult in knowing. It's as if I could predict the news.

I am now enough of a fan that I buy a twenty-five-dollar ticket to hear a famous orchestra play the *Eroica* live. It is not a very heroic experience. I feel dispirited from the moment I walk in the hall. My black jeans draw disapproving glances from men who seem to be modeling the Johnny Carson collection. I look around warily at the twenty shades of beige in which the hall is decorated. The music starts, with the imperious chords that say, "Listen to this." Yet I somehow find it hard to think of Beethoven's detestation of all tyranny over the human mind when the man next to me is a dead ringer for my dentist. The assassination sequence in the first movement is less exciting when the musicians have no emotion on their faces. I cough; a thin man, reading a dog-eared score, glares at me. When the movement is about a minute from ending, an ancient woman creeps slowly up the aisle, a look of enormous dissatisfaction on her face, followed at a few paces by a blank-faced husband. Finally, three smashing chords to finish, obviously intended to set off a roar of applause. I start to clap, but the man with the score glares again. One does not applaud in the midst of greatly great great music, even if the composer wants one to! Coughing, squirming, whispering, the crowd suppresses its urge to express pleasure. It's like mass anal retention. The slow tread of the Funeral March, or Marcia funebre, as everyone insists on calling it, begins. I start to feel that my newfound respect for the music is dragging along behind the hearse.

But I stay with it. For the duration of the Marcia, I try to disregard the audience and concentrate on the music. It strikes me that what I'm hearing is an entirely natural phenomenon, the sum of the vibrations of various creaky old instruments reverberating around a boxlike hall. Each scrape of a bow translates into a strand of sound; what I see is what I hear. So when the cellos and basses make the floor tremble with their big low note in the middle of the march (what Bernstein calls the "wham!") the impact of the moment is purely physical. Amplifiers are for sissies, I'm starting to think. The orchestra isn't playing with the same cowed force as Klemperer's heroes, but the tone is warmer and deeper and rounder than on the CD. I make my peace with the stiffness of the scene by thinking of it as a cool frame for a hot event. Perhaps this is how it has to be: Beethoven needs a passive audience as a foil. To my left, a sleeping dentist; to my right, a put-upon aesthete; and, in front of me, the funeral march that rises to a fugal fury, and breaks down into softly sobbing memories of themes, and then gives way to an entirely new mood—hard-driving, laughing, lurching, a bit drunk.

Two centuries ago, Beethoven bent over the manuscript of the *Eroica* and struck out Napoleon's name. It is often said that he made himself the protagonist of the work instead. Indeed, he fashioned an archetype—the rebel artist hero—that modern artists are still recycling. I wonder, though, if Beethoven's gesture meant what people think it did. Perhaps he was freeing his music from a too specific interpretation, from his own preoccupations. He was setting his symphony adrift, as a message in a bottle. He could hardly have imagined it traveling two hundred years, through the dark heart of the twentieth century and into the pulverizing electronic age. But he knew it would go far, and he did not weigh it down. There was now a torn, blank space on the title page. The symphony became a fragmentary, unfinished thing, and unfinished it remains. It becomes whole again only in the mind and soul of someone listening for the first time, and listening again. The hero is you.

2

CHACONA, LAMENTO, WALKING BLUES

BASS LINES OF MUSIC HISTORY

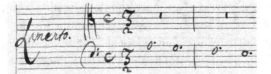

At the outset of the seventeenth century, as the Spanish Empire reached its zenith, there was a fad for the chacona, a sexily swirling dance that hypnotized all who heard it. No one knows for certain where it came from, but scattered evidence suggests that it originated somewhere in Spain's New World colonies. In 1598, Mateo Rosas de Oquendo, a soldier and court official who had spent a decade in Peru, included the chacona in a list of locally popular dances and airs whose names had been "given by the devil." Because no flesh-and-blood person could resist such sounds, Oquendo wrote, the law should ignore whatever mischief they might cause.

The devil did fine work: the chacona is perfectly engineered to bewitch the senses. It is in triple time, with a stress on the second beat encouraging a sway of the hips. Players in the chacona band lay down an ostinato—a motif, bass line, or chord progression that repeats in an insistent fashion. ("Ostinato" is Italian for "obstinate.") Other instruments add variations, the wilder the better. And singers step forward to tell bawdy tales of *la vida bona*, the good life. The result is a little sonic tornado that spins in circles while hurtling forward. When an early-music group reconstructs the form—the Catalan viol player Jordi Savall often improvises on the chacona with his ensemble Hespèrion XXI—centuries melt away and modern feet tap to an ancient tune.

The late Renaissance brought forth many ostinato dances of this type—the passamezzo, the bergamasca, the zarabanda, *la folia*—but the chacona took on a certain notoriety. Writers of the Spanish Golden Age savored its exotic, dubious reputation: Lope de Vega personified the dance as an old lady "riding in to Seville from the Indies." Cervantes's novella *La ilustre fregona* (*The Illustrious Scullery-Maid*), published in 1613, has a scene in which a young nobleman poses as a water carrier and plays a chacona in a common tavern, to the stamping delight of the maids and mule boys. He sings:

> So come in, all you nymph girls,
> All you nymph boys, if you please,
> The dance of the chacona
> Is wider than the seas.

Chacona lyrics often emphasize the dance's topsy-turvy nature—its knack for disrupting solemn occasions and breaking down inhibitions. Thieves use it to fool their prey. Kings get down with their subjects. When a sexton at a funeral accidentally says "*Vida bona*" instead of "*Requiem*," all begin to bounce to the familiar beat—including, it is said, the corpse. "Un sarao de la chacona," or "A Chaconne Soirée," a song published by the Spanish musician Juan Arañés, presents this busy tableau:

> When Almadán was married,
> A wild party was arranged,
> The daughters of Anao dancing
> With the grandsons of Milan.
> A father-in-law of Don Beltrán
> And a sister-in-law of Orfeo
> Started dancing the Guineo,
> With the fat one at the end.
> And Fame spreads it all around:
> To the good life, la vida bona,
> Let's all go now to Chacona.

A surreal parade of wedding guests ensues: a blind man poking girls with a stick, an African heathen singing with a Gypsy, a doctor wearing pans around his neck. Drunks, thieves, cuckolds, brawlers, and men and women of ill repute complete the scene.

King Philip II, the austere master of the Spanish imperium, died in 1598, around the time that the chacona first surfaced in Peru. In the final months of his reign, Philip took note of certain immoral dances that were circulating in Madrid; religious authorities had warned him that the frivolity rampant in the city resembled the decadence of the Roman Empire. The debate continued after Philip's death. In 1615, the King's Council banned from public theaters the chacona, the zarabanda, and other dances that were deemed "lascivious, dishonest, or offensive to pious ears." In truth, officialdom had little to fear from these naughty little numbers. They give off a frisson of rebellion, yet the established order remains intact. The errant nobles in Cervantes's story resume their proper roles; the characters in "Un sarao de la chacona" surely return to their usual places the following day. Tellingly, Arañés dedicated his collection of songs to his employer, the Spanish ambassador to the Holy See. Courtly life had no trouble assimilating the chacona, which soon became a respectable form in what we now call classical music.

The subsequent history of the chacona cuts a cross-section through four centuries of Western culture. As the original fad subsided, composers avidly explored the hidden possibilities of the dance, ringing intricate variations on a simple idea. It passed into Italian, French, German, and English hands, assuming masks of arcane virtuosity, aristocratic elegance, minor-key cogitation, and high-toned yearning. Louis XIV, whose empire eclipsed Philip's, danced *la chaconne* at the court of Versailles; in the modern era, the French term for the dance has generally prevailed. Johann Sebastian Bach, in the final movement of his Second Partita for solo violin, wrote a chaconne of almost shocking severity, rendering the form all but unrecognizable. In the Romantic age, the chaconne fell from fashion, but amid the terrors of the twentieth century composers once again picked it up, associating it with the high seriousness of Bach rather than the ebullience of the original. The chaconne has continued to evolve in music of recent decades. In 1978, György Ligeti, an avant-gardist with a long historical memory, wrote a harpsichord piece titled *Hungarian Rock (Chaconne)*, which revived the Spanish bounce and infused it with boogie-woogie.

The circuitous career of the chaconne intersects many times with that of another ostinato figure, the *basso lamento*. This is a repeating bass line that descends the interval of a fourth, sometimes following the steps of the minor mode (think of the piano riff in Ray Charles's "Hit the Road

Jack") and sometimes inching down the chromatic scale (think of the "Crucifixus" of Bach's B-Minor Mass, or, if you prefer, Bob Dylan's "Simple Twist of Fate"):

If the chaconne is a mercurial thing, radically changing its meaning as it moves through space and time, these motifs of weeping and longing bring out profound continuities in musical history. They almost seem to possess intrinsic significance, as if they were fragments of a strand of musical DNA.

Theorists warn us that music is a non-referential art, that its affective properties depend on extra-musical associations. Indeed, with a change of variables, a rowdy chaconne can turn into a deathly lament. Nothing in the medium is fixed. "I consider music by its very nature powerless to *express* anything," Stravinsky once said, warding off sentimental interpretations. Then again, when Stravinsky composed the opening lament of his ballet *Orpheus*, he reached for the same four-note descending figure that has represented sorrow for at least a thousand years.

FOLK LAMENT

Across the millennia, scholars have attempted to construct a grammar of musical meaning. The ancient Greeks believed that their system of scales could be linked to gradations of emotion. Indian ragas include categories of *hasya* (joy), *karuna* (sadness), *raudra* (anger), and *shanta* (peace). In Western European music, songs in a major key are thought to be happy, songs in a minor key sad. Although these distinctions turn hazy under close inspection—Beethoven's Fifth Symphony, in muscular C minor, defies categorization—we are, for the most part, surprisingly adept at picking up the intended message of an unfamiliar musical piece. Psychologists have found that Western listeners can properly sort Indian ragas by type, even if they know nothing of the music. Likewise, the Mafa people of Cameroon, who inhabit remote parts of the Mandara Mountains, easily performed a similar exercise with Western samples.

The music of dejection is especially hard to miss. When a person cries, he or she generally makes a noise that slides downward and then leaps to an even higher pitch to begin the slide again. Not surprisingly, something similar happens in musical laments around the world. Those stepwise falling figures suggest not only the sounds that we emit when we are in distress but also the sympathetic drooping of our faces and shoulders. In a broader sense, they imply a spiritual descent, even a voyage to the underworld. In a pioneering essay on the chromatic lament, the composer Robert Müller-Hartmann wrote, "A vision of the grave or of Hades is brought about by its decisive downward trend." At the same time, laments help to guide us out of the labyrinth of despair. Like Aristotelean tragedy, they allow for a purgation of pity and fear: through the repetitive ritual of mourning, we tame the edges of emotion, give shape to inner chaos.

In 1917, the Hungarian composer Béla Bartók, a passionate collector of folk music, took his Edison cylinder to the Transylvanian village of Mânerău and recorded the *bocet*, or lament, of a woman pining for her absent husband: "Change me to a rainbow, Lord, / To see where my husband is." The melody goes down four sobbing steps:

This pattern shows up all over Eastern European folk music. In a village in the Somogy region of Hungary, a woman was recorded singing a strikingly similar tune as she exclaimed, "Woe is me, what have I done against the great Lord that he has taken my beloved spouse away?" At Russian weddings, where a symbolic "killing the bride" is part of the nuptial rite, the wailing of the bride often presses down a fourth. Comparable laments have been documented in the Mangystau region of Kazakhstan and in the Karelian territories of Finland and Russia, with more distant parallels appearing among the Shipibo-Conibo people, in the upper Amazon, and the Kaluli of Papua New Guinea.

If you twang those four descending notes forcefully on a guitar, you have the makings of flamenco. The motif is especially prominent in the flamenco genre known as siguiriya, which stems from older genres of Gypsy lament. On a 1922 recording, Manuel Torre sings a classic siguiriya, with the guitarist El Hijo de Salvador repeatedly plucking out the fateful figure:

Siempre por los rincones	I always find you
te encuentro llorando . . .	weeping in the corners . . .

Flamenco is more than lament, of course; it is also music of high passion. As Federico García Lorca wrote of the siguiriya, "It comes from the first sob and the first kiss."

Of course, not every descending melody has lamentation on its mind. Lajos Vargyas's treatise *Folk Music of the Hungarians* contains a song called "Hej, Dunaról fuj a szél," whose slow-moving, downward-tending phrases display the markers of musical sadness. But it is actually a song of flirtation, with the singer turning a bleak situation to her advantage: "Hey, the wind's blowing from the Danube / Lie beside me, it won't reach you." Likewise, certain laments lack telltale "weeping" features: the aria "Che farò senza Euridice?" from Gluck's opera *Orfeo ed Euridice*, begins with a decorous, upward-arching phrase in a sunny major mode.

In other words, there are no globally consistent signifiers of emotion. Music is something other than a universal language. Nonetheless, the lament topos occurs often enough in various traditions that it has become a durable point of reference. Peter Kivy, in his book *Sound Sentiment*, argues that musical expression falls into two categories: "contours," melodic shapes that imitate some basic aspect of human speech or behavior; and "conventions," gestures that listeners within a particular culture learn to associate with particular psychological states. The falling figure of lament is more contour than convention, and it is a promising thread to follow through the musical maze.

THE ART OF MELANCHOLY

Emotional archetypes came late to notated or composed music. In the late Middle Ages, a stylized array of chantlike lines worked equally for texts of lust, grief, and devotion. Hildegard of Bingen, abbess of Rupertsberg (1098–1179), exhibited one of the first strongly defined personalities in music history, yet the fervid mysticism of her output emanates more from the words than from the music. The opening vocal line of Hildegard's "Laus Trinitati" ("Praise be to the Trinity, who is sound, and life") has much the same rising and falling shape as "O cruor sanguinis" (O bloodshed that rang out on high"). Still, you can identify a few explicitly emotional effects in medieval music—"not mere signs but actual *symptoms* of feeling," in the words of the scholar John Stevens. The lament contour might be among the oldest of these. In the twelfth-century liturgical drama *The Play of Daniel*, the prophet lets out a stepwise descending cry as he faces death in the lion's den: "Heu, heu!"

As the Middle Ages gave way to the Renaissance, "symptoms of feeling" erupted all over the musical landscape. Guillaume de Machaut (d. 1377), the most celebrated practitioner of the rhythmically pointed style of Ars Nova, dilated on the pleasures and pains of love, and you can hear a marked difference between the gently rippling figures of "Tant doucement" ("So sweetly I feel myself imprisoned") and the stark descending line of "Mors sui" ("I die, if I do not see you"). This emphasis on palpable emotion, bordering on the erotic, was probably connected to the growing assertiveness of the independent nobility and of the merchant classes. In the following century, Marsilio Ficino, the Florentine Neoplatonist philosopher, described music as presenting "the intentions and passions of the soul as well as words . . . so forcibly that it immediately provokes both the singer and the audience to imitate and act out the same things." The conception of music as a spur to individual action was an implicit challenge to medieval doctrine, and, indeed, Ficino's revival of Greek ideas led to suspicions of heresy.

When secular strains infiltrated sacred music, a major new phase in composition began. The high musical art of the later Renaissance was polyphony, the knotty interweaving of multiple melodic strands. A cadre of composers from the Low Countries—cultivated first by the dukes of Burgundy and later by such patrons as Louis XI of France and Lorenzo the Magnificent of Florence—wrote multi-movement masses of unprecedented complexity, perhaps the first purposefully awe-inducing works in the classical tradition. These composers adopted a new practice, English in origin, of letting a preexisting theme take control of a large-scale piece. At first, the melodies were taken from liturgical chant, but popular tunes later came into play. The master of the game was Johannes Ockeghem (d. 1497), who is said to have sung with a deep bass voice and who lived to a grand old age. Around 1460, Ockeghem wrote a chanson titled "Fors seulement," whose lovelorn text begins with the lines "Save only for the expectation of death / No hope dwells in my weary heart." Its opening notes match up with the lament contour of various folk traditions:

Ockeghem's song became widely popular, inspiring dozens of arrangements; a version by Antoine Brumel added a text beginning with the words "Plunged into the lake of despair." In due course, the tune served as a *cantus firmus*, or "fixed song," for settings of the Mass. The Kyrie of Ockeghem's own *Missa Fors seulement* begins with a terraced series of descents, the basses delving into almost Wagnerian regions. The illusion of three-dimensional space resulting from that vertical plunge is one novel sensation that Ockeghem's music affords; another is the cascading, overlapping motion of the voices, an early demonstration of the magic of organized sound. As the Mass goes on, the song of despair is transformed into a sign of Christ's glory.

After reaching a peak of refinement in the works of Ockeghem's disciple Josquin Desprez, polyphony faded in importance in the later sixteenth century. Listeners demanded new, often simpler styles. The marketplace for music expanded dramatically, with the printing press fostering an international, nonspecialist public. Dance fads such as the chaconne indicated the growing vitality of the vernacular. The Church, shaken by the challenge of the Reformation and its catchy hymns of praise, saw the need to make its messages more transparent; the Council of Trent decreed that church composers should formulate their ideas more intelligibly, instead of giving "empty pleasure to the ear" through abstruse polyphonic designs.

For a host of reasons, then, emotion in music became a hot topic. The theorist Gioseffo Zarlino, in his 1558 text *Le istitutioni harmoniche*, instructed composers to use "cheerful harmonies and fast rhythms for cheerful subjects and sad harmonies and grave rhythms for sad subjects." Zarlino went on: "When a composer wishes to express effects of grief and sorrow, he should (observing the rules given) use movements which proceed through the semitone, the semiditone, and similar intervals"—a reference to the sinuous chromatic scale, which had long been discouraged as musically erroneous but which in these years became a modish thing. Various scholars promoted the idea of a *stile moderno*, or "modern style"— music strong in feeling, alert to the nuances of texts, attentive to the movement of a singing voice.

The passions of the late Renaissance primed the scene for opera, which emerged in Italy just before 1600. In the decades leading up to that breakthrough, the great laboratory of musical invention was the madrigal—a secular polyphonic genre that allowed for much experiment in the blending of word and tone. While early madrigals tended to be straightforwardly songful, later ones were at times willfully convoluted, comparable in spirit to Mannerist painting. High-minded patrons encouraged innovation, even an avant-garde mentality; the dukes of Ferrara commissioned a repertory of *musica secreta*, or "secret music." The arch-magus of musical Mannerism was Carlo Gesualdo, a nobleman-composer who put forward some of the most harmonically peculiar music of the premodern epoch. His madrigal *Moro lasso*—"I die, alas, in my grief"—begins with a kaleidoscopic sequence of chords pinned to a four-note chromatic slide; *Dolcissima mia vita* ends with a briar patch of chromatic lines around the words "I must love you or die." The words are ironic in light of Gesualdo's personal history: in 1590, he discovered his wife in bed with another man and had both of them slaughtered.

The madrigal fad spread to England, where Elizabethan intellectuals were raising their own banners of independence. Drowning oneself in sorrow was one way of resisting the outward hierarchy of late-Renaissance society, the beehive ideal of each human worker performing his assigned task. Shakespeare's *Hamlet*, which was first performed around 1601, is the obvious case in point. The grief of the Prince of Denmark shines like a grim lantern on Claudius's rotten kingdom, exposing not only Hamlet's private loss but the hollowness of all human affairs: "I have that within, which passeth show; / These, but the trappings and the suits of woe." Music was a favorite site for brooding in the Danish style. The composer Thomas Morley set down some guidelines in his 1597 textbook *A Plaine and Easie Introduction to Practicall Musicke*: "If [the subject] be lamentable, the note must goe in slow and heavy motions, as semibriefs, briefs, and such like . . . Where your dittie speaketh of descending, lowenes, depth, hell, and others such, you must make your musick descend." This echoed Zarlino's literal-minded directive of 1558. In Elizabethan England, an inordinate number of ditties spoke of lowness, depth, and hell, leaving the heavenly register somewhat neglected.

The supreme melancholic among English composers was the lutenist John Dowland. Like so many of his international colleagues, Dowland indulged in chromatic esoterica, but he also showed a songwriter's flair for hummable phrases: his lute piece *Lachrimae*, or *Tears*, achieved hit status across Europe in the last years of the sixteenth century. When, in 1600, Dowland published his Second Book of Songs, he included a vocal version of *Lachrimae*, with words suitable for a Hamlet soliloquy:

> *Flow my tears, fall from your springs,*
> *Exil'd forever let me mourn*
> *Where night's black bird her sad infamy sings,*
> *There let me live forlorn.*

The first four notes of the melody have a familiar ring: they traverse the same intervals—whole tone, whole tone, semitone—that usher in Ockeghem's "Fors seulement." Underscoring the personal significance of the theme, Dowland made it the leitmotif of his 1604 cycle of pieces for viol consort, also titled *Lachrimae*.

In Dowland's instrumental masterpiece, no reason for the flow of tears is given, no biblical or literary motive. Music becomes self-sufficient, taking its own expressive power as its subject. *Lachrimae* could have been cited as an illustration in Robert Burton's 1621 treatise *The Anatomy of*

Melancholy, which meditates on music's capacity to conquer all human defenses: "Speaking without a mouth, it exercises domination over the soul, and carries it beyond itself, helps, elevates, extends it." Music might inject melancholy into an otherwise happy temperament, Burton concedes, but it is a "pleasing melancholy." That phrase encapsulates Dowland's aesthetic. His forlorn songs have about them an air of luxury, as if sadness were a place of refuge far from the hurly-burly, a twilight realm where time stops for a while. The *Lachrimae* tune becomes, in a way, the anthem of the eternally lonely man. Indeed, as the musicologist Peter Holman points out, Dowland anticipated Burton's thought in the preface to his collection: "No doubt pleasant are the tears which Musicke weeps."

It has long been understood that music has the ability to stir feelings for which we do not have a name. The neurobiologist Aniruddh Patel, in his book *Music, Language, and the Brain,* lays out myriad relationships between music and speech, and yet he allows that "musical sounds can evoke emotions that speech sounds cannot." The dream of a private kingdom beyond the grasp of ordinary language seems to have been crucial for the process of self-fashioning that so preoccupied Renaissance intellectuals: through music, one could make an autonomous, unknowable self that stood apart from the order of things. In a wider sense, Dowland forecast the untrammeled emotionalism of the Romantic era, and even the moodier dropout anthems of the 1960s, the likes of "Nowhere Man" and "Desolation Row." As Oscar Wilde wrote of *Hamlet,* "The world has become sad because a puppet was once melancholy."

OPERA

In 1589, Ferdinando de' Medici, the grand duke of Tuscany, married Christine of Lorraine. The duke had acquired his title two years earlier, after the sudden demise of his older brother, Francesco. Modern analysis has confirmed what rumor long held: Francesco died of arsenic poisoning. Against this suitably sinister backdrop the art of opera arose. For decades, Medici festivities had offered dramatic musical interludes within a larger theatrical presentation. These *intermedi,* as they were called, grew ever more extravagant as the century went on, serving, in the words of the poet Giovanni Battista Strozzi the Younger, to "stun the beholder with their grandeur." The play accompanied the music rather than the other way around. The writers and composers of Florence eventually decided to let the music run continuously. It was a new kind of sung drama, modeled on the theater of ancient Greece.

The first true opera was apparently Jacopo Peri's *Dafne*, presented in Florence in 1598, with a text by Ottavio Rinuccini. Two years later, for another Medici wedding, Peri set Rinuccini's *Euridice*, telling of the unhappy adventures of the poet and musician Orpheus. In a preface to the score, Peri announced the ascendancy of "a new manner of song," through which grief and joy would speak forth with unusual immediacy. Peri's chief rival, the singer-composer Giulio Caccini, wrote an opera on the same *Euridice* libretto not long after, and managed to get his version into print first. Claudio Monteverdi, an ambitious younger composer from Cremona, trumped them both with his five-act opera *Orfeo*, which had its premiere in 1607, at the court of the Gonzagas in Mantua, and which still holds the stage more than four centuries later.

Without the lament, opera might never have caught fire. The story of Orpheus is little more than a string of lamentations: the bard bewails the loss of Euridice, goes down into the underworld to rescue her (his plaint wins Hades over), and then, with one ill-timed backward glance, loses her again. Both *Euridice* operas, despite their tacked-on happy endings, perform familiar gestures of musical weeping. Peri briefly applies the falling four-note figure to Orpheus's words "Chi mi t'ha tolto, ohime" ("Who has torn you from me, alas"). There's a noteworthy expansion of the motif in Caccini's treatment of the same text. After Orpheus finishes his lament, a nymph and various other voices echo him, bemoaning "Cruel death." Caccini's version is slower and grander than Peri's, making more deliberate use of repetition. Seven times the chorus sings the formula "Sospirate, aure celesti, / lagrimate, o selve, o campi" ("Sigh, heavenly breezes / Weep, o forests, o fields"), with four-note laments threaded through the voices. The spaciousness of the sequence seems essentially operatic.

The next step was to back away from aristocratic refinement and incorporate elements of popular song and dance. Spain served as a primary source. Back in 1553, the viol player Diego Ortiz published a set of improvisations over a repeating bass line—a *basso ostinato*, or ground bass. The art of improvising on an ostinato went back centuries, although it had gone largely undocumented in notated music. When composers finally took hold of it, the effect was exhilarating, as if someone had switched on a rhythmic engine. Renaissance harmony in all its fullness was wedded to the dance. As Richard Taruskin observes, in his *Oxford History of Western Music*, this mammoth event—the birth of modern tonal language—was a revolution from below. A "great submerged iceberg" of unrecorded traditions, in Taruskin's phrase, came into view, not least because publishers realized there was money in it.

The chaconne was one such bass-driven dance. The first major composer to impose his personality on the form was the magisterial Italian organist Girolamo Frescobaldi, another beneficiary of the largesse of the dukes of Ferrara. In 1627, Frescobaldi published *Partite sopra ciaccona*, or *Variations on the Chaconne*, in which the popular formula is sent through the compositional wringer: the bass line breaks away from its mold, the rhythmic pulse speeds up and slows down, and the harmony darkens several times from major to minor, with a spooky dissonance piercing the texture just before the end. Frescobaldi also wrote *Partite* on a related ostinato dance, the passacaglia, holding to the minor mode until the very end. (Chaconnes were generally in major keys and passacaglias in minor ones, although composers enjoyed subverting the rule.) A decade later, Frescobaldi upped the ante with his *Cento partite*, a dazzling sequence of one hundred variations that includes both passacaglias and chaconnes. In the words of the scholar Alexander Silbiger, *Cento partite* is "a narrative of the flow and unpredictability of human experience." It deserves comparison with Bach's *Goldberg Variations*, Beethoven's *Diabelli Variations*, and other consummate displays of compositional virtuosity.

Monteverdi, the reigning Italian master, appropriated the chaconne at around the same time. Although he held the lofty title of *maestro di cappella*, or director of music, at the Basilica of San Marco in Venice, he never lost his ear for the music of the streets. A rocketing chaconne propels the 1632 duet *Zefiro torna*, on a Rinuccini text:

> *Zephyr returns and blesses the air*
> *with his soft perfume, draws bare feet to the shore,*
> *and, murmuring among the green branches,*
> *makes the flowers dance in the meadows to his pretty tune.*

The buoyant rhythm neatly captures Rinuccini's springtime imagery. The voices imitate one another and tease against the beat, like dancers weaving around a maypole. In the final lines, the sonnet takes a surprising turn: the protagonist of the poem reveals himself to be a disconsolate loner, singing and weeping over the absence of two fair eyes. And the bouncing beat gives way to a heaving lament. As in Lorca's flamenco, sobs and kisses, pleasure and anguish, coincide.

Zefiro torna was a certifiable hit of the 1630s, grabbing the attention of many rival composers. Monteverdi deployed ostinato basses in several other pieces, most memorably in *Lamento della ninfa*, or *Lament of the Nymph*, which he published in his Eighth Book of Madrigals, of 1638. In an introduction to the volume, Monteverdi declared that he wished to give a complete musical picture of what he called the three passions—"anger, temperance, and humility or supplication." Anger, he said, had never been properly depicted in music before, and he proudly underlined the groundbreaking achievement of his "madrigals of war." But the *Lamento* is no less inventive in the way it goes about illustrating the third passion, that of the humbled soul. A solo female voice, representing a distraught nymph, sings a plaint—

> *Let my love return to me*
> *as he was before*
> *or take me then and kill me*
> *so I rack myself no more.*

—while three male voices paraphrase her woe ("unhappy one, ah, no more, she cannot suffer so much ice"). The bass line follows the classic lamenting shape. The notes A-G-F-E are heard thirty-four times in succession, never yielding.

The ostinato in *Zefiro torna* exudes a giddy, carefree air. The one in *Lamento della ninfa* is different. First, obsessive repetition focuses and magnifies the melancholy affect of the stepwise descent. Indeed, as the musicologist Ellen Rosand maintains, this work made the association almost official; the falling motif became an "emblem of lament," one that composers employed consciously, with reference to Monteverdi's model. Second, the ostinato has a symbolic function, carrying a tinge of psychological compulsion. The voice keeps tugging against the bass line, pushing upward, stretching its phrases beyond the two-bar unit, giving rise to dissonant clashes, breaking down into chromatic steps. The implacability of the bass suggests that these attempts at escape are in vain. Instead, the piece ends in a mood of shattered acquiescence, as the voice subsides to the note from which it began. Even so, there is no denying the seduction of repetition, the psychic pull of the circling motion. The ceremony of lament interrupts the ordinary passage of time, and therefore, paradoxically, holds mortality at bay.

In the early seventeenth century, opera spread across Italy, becoming more of a commercial entertainment in the process. In 1637, one year before Monteverdi published *Lamento della ninfa*, a touring troupe brought opera to the republic of Venice. The season took place during Carnival, the time of dissolution and self-reinvention. Opera was reborn as a many-layered, stylistically ravenous form, combining lyric tragedy with lewd comedy— the musical counterpart of the high-low drama of Shakespeare and Lope de Vega. Mythological subjects took on a modern edge; castrato singers flamboyantly restyled classical heroes; star divas enacted scenes of madness and lament; and a diverse public showed lusty approval. For the remainder of the century, up to five theaters were operating in Venice at one time, drawing an audience that included not only the upper crust but also courtesans, tourists, well-born students, and a smattering of ordinary people. In Ellen Rosand's words, "opera as we know it assumed its definitive identity."

Monteverdi was nearly seventy when opera came to Venice, but the phenomenon allowed him to experience a second youth. His two surviving late operas, *The Return of Ulysses* and *The Coronation of Poppea*, revel in extreme emotions, oscillating between suicidal angst and orgiastic joy. The two extant scores of *Poppea*—a drama of lust and greed in the high Roman Empire—both end with a disarmingly blissful duet between Nero and his lover Poppea, "Pur ti miro" ("I gaze upon you"), over a caressing major-key ground bass. Although scholars now believe that this duet was added by another composer, it communicates the heady allure of opera in its early days.

When Monteverdi died, in 1643, Francesco Cavalli, a gifted protégé, took his place. No less than his mentor had, Cavalli shaped the opera genre as we know it today, perfecting the transition from speechlike recitative to fully lyrical arioso singing. He had a particular gift for arias of lament, embedding them in velvety harmonic progressions. An early example appears in the 1640 opera *Gli amori d'Apollo e di Dafne*, which tells of Daphne's transformation into a laurel tree. Toward the end, the god Apollo realizes that his beloved nymph has slipped from his grasp, and he declares himself miserable. Cavalli promptly unfurls the A-G-F-E bass line from *Lamento della ninfa*, making it the motor of a truncated arioso passage that bears the title Lamento:

As in Monteverdi, the repetition in the bass mimics the obsessive, circular thinking of the unhappy lover—the painful recollection of happy moments, the sick-hearted imagining of alternate outcomes. It follows the psychological rhythm of depression: the spirit sinking step by step, straining to recover, then sinking again.

The Venetian public evidently enjoyed Apollo's monologue of misery, for *Didone*, Cavalli's opera for the following season, features laments galore. In the first act, survivors of the fall of Troy—Hecuba, King Priam's widow; her daughters Cassandra and Creusa; and the hero Aeneas, Creusa's husband—bewail the end of their world even as more mayhem descends on them. Cassandra has hardly finished mourning for her beloved Coroebus when Creusa is abruptly slain. Hecuba enters, seeking to voice a feeling "beyond the tears," and she finds release in an incantation that seems to portray not only the recent fall of Troy but also the future demise of Greece:

> *Porticos, temples are*
> *Shaking and trembling,*
> *Burning and tumbling.*
> *Purple and empire,*
> *Turn into dust,*
> *Make clothes of ashes!*

At this point Cavalli had a stroke of genius, one that reverberated through the centuries. He prolonged Monteverdi's ostinato bass, so that it moved down by chromatic steps (G–F-sharp–F-natural–E–E-flat–D). There's something claustrophobic about those close-set intervals: they give the feeling of a dismal shuffle, the gait of a lost soul.

The laments of *Didone* come mainly from the throats of women: Cassandra and Hecuba in the first act, Dido at the end. Almost from the start, male opera composers depended on the figure of the abandoned, vengeful, and/or maddened female. The musicologist Susan McClary, in her pioneering study *Feminine Endings*, identifies Monteverdi's *Lamento della ninfa* as a harbinger of operatic mad scenes, describing the piece as "a display designed by men, chiefly for the consumption of other men." McClary compares the music to a grille on an old asylum window through which passersby could watch mad people. Other scholars, though, have detected a certain defiant self-assertion in the female portraits set forth by Cavalli and other early operatic composers. Wendy Heller, in a discussion of *Didone*, describes the title character as a tragically constrained woman, but celebrates Hecuba as an intriguingly dangerous force of nature, her music charged with "a sense of the supernatural and the other-worldliness of [her] strength."

The singer and composer Barbara Strozzi (1619–77), one of the few publicly recognized female composers of the Baroque period, reversed the standard equation in her cantata *L'Eraclito amoroso* ("The Amorous Heraclitus"). The text for this piece shows the Greek philosopher Heraclitus in a perpetual fit of despondency:

> *My only pleasure is in weeping,*
> *I feed on tears alone.*
> *Dolor is my delight,*
> *And my joy is sighing.*

Strozzi presumably sang the cantata herself, impersonating a male in extremis. An ornate vocal line unfolds over a steady iteration of the *Lamento della ninfa* bass. It is an ambiguous, even androgynous scene, with gender identity melting away into a purely musical space of lamentation. For Strozzi, as for Dowland, melancholy may have been a site of self-creation, even giving hints of future freedom.

FRENCH AND ENGLISH CHACONNES

The chaconne had its apotheosis at Versailles. The music master at the court of Louis XIV was Jean-Baptiste Lully, who, like the chaconne itself, came from lowly circumstances; the son of a Florentine miller, he started out laboring as a servant and tutor to a princess who was a cousin of the king. When Lully exhibited performing talent, Louis hired him as a dancer, and shortly after set him to work composing. Lully created a series of grand ballets that he and Louis danced side by side; in later years, he became the chief opera composer of the kingdom, his clout confirmed by his friendship with the sovereign and his scandalous homosexual affairs largely excused. Productions at Versailles were so staggeringly lavish that many in the audience came principally to see the theatrical machinery. Plots were taken from mythology and chivalric tales, with unhappy endings modified to meet the harmonious ideals of the Sun King's world.

Lully's theater works routinely culminate in a majestic chaconne or passacaille. The flowing motion of these dances symbolizes the reconciliation of warring elements and the restoration of happiness. At the same time, an exotic association remains; a scholarly study by Rose Pruiksma notes that Lully's chaconnes and passacailles are linked to Italian, Spanish, North African, even Chinese characters and locales. In *Cadmus*, a chaconne is performed by "thirteen Africans dancing and playing the guitar." In *Armide*, a four-note passacaglia bass stands for the sorcery of the title character. And in the *Ballet d'Alcidiane*, from 1658, the union of the island princess and the hero Polexandre prompts a Chaconne des Maures, or Chaconne of the Moors. Louis himself performed as one of eight Moorish dancers, donning a black mask. The verses for the scene invoke the irresistible attraction of the darker-skinned males:

> One dreads the arms of these lovely shadowed ones
> And everything gives way to their charms,
> Blondes, I say farewell to you.

As Pruiksma explains, the sight of world cultures happily intermingling provided a mythological justification for Louis XIV's marriage into the Spanish Habsburg family in 1660. Given the Hispanic origins of the chaconne, the music fit the occasion.

In these same years, the chaconne underwent its epic mutation, taking on a markedly more serious visage. Other dances of the day evolved in much the same way: the racy zarabanda became the stately sarabande, a medium of sober reflection for the likes of J. S. Bach and George Frideric Handel. Composers seemed to compete among themselves to see who could most effectively distort and deconstruct the popular music of the seventeenth century. They must have done so in a spirit of intellectual play, demonstrating how the most familiar stuff could be creatively transformed; such is the implicit attitude of Frescobaldi's *Partite sopra ciaccona* and *Cento partite*. Louis Couperin, a keyboard composer of questing intellect, carried on the game by writing chaconnes that, in the words of Wilfrid Mellers, "proceed with relentless power, and are usually dark in color and dissonant in texture." The same dusky aura hangs over a *Chaconne raportée* by the august viol player Sainte-Colombe, which, in a fusion of the chaconne and lamento traditions, begins with a lugubrious chromatic line.

English chaconnes, too, assumed both light and dark shades. The restoration of the English monarchy in the wake of Oliver Cromwell's republican experiment called for musical spectaculars in the Lully vein, replete with sumptuous dances of enchantment and reconciliation. Several exquisite specimens came from the pen of Henry Purcell, the leading English composer of the late-seventeenth century. In his semiopera *King Arthur*, nymphs and sylvans in the employ of an evil magician attempt to lure the hero king with a gigantic passacaglia on a *Lamento della ninfa* bass. Purcell's *The Fairy Queen*, a very free adaptation of *A Midsummer Night's Dream*, culminates in a decorous, Lullyesque chaconne titled "Dance for Chinese Man and Woman." (The play ends in a not very Shakespearean Chinese Garden.) In works of more intimate character, Purcell often reverted to the lachrymose manner of Dowland and other Elizabethan masters. The lamenting chromatic fourth worms its way through the anthem "Plung'd in the confines of despair" and the sacred song "O I'm sick of life."

In 1689 or shortly before, Purcell produced the most celebrated ground-bass lament in history: "When I am laid in earth," Dido's aria at the end of the short opera *Dido and Aeneas*. Could Purcell have known Cavalli's *Didone*? Probably not, but he did make unforgettable use of the same chromatic-ostinato device that Cavalli implanted in Hecuba's song. Purcell takes care first to introduce the bass line on its own, so there is no mistaking its expressive role. This is from an eighteenth-century copy:

The notes are like a chilly staircase stretching out before one's feet. In the fourth full bar there's a slight rhythmic unevenness, a subtle emphasis on the second beat (one-*two*-three). You can hear the piece almost as an immensely slow, immensely solemn chaconne. Nine times the ground unwinds, in five-bar segments. Over it, Dido sings her valediction, a blanket of strings draped over her:

> *When I am laid in earth, may my wrongs create*
> *No trouble in thy breast,*
> *Remember me, but ah! forget my fate.*

The vocal line begins on G, works its way upward, and retreats, with pointed repetitions of the phrases "no trouble" and "remember me." Dido's long lines spill over the structure of the ground, so that she finds herself arching toward a climactic note just as the bass returns to the point of departure. First she reaches a D, then an E-flat. With the final "remember me" she attains the next higher G, the "me" falling on the second beat. When the song is done, there is a debilitating chromatic slide, undoing, step by step, the effort of the ascent. The ostinato of fate seems triumphant. Yet Dido's high, brief cry is the sound we remember—a Morse-code signal from oblivion.

CIACCONA IN D MINOR

Bach's Ciaccona for unaccompanied violin, a quarter-hour-long soliloquy of lacerating beauty, stands at such a distance from the hijinks of the Spanish chacona that the title seems almost ironic. With its white-knuckle virtuosity, its unyielding variation structure, and its tragic D-minor cast, this is a piece from which *la vida bona* appears to have been banished utterly. Yet the ghost of the dance hovers in the background. The image of Bach as a bewigged, sour-faced lawgiver of tradition has caused both performers and listeners to neglect the physical dimension of his work. To hear the Ciaccona played on the guitar—there are richly resonant recordings by Andrés Segovia and Julian Bream—is to realize that bodily pleasure has its place even in the blackest corners of Bach's world.

Bach made his name as an organist, joining a starry lineage of northern European organ players that went back to the Dutch composer Jan Pieterszoon Sweelinck (1562–1621). Sweelinck, in turn, drew on the tortuous chromatic techniques of late-Renaissance Italy and Elizabethan England. In his *Fantasia chromatica*, Sweelinck subjects a descending chromatic figure and two companion themes to various contrapuntal manipulations, forming a spidery mass of intersecting lines. The finger-twisting brilliance of the writing is held in check by a taut tripartite scheme: in the first third, the theme proceeds at a regular tempo; in the second, it is slowed down; in the third, it goes faster and faster still. Such music marks the beginning of the Bachian art of the fugue.

The organists of the German Baroque, who included Dietrich Buxtehude and Johann Pachelbel, embraced the practice of "strict ostinato," in which a short motif repeats in the bass while upper voices move about more freely. (The inescapable Pachelbel Canon is an ostinato exercise in a lulling major key.) The interplay between independent treble and locked-in bass acquires additional drama when the bass lines are bellowed out on the organ's pedal notes—sixteen- and even thirty-two-foot pipes activated by the feet. Bach's Passacaglia in C Minor, a looser kind of ostinato piece, begins with the bass alone, in a pattern that winds upward from the initial C before spiraling down an octave and a half to a bottom C that should be heard less as a note than as a minor earthquake. Bach was especially attracted to bass lines that crawled along chromatic steps. One of these shows up in the third movement of the playful little suite *Capriccio on the Departure of a*

Beloved Brother, one of Bach's earliest extant works. In the 1714 cantata "Weinen, Klagen, Sorgen, Zagen," a corkscrew chromatic bass portrays the "weeping, wailing, fretting, and quaking" of Christ's followers.

When, in 1723, Bach took up the position of cantor at St. Thomas School in Leipzig, he pledged that his music would be "of such a nature as not to make an operatic impression, but rather incite the listeners to devotion." In employing Italian opera devices such as the lamento bass, he might have been trying to sublimate them, taming a dangerously sultry form. A man of religious convictions, Bach wrote in the margins of his Bible commentary that music was "ordered by God's spirit through David" and that devotional music showed the "presence of grace." At the same time, though, his arioso melodies had the potential to undermine the austerity of the Lutheran service; even if he never wrote an opera, he displayed operatic tendencies. He presumably understood these contradictions, and possibly relished them. His comment about the "presence of grace" pertained to a faintly occult description of music-making at the Temple, in the second book of Chronicles: "It came even to pass, as the trumpeters and the singers were as one, to make one sound to be heard in praising and thanking the Lord . . . The house was filled with a cloud, even the house of the Lord."

The Ciaccona for solo violin, which Bach composed in 1720 as part of his cycle of Sonatas and Partitas, possesses something like that ominous, cloudlike presence. It takes the form of sixty-four variations on a four-bar

theme in D minor, with each four-bar segment generally repeated before the next variation begins. But the melodic strands of the opening bars— both treble and bass—disappear for long stretches as Bach explores new material. The "theme" is really a set of chords, framing limitless flux. (The copy reproduced on the previous page was probably made not long after Bach's death.) Lament figures crop up throughout, sometimes plainly presented and sometimes hidden in the seams. A D-major middle section functions as a respite from the prevailing gloom of the piece, yet the apparition of a descending chromatic line high in the treble hints that these brighter days won't last. Soon after, D minor returns, with a four-note lament motif planted firmly in the bass—the shade of "Fors seulement," *Lachrimae*, and *Lamento della ninfa*.

It would appear that Bach has gone beyond rituals of mourning to a solitary, existential agony. In the words of Susan McClary, "the lone violinist must both furnish the redundant ostinato and also fight tooth and nail against it." For McClary, the chaconne has become a formal prison for the struggling self. But Bach hasn't entirely forgotten the sway of the dance. Alexander Silbiger, in a revealing essay, draws attention to passages of "repeated strumming," "rustling arpeggiations," "sudden foot-stamping." Often Bach tests the limits of his variation scheme and lands back in D minor with a precarious lunge: "Some of these ventures bring to mind a trapeze artist, who swings further and further, reaching safety only at the last instant and leaving his spectators gasping." The violin's more florid gestures also make Silbiger think of jazz artists and sitar players, who "create the illusion of taking momentary flight from the solid ground that supports their improvisations, to the occasional bewilderment of their fellow performers." In the end, the Ciaccona might be a grave dance before the Lord, the ballet of the soul in the course of a life.

In 1748 and 1749, the last full years of his earthly existence, Bach assembled his Mass in B Minor, rearranging extant works and writing new material in a quest for a comprehensive union of Catholic and Lutheran traditions. At the heart of the Mass is the section of the Credo that deals with the death of Jesus Christ on the cross:

Crucifixus etiam pro nobis	He was also crucified for us
sub Pontio Pilato, passus	under Pontius Pilate, suffered,
et sepultus est.	and was buried.

To find music for this text, Bach went back thirty-five years in his output, to the "Weinen, Klagen, Sorgen, Zagen" chorus, with its twelve somber soundings of a chromatic bass. But he stepped up the pulsation of the ground, so that instead of three half notes per bar we hear a faster, tenser rhythm of six quarter notes per bar. He changed the instrumentation, adding breathy flutes to tearful strings. He inserted a brief instrumental prelude, so that, as in Purcell, we first hear the bass line without the voices. Bach thus expanded the structure from twelve to thirteen parts. Whether he intended any symbolism in the number thirteen is unknown, although most of his listeners would have been aware that the Last Supper had thirteen guests. This is in Bach's own hand:

As in *Didone* and *Dido and Aeneas*, the chromatic pattern evokes an individual pinned down by fate. This time, the struggler is not a woman but a man, one who knows full well what fate has in store. Bach makes Jesus Christ seem pitiably human at the moment of his ultimate suffering, so that believers may confront more directly their own grief and guilt. (Martin Luther vilified the Jews, but he also preached that Christians should hold none but themselves responsible for Christ's killing.) It is a quasi-operatic scene, although it is witnessed at a properly awed distance. The voices wend away from the bass, moving in various directions. There are slowly pulsing chords of strings on the first and third beats, flutes on the second and third: they suggest something dripping, perhaps blood from Christ's wounds, or tears from the eyes of his followers. In the thirteenth iteration, the bass singers give up their contrary motion and join the trudge of the continuo section. The sopranos, too, follow a chromatic path. The upper instruments fall silent, as if the dripping has stopped and life is spent. Fate's victory seems complete. But then the bass suddenly reverses direction, and there is a momentous swerve from E minor into the key of G major. On the next page, the Resurrection begins.

ROMANTIC VARIATIONS

Bach died in 1750, and the Baroque era more or less died with him. Forms of rigid repetition lost their appeal as the Baroque gave way to the Classical period and then to the Romantic: increasingly, composers valued constant variation, sudden contrast, unrelenting escalation. Music became linear rather than circular, with large-scale structures proceeding from assertive thematic ideas through episodes of strenuous development to climaxes of overwhelming magnitude. "Time's cycle had been straightened into an arrow, and the arrow was traveling ever faster," the scholar Karol Berger writes. Music would no longer react to an exterior order; instead, it would become a kind of aesthetic empire unto itself. In 1810, E.T.A. Hoffmann wrote a review of Beethoven's Fifth Symphony in which he differentiated the Romantic ethos from the more restrained spirit of prior centuries: "Orpheus's lyre opened the gates of Orcus. Music reveals to man an unknown realm, a world quite separate from the outer sensual world surrounding him, a world in which he leaves behind all feelings circumscribed by intellect in order to embrace the inexpressible."

For composers of Mozart's time and after, the chaconne, the passacaglia, and the lamento aria would have been antique devices learned from manuals of counterpoint and the like. Yet they never disappeared entirely. Beethoven studied Bach in his youth, and at some point he came across the B-Minor Mass, or a description of it; in 1810 he asked his publisher to send him "a Mass by J. S. Bach that has the following Crucifixus with a *basso ostinato* as obstinate as you are"—and he wrote out the "Crucifixus" bass line. Beethoven was undoubtedly thinking of Bach when, in his Thirty-two Variations in C Minor of 1806, he elaborated doggedly on the downward chromatic fourth. Eighteen years later, a "Crucifixus" figure cropped up in the stormy D-minor opening movement of the Ninth Symphony. Thirty-five bars before the end, the strings and bassoons churn out a *basso lamento* that has the rhythm of a dirge: you can almost hear the feet of pallbearers dragging alongside a hero's casket.

Yet the ostinato is a nightmare from which Beethoven wishes to wake. The finale of the Ninth rejects the mechanics of fateful repetition: in the frenzied, dissonant music that opens the finale, the chromatic descent momentarily resurfaces, and when it is heard again at the beginning of the vocal section of the movement the bass soloist intones, "O friends, not these tones!" At which point the Ode to Joy begins. Beethoven might have been echoing the central shift of the B-Minor Mass—the leap from the chromatic "Crucifixus" to the blazing "Et resurrexit."

The lamento bass would not stay buried. It rumbles in much music of the later nineteenth century: in various works of Brahms, in the late piano music of Liszt, in the songs and symphonies of Mahler. It is a dominating presence in Tchaikovsky's *Pathétique* Symphony, which ends with a slow movement marked Adagio lamentoso. Even in the first bars of the first movement, double basses creep down step by chromatic step while a single bassoon presses fitfully upward. (The scenario is much like the contrary motion of the upper and lower voices in Dido's Lament.) The final Adagio begins with a desperately eloquent theme that contains within it the time-worn contour of folkish lament. In the coda, Tchaikovsky combines the modal and chromatic forms of the lamento pattern, creating a hybrid emblem of grief, somewhat in the manner of Bach's chaconne. The passage plays out over a softly pulsing bass note that recalls the eternal basses of Bach's Passions.

The affect of the Adagio lamentoso could hardly be clearer. Tchaikovsky seems to have reverted to the mimetic code of Renaissance writers such as Ficino: as the music droops, so droops the heart, until death removes all pain. Indeed, the tone of lament is so fearsomely strong that many listeners have taken it to be a direct transcription of Tchaikovsky's own feelings. The work had its premiere nine days before the composer's sudden death, of cholera, in 1893, and almost immediately people began to speculate that it was a conscious farewell. Wild rumors circulated: according to one tale, Tchaikovsky had committed suicide at the behest of former schoolmates who were scandalized by his homosexuality. That last story is a fascinating case of musically induced hallucination, for the biographer Alexander Poznansky has established that no such plot could have existed and that Tchaikovsky was actually in good spirits before he fell ill. The *Pathétique* is best understood not as a confession but as a riposte to Beethoven's heroic narrative, the progression from solitary struggle to collective joy. In the vein of Dowland, Tchaikovsky asserts the power of the private sphere—the contrary stance of the happily melancholy self. Indeed, lament has never made so voluptuous a sound.

THE LIGETI LAMENTO

In the twentieth century, time's arrow again bent into a cycle, to follow Karol Berger's metaphor. While some composers pursued ever more arcane musics of the future, others found a new thrill in archaic repetition. Chaconne and related forms returned to fashion. Schoenberg, hailed and feared as the destroyer of tonality, actually considered himself Bach's heir, and his method of twelve-tone writing, which extracts the musical material of a piece from a fixed series of twelve notes, is an extension of the variation concept. (So argued Stefan Wolpe, an important Schoenberg disciple, in an essay on Bach's Passacaglia in C Minor.) "Nacht," the eighth song of Schoenberg's melodrama *Pierrot lunaire*, is subtitled "Passacaglia," its main theme built around a downward chromatic segment. The revival of Baroque forms quickened after the horror of the First World War, which impelled young composers to distance themselves from a blood-soaked Romantic aesthetic. The circling motion of the chaconne and the passacaglia also summons up a modern kind of fateful loop—the grinding of a monstrous engine or political force. In Berg's *Wozzeck*, a passacaglia reflects the regimented madness of military life; in Britten's *Peter Grimes*, the same form voices the mounting dread of a boy apprentice in the grip of a socially outcast fisherman.

No modern composer manipulated the lament and the chaconne more imaginatively than György Ligeti, whose music is known to millions through Stanley Kubrick's film *2001: A Space Odyssey*. Indeed, Ligeti inspired the present essay. In 1993, I heard the composer give a series of dazzlingly erudite talks at the New England Conservatory, in Boston, during which he touched many times on the literature of lament. At one point Ligeti sang the notes "La, sol, fa, mi"—A, G, F, E, the *Lamento della ninfa* bass—and began cataloguing its myriad appearances in Western music, both in the classical repertory and in folk melodies that he learned as a child. He remembered hearing the *bocet* in Transylvania: "I was very much impressed by these Romanian lamentos, which old women sing who are paid when somebody is dead in a village. And maybe this is some musical signal which is very, very deep in my subconscious." He noted a resemblance between Eastern European Gypsy music and Andalusian flamenco. He also spoke of Gesualdo's madrigals, Purcell's "When I am laid in earth," Bach's "Crucifixus," and Schubert's Quartet in G Major—about which more will be said in a later chapter.

Ligeti first encountered the older repertory while studying at the Kolozsvár Conservatory, in the early 1940s. The Second World War interrupted his schooling: after serving in a forced-labor gang, he returned home to discover that many of his relatives, including his father and his brother, had died in the Nazi concentration camps. His first major postwar work, *Musica ricercata* for piano (1951–53), dabbled in various Renaissance and Baroque tricks; the final movement, a hushed fugue, draws on one of Frescobaldi's chromatic melodies. After leaving Hungary, in 1956, Ligeti entered his avant-garde period, producing scores in which melody and harmony seem to vanish into an enveloping fog of cluster chords, although those masses of sound are in fact made up of thousands of swirling microscopic figures. In the 1980s, Ligeti resumed an eccentric kind of tonal writing, in an effort to engage more directly with classical tradition; perhaps he also wished to excavate his tortured memories of the European past. The finale of his Horn Trio is titled "Lamento"; at the outset, the violin softly wails in a broken chromatic descent. Although the motif recurs in chaconne style, this is a somewhat unhinged ceremony of mourning, its funereal tones giving way to outright delirium. In the climactic passage, the three instruments execute musical sobs in turn, as if mimicking village cries that Ligeti heard as a child.

In the last phase of his career, Ligeti devised his own lament signature. Richard Steinitz, the composer's biographer, defines it as a melody of three falling phrases, dropping sometimes by half-steps and sometimes by wider intervals, with the note of departure often inching upward in pitch and the final phrase stretching out longer than the previous two. That heightening and elongating of the phrases is another memory of folk practice. The Ligeti lamento cascades through all registers of the piano etude "Automne à Varsovie"; it also figures in several recklessly intense passages of the Violin Concerto (whose fourth movement is a Passacaglia) and of the Piano Concerto. And in the Viola Sonata, chaconne and lament once again intersect. The final movement of the sonata is titled "Chaconne chromatique," and the rhythm of the principal theme—short-long, short-long, short-short-short-short long—recalls the languid motion of Dido's Lament. Then the motif begins to accelerate, becoming, in Steinitz's words, "fast, exuberant, passionate." As in *Hungarian Rock*, Ligeti's rollicking chaconne for harpsichord, the specter of the old Spanish dance returns, writhing behind a modernist scrim.

THE BLUES

In 1903, the African-American bandleader W. C. Handy was killing time at a train depot in Tutwiler, Mississippi—a small town in the impoverished, mostly black Mississippi Delta region—when he came upon a raggedly dressed man singing and strumming what Handy later described as "the weirdest music I had ever heard." The nameless musician, his face marked with "the sadness of the ages," kept repeating the phrase "Goin' where the Southern cross' the Dog," and he bent notes on his guitar by applying a knife to the strings. The refrain referred to the meeting point of two railway lines, but it conjured up some vaguer, supernatural scene. Handy tried to capture the phantom singer of Tutwiler in such numbers as "The Memphis Blues," "The Yellow Dog Blues," and "The St. Louis Blues." The last, in 1914, set off an international craze for the music that came to be known as the blues.

One feature common to many early blues, whether commercial or rural, is the old downward chromatic slide. It runs in an almost subliminal way through the opening sequence of "St. Louis Blues," and makes an unmistakable appearance in Bessie Smith's 1925 recording of the song, where the young Louis Armstrong traces rapierlike solos on his trumpet. In Mamie Smith's "Crazy Blues," it takes on burlesque exuberance, merging with the sassy glissando of the slide trombone.

In the late twenties and thirties, recording technology captured the voices of numerous authentic practitioners of the Delta blues: Charley Patton, Willie Brown, Son House, Skip James, Robert Johnson, and others. These singers made a living variously as field hands, laborers, drifters, and bootleggers, playing in their spare time. All over their records you hear a rapid articulation of the descending chromatic figure—think of the "Crucifixus" bass line sped up and stripped down. When Willie Brown plays it on "Future Blues," the strings snap violently in emphasis:

> *Can't tell my future, I can't tell my past*
> *Lord, it seems like every minute sure gon' be my last.*

Skip James, the canniest musician among Delta blues singers, uses the chromatic riff for ironic effect in "I'm So Glad"; it's an ostensibly uplifting number with a gospel tinge, but the continual chromatic undertow undercuts the singer's claim to be "tired of weeping, tired of moaning, tired of groaning for you." Chromatic lines snake through James's "Devil Got My Woman," a beautifully baleful ode to love gone wrong: "I'd rather be the devil than be that woman['s] man . . ." Robert Johnson, rumored to have sold his soul to the devil for the sake of his art, leaned heavily on the chromatic slide in such numbers as "Cross Road Blues," "Me and the Devil Blues," and "Walkin' Blues."

The origins of the riff are obscure. It seems to have deep roots in black music, reaching back through ragtime to the sketchily documented repertories of nineteenth-century African-American song. It might even be related to slithery chromatic lines that have been recorded in chants of the Ewe and Yoruba peoples, in West Africa. Although it holds to the classic devil's-staircase shape, it has little apparent connection to the ostinato laments of previous eras: it's a decorative element, not a bass line. And it gives off a different vibe, in keeping with the emotional complexity of blues form. A blues is sensual, knowing, tough; it's full of resilience, even as it heeds the power of fate. The gesture of lament annuls itself and engenders its opposite. This is the subtext of Duke Ellington's pathbreaking 1935 piece *Reminiscing in Tempo*, a thirteen-minute jazz fantasia propelled by a short chromatic ostinato. It was written in the wake of the death of the composer's mother, but it keeps sorrow at bay, ending in a jaunty, urbane mood. The trudging ostinato becomes a walking, dancing bass.

Blues chromaticism entered the American mainstream through the hot jazz of the Roaring Twenties. It was also a favorite tool in the workshops of Tin Pan Alley: Gershwin loved to introduce half-step motion into the inner voices of songs like "Someone to Watch Over Me." A hint of the descending chromatic bass shadows the opening of Richard Rodgers's "My Funny Valentine." Of course, Tin Pan Alley writers, many of them from Russian-Jewish backgrounds, had multiple sources for these tricks of the trade; they drew liberally on late-Romantic classical music and also on Yiddish song. One way or another, the sighing chromatic line became so widespread as a sign of worldly-wise sophistication that it turned into a journeyman cliché. Sometimes, though, it came bearing a more urgent message. When Frank Sinatra began making downcast concept albums in the later 1950s—*In the Wee Small Hours, Only the Lonely, No One Cares,* and other studies in Cold War melancholia—he seemed to require morose chromatic lines to set the tone. A lamenting pizzicato bass prowls through Sinatra's "Angel Eyes," whose Scotch-soaked emotional state goes from the vengeful to the suicidal ("Excuse me while I disappear").

Sinatra's nocturnal ballads of the fifties forecast a weird and wonderful twist of musical history: the return, circa 1965, of the chromatic *basso lamento,* in strict, almost neo-Baroque guise. Why it came back is difficult to explain. For one thing, the American folk-music revival of the fifties gave new life to ancient ballad forms, which depended on strophic repetition. Also, Baroque music was much in vogue in the later fifties, with I Musici's recording of Vivaldi's *Four Seasons* and Glenn Gould's account of the chaconnelike *Goldberg Variations* selling in mass quantities. And perhaps Brazilian bossa nova played an assisting role; as Peter Williams points out, in his wide-ranging survey *The Chromatic Fourth,* liquid chromatic lines course through Antônio Carlos Jobim's "Corcovado," also known as "Quiet Nights of Quiet Stars."

Whatever the reason, by the mid-sixties the lamento bass was again the rage. You hear it in "Chim Chim Cher-ee," the waltzing chimney-sweep song in Richard and Robert Sherman's movie musical *Mary Poppins.* You hear it also in "Michelle," on the Beatles' *Rubber Soul,* and in various later Beatles songs. It sounds seven times in Bob Dylan's psychedelic manifesto "Ballad of a Thin Man," setting up the refrain "Something is happening here / But you don't know what it is / Do you, Mr. Jones?" (The song's dramatis personae, consisting of one-eyed midgets, circus geeks, and sword swallowers in high heels, vaguely resembles the guest list for the wedding of Almadán, as described in Juan Arañés's "Un sarao de la chacona.") The rock scholar Walter Everett has catalogued dozens of chromatic basses in sixties and seventies pop: a peculiar playlist could be assembled from the likes of "How Could I Be Such a Fool?" "Can't Take My Eyes off You," "My Way," "Hooked on a Feeling," "Time in a Bottle," and the Eagles' "Hotel California." As Everett notes, the last song is fittingly set in a decadent Spanish-mission town, by the side of a desert highway.

It fell to Led Zeppelin, the behemoth hard-rock band of the seventies, to perfect the rock Baroque. Dylan and the Beatles may have won the plaudits of the intellectuals, but Led Zeppelin launched a no less ambitious raid on music history, commandeering rock, folk music, Delta blues, Indian and other non-Western music, and smatterings of classical tradition. "Babe I'm Gonna Leave You" and "Stairway to Heaven" both take off from meticulous finger-picking exercises for semi-classical guitar, with descending chromatic lines interwoven; washes of Bachian organ playing give a churchy aura to "Your Time Is Gonna Come" and "Since I've Been Loving You." Several of the band's weightiest creations rest on artfully repeating bass lines: "Kashmir" is built on a riff that climbs step by chromatic step.

Led Zeppelin's early magnum opus was "Dazed and Confused," a tormented love song that Jimmy Page, the band's fleet-fingered, mildly satanic guitarist, first started playing when he was in the Yardbirds. Page borrowed many elements of the piece from a New York singer-songwriter named Jake Holmes, who included a track with the same name on his 1967 album *"The Above Ground Sound" of Jake Holmes*. Holmes's song is anchored in consecutive chromatic descents; they were the work of an itinerant bass guitarist named Rick Randle, whom Holmes later described as "absolutely stone, raving mad," and who was last reported living in Utah with a witch.

In the Led Zeppelin version, which appeared on the band's debut album of 1969, John Paul Jones gave the bass line a forbidding, organlike sound— the Delta blues riff monumentalized. In recordings from the band's stadium tours of the early seventies, where the song stretches on for half an hour or more, the bass motto undergoes ostentatious transformations, sometimes shimmering on Page's bowed guitar, sometimes shrieking in the high falsetto zone of Robert Plant's voice. For long stretches, the bass falls silent while singer and guitarist call out to each other, like wanderers lost in a desolate landscape. Finally, in a climactic passage, the theme is thundered out on guitar and bass in tandem, saturating the musical space.

When the chacona first surfaced, at the end of the sixteenth century, it promised an upending of the social order, a liberation of the body. The same outlaw spirit animates modern rock and pop: the swirl of a repeating bass line allows a crowd of dancing fans to forget, for a little while, the linear routines of daily life. When Frescobaldi and Bach recast the dance as a stern, inward-turned form, bending it toward lament, they hinted at a different sort of freedom, that of the individual defining himself in opposition to the mass. "Dazed and Confused," in its inner sections, implies a similar quest for self: the raw drive of rock and roll gives way to spacey variations. It's a big, brash rock anthem at heart, but, just as the dance abides in Bach's chaconne, the lament lingers in the rock arena. Above all, the song demonstrates how the same deep musical structures keep materializing across the centuries. If a time machine were to bring together some late-sixteenth-century Spanish musicians, a continuo section led by Bach, and players from Ellington's 1940 band, and if John Paul Jones stepped in with the bass line of "Dazed and Confused," they might, after a minute or two of confusion, find common ground. The dance of the chacona is wider than the sea.

3

INFERNAL MACHINES

HOW RECORDINGS CHANGED MUSIC

More than a century ago, the composer and bandleader John Philip Sousa warned that technology would destroy music. Testifying before the United States Congress in 1906, he said, "These talking machines are going to ruin the artistic development of music in this country. When I was a boy . . . in front of every house in the summer evenings you would find young people together singing the songs of the day or the old songs. Today you hear these infernal machines going night and day. We will not have a vocal cord left." Sousa expanded on the theme in subsequent articles and interviews. "The time is coming when no one will be ready to submit himself to the ennobling discipline of learning music," he declared. "Everyone will have their ready made or ready pirated music in their cupboards." Something is irretrievably lost when we are no longer in the presence of bodies making music, Sousa also said. "The nightingale's song is delightful because the nightingale herself gives it forth."

Before you dismiss Sousa as a curmudgeon, you might consider how drastically music has changed in the past hundred years. It has achieved onrushing omnipresence in our world: millions of hours of its history are available on disc; rivers of digital melody flow on the Internet; MP3 players with forty thousand songs can be tucked in a back pocket or a purse. Yet, for most of us, music is no longer something we do ourselves, or even watch other people do in front of us. It has become a radically virtual medium, an art without a face. When we walk around the city on an ordinary day, our ears will register music at almost every turn—bass lines pumping from passing cars, bits of hip-hop seeping out of the headphones of teenagers on the subway, a lawyer's cell phone tweeting Beethoven's

"Ode to Joy"—but almost none of it will be the immediate result of physical work by human hands or voices. Fewer and fewer people seem to know how to play traditional instruments or read music. In the future, Sousa's ghost might say, reproduction will displace production. Zombified listeners will shuffle through the archives of the past, and new music will consist of rearrangements of the old.

Ever since Edison invented the phonograph cylinder, in 1877, people have been assessing what the medium of recording has done for and to the art of music. Inevitably, the conversation has veered toward rhetorical extremes. Sousa was a pioneering spokesman for the party of doom, which was later filled out by various reactionaries, contrarians, Luddites, and post-Marxist theorists. In the opposite corner are the utopians, who argue that technology has not imprisoned music but liberated it, bringing the art of the elite to the masses and the art of the margins to the center. Before Edison came along, the utopians say, Beethoven's symphonies could be heard only in select concert halls. Now recordings carry the man from Bonn to the corners of the earth, summoning the throng hailed in the "Ode to Joy": "Be embraced, millions!" Glenn Gould, after renouncing live performance in 1964, predicted that within a century the public concert would disappear into the electronic ether, with a largely beneficial effect on musical culture.

Having discovered much of my favorite music through LPs and CDs, I am not about to join the lamenting party. Modern urban environments are often so soulless or ugly that I'm grateful for the humanizing touch of electronic sound. But neither can I accept Gould's slashing futurism. I want to be aware of technology's effects, positive and negative. I want a pragmatic theory that mediates between live performance and reproduction, without either apocalyptic screeching or corporate hype. Fortunately, scholars and critics have been methodically exploring this terrain for many decades, trying to figure out exactly what happens when we listen to music with no musicians in the room. They have reached no unshakable conclusions, but they give us most of the conceptual tools we need in order to listen with the alertness—and the ambivalence—that this magical medium demands.

The principal irony of the history of recording is that Edison did not make the phonograph with music in mind. Rather, he conceived of his cylinder as a business gadget, one that would supersede the costly, imperfect practice of stenography and have the added virtue of preserving in perpetuity the voices of the deceased. In an 1878 essay titled "The Phonograph and Its Future," Edison or his ghostwriter proclaimed that his invention would "annihilate time and space, and bottle up for posterity the mere utterance of man." "Annihilation" is an interestingly ambiguous figure of speech. Recording opened lines of communication between far-flung worlds, but it also placed older art and folk traditions in danger of extinction. With American popular culture as its house god, it brought about a global homogenization of taste, the effects of which are still spreading.

Although Edison mentioned the idea of recording music in his 1878 article, he had no inkling of a music industry. He pictured the phonograph as a tool for teaching singing and as a natural extension of domestic music-making: "A friend may in a morning-call sing us a song which shall delight an evening company." By the 1890s, however, alert entrepreneurs had installed phonographs in penny arcades, allowing customers to listen to assorted songs over ear tubes. In 1888, Emile Berliner introduced the flat disc, a less cumbersome storage device, and envisioned with it the entire modern music business—mass distribution, recording stars, royalties, and the rest. In 1902, the first great star was born: the tenor Enrico Caruso, whose voice remains one of the most transfixing phenomena in the history of the medium. The ping in Caruso's tone, that golden bark, made the man himself seem viscerally present, proving Edison's theory of the annihilation of space and time. Not so lucky was Johannes Brahms, who, in 1889, attempted to record his First Hungarian Dance. The master seems to be sending us a garbled message from a spacecraft disintegrating near Pluto.

Whenever a new gadget comes along, salespeople inevitably point out that an older gadget has been rendered obsolete. The automobile pushed aside the railroad; the computer replaced the typewriter. Sousa feared that the phonograph would supplant live music. His fears were excessive but not irrational. The Victor Talking Machine Company, which the engineer Eldridge Johnson founded in 1901, marketed its machines not just as vessels for music but as instruments in themselves. In a way, Victor was taking direct aim at the piano, which, around the turn of the century, dominated domestic musical life, from the salon to the tavern. The top-selling Victrola of 1906, a massive object standing four feet tall and weighing 137 pounds, was encased in "piano-finished" mahogany, if any-

one was missing the point. Ads showed families clustered about their phonographs, no piano in sight. Edison, whose cylinders soon began to lag
behind flat discs in popularity, was so determined to demonstrate the
verisimilitude of his machines that he held a nationwide series of Tone
Tests, during which halls were plunged into darkness and audiences were
supposedly unable to tell the difference between Anna Case singing live
and one of her records.

Each subsequent leap in audio technology—microphones, magnetic
tape, long-playing records, stereo sound, transistors, digital sound, the
compact disc, and the MP3—has elicited the same kind of over-the-top
reaction. The latest device inspires heady confusion between reality and
reproduction, while yesterday's wonder machine is exposed as inadequate,
even primitive. When, in 1931, the composer and critic Deems Taylor
heard a pioneering example of stereophonic recording, he commented,
"The difference between what we usually hear and what I heard was,
roughly, the difference between looking at a photograph of somebody and
looking at the person himself." Twenty years later, Howard Taubman
wrote of a long-playing record on the Mercury label: "The orchestra's tone
is so lifelike that one feels one is listening to the living presence." (Mercury promptly adopted "Living Presence" as its slogan.) A high-fidelity ad
of the 1950s offered users "the finest seat in the house"—an experience
not simply equal to the concert hall but superior to it, cleansed of the in-
convenience of "audience distraction." A television commercial of the seventies, starring Ella Fitzgerald, famously asked, "Is it live or is it Memorex?"
Compact discs promised "perfect sound forever."

Just as inevitably, audiophile happy-talk leads to a backlash among
listeners who doubt the rhetoric of fidelity and perfection. Dissenters
complain that the latest device is actually inferior to the old—artificial,
inauthentic, soulless. Greg Milner has documented this never-ending
back-and-forth in his book *Perfecting Sound Forever*, a smartly skeptical
account of the ideology of audio progress. Some enthusiasts of the Edison
cylinder felt that no other machine gave such a faithful sensation of the
warmth of the human voice. When electrical recording came in, a few
stalwarts detected nothing but fakery in the use of microphones to am-
plify soft sounds and invent a sonic perspective that does not exist for
human ears. "I wonder if pure tone will disappear from the earth sometimes," a British critic wrote in 1928.

Magnetic tape led to the most crucial shift in the relationship between recordings and musical reality. German engineers perfected the magnetic tape recorder, or Magnetophon, during the Second World War. Late one night, an audio expert turned serviceman named Jack Mullin was monitoring German radio when he noticed that an overnight orchestral broadcast was astonishingly clear: it sounded "live," yet not even at Hitler's whim could the orchestra have been playing in the middle of the night. After the war was over, Mullin tracked down a Magnetophon and brought it to America. He demonstrated it to Bing Crosby, who used it to tape his broadcasts in advance. Crosby was a pioneer of perhaps the most famous of all technological effects, the croon. Magnetic tape meant that Bing could practically whisper into the microphone and still be heard across America; a marked drop-off in surface noise meant that vocal murmurs could register as readily as Louis Armstrong's pealing trumpet.

The magnetic process also allowed performers to invent their own reality in the studio. Errors could be corrected by splicing together bits of different takes. In the sixties, the Beatles and the Beach Boys, following in the wake of electronic compositions by Cage and Stockhausen, constructed intricate studio soundscapes that could never be replicated onstage; even Glenn Gould might have had trouble executing the mechanically accelerated keyboard solo in "In My Life." The great rock debate about authenticity began. Were the Beatles pushing the art forward by reinventing it in the studio? Or were they losing touch with the rugged intelligence of folk, blues, and rock traditions? Bob Dylan stood at a craggy opposite extreme, turning out records in a few days' time and avoiding any vocal overdubs until the seventies. The Dylan scholar Clinton Heylin points out that while the Beatles spent 129 days crafting *Sgt. Pepper*, Dylan needed only 90 days to make his first *fifteen* records. Yet frills-free, "lo-fi" recording has no special claim on musical truth; indeed, it easily becomes another effect, the effect of no effect. Today's neoclassical rock bands pay good money to sound old.

The advent of digital recording was, for many skeptics, the ultimate outrage. The old machines vibrated in sympathy with their subjects: the hills and valleys on a cylinder or a flat disc followed the contours of the music. Digital technology literally chopped the incoming vibrations into bits—strings of 0's and 1's that were encoded onto a compact disc and then reconstituted on a CD player. Traditionalists felt that the end product was a kind of android music. Neil Young, the raw-voiced Canadian singer-songwriter, was especially withering: "Listening to a CD is like looking at the world through a screen window." Step by step, recordings have become an ever more fictional world, even as they become ever more "real." The final frontier—for the moment—has been reached with Auto-Tune, Pro Tools, and other forms of digital software, which can readjust out-of-tune playing and generate entire orchestras from nowhere. At the touch of a key, a tone-deaf starlet becomes dulcet and a college rock band turns Wagnerian.

Yet some audio equivalent of the law of conservation of energy means that these incessant crises have a way of balancing themselves out. Fakers, hucksters, and mediocrities prosper in every age; artists of genius manage to survive, or, at least, to fail memorably. Technology has certainly advanced the careers of nonentities, but it has also lent a hand to those who lacked a foothold in the system. Nowhere is this more evident than in the story of African-American music. Almost from the start, recording permitted black musicians on the margins of the culture—notably, the blues singers of the Mississippi Delta—to speak out with nothing more than a voice and a guitar. Many of these artists were robbed blind by corporate manipulators, but their music got through. Recordings gave Armstrong, Ellington, Chuck Berry, and James Brown the chance to occupy a global platform that Sousa's idyllic old America, racist to the core, would have denied them. The fact that their records played a crucial role in the advancement of African-American civil rights puts in proper perspective the debate about whether or not technology has been "good" for music.

Hip-hop, the dominant turn-of-the-century pop form, gives the most electrifying demonstration of technology's empowering effect. As Jeff Chang recounts, in his book *Can't Stop Won't Stop: A History of the Hip-Hop Generation*, the genre rose up from desperately impoverished high-rise ghettos, where families couldn't afford to buy instruments for their kids and even the most rudimentary music-making seemed out of reach. But music was made all the same: the phonograph itself became an instrument. In the South Bronx in the 1970s, DJs like Kool Herc, Afrika Bambaataa, and Grandmaster Flash used turntables to create a hurtling collage of effects—loops, breaks, beats, scratches. Later, studio-bound DJs and producers used digital sampling to assemble some of the most densely packed sonic assemblages in musical history: Eric B. and Rakim's *Paid in Full*, Public Enemy's *Fear of a Black Planet*, Dr. Dre's *The Chronic*.

Sooner or later, every critique of recording gets around to quoting Walter Benjamin's essay "The Work of Art in the Age of Its Technological Reproducibility," written in the late 1930s. The most often cited passage is Benjamin's discussion of the loss of an "aura" surrounding works of art—the "here and now" of the sacred artistic object, its connection to a well-defined community. This formulation seems to recall the familiar lament, going back to Sousa, that recordings have leeched the life out of music. But when Benjamin spoke of the withering of aura and the rise of reproducible art, lamentation was not his aim. While he stopped short of populism, he voiced a nagging mistrust of the elitist spiel—the automatic privileging of high-art devotion over mass-market consumption. The cult of art for art's sake, Benjamin noted, was deteriorating into fascist kitsch. The films of Charlie Chaplin, by contrast, mixed comic pratfalls with subversive political messages. In other words, mechanical reproduction is not an inherently cheapening process; an outsider artist may use it to bypass cultural gatekeepers and advance radical ideas. That the thugs of commerce seldom fail to win out in the end does not lessen the glory of the moment.

Although classical performers and listeners like to picture themselves in a high tower, remote from the electronic melee, they, too, are in thrall to the machines. Some of the most overheated propaganda on behalf of new technologies has come from the classical side, where the illusion of perfect reproduction is particularly alluring. Classical recordings are supposed to deny the fact that they are recordings. That process involves, paradoxically, considerable artifice. Overdubbing, patching, knob-twiddling, and, in recent years, pitch correction have all come into play. The phenomenon of the dummy star, who has a hard time duplicating in the concert hall what he or she purports to do on record, is not unheard of.

Perhaps there is something unnatural in the very act of making a studio recording, no matter how intelligent the presentation. At the height of the hi-fi era, leading classical producers and executives—Walter Legge, at EMI; Goddard Lieberson, at Columbia Records; and John Culshaw, at Decca, to name three of the best—spent many millions of dollars engaging top-of-the-line orchestras, soloists, and conductors in an effort to create definitive recordings of the peaks of the repertory. They met their goal: any short list of gramophone classics would include Maria Callas's *Tosca*,

Wilhelm Furtwängler's *Tristan und Isolde*, Georg Solti's *Ring*, and Glenn Gould's *Goldberg Variations*, all recorded or set in motion in the fifties. Yet the excellence of these discs posed a problem for the working musicians who had to play in their wake. Concert presenters began to complain that record collectors had formed a separate audience, one that seldom ventured into the concert hall. Recordings threatened to become a phantasmagoria, a virtual reality encroaching on concert life. (Gould claimed that the Decca *Ring* achieved "a more effective unity between intensity of action and displacement of sound than could be afforded by the best of all seasons at Bayreuth.") When people did venture out, they brought with them the habits of home listening. The solitary ritual of absorbing symphonies in one's living room almost certainly contributed to the growing quietude of the classical public; that applause-free spell after the first movement of the *Eroica* matches the whispery groove on the long-playing record.

Like Heisenberg's mythical observer, the phonograph was never a mere recorder of events: it changed not only how people listened but also how they sang and played. Mark Katz, in his book *Capturing Sound*, calls these changes "phonograph effects." (The phrase comes from the digital studio, where it is used to describe the crackling, scratching noises that are sometimes added to pop-music tracks to lend them an appealingly antique air.) Katz devotes one chapter of his book to a shift in violin technique that occurred in the early twentieth century. It involved vibrato—the trembling action of the hand on the fingerboard, whereby the player is able to give notes a warbling sweetness. Early recordings and written evidence suggest that in prior eras vibrato was used more sparingly than it is today. By the twenties and thirties, many leading violinists had adopted continuous vibrato, which became the approved style in conservatories. Katz proposes that technology prompted the change. When a wobble was added to violin tone, the phonograph was able to pick it up more easily; it's a "wider" sound in acoustical terms, a blob of several superimposed frequencies. Also, the fuzzy focus of vibrato enabled players to cover up inaccuracies of intonation, and, from the start, the phonograph made players more self-conscious about intonation than they were before. What worked in the studio then spread to the concert stage.

Robert Philip, a British scholar who specializes in performance practice, tackles the same problem in his book *Performing Music in the Age of*

Recording. He proposes that when musicians listened to records of their own playing they passed through a kind of mirror stage; for the first time, they were forced to confront their "true" selves. "Musicians who first heard their own recordings in the early years of the twentieth century were often taken aback by what they heard, suddenly being made aware of inaccuracies and mannerisms they had not suspected," Philip writes. When they went back onstage, he says, they tried to embody the superior self that they glimpsed in the phonographic mirror, and never again played in quite the same way.

Philip gives a riveting description of what classical performances sounded like at the turn of the last century. "Freedom from disaster was the standard for a good concert," he writes. Rehearsals were brief, mishaps routine. Precision was not a universal value. Pianists rolled chords instead of playing them at one stroke. String players slid expressively from one note to the next—portamento, the style was called—in imitation of the slide of the voice. In a 1912 recording, the great Belgian violinist Eugène Ysaÿe "sways either side of the beat, while the piano maintains an even rhythm." Orchestras flirted with chaos in an effort to generate maximum passion—witness Edward Elgar's recordings of his music. And the instruments themselves sounded different, depending on the nationality of the player. French bassoons had a pungent tone, quite unlike the rounded timbre of German bassoons. French flutists, by contrast, used more vibrato than their German and English counterparts, supplying a warmer, mellower quality. American orchestral culture, which brought together immigrant musicians from all European countries, began to erode the differences, and recordings helped to cement the new standard practice. Whatever style sounded cleanest on the medium—in these cases, German bassoons and French flutes—became the golden mean. Young virtuosos today may have recognizable idiosyncrasies, but their playing seldom indicates that they have come from any particular place or that they have emerged from any particular tradition.

Opera is prey to the same standardizing trend. The conductor and scholar Will Crutchfield cites a startling example of a "phonograph effect" in an essay on changing perceptions of operatic style. He once sat down to compare all extant recordings of "Una furtiva lagrima," the plaintive tenor aria from Donizetti's bel-canto comedy *L'elisir d'amore.* Crutchfield wanted to know what singers of various eras have done with the cadenza—

the passage at the end of the aria where the orchestra halts and the tenor engages in a few graceful acrobatics. Early recordings show singers trying out a range of possibilities, some contemplative, some florid, none the same. Then came Caruso. He first recorded "Una furtiva lagrima" in 1902, and returned to it three more times in the course of his epochal studio career. After that, tenors began imitating the stylish little display that Caruso devised: a quick up-and-down run followed by two slow, tender phrases. Out of more than two hundred singers who have recorded the aria since Caruso's death, how many try something different? Crutchfield counts four. Many operagoers would identify Caruso's cadenza as the "traditional" one, but Crutchfield calls it the "death-of-tradition" cadenza, the one that stifled a long-flourishing vocal practice.

The tics and traits of old-school performance—moving ahead or behind the beat, sliding between notes, breaking chords into arpeggios, improvising cadenzas, adding ornaments as the style demands—are alike in bringing out the distinct voices of the performers, not to mention the mere fact that they are fallible humans. Most modern playing tends to erase all evidence of the work that has gone on behind the scenes: virtuosity is defined as effortlessness. One often-quoted ideal is to "disappear behind the music." But when precision is divorced from emotion it can become anti-musical, inhuman, repulsive. Is there any escape from the cycle? Robert Philip, having blamed recordings for a multitude of sins, ends by saying that they may be able to come to the rescue. By studying artifacts from the dawn of the century, musicians might recapture what has gone missing from the perfectionist style. They can rebel against the letter of the score in pursuit of its spirit. There are, however, substantial psychic barriers in the way of such a shift: performers will have to be unafraid of trying out mannerisms that will sound sloppy to some ears, of committing what will sound like mistakes. They will have to defy the hyper-competitive conservatory culture in which they came of age, and also the hyper-professionalized culture of the ensembles in which they find work.

In at least one area, performance style has undergone a sea change. Early music long had the reputation of being the most pedantically "correct" subculture in classical music, but in recent years the more dynamic Renaissance and Baroque ensembles—Jordi Savall's Hespèrion XXI, William Christie's Les Arts Florissants, Rinaldo Alessandrini's Concerto

Italiano, and various groups led by the violinist Andrew Manze and the keyboard player Richard Egarr, to name a few—have begun exercising all the freedoms that have gone missing in much modern performance. They execute some notes cleanly and others roughly, they weave around the beat instead of staying on top of it, they slide from note to note when they are so moved. If the score calls for or expects a cadenza or improvisation, they execute one of their own invention. As a result, the music feels liberated, and audiences respond in kind, with yelps of joy. Christie has said that his group is modeled on Duke Ellington's band of 1929: players amble in and out of the spotlight, adding daubs of color before rejoining the background. If, in coming years, the freewheeling spirit of the early-music scene enters into performances of the nineteenth-century repertory, classical music may finally kick away its cold marble façade.

For those of us who grew up during the extended heyday of recordings, the digital landscape of the early twenty-first century presents a confusing picture. The record labels, which long held sway with an iron or velvet fist, are reeling, their products downloaded everywhere on file-sharing networks, their attempts to police piracy verging on the fascistic. The concept of a discrete album of songs or works is probably in terminal decline. In pop, the main money is now to be made in the packaging of tours and the selling of merchandise. Prince gave away millions of copies of his 2007 album *Planet Earth* as a way of luring audiences to his shows. In the same year, Radiohead offered its album *In Rainbows* through its own website, instructing fans to pay whatever they wished. The technology of easy access has become so sophisticated that it is undermining the corporate structure which brought it into being—a development that might have delighted Walter Benjamin. The brainy moguls of decades past are to be mourned, but in the long run it may not be a bad thing that young people have stopped hoarding music in the form of packaged objects. Music is no longer a prize in a collection; it is returning to its natural evanescent state.

Classical music, or a portion thereof, is thriving online in unexpected ways. Perhaps no one should be surprised; if, as people say, the Internet is a paradise for geeks, it would logically work to the benefit of one of the most opulently geeky art forms in history. The more resourceful organizations are offering live and archived audio (you can hear almost every event in London's summertime Proms series through the website of the BBC), setting up online listening guides (the San Francisco Symphony has high-tech maps of the *Eroica* and *The Rite of Spring*), assembling fastidious archives (the Metropolitan Opera site can tell you in a matter of seconds when any singer made his or her debut), and peddling studio-master-quality audio downloads (the Tallis Scholars sell their impeccable record-ings of Renaissance masses). Web-savvy young composers, meanwhile, no longer depend on publishers to reach their public, distributing their wares through blogs, MySpace, YouTube, Facebook, Twitter, and whatever so-cial network becomes fashionable after this book goes to press.

The diffusion of classical music online is a boon for fans, and it may also ease the fears of the infamous "culturally aware non-attenders." Nov-ice concertgoers and operagoers can shop for tickets, read synopses of unfamiliar plots, listen to snippets of unfamiliar music, read performers' blogs, and otherwise get their bearings out on the tundra of the classical experience. First-time record-buyers can read reviews, compare audio sam-ples, and decide on, for example, a Beethoven recording by Furtwängler, all without risking the humiliation of mispronouncing the conductor's name under the gaze of a grumpy record clerk. In the days before the collapse of the record business, when megastores like Tower Records were thriv-ing, sepulchral soundproofed doors divided the classical department from the rest of humanity. For better or worse, classical music no longer inhab-its a separate room; it is in the mix.

At the same time, classical music stands partly outside the technologi-cal realm, because most of its repertory is designed to resonate naturally within a room. By contrast, almost all pop music is written for micro-phones and speakers. In a totally mediated society, where some form of electronic sound saturates nearly every minute of our waking lives, the act of sitting down in a concert hall, joining the expectant silence in the mo-ments before the music begins, and surrendering to the elemental proper-ties of sound can have an almost spiritual dimension. Classical supremacists of prior years might have described it as a rite of elevation, but for me it is something more primal and enigmatic. Forms coalesce and then vanish, like Rimsky-Korsakov's phantom city of Kitezh.

• • •

In 1926, twenty years after Sousa foretold doom, the critic Hans Heinz Stuckenschmidt reflected on the mechanization of music and came to this eminently sane conclusion: "The machine is neither a god nor a devil." Mark Katz uses that quotation as an epigraph to *Capturing Sound*, and it nicely sums up the whole shebang. Neither the utopian nor the apocalyptic vision of the musical future has come to pass. People have plenty of pirated music in their cupboards, but they are still turning out for live performances, paying hundreds or even thousands of dollars to catch a glimpse of their idols. Music education is in tatters, but the impulse to make music with the voice, with an instrument, or on a computer remains. The critic David Hajdu, in an essay on the phenomenon of home remixing (creating new versions of songs on home computers), notes a curious throwback. "Members of the musical public are again assuming participatory roles, interpreting compositions at home, much as late Victorians played sheet music in parlor musicales," he writes. In other words, we are almost back to where we started.

When I sift through my musical memory, I find that real and virtual events are inextricably jumbled. The strongest echoes are of live performances that shook me to the core: Mahler's Eighth Symphony at Carnegie Hall, under the direction of the incomparable choral conductor Robert Shaw, with more than four hundred singers roaring forth in the first- and second-tier boxes; the post-punk bands Fugazi and the Ex in a sweat-drenched church basement in Washington, D.C., firing up a mass of youthful bodies; Gidon Kremer and five other musicians in an Austrian village church at midnight, presenting an extraordinarily eerie chamber arrangement of Shostakovich's Fifteenth Symphony. Then again, certain recordings carry an acute emotional charge: I think of the Bernstein *Eroica* that I pretended to conduct as a child, the LPs of Mahler's Sixth that I blasted in high school late at night, the Pere Ubu CD that forced me to abandon my cavalier dismissal of rock music. But I can't replicate the psychic impact of those first encounters. They were unrepeatable events on a private stage. As the composer and theorist Benjamin Boretz has written, "In music, as in everything, the disappearing moment of experience is the firmest reality."

Nothing in my listening life can compare to the experience of Hans Fantel, an author and critic who for many years covered audio matters for *The New York Times*. In 1989 he wrote about what it was like for him to listen to a CD reissue of a classic disc: a live recording, made on January 16, 1938, of the Vienna Philharmonic playing Mahler's Ninth Symphony, under the direction of Bruno Walter. Fantel spent his childhood in Vienna, and he attended that performance with his father.

"We could not know on that winter Sunday that this would turn out to be the last performance of the Vienna Philharmonic before Hitler crushed his homeland to make it part of the German Reich," Fantel wrote. "The music, captured that day by the bulky old microphones I remember strung across the stage, was the last to be heard from many of the musicians in the orchestra. They and their country vanished." Fantel put on the record and relived the occasion. "I could now recognize and appreciate the singular aura of that performance: I could sense its uncanny intensity—a strange inner turmoil quite different from the many other recordings and performances of Mahler's Ninth I had heard since."

Some of the turmoil was Fantel's own. "This disc held fast an event I had shared with my father: seventy-one minutes out of the sixteen years we had together. Soon after, as an 'enemy of Reich and Führer,' my father also disappeared into Hitler's abyss. That's what made me realize something about the nature of phonographs: they admit no ending. They imply perpetuity . . . Something of life itself steps over the normal limits of time."

PART II

PART II

4

THE STORM OF STYLE

MOZART'S GOLDEN MEAN

Wolfgang Amadè Mozart, as he usually spelled his name, was a small man with a plain, pockmarked face, whose most striking feature was a pair of intense blue-gray eyes. When he was in a convivial mood, his gaze was said to be warm, even seductive. But he often gave the impression of being not entirely present, as if his mind were caught up in some invisible event. Portraits suggest a man aware of his separation from the world. In one, he wears a hard, distant look; in another, his face glows with sadness. In several pictures, his left eye droops a little, perhaps from fatigue. "As touchy as gunpowder," one friend called him. Nonetheless, he was generally well liked.

He was born in the archbishopric of Salzburg in 1756, and he died in the imperial capital of Vienna in 1791. He was a thoroughly urban creature, one who never had much to say about the charms of nature. A product of the artisan classes—his ancestors were bookbinders, weavers, and masons—he adopted aristocratic fashions, going around Vienna in a gold-trimmed hat and a red coat with mother-of-pearl buttons. He was physically restless, quick-witted, sociable, flirtatious, and obscene; one of the more provocative items in his catalogue is a canon for six voices titled *Leck mich im Arsch* (K. 231/382c). He frittered away money, not least on apartments that he could ill afford. He had considerable success, although he knew that he deserved more. If audiences were occasionally perplexed by his creations, listeners in high places recognized his worth. Emperor Joseph II was a fan of Mozart's work, and, in 1787, to prevent "so rare a genius" from going abroad, he gave the composer a well-paying position that required little more than the writing of dances. In a letter to his father, Leopold, Mozart had warned that "the Viennese gentry, and in particular the Emperor, must not imagine that I am on this earth solely for the sake of Vienna."

As a child, Mozart was advertised in London as "the most extraordinary Prodigy, and most amazing Genius, that has appeared in any Age." Leopold dubbed him "the miracle whom God allowed to be born in Salzburg." Prince Kaunitz, Joseph II's chief minister, said, "Such people only come into the world once in a hundred years." Praise at this level, however justified, takes its toll on a man's humility. Mozart, by his own admission, could be "as proud as a peacock," and the Archbishop of Salzburg, whose service he quit in 1781, was not the only person who considered him "dreadfully conceited." Conceit edges easily into paranoia, and Mozart was not immune. "I think that something is going on behind the scenes, and that doubtless here too I have enemies," he wrote from Paris, in 1778. "Where, indeed, have I not had them?" As he traces conspiracies, mocks the French, and extols the Germans, he sounds curiously like Richard Wagner.

Later, in Vienna, Mozart clung to the idea that Antonio Salieri, the Imperial Kapellmeister, was plotting against him. Whether or not such intrigues existed—John Rice's biography of the supposedly dastardly Salieri portrays him as a likable character, and an intermittently imaginative composer—Mozart himself was not above politicking: when he applied for the job of second Kapellmeister, he pointedly observed that "Salieri, that very gifted Kapellmeister, has never devoted himself to church music."

Playfulness was Mozart's saving grace. His counterpart in modern times is perhaps George Gershwin, who was charming and self-infatuated in equal measure. Latter-day attempts to find a dark, despondent layer in Mozart's psychology have been unconvincing. In his correspondence, he once or twice displays depressive symptoms—alluding to his "black thoughts," describing sensations of coldness and emptiness—but context is all-important: in the first instance, he is begging for money, and in the second he is telling his wife, the demanding Constanze, how much he misses her. Nor should too much be made of a letter in which Mozart tells his dying father that death is the "true goal of our existence," the "best and truest friend of mankind." These sentiments were commonplace in a world where lives ended early and without warning. Of the seven children born to Leopold and Maria Anna Mozart, Wolfgang was one of two who survived infancy; only two of his own six children lived to adulthood. Against this backdrop, Mozart seems, if anything, indefatigably optimistic.

Leopold Mozart said of his son, "Two opposing elements rule his nature, I mean, there is either too *much* or too *little*, never the golden mean." Often, an artist sets forth in his work what he cannot achieve in life, and Mozart's music is the empire of the golden mean. Nicholas Kenyon, in *The Pegasus Pocket Guide to Mozart*, writes, "Other great composers have expressed the extremes of life: affirmation, despair, sensual pleasure, bleak emptiness, but only in Mozart can all these emotions coexist within the space of a short phrase." Mozart inhabits a middle world where beauty surges in and ebbs away, where everything is contingent and nothing pure, where, as Henry James's Madame Merle says, an envelope of circumstances encloses every human life. It is a place where genres meld; where concertos become operatic and arias symphonic; where comedy and tragedy, and the sensual and the sacred, are one.

You can find the golden mean running through the Andante of the Sinfonia Concertante for Violin and Viola, from 1779–80. A beguiling four-bar melody appears twice, in E-flat major in the middle and in C minor at the end. The first time, the major mode is briefly shadowed by a turn into the relative minor. The second time, minor is flecked by major, creating the effect of a light in the night. The two passages are more or less the same, but the space between them could contain a novel.

The musicologist Scott Burnham has observed that Mozart offers the "sound of the loss of innocence, the ever renewable loss of innocence." There is no more potent subject for an artist, and it explains why Mozart remains so vivid a presence. As ever, the slow movement of the Piano Concerto No. 23 sends us into a pensive trance, the finale of the "Jupiter" Symphony wakes us up into a uniquely Mozartian kind of intelligent happiness, and the catastrophic climax of *Don Giovanni* stirs our primal fear of being weighed in the balance and found wanting. The loss of innocence was Mozart's, too. Like the rest of us, he had to live outside the complex paradise that he created in sound.

Thousands of books have been written about Mozart, and they present a bewildering variety of images. For a long time, well into the twentieth century, many people pictured Mozart as the "eternal child"—an antic

boy-man who happened to write sublime music. This was a theme of Alfred Einstein's 1945 biography, long considered the standard work. Pushkin, in his play *Mozart and Salieri*, came up with an influential variant:
Mozart as "idle hooligan." This led to the eternal adolescent of the play
and movie *Amadeus*—a potty-mouthed punk who happened to write sublime music. Other commentators have made Mozart out to be a Romantic
in the making or a modernist before the fact—an aloof, tortured character, an agent of sexual subversion, or a clandestine social revolutionary.

Present-day scholars are picking away at the myths and fantasies that
have encrusted the composer. They describe him not as a naïve prodigy or
a suffering outcast but as a hardworking, ambitious, successful musician—
"Mozart as a Working Stiff," to borrow the title of an essay by Neal Zaslaw.
One notable upshot has been the rehabilitation of Leopold Mozart, who
long loomed over his son's life story as an oppressive, even abusive, figure.
Maynard Solomon, in his 1995 biography, presented damning evidence
against Leopold, writing of the father's "erotically tinged drive to dominate" his son. Leopold is said to have exploited Wolfgang in his early
years, squirreling away profits from their European tours. When the gifted
child became a problematic teen, Leopold exhibited an unhealthy posses-
siveness, opposing his son's marriage plans and berating him for what he
considered spendthrift behavior. His letters contain passages of world-class
manipulation. "Your whole intent is to ruin me so you can build your
castles in the air," Leopold wrote in 1778, not long after his wife died
while accompanying her son to Paris. "I hope that, after your mother had
to die in Paris already, you will not also burden your conscience by expe-
diting the death of your father."

Leopold was a bit of a monster, but the job of raising the Miracle of
Salzburg would have sapped anyone's patience. Ruth Halliwell made the
case for Leopold in her illuminating 1998 book, *The Mozart Family*. The
father didn't so much exploit the son as make him possible. Those long
European tours gave Mozart an incomparable education; he went to London, Paris, Vienna, Milan, and Munich, met the monarchs and princes of
the day, and talked to most of the leading composers. Knowing that his
son's musical gifts far exceeded his own, Leopold offered advice on the
practical aspects of art and life, in which he was rather better versed. Who
can deny the truth of Leopold's maxim "Where money is plentiful, everything is dear, and where living is cheap, money will be scarce"? Or: "The

best way to make people feel ashamed of themselves is to be extremely friendly and polite to those who are your enemies"? Mozart's path would have been easier if he had absorbed a few of the bland but useful adages that his father passed along.

The letters between father and son become much livelier when music is the subject. On musical matters, the Mozarts are essentially of one mind; Leopold never seems to be reining in his son's imagination. In late 1780 and early 1781, Mozart was in Munich, preparing his first major opera, *Idomeneo*, while Leopold was in Salzburg, supervising the librettist. The young composer was unleashing every expressive device available to him: as David Cairns writes, in his 2006 book *Mozart and His Operas*, *Idomeneo* touches on "love, joy, physical and spiritual contentment, stoicism, heroic resolution; the ecstasy of self-sacrifice, the horrors of dementia, the agonizing dilemma of a ruler trapped in the consequences of his actions; mass hysteria, panic in the face of an unknown scourge, turning to awe before the yet more terrible fact; the strange peace that can follow intense grief; the infinite tenderness of a father's last farewell to his son." Leopold was mostly a bystander to Mozart's feat, but he did make one crucial contribution: for a pivotal scene in Act III, when the voice of Neptune's oracle rises from the depths, he requested "moving, terrifying, and altogether unusual" music, and went on to suggest a series of sudden crescendos and decrescendos in the brass and winds, bracketing the vocal phrases. Exactly this effect appears in the finished score.

Perhaps Leopold's greatest gift to his son was the instruction to compose with both musical insiders and the general public in mind. In a letter from 1782, Mozart takes that favorite concept of his father's—"the golden mean"—and weaves around it a pragmatic philosophy that is just as relevant now as it was in the eighteenth century:

> These concertos [Nos. 11, 12, and 13] are a happy medium between what is too easy and too difficult; they are very brilliant, pleasing to the ear, and natural, without being vapid. There are passages here and there from which the connoisseurs alone can derive satisfaction; but these passages are written in such a way that the less learned cannot fail to be pleased, though without knowing why . . . The golden mean of truth in all things is no longer either known or appreciated. In order to win applause one must write stuff which

is so inane that a coachman could sing it, or so unintelligible that it pleases precisely because no sensible man can understand it.

One wonders what Mozart would have made of today's musical scene, where the gap between inanity and unintelligibility is spectacularly wide.

Scholars have also demolished the old picture of Mozart as an idiot savant who transcribed the music playing in his brain. Instead, he seems to have refined his ideas to an almost manic degree. Examination of Mozart's surviving sketches and drafts—Constanze threw many manuscripts away—reveals that the composer sometimes began a piece, set it aside, and resumed it months or years later; rewrote troubling sections several times in a row; started movements from scratch when a first attempt failed to satisfy; and waited to finish an aria until a singer had tried out the opening. Ulrich Konrad calls these stockpiles of material "departure points"—"a delineation of intellectual places to which Mozart could return as necessary." In other words, the music in Mozart's mind may have been like a huge map of half-explored territories; in a way, he was writing all his works all the time. The new image of him as a kind of improvising perfectionist is even more daunting than the previous one of God's stenographer. Ambitious parents who play the *Baby Mozart* video for their toddlers may be disappointed to learn that Mozart became Mozart by working furiously hard, and, if Constanze was right, by working himself to death.

In 1991, the Philips label issued a deluxe, complete Mozart edition—180 CDs—employing such distinguished interpreters as Mitsuko Uchida, Alfred Brendel, and Colin Davis. The set was later reissued in a handsome and surprisingly manageable array of seventeen boxes. One day I transferred it to my iPod and discovered that Mozart requires, at the minimum listenable bitrate, 9.77 gigabytes.

On a computer, you can use search functions to create cross-sections of Mozart—a dreamworld of adagios, a neo-Baroque swirl of fantasias and fugues, a nonet of quintets (all major works). To listen to his twenty-seven settings of the *Kyrie* is to appreciate his inexhaustible invention: they range from the ravishingly sweet to the forbiddingly severe, each a convincing simulacrum of the power of the Lord. But the obvious challenge

was to go through the whole megillah—to begin with the Andante in C
Major (K. 1a), which Mozart wrote when he was five, and proceed to the
bitter end, the Requiem (K. 626), which he left unfinished at his death, at
thirty-five. It took me three months. I can't claim to have given every bar
close attention—a patch of recitative in the early opera *La finta semplice*
(*The Pretend Simpleton*) was disrupted by a protracted public-address announcement at Detroit Metro Airport, and most of the Contredanse No. 4
in F (K. 101) was drowned out by the crack drum corps Drumedies performing in the Times Square subway station—but I did get a bird's-eye view
of Mozart's achievement, and was more in awe than ever.

From the start, the music is astonishingly well made. (A caveat from
the scholarly demythologizers: most of the earliest works were "corrected"
by Leopold.) Young Mozart shows an uncanny ability to mimic the styles
and forms of the day: Baroque sacred music, opera buffa and opera seria,
Gluckian reform opera, Haydn's classicism, the Mannheim symphonic
school, Sturm und Drang agitation, and so on. Quite a bit of the music is
reassuringly routine; Hermann Abert writes, in his massive 1921 biography of the composer, that Mozart "evolved along sound lines, without any
supernatural leaps and bounds." But very early there are flashes of individuality. Some of the first come in the London Sketchbook, which dates
from Mozart's London sojourn of 1764 and 1765 (and which Leopold did
not touch). A piece in G minor (K. 15p) features a stormily descending chromatic bass line—a Bachian gesture with a trace of boyish impudence. A
piece in E-flat major (K. 15kk) has gently murmuring chords and mournful slips into the minor, forecasting time-suspending andantes and adagios to come.

Hearing so many premonitions of future masterworks, I got the feeling
that Mozart's brain contained an array of musical archetypes that were
connected to particular dramatic situations or emotional states—figures
connoting vengeance, reconciliation, longing, and so on. One example appears in *La finta semplice*, the merry little opera buffa that Mozart wrote
when he was twelve. In the finale, when all misunderstandings are re-
solved, there is a passage marked "*un poco adagio*," in which Giacinta and
her maid Ninetta ask forgiveness for an elaborate ruse that they have
pulled on Giacinta's brothers. "Perdono," they sing—"Forgive." Not just the
words but the music prefigures the stupendous final scene of *The Marriage
of Figaro*, in which the wayward Count asks the Countess's forgiveness—

"Contessa, perdono!"—and she grants it, in a half-hopeful, half-heartbroken phrase. I looked at the New Mozart Edition scores side by side, and noticed that the two passages not only waver between the same happy-sad chords (G major and E minor) but pivot on the same rising bass line (B-C-D-E). It is unlikely that Mozart thought back to *La finta semplice* when he composed *Figaro*, but the idea of forgiveness apparently triggered certain sounds in his mind.

As Mozart grows toward adulthood, there is a palpable thrill of emergence. The routine becomes rare, the extraordinary ordinary. Having proved himself as an able technician of theatrical and sacred music (*Lucio Silla*, of 1772, and the Sacramental Litany, of 1776, are high-water marks of his youth), Mozart now imports exterior drama and interior reflection to instrumental genres: the hard-driving Symphony No. 25 in G Minor, the swashbuckling violin concertos of 1775, the spacious String Quintet No. 1 in B-flat, and, most strikingly, the Piano Concerto No. 9, which is a three-act instrumental opera of energetic play, melancholy withdrawal, and happy return. Whether any of these forward leaps can be connected with events in Mozart's life remains a matter of debate. Did the traumas of 1778—the failure of his venture to Paris, the death of his mother, Leopold's scathing criticism—create in Mozart a new musical maturity? During that Paris summer, Mozart wrote his taut, tense Piano Sonata in A Minor, another landmark in his development. The trouble is that we don't know whether it was written before or after Maria Anna's death, and, in the absence of other information, we have to assume that one day Mozart banged an A-minor chord like a wedge into the middle range of the piano and liked the way it sounded. Stanley Sadie, in his 2005 book *Mozart: The Early Years*, concludes unsentimentally, "There is no real reason to imagine that [Mozart] used his music as a vehicle for the expression of his own personal feelings."

Then again, it's hard not to see some connection between the life and the art in the period from 1781 to 1786, when a series of independent acts—Mozart's escape from Salzburg to Vienna, his marriage to Constanze, his defiant response to Leopold's objections to the above—coincides with a staggering outpouring of inspiration: the six string quartets dedicated to Haydn, fifteen concertos for piano and orchestra, the "Haffner" and "Linz" and "Prague" Symphonies, the Mass in C Minor, the operas *The Abduction from the Seraglio* and *The Marriage of Figaro*, and a dozen other pieces

without which classical programming would grind to a halt. The instrumental works, with their architecturally imposing first movements and
their slow movements that open up multiple inner worlds, are the most
expansive of their time, looking forward to Beethoven only insofar as
Beethoven looked back at them. Yet the futuristic broadening of scope is
made possible by a study of the past; Mozart immerses himself in the art
of Bach, prompted by a fad for old music in aristocratic circles. (The emperor liked fugues.) Also, in the slow movements spasms of dissonance
are used to offset the surplus of beauty; Scott Burnham notes that the
famous Andante of the Concerto No. 21 contains a quietly shuddering
five-note collection that is not so much a chord as a cluster. Counterpoint
and dissonance are the cables on which Mozart's bridges to paradise hang.

Mozart's operas, meanwhile, abandon artifice in favor of moment-to-
moment psychological realism. In *The Abduction from the Seraglio*, Bel-
monte ventures into the Ottoman Empire in search of his kidnapped love,
Constanze. Having learned that she is nearby, he sings of the anxious
beating of his heart ("O wie ängstlich, o wie feurig"). The heartbeat is
indicated in a soft but insistent pattern of falling thirds, in which, Mozart
wrote proudly to his father, "you see the trembling, the faltering." A fluttering, innocent-sounding kind of worry is suggested by rapid runs of flute
and muted violins. Toward the end of the aria, the "throbbing" figure
comes back in the minor mode, and it is reinforced by winds in unison. It
ends up sounding obsessive and fearful—a lover's paranoia creeping in.
This insistent deepening of an ostensibly comic situation would become
Mozart's signature in the next several years; *The Marriage of Figaro, Don
Giovanni*, and *Così fan tutte*, the three operas that he created in tandem
with his ideal librettist, the Italian Jewish polymath Lorenzo Da Ponte,
sprawl across the boundary between the comic and the tragic, defining
life as what happens in between.

After 1786, the storm of style abates slightly. In this period, Mozart
was no longer attracting sufficient numbers of subscribers to his public
concerts, in part because of the economic effects of an expensive war
with Turkey. So the production of piano concertos tapers off, and there
are no symphonies after the "Jupiter," of 1788. Instead, the completist
listener must get through thickets of minuets, contredanses, and other
popular dances, the result of Mozart's new, revenue-enhancing job as the
emperor's Kammermusicus. These pieces are a little exasperating in large

quantity, but they are full of witty, even zany details, and serve as a reminder that eighteenth-century composers were expected to be adept at producing both "popular" and "serious" styles. Period dances are deployed to dramatic effect in the ballroom scene in *Don Giovanni*, in which an aristocratic minuet, a popular contredanse, and a working-class Deutscher unfold simultaneously, in three different meters. The episode demonstrates Mozart's ability to move as a free agent through the social and cultural hierarchies of his time.

In his last years, Mozart is less prolific than before. He seems to be groping his way toward a new style, more concise in form and more melodically compressed. Charles Rosen, in his book *The Classical Style*, isolates a telltale episode in the Adagio of the String Quintet in D (1790)—a quietly radical sequence in which, as Rosen writes, "four completely different kinds of rhythm [are] superimposed in a contrapuntal texture at once complex and deeply touching." One violin moves up by steps, the other moves haltingly down, the two violas sigh on repeated seconds and thirds, and the cello undermines the harmony with a jazzy pizzicato figure that plunges down an octave and a half. Right afterward comes a radiant little theme of rising-and-falling phrases, which brings back one of the oldest recurring motifs in Mozart's language—an archetype of love or longing. There is something elegiac in this gesture toward the past; Mozart, near the end, goes back to his beginnings. Yet it is hazardous to connect the elusive emotions of the late works with the fact of the composer's approaching death. Julian Rushton wryly notes that critics used to detect "feelings of impending doom" in the Clarinet Concerto and the Piano Concerto No. 27, both of which appeared in Mozart's final year; it turns out that the first movement of each was sketched several years earlier.

What Mozart might have done next is no one's guess. The pieces that emerged from the suddenly productive year 1791—*The Magic Flute*, the ultimate Leopoldian synthesis of high and low; *La clemenza di Tito* (*The Clemency of Titus*), a robust revival of the aging art of opera seria; the silken lyricism of the Clarinet Concerto; the Requiem, at once cerebral and raw—form a garden of forking paths. Mozart was still a young man, discovering what he could do. In the unimaginable alternate universe in which he lived to the age of seventy, an anniversary-year essay might have contained a sentence such as this: "Opera houses focus on the great works of Mozart's maturity—*The Tempest*, *Hamlet*, the two-part *Faust*—but it would be a good thing if we occasionally heard that flawed yet lively work of his youth, *Don Giovanni*."

With the Mozart myths perpetually rising out of the ground where scholars have tried to bury them, the usefulness of *Don Giovanni* is that it puts a stake through the heart of the chocolate-box Mozart, the car-radio Mozart, the Mozart-makes-you-smarter Mozart. If the opera were played in bus stations or dentists' waiting rooms, it would spread fear. It might cause perversion in infants. No matter how many times you hear the punitive D-minor chord with which the opera begins, or the glowering diminished seventh that heralds the arrival of the stone statue of the Commendatore ("Don Giovanni, you invited me to dinner, and I have come"), it generates a certain mental panic. Mozart's harmonies of disaster are all the more terrifying because they break through the frame of what purports to be a saucy comedy about an aristocratic rake—a successor to *Figaro*. The fact that *Figaro* is actually quoted in the score—"Non più andrai" is one of the airs that the Don enjoys at dinner, just before the Commendatore arrives—suggests that Mozart is consciously subverting his reputation as a supplier of ambient musical pleasure.

The scholars Lydia Goehr and Daniel Herwitz have put together an anthology titled *The Don Giovanni Moment*, which leaves aside the discussion of who Mozart really was and addresses the music's impact on Western culture. That influence is enormous; if you wanted to locate the moment at which the Enlightenment gave way to the Romantic age, you might well settle on *Don Giovanni*. As various writers in *The Don Giovanni Moment* recount, Goethe set to work in earnest on his *Faust* after seeing a performance of *Don Giovanni*, in 1797; Kierkegaard was excited by the "sensuous genius" of Mozart's music, and by the Don's chase after erotic release; the ambivalent liberal Pushkin was torn between the Don's swagger and the Commendatore's rectitude; George Bernard Shaw riffed on the opera in *Man and Superman*, letting the Don end up in heaven. Wagner was deeply in Mozart's debt; when the tragic god Wotan sings the words "Das Ende!" in the *Ring*, he traverses the same intervals with which the Commendatore intones Don Giovanni's name.

The leading Romantic rhapsodist of *Don Giovanni* was the novelist, storyteller, critic, and composer E.T.A. Hoffmann, whose 1813 story-essay

"Don Juan" is analyzed by Richard Eldridge in the anthology. For Hoffmann, the character of the Don is uninteresting on paper—"a bon vivant who loves wine and girls immoderately, who arrogantly invites the stone man, who portrays the old father whom he cut down in self-defense, to join him at his festive table." Mozart's music transforms the Don into a radical sensualist, a seeker of extremes. But he is a Romantic gone to seed: infinite longing devolves into sexual predation, a contempt for the ordinary curdles into cynicism. On the other side stands Donna Anna, the Commendatore's daughter, whom the Don attempts to rape in the first scene of the opera. Hoffmann's narrator speculates that Donna Anna actually succumbed to the Don's advances, and swears vengeance to cover up her shame. Hoffmann is right in hearing something weirdly violent in Donna Anna's utterances, especially the aria "Or sai chi l'onore" and the ragged recitative that introduces it. There is a blackness at the heart of her righteousness, just as there is a life force in the Don's malice. Mozart's quest for middle ground takes him into the risky space between good and evil. Both the terms and the outcome of this "conflict between godly and demonic powers," as Hoffmann called it, are murky.

When the Don finally goes down to hell, you are not sure whether you are hearing infernal legions celebrating his arrival or the armies of heaven rather too enthusiastically enjoying their capacity for destruction—or, perhaps, some unholy concert of the two. The scene is structured around a staggered sequence of upward-creeping lines, sometimes in the bass and sometimes in the treble. Twice, the strings embroider that pattern with vehement up-and-down scales, and the fact that each scale is a half-step higher than the previous one gives the impression that the music is obliterating everything in its path, like a death machine in a medieval etching. Toward the end, a thumping four-note figure comes to the fore; it recalls the Commendatore knocking at the door but ends up sounding like the stomping of feet.

At the same time, as Michel Noiray observes in *The Cambridge Mozart Encyclopedia*, the scene has an archaic, religious aspect, echoing Renaissance and Baroque sacred music. In the first bars of the opera, immediately after the colossal opening chords, Mozart revives the device of the chromatic lamento bass. There might be a certain irony in the gesture; Peter Williams calls it "fate being underlined with a familiar and mundane formula, like doggerel verse in *Faust*." When the Commendatore exacts his revenge, the formula is reversed: instead of trudging down, as in the "Crucifixus" of Bach's B-Minor Mass, the bass line plows relentlessly upward. As it happens, the same effect appears in several of Mozart's youthful masses, in settings of the word "Crucifixus." In addition, Mozart probably took inspiration from the hectic, dissonant dance that concludes Gluck's 1761 ballet *Don Juan*—a diabolical chaconne in the key of D minor. For perhaps the first time in musical history, references to the past become a modernist gesture, a radical haunting.

The Don's almost existential fate, his crucifixion without resurrection, is a singular event in Mozart's world. Most of his operas end in a great scene of reconciliation, in keeping with Enlightenment ideals. In *Figaro*, the Countess pardons the Count; in *Idomeneo*, Neptune's oracle, in whose music Leopold Mozart took such an interest, proclaims the power of love; in *The Abduction from the Seraglio*, Pasha Selim forgives his enemy's son; and in *The Magic Flute* and *La clemenza di Tito*, both Sarastro and the Emperor rise above vengeance. (*Così fan tutte* is the other problem case; its reuniting of lovers is troubled by the fact that Fiordiligi has expressed high passion for the wrong man.) Jessica Waldoff, in her 2006 study *Recognition in Mozart's Operas*, connects these scenes to Aristotle's concept of anagnorisis, or recognition, the "change from ignorance to knowledge." In *Don Giovanni*, Waldoff points out, the moment of recognition is withheld: the Don remains "unflinching, unreflecting." That is why the Romantics revered him: he does not stray from the extreme path that he has chosen. He is more Faustian than Goethe's Faust—who does, in the end, repent.

A final twist awaits. In a cosmically laughing epilogue, the remaining principals gather to proclaim, in bouncy, up-tempo music, that evildoers always meet the same bad end. The Romantics had such difficulty accepting this seeming anticlimax that they routinely cut it from the opera. Richard Strauss was one of the first to recognize its ironic intelligence, and to restore it in performance. The scholars Philip Kitcher and Richard Schacht write that the ending imagines "life without awe," a truly human existence beginning on the other side of tragedy. The world may be a duller place without the Don and his occult nemesis, but it is still suffused with Mozartian bliss. We can live without extremists, however much they may stimulate our faculties of lust and rage.

Don Giovanni, which is many people's choice for the greatest opera ever written, ends with something like a humble gesture: it dissolves its own aura of greatness. Having marched us to the brink of heaven and hell, Mozart abruptly pulls us back, implying that, in the manner of Shakespeare's epilogues, all is show, a pageant melting into air. "I'm just the composer, I don't have any answers," he seems to say. "Life goes on!" And he walks away at a rapid pace, his red coat flapping behind him.

5

ORBITING

RADIOHEAD'S GRAND TOUR

On a hot day in May 2001, the city of Bilbao was shaken by a velvety roar, not unlike the sound of a jet plane waiting on a tarmac. At one end of Calle de Iparraguirre, which cuts across the town, the silver shell of Frank Gehry's Guggenheim Museum was glistening in the sun. For a moment, it seemed as if the noise were coming from there—as if the building were about to lift off and rocket elsewhere. In fact, the source of the disturbance was a local bullring, the Vista Alegre, where a German experimental DJ named Christoph de Babalon was testing his gear. He was the opening act for Radiohead, a five-man British group that had the reputation of being the most artistically formidable rock band since the Beatles. Radiohead fans were gathered at the entrance, staring up at the sound and asking what it meant. One had on a Kafka T-shirt, and others wore shirts with a Radiohead logo, which can only be described as a demon in tears.

A side door led to a concrete corridor, where the bulls run on an ordinary day. From there, planks reached out to a temporary stage. Christoph was in the center, eyeing his mixer and his CD players. With ice-blond hair and black sunglasses, he looked like a young Bond villain, but he turned out to be a friendly, chatty sort of sonic terrorist. "I am familiar with dark, small clubs," he said after the sound check. "Now it is like I am in a gladiator film." He mentioned some of his musical influences, which included avant-garde figures like Merzbow and the composer Morton Feldman. "Sometimes I work with beats, sometimes with layers," he said. "Tonight I do layers."

Christoph went to his dressing room, and the stage was empty for a while. Two shirtless old men sat on stone steps, looking as though they

had not moved since Franco died. Radiohead's gear basked in the sun. On
the left-hand side was a rack of guitars—twenty-three in all. Up front, in
an area set aside for Ed O'Brien, one of three guitarists in the band, was
a tangle of pedals, samplers, and inch-thick cords. In the center of the
stage, to be shared by Colin Greenwood, the bass player, and Thom Yorke,
the singer, were various keyboards, a piano, and an upright bass. Equipment for Colin's younger brother, Jonny Greenwood, stood on the right:
more guitars, more keyboards, a xylophone, a transistor radio, a sci-fi stack
of analog synthesizers, and a modified ondes Martenot, one of the earliest
electronic instruments. The ondes Martenot is controlled by a ring that
slides along a wire; fewer than a hundred people have mastered it, and
Jonny is one. The only really conventional-looking apparatus was the drum
set, although you could tell by some distress on the edges of the drums
that the player, Phil Selway, had attacked the sides as well as the skins.

Backstage, the members of Radiohead were eating dinner. Colin Greenwood hovered over the catering table, inspecting an array of Basque dishes.
He is typical of the group in that he looks nothing like a celebrity who has
sold fifteen million records. He is a pale, slender man with jet-black hair
and large, kindly eyes. He is easily distracted and delighted by the world
around him, favoring the words "mad," "brilliant," and "amazing"—the
last spoken with a long, liquid stress on the second syllable. He has a habit
of suddenly burying his face in his hands, as if he were sinking into despair or falling asleep; after a moment, his face lights up again. Lavishly
well-read, he can talk at length about almost any topic under the sun—
Belgian fashion, the stories of John Cheever, the effect of different types
of charcoal on barbecued meat—but he gets embarrassed by his erudition
and cuts himself off by saying, "I'm rambling." He is not above wearing a
T-shirt that says "Life's a beach and then you shag." You might peg him as
a cultish young neo-Marxist professor, or as the editor of a hip quarterly.
But he is a rock star, with several Web pages devoted to him.

"It's full on out there, isn't it?" Greenwood said, looking toward the
bullring, which was filling up with fans. "I'm scared." He occupied himself by talking about *Faust's Metropolis*, Alexandra Richie's thousand-page
history of Berlin. Outside, Christoph began to play for real, and was received in bemused silence.

An hour later, Radiohead hit the stage with a confidence that had been
invisible before the show. The sound was huge, but it was awash in colors,

contrasts, and detail. It was grand in effect, cool in tone, dark in mood. The set combined music from the band's breakthrough albums of the mid-nineties—*The Bends* and *OK Computer*—with more recent material from the albums *Kid A* and *Amnesiac*. The older songs had choruses that the fans knew by heart, but the newer ones, which some rock critics had described as "anticommercial," made the crowd dance harder. (In a demolition of conventional wisdom, *Kid A*, a hypnotic blend of rock riffs, jazz chords, classical textures, and electronic noise, had gone to the top of the Billboard chart the previous year.) "Idioteque" set off fierce rhythmic clapping, even though it was dominated by jagged beats, computer-music samples, and squawks from the analog synths. It must have helped that the singer, when he was done singing, launched into a demonically silly dance, kicking his legs as if someone were firing a gun at his feet. It may also have helped, on an unconscious level, that love-drunk chords from *Tristan und Isolde* lurked at the heart of the song, courtesy of Paul Lansky's 1973 computer composition *mild und leise*.

In the middle of the set, Radiohead played a song called "Airbag," which typifies the band's crafty balance of art and pop. Jonny started off with a melody that snaked along in uneven time—*one*-two-three-*one*-two-three-*one*-two—and swayed between A major and F major. O'Brien added leaner, brighter curlicues on guitar. Selway came in with a precise but heavily syncopated beat. Then Yorke began to sing, in a well-schooled, plaintive voice, an oblique account of a near-fatal collision: "In the next world war / In a jackknifed juggernaut / I am born again." At the mention of war, Colin let loose a jumpy bass line, giving a funky spin to the hymns in the treble. The music cut through a jumble of verses and choruses, then held fast to a single chord, as Yorke fell into sync with O'Brien's chiming lines. Just before the end, Colin grinned, leaped in the air a couple of times, and seized hold of his brother's tune, the one that had set the song in motion. The doubling of the theme, a very Led Zeppelin move, had thunderous logic, as if an equation had been solved. The interplay was as engaging to the mind as anything that had been done in classical music recently, but you could jump up and down to it.

In the old days, rock bands had a haircut, a lingo, a house style. The disconcerting thing about Radiohead is that its members aren't much alike.

They have in common the fact that they were born between 1967 and 1971, and that they grew up in Oxfordshire, England, where most of them still live, but beyond that their personalities diverge. Yorke, who writes most of the songs, is compact, boyish, and impish; he has a lethally quick mind and a subtly potent charisma. O'Brien, almost a foot taller than Yorke, has the jutting jaw and floppy bangs of an actor in a period war movie; he is suave and direct and seems to have rolled in from a different posse. Jonny Greenwood, a lanky figure with unruly black hair, is more cautious than his brother, Colin, but when he starts talking he excitedly involves himself in dense, Victorian sentences, biting clauses out of the air. Phil Selway, the oldest, is bald and sweet-faced, and talks in a gentle voice. He looks like the nice, ordinary one, but he often has a trace of a wicked smile.

How these five quirky Englishmen became the Knights Templar of rock and roll—the most closely analyzed, fervently admired, hotly debated, and slavishly imitated band of the modern era—is anyone's guess. They are not too sure themselves. "Everyone comes to us with their heads bowed, expecting to be inducted into the mystery of Radiohead," Selway said. He made a King Tut gesture with his arms. "We were hoist on our own petard with that. At a certain point, around 1997, we were simply overwhelmed and had to vanish for a bit. This was our honest reaction to the situation we were in. But some people thought we were playing a game, or had started taking ourselves too seriously. Really, we don't want people twiddling their goatees over our stuff. What we do is pure escapism."

What happened to Radiohead in 1997 was that they caught a wave of generational anxiety. The album OK Computer, with titles like "Paranoid Android," "Karma Police," and "Climbing Up the Walls," pictured the onslaught of the information age and a young person's panicky embrace of it. Yorke's lyrics seemed a mixture of overheard conversations, techno-speak, and fragments of a harsh diary. The songs offered images of riot police at political rallies, anguished lives in tidy suburbs, yuppies freaking out, sympathetic aliens gliding overhead. In "Let Down," Yorke even dared to describe the feeling of disappointment that follows a blast of hype, such as the one his band was producing. The album sold more than four million copies worldwide, enabling the group to become, by 1999, an independent operation. Radiohead were the poster boys for a certain kind of knowing alienation—as Talking Heads and R.E.M. had been before.

Radiohead remain a magnet for misfits everywhere, but their outsider status is only a part of their appeal. What fans seem to like, even more than the content of the songs, is the sense that the band members have labored over every aspect of the product. They are skilled, first of all, at inventing the kinds of riddles that people enjoy unraveling. The records, the videos, the official website, even the T-shirts all cry out for interpretation. Why are words spelled funny? What are all these charts and diagrams? What about the grinning bears and crying Minotaurs? "We liked worrying over that kind of thing when we were kids, and we're still in the same mind-set a lot of the time," Selway said. "But it's a bit incidental. We're dead set on the music. That's the thread running through this whole thing. We met at school playing music together, and we still get together over music now. We like solving musical puzzles. That's what Thom gives us."

A Radiohead song is usually written in three stages. First, Yorke comes up with a rough sketch; then, Jonny, who studied composition briefly at Oxford Brookes University, fleshes out the harmony; finally, the others digest it for a while, working out their parts on their own. It can be months, even years, before a song comes together in a way that satisfies all of them. Take away any one element—Selway's flickering rhythmic grid, for example, crisp in execution and trippy in effect—and Radiohead is a different band. The five together form a single mind, with its own habits and tics—the Radiohead Composer. This personality can be glimpsed in the daily bustle of the group, but you can never meet it face-to-face, because it lives in the music. A lot of what has been written about Radiohead—there are a dozen books, hundreds of magazine articles, and millions of words on the Internet—circles around an absent center.

During Radiohead's tours of 2001, the best picture of the band at work came during the sound checks. Yorke led these preshow rituals with the assurance of a seasoned conductor with limited rehearsal time. He'd shout "Next!" just as a song was building to its climax. All problems had to be addressed on the spot. At one point, Colin said, "That's something we can work on later," whereupon Yorke muttered to himself, and Colin added, a little wearily, "It is also something we can work on now." There were moments, though, when Yorke was at a loss. Once, during a run-through of "The Tourist," he forgot the final chord, and so did everyone else—including Jonny, who had written the song. "Does anyone have a copy of

OK Computer?" Yorke called out. No one did. The Composer was taking a nap. A couple of weeks later, the problem still hadn't been solved. "Shall we nominate an ending and play through it to see what it sounds like?" O'Brien said, impatiently. "What do you have in mind?" Yorke said. "D7, perhaps?" "OK, let's try it."

On their days off, Radiohead dissolve into literate anarchy. They buzz with curiosity, pepper strangers with questions, digest the answers, and wander off on their own. On the day after the Bilbao show, they took a ramble around the city, and the city was caught off guard. One stop was the Guggenheim, where they had an unsuspecting tour guide named Maria. While Maria was still trying to muster everyone in one place, Colin began reciting facts about the structure: "The limestone had to be cut by a computer. Each curve has its own algorithm. I read an article somewhere. The A/C is fucking brilliant, man. Air pumps out of that vent way up there and goes all the way down here." When Colin arrived in front of Richard Serra's massive steel sculptures, he declared that one of the pieces had gone missing from its usual place. "This is wrong," he said. "There should be a second plate bisecting the first." Selway and O'Brien started making fun of him—"Can't have gone far"; "Call Lost and Found"—but Maria confirmed that, in fact, the sculptures had been rearranged.

As Radiohead fanned out through the museum, clumps of fans in *Kid A* T-shirts followed at a respectful distance. "Cool that our blokes like art," O'Brien said. Yorke walked alone through the Serra installation, singing, "We're bad, we're bad." The group had disintegrated, and Maria gave up. At the exit, she said sternly, "Not once this entire time have you all been together." Yorke smiled sympathetically and replied, "Not the first time, won't be the last."

The same day, the band had a meal at a restaurant called Etxebarri, in the hills above Bilbao. The conversation was an intelligent blur, jumping from high to low and back again. On one side of the table, Jonny was picking at a plate of lettuce and talking about favorite twentieth-century classical composers, notably Alban Berg and Olivier Messiaen. "I've been listening to a CD of Berg's *Lulu* Suite," he said. "I'm killing myself because I forgot to bring my Messiaen." It is because of Messiaen—the Catholic avant-gardist who composed in explosively vibrant colors—that Jonny became interested in the ondes Martenot, which is featured in many of the composer's works. "I heard the *Turangalîla Symphony* when I was fifteen,"

Jonny went on, "and I became round-the-bend obsessed with it. I wish I could have met him or shaken his hand."

On the other side of the table, Yorke, whose meal consisted of a bowl of bean soup, started complaining about pop-music conglomerates. He and the rest of the band had become politically outspoken, protesting globalization and corporate capitalism. The previous night, he had dedicated "No Surprises"—which contains the line "Bring down the government"—to George W. Bush. In the summer of 2001, Radiohead chose to play a number of open-air venues—such as Liberty State Park, in Jersey City—because these sites had so far escaped the tentacles of an aggressive promotion company called S.F.X., whose parent corporation, Clear Channel, also operated more than a thousand radio stations.

"S.F.X. is a parasite that needs a host to feed on," Yorke said.

"It's effective only as long as it keeps growing," O'Brien added. "At some point, it will cease growing, and then its reason to exist will disappear."

"No," Yorke said, "it's a virus that's just going to keep spreading forever."

Chris Hufford, one of the band's managers, who has to negotiate with viruses on the phone, grew impatient. "This is reality, Thom," he said. "This is the marketplace we're in."

"No," Yorke replied, "the marketplace is where we sell records. This isn't the marketplace. It's an area of, I don't know, oversight."

"Come on," Hufford said, "it's capitalism, it's what we have to work with."

"Bollocks!"

"Capitalism!"

"Bollocks!" Yorke yelled. He got up in a mock huff to go to the bathroom. Colin looked up from his steak and gestured toward the wine in the middle of the table. "Brilliant!" he exclaimed. "Booze in the afternoon!"

That night, Radiohead got on a bus to go to their next gig, in the French village of Vaison-la-Romaine. They played a show at a magnificent Roman amphitheater there, and then went to Verona, in Italy, where they performed for a crowd of fifteen thousand in the legendary Arena, displacing scenery for *Aida* onto the piazza. Along the way, they made on-the-fly recordings with Nigel Godrich, their young, wizardly producer, on assorted Apple PowerBooks; appeared on a popular BBC radio show called *Mark & Lard*, where they were required to shout the phrase "Biggity-biggity-bong!"; greeted a radio-contest winner who hailed Yorke as "a genius" and "sincere";

and avoided some overzealous fans who hollered, "We have come all the way from Venezuela, give us your autograph!" even though they had French accents and were not from Venezuela. There were also quiet moments here and there, as when they sat in a hotel lobby reading the English papers, sun streaming on the marble, and seemed to be fulfilling Colin's notion of the band as "the E. M. Forster of rock."

Radiohead began at Abingdon School, a private boys' school outside Oxford. Abingdon has a history dating back to the twelfth century, but it is not a national bastion on the order of Eton or Winchester. Its students tend to come from the Thames Valley region, rather than from all over England, and many rely on scholarships. The members of Radiohead were born into ordinary middle-class families: Yorke's father was a chemical-equipment supplier; Jonny and Colin's father served in the army. They were, basically, townies—the kids on the other side of the ancient walls. Even at Abingdon, they felt out of place. The longtime headmaster of the school, Michael St. John Parker, cultivated a pompous manner that many alumni—not just Radiohead—remember less than fondly. Parker described the school spirit in these terms: "Competition is promoted, achievement is applauded, and individual dynamism is encouraged."

In schools of this kind, many students gravitate to the art, music, and drama departments, where the sense of discipline is looser. For Radiohead, the saving grace of Abingdon was an exceptional teacher named Terence Gilmore-James, who headed the music program. "I was a sort of leper at the time," Yorke recalled, "and he was the only one who was nice to me." Yorke was born with his left eye paralyzed; in his childhood, he endured a series of not entirely successful operations to correct it, and the oddity of his half-open eye made him a target for bullies. Tougher than he looked, he often fought back, but he preferred to disappear. "School was bearable for me because the music department was separate from the rest of the school," he said. "It had pianos in tiny booths, and I used to spend a lot of time hanging around there after school, waiting for my dad to come home from work." Other members of the band also studied with Gilmore-James and were encouraged by him. "When we started, it was very important that we got support from him," Colin said, "because we weren't getting any from the headmaster. You know, the man once sent us a bill, charging us for the use of school property, because we practiced in one of the music rooms on a Sunday."

Radiohead's sound owes much to Gilmore-James, who immersed his students in twentieth-century classical music, avant-garde music of the postwar era, classic jazz, and film scores. Once, he had the school orchestra perform Richard Rodney Bennett's score for *Murder on the Orient Express* while the film was playing. He left Abingdon in 1987 to devote himself to the legacy of his father-in-law, the Welsh composer Mansel Thomas, whose music he was editing for publication. "I watch over Radiohead much as I watch over my children," he said in a phone call. He spoke with the fastidiousness of a lifelong teacher, and yet his tone was enthusiastic rather than dogmatic. "They were all of them talented boys, in the sense that they had more than average abilities to think for themselves. I was of a different generation, and I did not always grasp what they were after, but I knew that they were serious. And they were delightful to be around, always getting carried away by their latest discoveries. Whenever I see them"—his voice became firm—"I tell them that they must continue to pursue their own original line."

In the schoolboy cadre of Radiohead, Yorke was the bossy one from the start. His very first words to Selway at rehearsal were "Can't you play any fucking faster?" The band's early songs were all over the map, sounding variously like the Smiths, R.E.M., Sonic Youth, the Pixies, and Talking Heads, whose song "Radio Head" gave the group its name. (At first, they performed under the name On a Friday, but they wisely changed their minds.) The strongest influence came from the Pixies, the great but never world-famous Boston band whose gritty songs, shaded soft and loud, also inspired Nirvana. Even as the boys wandered off to university, they got together over weekends, practicing, arguing, and searching for a style. In 1991, Hufford, the co-owner of an Oxford sound studio, came to hear them play, at a place called the Jericho Tavern, and was fascinated by Yorke's dire energy onstage. He and his partner Bryce Edge produced a demo tape and signed on as managers. Colin, who was working at a record store, gave the tape to Keith Wozencroft, a sales rep for EMI, who moved to A&R shortly afterward and began to tout the band. They signed with EMI later that year.

"I was getting ready to quit EMI when these lads appeared," Carol Baxter, Radiohead's international record-company representative, recalled.

"Bunch of disturbed consumptives, I thought. But they were ambitious and smart. At first, I had to hide my Radiohead paperwork behind the Tina Turner and Queensrÿche files, because my boss thought I was wasting my time. Then the call came in, from Israel, actually, saying that the band had a hit." Tim Greaves, Radiohead's longtime tour manager, commented on the band's overnight success. "The funny thing about Radiohead early on was that they were more famous abroad than in England," he said. "They'd go around in a van, playing in sweaty little clubs. Then they'd go to Israel and they were rock stars. Same in America. Then it was back to England, back to the van, back to the clubs. They had a good early introduction to the relativity of fame. Fame for this band is a holiday that lasts a few weeks."

Radiohead's ticket to fame was a song called "Creep." It became a worldwide hit in 1993, when grunge rock was at its height. The lyrics spelled out the self-lacerating rage of an unsuccessful crush:

> *You're so fucking special*
> *I wish I was special*
> *But I'm a creep.*

The music was modeled on Pixies songs like "Where Is My Mind?": stately arpeggios, then an electric squall. What set "Creep" apart from the grunge of the early nineties was the grandeur of its chords—in particular, its regal turn from G major to B major. No matter how many times you hear the song, the second chord still sails beautifully out of the blue. The lyrics may be saying, "I'm a creep," but the music is saying, "I am majestic." The sense of coiled force is increased by several horrible stabs of noise on Jonny Greenwood's guitar. Radiohead have stopped playing "Creep," more or less, but it still hits home when it comes on the radio. When Beavis of *Beavis and Butt-Head* heard the noisy part, he said, "Rock!" But why, he wondered, didn't the song rock from beginning to end? "If they didn't have, like, a part of the song that sucked, then, it's like, the other part wouldn't be as cool," Butt-Head explained.

"Creep," as Butt-Head must have noticed, was the first of many Radiohead songs that used pivot tones, in which one note of a chord is held until a new chord is formed around it. (In the turn from G to B, the note B is the pivot point.) "Yeah, that's my only trick," Yorke said, when this was pointed out to him. "I've got one trick and that's it, and I'm really going to have to learn a new one. Pedals, banging away through everything." But a reliance on pedal tones and pivot tones isn't necessarily a limitation: the Romantic composers worked to death the idea that any chord could turn on a dime toward another. Yorke's "pedals" help give Radiohead songs a bittersweet, doomy taste. ("Airbag," for example, being in A major, ought to be a bright thing, but the intrusion of F and C tones tilts the music toward the minor mode. "Morning Bell" wavers darkly between A minor and C-sharp minor.) It's a looser, roomier kind of harmony than the standard I-IV-V-I, and it gives the songs a distinct stamp. It also helps sell records: whether playing guitar rock or sampling spaced-out electronica, Radiohead affix their signature.

Through the years, many bands have thrown bits and pieces of jazz and classical into their mix. The Beatles were by far the best at this kind of genre assimilation. Lesser psychedelic and prog-rock bands turned orchestral crescendos and jazz freak-outs into another brand of kitsch, but Radiohead's classical sensibility isn't pasted on the surface; it's planted at the core. If you did a breakdown of the music, you'd find the same harmonic DNA everywhere. Another trademark is the band's use of musical space. Riffs are always switching registers, bouncing from treble to bass, breaking through the ceiling or falling through the floor. In "Just," from *The Bends*, the Greenwood brothers play octatonic scales—whole steps and half-steps in alternation—that extend over four octaves; the effect is of music looming miles above you.

There are times when Radiohead seem to be practicing a new kind of classical music for the masses. In the sessions for *Kid A* and *Amnesiac*, which began in 1999 and dragged on for a year and a half, their sound became mesmerizingly intricate. On "Pyramid Song," for example, a string section played glissando harmonics, a texture that Stravinsky's *Firebird* made famous, while Selway laid on a shuffling rhythm that defies description, because, as he said, "there is no time signature." On "Dollars and Cents," O'Brien used a pedal to bend a chord from major to minor and back again. For "Like Spinning Plates," Yorke learned the vocal line of an unused song backward and made up new words while driving around in his car. The guitarists set aside their instruments for a while and taught themselves to use heaps of electronic equipment. In "Treefingers," on *Kid A*, O'Brien generated something that sounded a lot like Jonny's beloved Messiaen. Both albums also drew on jazz, especially on Charles Mingus, Alice Coltrane, and Miles Davis in his fusion phase.

Behind this creative tumult, however, was an ongoing debate about the direction of the band. The five of them often have to thrash out issues among themselves: how to balance tours with family life; how to keep the media at bay; how, simply, to get along. In this case, Yorke was fed up with verse-and-chorus music, and not everyone else agreed. O'Brien thought that the band should return to classic guitar rock, which, by the end of the nineties, had become an endangered species. "There was a lot of arguing," Nigel Godrich recalled. "People stopped talking to one another. 'Insanity' is the word. In the end, I think the debate was redundant, because the band ultimately kept doing what it has always done—zigzagging between extremes. Whenever we really did try to impose an aesthetic from the outside—the aesthetic being, say, electronic—it would fail. All the drama was just a form of procrastination. Next time, three weeks, and we're out."

In the summer of 2001, Radiohead seemed prepared to change direction once again. Several songs on *Amnesiac* stood out for their straight-ahead pop appeal. "I Might Be Wrong" is all snarling guitars; "Knives Out" goes back to the clean-cut heartbreak of the Smiths. The narcotically beautiful "Pyramid Song" could almost be a variation on "Swing Low, Sweet Chariot":

> *I jumped in the river, what did I see?*
> *Black-eyed angels swam with me . . .*
> *We all went to heaven in a little rowboat*
> *There was nothing to fear and nothing to doubt.*

This is very much Yorke's song, and it sounds best when he performs it alone, on an upright piano. You notice that he sings from the chest, breathing through his phrases. You also notice the unusual makeup of his piano chords. Laced with suspended tones, they hang ambiguously in the air, somewhere between serenity and sadness. "I bought a piano after *OK Computer*, at a time when picking up a guitar just didn't do anything for me at all," he says. "I bought a really flashy piano that I couldn't play at all. In true rock-star style." In fact, he gets a warm, mellow tone out of the piano, caressing rather than pounding the keys, keeping his wrists high.

Yorke is the essential spark of the Radiohead phenomenon. Like all greatly gifted people, he is not always easy to be around. When a stranger approaches him, wanting unscheduled attention, he can fall unsettlingly mute. He is, by his own admission, temperamental and chronically dis-satisfied. But his fault-finding circles back to the music, which is why the other band members go along with it. When he is happy, it feels like his-tory in the making. Curled up on a dressing-room sofa after a show, he comes across as warm, alert, and faintly mischievous. "It's nice when peo-ple talk to you as if you're a human being, rather than as if you'd just landed from another planet," he said. "We're fallible, this is fallible, some-times we're shit, sometimes we're not. We want to kind of mellow it all out a bit. Just chill the fuck out." He grinned quickly, perhaps realizing that the last phrase was a contradiction in terms.

At the beginning of June 2001, *Amnesiac* went on sale in the United States. There was low-level Radiohead mania around New York. Helen Weng, an eighteen-year-old from Long Island, waited at the Union Square Virgin Megastore with her friend Melissa Torres to buy *Amnesiac* at a midnight sale. In her bag, she carried a letter from Thom Yorke, written in his own hand, with advice on how to make yourself happy. "It's good to know someone else has had the same feelings," she said, clutching the paper. Over at Fez, Justin Bond, the cross-dressing star of the cabaret duo Kiki and Herb, sang "Life in a Glasshouse," from *Amnesiac*, even though the record was not yet in the stores. He attributed it to "Rodeohead, a very exciting young English rock ensemble," and rendered it as a demented torch song, which it already mostly was.

   Much modern British pop has failed to translate to the American pub-lic. Steve Martin, a publicist for Radiohead, puts it this way: "Americans don't go for 'cheeky.' We like earnest." Radiohead may be cagey, but they are never cheeky, and they are massively earnest. They have worked hard in America, logging time in the middle of the country as well as on the coasts. They are noted in the music business for being polite and unprob-lematic. A French hotel reservation of theirs extravagantly requested "ex-tra towels." One hotel doorman described them as "nice, sharp-witted, entertaining young men. Not trash-headed and stupored, as you might expect." Despite the fatigue of their previous big tours, in 1997 and 1998, they were game for America.

   "Sure, the last tour was bloody awful," Ed O'Brien said, "but that was where we were at mentally, not a reaction to America. This place is just too huge to generalize about. When I was in college, I took six months off to ride around in Greyhound buses, and I got a sense of it." He was eager to play at Red Rocks Amphitheatre, in the foothills of the Rockies. "Basically, we've had a fantasy scenario of reenacting U2 live at Red Rocks," he said. "We watched the video a million times when we were kids and know every frame. 'This song is not a rebel song!'" He lifted his fist and let out a soft roar. Fans who worry that Radiohead are losing touch with rock and roll can always look to this man, who enjoys the role of the guitar hero, even if he also sometimes kneels down in front of his samplers and molds the music into a smear of color.

Radiohead checked into a Denver hotel on June 19. Fans descended on Red Rocks the following morning, squatting on a half-mile flight of steps that leads to the arena. Down at the bottom was a group of college students, from Pepperdine and the University of Colorado at Boulder. Their names were Elke Goldstein, Amber Hollingsworth, Matt Duffy, and Kendall Lux. "Radiohead is music for miserable people who were dropped on the floor when they were little," Amber explained. "I don't know about that," Elke said. "I mean, that's the reputation, but are we miserable?" Munching on carrots, they did not look miserable.

Matt delivered a critique of the band, speaking rapidly, as if from memory. "Thom is suffering from Bono syndrome," he said. "Getting political. What's he doing hanging out with Bono? What's Bono doing hanging out with presidents and the Pope? He's a rock singer, damn it! Here's the difference between U2 and Radiohead: U2 says, 'The world sucks, and we have to change it,' whereas Radiohead says, 'The world sucks and not much can be done about it. The world is lame, ridiculous.'" Elke rolled her eyes. "*May*-be," she said. Matt barreled on: "Their records are put out by EMI, a multinational conglomerate, so it's hard to see how they can attack capitalism from that position. *Kid A* and *Amnesiac*? Ambient blueprints for music we haven't quite heard yet. Thom listens to Brian Eno, Aphex Twin, the whole Warp Records back catalogue. 'Packt Like Sardines'—what's that, one pattern stuck in a groove? But when they play it we're all going to go, 'Yeah!' No one can really say why they like them. Yet here we are."

In a matter of minutes, Matt had summed up the state of Radiohead criticism. Rock critics, like adolescent fans, have feisty friendships with the bands they admire, lacing hero worship with contempt. The magazine *Q*, for example, gave *Amnesiac* four stars and then called it "numb, petty, desolate." Some of the criticism has been peculiarly personal, especially in Britain. As a result, the singer has developed an aversion to most rock writers, and they, in turn, have goaded him at every turn. Ill feelings all around have led to unrecognizable profiles in which the band seems to be composed of antisocial curmudgeons.

At Red Rocks, Radiohead agreed to sit down for a rare collective interview with a journalist. A brave young MTV correspondent named Gideon Yago showed up to interrogate them. A Queens native who started working at MTV at the age of twenty-one, Yago had loved Radiohead since his teens. He had a sheaf of notes on his clipboard, including a chart of the band members' personalities. O'Brien and Selway struck him as "the sensible ones"; the Greenwood brothers he pegged as "will eat you alive." He wasn't sure what to make of Yorke. His impressions were based largely on a Radiohead tour documentary, *Meeting People Is Easy*, which came out in 1998. This unpleasant film was a kind of counterstrike against the music press, recording scores of pointless interviews with dead-tired members of the band. During one of them, Colin seemed ready to lapse into a coma. "I don't want to be just another dolt with a microphone," Yago said. "Like the guy in the movie who asks Thom if he got to talk to Calvin Klein."

Yago had read up on Radiohead, but when the cameras rolled he elected to keep much of his knowledge hidden. "Remember," his producer, Liane Su, told him, "you're not an expert, you're just a fan." The fans wanted to know whether the band thought it was experimenting too much, why *Kid A* and *Amnesiac* hadn't been released as a double album, what all the songs on *Amnesiac* meant. Radiohead did snap at Yago once or twice, as when he characterized *Amnesiac* as "a collection of outtakes from the *Kid A* sessions," and Selway shot back, "Try again!" But the mood was relaxed, for the most part. Yago got them all to laugh when he introduced a question from a so-called "Stanley from Coney Island," which read, "How do you guys feel about the fact that bands like Travis, Coldplay, and Muse are making a career sounding exactly like your records did in 1997?" Yorke cupped his hand around his mouth and called out, "Good luck with *Kid A*!"

When the interview was over, Yago looked shell-shocked but relieved. "That was relatively painless," the journalist said, gulping down a Molson.

In July 2001, Radiohead returned home to play in South Park, a broad meadow outside the center of Oxford. It was a drizzly day, and the towers of the university were gray lumps in the distance. The event was a kind of mini-festival, mostly given over to performances by bands that Radiohead admired. Like other summer festivals, it had kebab stands, beer huts, and T-shirt booths. Forty-four thousand fans, mostly in their teens and twenties, sat on the lawn. After a few hours, the grass was carpeted with plastic-foam cups, each one displaying the *Amnesiac* logo.

At about four o'clock, Humphrey Lyttelton, the venerable English jazz trumpeter, appeared onstage. After a few words of introduction, he and his band launched into a deft set of Armstrong and Ellington numbers. A guy in a BLUR: ARE SHITE T-shirt shouted, "You're great!" Next up was Sigur Rós, a group of Icelandic musicians, who play a kind of mystic-minimalist rock that builds to climaxes over five- and ten-minute spans. In the half-mile-long line of people who were shuffling toward the "Alcoholic Fresh Juices" stand, every other face was lost in wonder at the gentle power of the chords.

The show may have looked and smelled like an ordinary outdoor rock festival, but it was marked with the Radiohead ethic—a love of far-flung sounds, a knack for head-turning juxtapositions, a faith in the audience's ability to take it all in. "We shouldn't be just a band, playing our music and getting paid for it," Colin said beforehand. "We should be an alternative radio station, broadcasting music that gets left out of the mainstream." Radiohead have promoted dozens of lesser-known, inventive acts, including Autechre, the Beta Band, Clinic, Kid Koala, Lali Puna, Low, Sparklehorse, and, of course, Christoph de Babalon. They have also boosted favorite authors, helping to sell thousands of copies of Naomi Klein's anti-globalization book *No Logo*. The members of this roster have little or nothing in common, and that is the point: they are a funky clamor of voices, not a line of products. Such guerrilla marketing is, in the end, a form of politics—a protest against the sameness of the cultural landscape.

"Lots of really talented artists are being thrown by the wayside," Yorke had said during the American tour. "They are not being given the time of day, because they're not doing things that fit the moment. Madmen with machetes are chopping away at the wood—any wood, deadwood, doesn't matter. You want to slap people and say, 'Why don't you go back and look at all the beautiful things that have been made in the music business and realize that you have to have faith in people?' In the long run, the industry wants to make money, but if a company wants to make money then it has to take a risk. These people don't take risks. They make quick money and then that's it. And the world isn't a nicer place for it. What really makes me fucking spit blood is when people in the industry start complaining about how there's no talent around. I know it's there and you know it's there. But you are too shit scared to do anything about it."

Radiohead walked onto the South Park stage at 8:30. It was not the most flawless show of recent weeks, but it may have been the most intense. Yorke's voice glowed with emotion. During "How to Disappear Completely," as Jonny bent over his ondes Martenot, a drenching rain began to fall. The crowd, religiously attentive, stayed in place. Yorke appeared alone for the last number, and hit a few plangent chords. His instrument went dead. "Es ist kaputt, ja?" he said. "I have another idea." The others returned, and together they launched into the familiar strains of "Creep," which had gone unplayed since 1998. G major wheeled majestically into B. Jonny made his Beavis-and-Butt-Head noise. Yorke sang, "What the hell am I doing here?"

Afterward, in the dressing room, Yorke looked happy. Someone had brought in a gigantic bottle of champagne, and he was struggling to pour himself a glass. "Don't know if you could tell," he said to Colin's wife, the poet and novelist Molly McGrann, "but I was in tears for the last part of it." Then the perfectionist in him reawakened. "Horrible diesel smell coming from somewhere," he said.

The next day, Colin invited some friends over for brunch. At the time, he and Molly lived in a semidetached house on an Oxford side street. This was the beginning of a three-week holiday for the band, and Colin faced the unfamiliar prospect of having nothing to do. "We might go to a movie," he said, as if he were going to the moon. He picked through some LPs and CDs, putting on Brad Mehldau. When someone asked him if he had got a sense of the crowd at South Park—it may have been the largest public gathering in the thousand-year history of Oxford—he rubbed his eyes and smiled. "'Fraid not," he replied. "I was too busy looking at Phil's calves. That's where the beats are."

6

THE ANTI-MAESTRO

ESA-PEKKA SALONEN AT THE

LOS ANGELES PHILHARMONIC

"I had this one morning—it was like a vision," the Finnish composer and conductor Esa-Pekka Salonen told an audience in Los Angeles in early 2007, at the end of one of those grand, warm Southern California days that you hope will never end. He was describing something that he had experienced not long after he became the music director of the Los Angeles Philharmonic, in 1992. "I woke up early, and my two little daughters were still asleep and so was my wife, and I saw the hummingbirds outside my window, and the sun was shining. And I felt this very strange thing. I couldn't quite know what it was. I went to the kitchen and I made myself a cup of coffee. As I was sitting there, I thought, Why do I feel like this? What is it? And then I realized that I felt—*free*. Nice feeling." Free, he explained, from the totems and taboos of modernism; free to investigate new canons in music and art; free to become himself.

Salonen was speaking at the Apple Store in Santa Monica. He had been invited there to discuss one of his recent works—*Helix*, a kaleidoscopic tone poem for orchestra—and the computer programs that he employs to notate and elaborate his ideas. More than a hundred people, ranging from longtime Philharmonic subscribers to college-age electronic-music enthusiasts, squeezed in among the iMacs and the iPods to see Salonen in person. He had become an unusual kind of celebrity—a fixed point of cerebral cool in a city of spectacle and flux.

Salonen is a short, lean man, preternaturally youthful in appearance. It didn't quite compute that he would turn fifty the following year. Some years ago, *People* magazine offered him the opportunity to be one of its "Most Beautiful People"; he declined. A native of Helsinki, he speaks in a polyglot diction made up, variously, of the fluid singsong of the Finnish language, a kind of BBC-announcer plumminess, bits of various Continental languages, and an array of American idioms, some of them picked up from his daughters, Ella and Anja (who were by this time teenagers). Reserved by nature, he is a winning speaker nonetheless, puncturing his maestro façade with deadpan jokes, whimsical digressions, "Who, me?" inflections, and a favorite facial expression of the cat-that-ate-the-canary type.

Salonen told the crowd about his first years with the Philharmonic. "I was then a little over thirty years old," he said. "And I was being given this orchestra to conduct. What other city would be prepared to do this—give one of the top orchestras in the world to some guy from Finland nobody has ever heard of? And yet they did that. And all along I felt this tremendous support. 'OK, show us. Do something with it. Just run with it.'"

Run with it he did: Salonen proceeded to make the L.A. Philharmonic the most contemporary-minded orchestra in America. Stravinsky's *Rite of Spring*, premiered in 1913, became the center of the repertory, not the outer limit. Conductor and listeners met each other halfway, the latter opening themselves to new sounds and the former softening his modernist edge. In 2003, with the opening of Walt Disney Concert Hall, in downtown L.A., the Philharmonic acquired the most architecturally striking and acoustically satisfying performance space of modern times. More good things followed: a festival called Minimalist Jukebox brought in thousands of new listeners, and Peter Sellars's production of *Tristan und Isolde*, set to a full-length film by Bill Viola, remade Wagner's medieval tragedy as a ritual of watery immersion and purification. Flush with money, free of contract disputes, playing to near-capacity audiences, capitalizing on new technologies, the L.A. Phil became that rare creature: a happy orchestra.

The one malcontent, ironically, was Salonen. His main ambition had always been to compose. Although he had found time to write some notable works during his Los Angeles tenure—L.A. *Variations*, *Wing on Wing*, the Piano Concerto—he lacked real creative freedom, his days still taken up with conducting, rehearsals, meetings, public appearances, and interviews. So, after a *Tristan* rehearsal on April 7, 2007, with the strains of Isolde's "Liebestod" still hanging in the air, Salonen told the orchestra that he would step down from the podium in two years' time, so that he could spend more time composing, and so that the players could have a fresh start. As he explained a couple of days later, "What I didn't want to see was that I'd sit on top of the orchestra like Jabba the Hutt and prevent every other life-form from emerging." He said that he would continue to conduct, though at a slower pace—he had recently signed up for a less time-consuming position with the Philharmonia Orchestra, in London, where his wife, Jane, was once a violinist—and that he would maintain ties with the Philharmonic.

The orchestra was still absorbing Salonen's news when Deborah Borda, the orchestra's chief executive, got up to make a second announcement. In secret consultation with the Artistic Liaison Committee, which consists of five Philharmonic musicians, the administration had selected as the orchestra's next music director Gustavo Dudamel, a twenty-six-year-old Venezuelan. In 2004, Salonen had served on the jury of a conducting competition in Bamberg, Germany, where Dudamel was among the entrants. After a performance of Mahler's Fifth Symphony, Salonen had called Borda to tell her that he had encountered a "real conducting animal," and that it might be good to engage Dudamel for a guest appearance in Los Angeles. Dudamel led the Philharmonic twice in the following three years. With an eye toward finding Salonen's successor, Borda had asked the members of the orchestra to evaluate every guest conductor who passed through. Dudamel received almost entirely positive responses.

The announcement of Dudamel's hiring was made official at a Monday morning press conference. Three nights later, in a hall thrown into darkness—the blue step lights glimmering like stars seen through the rigging of a ship—Salonen set Act I of *Tristan* in motion. Like so many of his performances in the past, it fell cleanly and richly on the ears; few conductors give as clear a beat or have so acute an ear for combinations of sounds. But there was also an unchecked heat in the playing that you didn't hear so often in the early years of Salonen's tenure, when his control of detail led to excitingly rigorous renditions of Stravinsky and Schoenberg and some emotionally constrained Mozart and Beethoven. Making wide, broadly curving gestures with the baton, he let himself be carried along by Wagner's music as much as he directed it.

The Salonen era in L.A., which ended on April 19, 2009, with a crystalline performance of Stravinsky's *Symphony of Psalms*, marked a turning point in the recent history of classical music in America. It was a story not of an individual magically imprinting his personality on an institution—what Salonen has called the "empty hype" of conductor worship—but of an individual and an institution bringing out unforeseen capabilities in each other, and thereby proving how much life remains in the orchestra itself, at once the most conservative and the most powerful of musical organisms.

Joseph Horowitz, in his 2005 book *Classical Music in America: A History of Its Rise and Fall,* explains in a three-word phrase why American classical music has had such a difficult time escaping the shadow of Europe. Shortly after the beginning of the twentieth century, Horowitz writes, the country's leading musical institutions, most conspicuously the great symphony orchestras of the East and Midwest, fell into a "culture of performance"—a concert ritual dedicated to the immaculate repetition of eighteenth- and nineteenth-century classics. Concert halls were explicitly designed as shrines to Beethoven and his brethren, with the great one's name customarily etched in block letters above center stage. Celebrity maestros and virtuosos assumed ersatz creative roles, lending a patina of novelty to superfamiliar music. Living composers became curiosities and nuisances. Almost nothing about the enterprise had any tangible connection to contemporary life. Small wonder that orchestras struggled to retain their audiences as the century went on: they were dealing in replicas, not in original work.

From time to time, forward-thinking conductors attempted to correct the necrophiliac leanings of the American classical audience. Leopold Stokowski may have been a scold when it came to suppressing noise in the audience, but he was wondrously open-minded when it came to programming contemporary music, not to mention exploiting new technologies and championing nonwhite composers and musicians. Serge Koussevitzky was hardly less adventurous during his tenure at the Boston Symphony, almost single-handedly commissioning an American orchestral repertory (major symphonies by Copland, Roy Harris, William Schuman) as well as calling forth such international masterpieces as the iconic *Symphony of Psalms,* Bartók's Concerto for Orchestra, Britten's *Peter Grimes,* and Messiaen's *Turangalîla Symphony.* Three consecutive music directors of the New York Philharmonic—Dimitri Mitropoulos, Leonard

Bernstein, and Pierre Boulez—tried with mixed success to convince New Yorkers of the power and beauty of twentieth-century scores. Boulez did draw crowds of jeans-clad youngsters to a special series of Rug Concerts, for which seats were removed from Philharmonic Hall, but the older subscription audience grumbled throughout his tenure.

Music professionals often cited Boulez's Philharmonic experiment as evidence that a modernistically oriented conductor, no matter how talented, could not conquer the mainstream orchestral world. The conventional wisdom held for some years, but it faltered in the 1990s, when two pathbreaking music directors arrived on the West Coast. One was Salonen; the other was Michael Tilson Thomas, who, in 1995, took over the San Francisco Symphony. That orchestra already prided itself on its progressive reputation; John Adams had served as composer-in-residence from 1978 to 1985, dumbfounding audiences with the neo-Romantic grandeur of his works *Harmonium* and *Harmonielehre*. Tilson Thomas added his pinpoint musicianship, his eclectic taste, his gift for explaining classical music to novice listeners, and his knack for elegant spectacle. His first season closed with a joyous American festival whose programs ranged from Ives's *Holidays Symphony* to a Cagean improvisation by surviving members of the Grateful Dead. Covering the event for *The New York Times*, I wrote, "The gravitational center of American orchestral life has shifted westward."

The rise of the L.A. Philharmonic was a more unexpected development. For much of the century, it had been considered an ensemble of the second rank—"not too much more than a glorified community orchestra," one veteran player told me. It was founded in 1919 by William Andrews Clark, Jr., the son of one of Montana's Copper Kings. Clark was a skilled amateur violinist, a collector of books and manuscripts (including a copious array of materials relating to Oscar Wilde), and an attentive companion to various handsome young men whom he had rescued from society's margins. In the thirties, the Philharmonic achieved distinction under the stern direction of Otto Klemperer, but the best orchestras in town belonged to the movie studios, where so many refugees from Hitler found employment. After the war, the Philharmonic subsided into an era of sleepy stasis, its finances in constant crisis. In the orchestra's archives, I found a forlorn report for the year 1963, showing a $125,000 deficit on a less than million-dollar budget.

The orchestra decided that it would have to take some risks. First, Dorothy Buffum Chandler, the wife of the publisher of the *Los Angeles Times*, raised money for what promised to be a splendid new concert hall, the Dorothy Chandler Pavilion. Second, the orchestra appointed its first whiz-kid music director—the twenty-six-year-old Zubin Mehta. And, most important, in 1969 it hired as its managing director Ernest Fleischmann, who, as the manager of the London Symphony, had made a name for himself as a hot-tempered revolutionary in the classical world, preaching the message that the modern orchestra could no longer run through the same old repertory for aging subscribers. It would have to become a more adaptable organism—a "community of musicians," Fleischmann later said, able to perform new-music and chamber concerts, make school appearances, and play all kinds of repertory. It would also have to submit to the will of a strong manager.

After a period of excitement, there was another tapering off. Mehta left for the New York Philharmonic. The Chandler Pavilion turned out to be acoustically deadening. Carlo Maria Giulini and André Previn had relatively short regimes—the first widely revered, the second inconsistent. Fleischmann, who was born to Jewish parents in Germany and grew up in South Africa, saw the need for a second revolution. He would require another hall and another conductor, both of a new kind. "We don't want a temple of culture—rather, a welcoming kind of place," Fleischmann said of the projected hall in 1988. A competition was held, and the winner was Frank Gehry, at that time a much talked about but underemployed deconstructionist, who, in the seventies, had contributed modifications to the Philharmonic's summer home, the Hollywood Bowl. As for the conductor, he would have to be a thinker as well as a virtuoso.

In 1983, on a flight from Marseilles to London, Fleischmann encountered an artist manager who told him that some Finnish singers had been raving about a young conductor with a funny name that he couldn't remember. Fleischmann spent the night in London before flying on to Los Angeles, and while there he learned that a man named Esa-Pekka, obviously the funnily named conductor in question, had been engaged at the last minute to conduct Mahler's gargantuan Third Symphony with the Philharmonia Orchestra.

"This was a Monday," Fleischmann told me at lunch, in his gravelly, courtly accent. "I had meetings scheduled on Tuesday with some L.A.

City Council people—grant proposal, that kind of thing. We needed the money. Halfway through the plane flight home, I thought to myself that I had made a terrible mistake. I should have stayed to hear the Finn. I couldn't ask the pilot to turn the plane around, so I went to my meetings on Tuesday and then on Wednesday I flew back to London. I heard Esa-Pekka's performance of the Mahler Third, and I was totally blown away. I went around backstage to meet him, and there was this guy with a can of beer in his hand, in short sleeves, and I thought he must be all right."

Salonen is characteristically wry when he recalls his first American visit, which took place in 1984, at Fleischmann's invitation. "I was a very European product," Salonen says. "By any measure, I was a piece of vintage Eurotrash." After conducting the Philharmonic in a program that included Witold Lutosławski's turbulent Third Symphony—"I suppose that you know the Lutosławski notation" was his unpromising salutation to the orchestra at the first rehearsal—Salonen let himself be taken out to a club by a staff member. After standing in a corner, he mustered the courage to approach an attractive woman who was sitting at the bar. She asked what he was doing in the city. "Well, I just conducted the L.A. Philharmonic," he said. "That's the dumbest line I ever heard," she said, and walked away.

This is a familiar genre of Salonen anecdote, in which the protagonist assumes an attitude of self-importance and then collides with reality. "In one presidential election in Finland," he told a group of friends at dinner, "I was actually a write-in candidate." He paused while eyebrows were respectfully raised. "I received, in fact, two votes, just behind Donald Duck."

From 2002 until 2009, when he moved with his family to London, Salonen lived in a white-walled, modern place in Brentwood. When I stopped by, he told me how the pianist Mitsuko Uchida once visited his home studio, which contained a Steinway piano that once belonged to the émigré conductor Bruno Walter. "Of course, I was very proud of this piano," Salonen said. "And so I said to Mitsuko"—he lowers his voice the interval of a fifth and brings out the Anglo element in his accent—"'You really have to try my piano. It used to belong to Bruno Walter.' 'Oh, yes?' Mitsuko said. She sat down, played a couple of things, and stopped. 'Esa-Pekka! Yuck!'"

These gestures of self-deprecation can go only so deep. Sheepish fellows do not become directors of major orchestras. Salonen's cool sometimes shades into coolness, even steeliness. He avoids gushing approval—"Very good!" is high praise from him—and he can cause agitation in subordinates by saying something like "That's actually not OK" and then falling silent. He lacks the American gift for filling in the holes in a conversation with reassuring blather, and one learns not to hear his silences as awkward pauses. He likes to cite an adage of his homeland: a Finnish introvert looks at his own shoes, while a Finnish extrovert looks at other people's shoes.

Salonen was born to middle-class, music-loving parents in 1958. When he was four, his mother tried to get him to play the piano, and he "refused point blank," he says, "because it was very clear to me that girls play piano and boys play the soccer." (He has now revised his opinion: "Girls can play the soccer as well.") He eventually started playing the French horn, because, an older musician told him, it was easier to get into an orchestra as a horn player. But it was the experience of hearing Messiaen's sublimely over-the-top *Turangalîla*, at the age of ten or eleven, that inflamed his desire to compose.

In the seventies, many Finnish composers were still writing brooding symphonies in the spirit of Sibelius, although some had fastened on to twelve-tone writing and other advanced techniques. By the time Salonen enrolled in composition and conducting classes at the Sibelius Academy, the country's main music school, he was eager to preach the gospel of the difficult; at one point, he wrote a paper on "the defeat of tonalism," and once disrupted a school party by putting on an LP of Boulez's very modern but not particularly danceable *Le Marteau sans maître*.

At the Sibelius Academy, Salonen fell in with a cadre of teenage avant-gardists, among them Magnus Lindberg and Kaija Saariaho. They formed a collective called Korvat auki, or Ears Open!, and began putting on concerts of new music for the people, at which the people did not always consent to appear. One legendary evening, devoted to the Argentine-German conceptual composer Mauricio Kagel, drew an audience consisting of two elderly ladies who had come by mistake; another attracted a janitor, his dog, and the mother of one of the composers, or so the story goes. Lindberg's youthful orchestral work *Kraft*, which includes an array of junk-metal percussion in its continuously seething orchestral textures, had its premiere on a nutty program that also featured the illustrious mezzo-soprano Teresa Berganza performing Handel arias. Berganza was forced to sing "Ombra mai fù" while auto parts, office-chair legs, and other metal objects dangled on wires behind her, waiting to be banged in the noise symphony to follow. "Only the extreme is interesting," Lindberg would say. Salonen agreed.

The Ears Open! composers have since moved away from the sonic edge. Their music is now less hard-nosed, more lyrical, more spacious, although it hardly counts as easy listening. Salonen has devised a personal vocabulary in which he customarily uses hexachords, or scale fragments made up of six notes; when all six sound together, ear-cleansing dissonances can result, although he likes to tease tonal melodies out of the material. He revealed a lyrical bent in 1999, in a song cycle called *Five Images After Sappho*, written for Dawn Upshaw. *Wing on Wing*, a vocal-orchestral work from 2004, evokes the swooping forms of Disney Hall itself, incorporating recorded samples of Frank Gehry's voice. There's a section toward the end of the score in which Gehry is heard saying "Go to the beginning," in a brief repeating loop, while drones and trills bubble up from the lower regions of the orchestra. Salonen seems to have followed this instruction in several recent pieces, sculpting rough-hewn melodies and forms that give elemental weight to fantastically sophisticated textures.

Just what role California played in Salonen's musical development remains to be determined by his official Finnish biographer. (The composer claims to be approaching what he calls, in an approximate translation from the Finnish, the "shitting deaf mute," or elderly notable, stage of his career, and therefore requires a biography.) Certainly, his work as a conductor and his residence in Los Angeles gave him new influences. Pulsating, pop-inflected rhythms can be heard in works such as *Foreign Bodies* and *Helix*. For a while, he listened to rock on his way home after concerts, letting his twentysomething drivers pick the CDs. He was impressed by Radiohead's *OK Computer*, and once went out for drinks with members of the band, although he had reservations about *Kid A* and *Amnesiac*. ("Too much ostinato crescendo," he told me.) Like most thinking people, he admires Björk, although at the gym he prefers Shakira. While he admits that most other pop music either baffles or bores him, he remains open to the idea that a pop album could floor him as *OK Computer* did, and wants to release similar forces in his own music, a mixture of the brainy and the visceral.

Salonen steeped himself in the culture of the Los Angeles émigrés—the throng of composers, musicians, writers, artists, and filmmakers who moved to neighborhoods like West Hollywood, Beverly Hills, Brentwood, and Pacific Palisades in the thirties and forties. He found out where Brecht lived, and Thomas Mann, and Rachmaninov, and, of course, Schoenberg and Stravinsky. (Salonen once considered buying Stravinsky's old house, on North Wetherly Drive, but he was spooked by the fact that there were still indentations on the carpet where the composer's piano had stood.) The émigrés fell into roughly two categories: those who Americanized themselves, such as Frederick Kohner, who wrote the novel *Gidget* and helped to codify surfer slang; and those who stayed aloof, such as Theodor Adorno, who sat in his house on South Kenter Avenue and pondered the interchangeability of totalitarianism and capitalism.

Salonen falls somewhere comfortably in the middle. His music threads together the aristocratic complexity of his European musical training and the blunt energy of his longtime California home. Plain chords come up against seething textures; a melody dances in and floats away. His conversation follows a similar cultural spiral. In front of an audience at Disney Hall in January 2007, he spoke briefly about Mahler's Seventh Symphony and Webern's Five Pieces for Orchestra; the progression from late-Romantic opulence to early modern austerity, he said, resembled the collapse of a giant star into a white dwarf. As he was unfurling this metaphor, he paused to note, "White Dwarf was actually what I was called on my school hockey team."

Salonen had his path mapped out from the moment he arrived in Los Angeles. When I first met him, in 1994, he told me, "There's this crowd who go to contemporary-art exhibitions and see art cinema—people who basically use their brains more than average people. But they don't come to classical-music concerts. It's a problem of perception. They don't see an orchestra as part of the contemporary art scene. It's not a conversation item in their circles, because symphony orchestras play Beethoven and audiences are eighty-five years old. Now people are realizing that the Philharmonic is moving into this century." In other words, he was aware of the problem of the culturally aware non-attender well before experts coined the phrase.

In the early years, the theory was better than the execution. Players recall a withdrawn young man who was inaudible in rehearsal and difficult to talk to afterward. Insistent programming of thorny European scores by Lutosławski, Berio, and Ligeti led to a drop in attendance. A couple of years in, members of the orchestra met with him and urged him to pay more attention to the subscribers' taste. If the usual story had unfolded, Salonen would have either caved in or gone back to Europe, muttering about the backwardness of the Americans. Instead, he stubbornly persisted, although he became savvier about mixing old and new in his programs. Fine-tuning an old Boulez strategy, he emphasized what he called "twentieth-century classics"—pieces such as the *Rite* and Bartók's Concerto for Orchestra—next to which a modern work by Ligeti or Lindberg or Steven Stucky, the orchestra's longtime composer-in-residence, made intuitive sense.

Gehry's new concert hall was crucial to Salonen's calculations, but for some years it seemed as though it might never be built. After ground was broken, in December 1992, projected costs mounted into the hundreds of millions of dollars, and few donors came forward to augment the original fifty-million-dollar gift from Lillian Disney, Walt Disney's widow. (The Disney Company has no connection to the hall, nor do most major Hollywood players; the Philharmonic has long been the province of old-money families from Pasadena.) Fleischmann and Salonen pressed ahead. In 1996, Salonen told Mark Swed, the chief classical-music critic of the *Los Angeles Times*, "Somehow I've ruled out the option of the hall not happening."

Fleischmann retired in 1998. Two years later, following a confusing interregnum involving a Dutch executive, Borda, a diminutive, propulsive Manhattanite, arrived. Salonen had sought her out, and at first she seemed an odd choice. She was at that time the executive director of the New York Philharmonic, a wealthier and more conservative institution. "It was like being president of Harvard, which I did not at first realize was not necessarily a good thing," Borda says. She'd had an often combative relationship with Kurt Masur, who was then the orchestra's music director. Earlier in her career, she had thrived in offbeat settings, managing a new-music ensemble in Boston and working alongside Edo de Waart and

John Adams at the San Francisco Symphony, but in New York she felt as if a box were closing in on her. "Esa-Pekka brought me back to life," she says. "This orchestra saved me."

Like Fleischmann before her, Borda is a formidable executive who runs the orchestra like a lean company, not like a flabby nonprofit. She is aggressive when she needs to be, as she proved when she snatched Gustavo Dudamel away from a half-dozen orchestras interested in retaining his services. She has put the organization on solid financial footing. When it moved to Disney Hall, in 2003, it actually expanded its operations, posting a one-year sales increase of 62 percent. The nightly sellouts of the first Disney season couldn't be sustained, but in the spring of 2007 the Philharmonic was still selling a very respectable 92 percent of its tickets. It depends less on charitable contributions than most big-league orchestras do; 75 percent of its $84 million 2007 budget was derived from regular-season ticket sales and other income, such as the lucrative summer season at the Hollywood Bowl. There has been a conspicuous lack of tension between the players and the management.

Yet, despite the on-message, on-budget managerial ethos, the L.A. Philharmonic remains an unpredictable place, still the most experimental of American orchestras. One crucial member of the staff is Chad Smith, a native of Gettysburg, Pennsylvania, who began his career as an operatic tenor of the fair-haired, dashing type and then took a sharp left turn into progressive music programming. He is now the vice president of artistic planning, which means that he is in charge of shaping the programs and cultivating visiting musicians. "I spent a couple of years listening to Esa-Pekka," Smith says, "and got the sense that the thinking always needed to be bigger, not big in scale but big in imagination. That's how we started thinking about minimalism."

The Minimalist Jukebox festival, which happened in the spring of 2006, was originally supposed to be a relatively conventional series of programs linking minimalist composers and earlier classical repertory— say, Steve Reich and Bach. But this seemed too boring for Disney Hall. What emerged instead was a two-week festival that ranged from classic minimalist pieces by Reich, Terry Riley, and Philip Glass to postminimalist works such as Michael Gordon's *Decasia* and Glenn Branca's *Hallucination City*, a symphony for a hundred electric guitars. The series kicked off with an all-night show by the Orb, a British group that plays ambient house music. Subscribers fled en masse, exchanging their tickets for other series, but the empty seats were filled by new, much younger listeners. The festival came close to breaking even, despite the fact that some ticket prices had been reduced to accommodate a less genteel crowd.

Perhaps Borda's boldest notion is to give visiting composers such as Adams and Thomas Adès the same royal treatment that is extended to the likes of Yo-Yo Ma and Joshua Bell; Borda talks about "hero composers." A 2007 performance of Adams's *Naïve and Sentimental Music* in the orchestra's Casual Fridays series—a shortened program in which the players skip formal dress and mingle with listeners afterward—drew a nearly full house. Borda's big-guns approach has invigorated the orchestra's long-running new-music series, called Green Umbrella, which Fleischmann established in 1982. In the early days, it drew modest audiences, but in recent years attendance has risen to the point where as many as sixteen hundred people show up for a concert that in other cities might draw thirty or forty. In 2006, the Australian composer Brett Dean walked onstage for a Green Umbrella concert and did a double take, saying that it was the largest new-music audience he'd ever seen.

One area in which the orchestra has done less well is in promoting younger composers. Speaking at an education conference in New York, Salonen said, "Institutions tend to play it safe. They are less willing to commission a large work by a young composer. They don't want to take the risk. It's the same old names that keep being circulated all the time." This is precisely what any number of composers who are not Adams, Adès, Stucky, or a half-dozen others might say about the Philharmonic itself. As the "hero composers" concept takes hold, the orchestra might want to challenge its own philosophy by taking chances on twenty-six-year-old composers, as it has on twenty-six-year-old conductors.

The Philharmonic is trying to solve the ultimate mystery of the orchestra business, which is how to attract new listeners without alienating established ones. The core audience will always be longtime lovers of classical music who mainly want to hear symphonies of Beethoven and concertos of Rachmaninov. Then there are Salonen's "people who basically use their brains more"—who ought to be at classical concerts but usually aren't. To serve both audiences, the orchestra becomes, in effect, two institutions folded into one: a museum of masterpieces and a gallery of new work. A number of music directors in other cities—notably,

David Robertson in St. Louis, Robert Spano in Atlanta, Marin Alsop in Baltimore, Osmo Vänskä in Minneapolis, and, since 2009, Alan Gilbert in New York—are moving in the same direction. Suddenly, it no longer makes sense to generalize about the hidebound attitude of the American orchestra.

As for the players themselves, their greatest resource is flexibility. The great orchestras of Cleveland and Chicago may possess a more flawlessly polished sound, but no American ensemble matches the L.A. Philharmonic in its ability to assimilate a wide range of music on a moment's notice. Adès, who first conducted his music in L.A. in 2006 and has become a regular visitor, told me, "They always seem to begin by finding exactly the right playing style for each piece of music—the kind of sound, the kind of phrasing, breathing, attacks, colors, the indefinable whole. That shouldn't be unusual, but it is." Adams calls the Philharmonic "the most *Amurrican* of orchestras. They don't hold back and they don't put on airs. If you met them in twos or threes, you'd have no idea they were playing in an orchestra, that they were classical-music people."

One day, I followed Ben Hong, the assistant principal cellist, as he went about his daily duties. A shaggy-haired thirty-eight-year-old who commutes on a motorcycle, he had been playing in the Philharmonic since he was twenty-four. He arrived at the hall at 9:00 a.m. to coach two students in a studio in the building. One of them was working on Elgar's Cello Concerto, and Hong, after working through issues of bowing and phrasing, tried to get his student to think about the piece in terms of "lost innocence" and the legacy of war.

Just before eleven, Hong reported to the main floor of Disney to play a matinee concert. The program consisted of Brahms's First and Third Symphonies, under the direction of Christoph von Dohnányi, who was visiting for two weeks. "We'll sell some tickets," Borda said of this concert in advance. "Plus, it will be good for the orchestra. Christoph will pick everything to pieces, rehearse in great detail, go back to basics."

After the concert, Hong had lunch with a few younger players: Eric Overholt, who had been playing French horn in the orchestra for only a few months; Ariana Ghez, the principal oboist, who had also started that season; and Joana Carneiro, the assistant conductor. They talked about the audition process ("It's pretty brutal, probably the most difficult thing you have to do as a musician," Hong said), the limits of a conservatory education (Ghez studied English at Columbia alongside music at Juilliard), and the intellectual pleasure of playing new works. Some orchestra veterans had never relished Salonen's favored diet of twentieth-century and contemporary fare, but several of the younger musicians identified it as one of the main attractions of the job. Ghez noted that older listeners no longer run for the exits when a little Ligeti appears on one of the regular programs. Instead, she said, they have been trained to say things like "I guess you have to take it like a Jackson Pollock."

Hong was thinking more deeply about the gaps in his conservatory training, and wondering what he might learn from other kinds of music-making. In particular, he had taken an interest in improvisation. After lunch, he drove up some twisting roads in the Laurel Canyon area to the home of Lili Haydn, a session violinist, singer-songwriter, and former child actress, who has been giving him guidance on how to improvise in a semi-jazz, semi-Indian style. This activity falls far outside his usual work with the orchestra, although it fits into the expanded mission of Salonen's Philharmonic, improvisation having a role in much avant-garde music after the Second World War and in quite a bit of alternative-minded contemporary work.

Hong joined Haydn in her studio, which was outfitted with wall hangings and antique lamps. There was a faint smell of incense. First, they worked on a track that will appear on Haydn's forthcoming album. She sang, "We all saw the water sweep the streets with the force that carried Noah." Hong played a doleful, arpeggiated accompaniment. Then the two improvised for twenty minutes or so over an Indian tamboura drone. Hong seemed hesitant at first, locking himself into a repeating figure or falling into rapid up-and-down scales that seemed exterior to the mood.

"Find the magic in the intervals," Haydn told him. She asked him to take hold of a figure of two or three notes, bend it this way and that against the regular rhythm, and then savor the effect of adding one more note. Hong promptly took off on a ruminative minor-key flight that sounded a little like the cello lines in Sibelius's *Swan of Tuonela* and, for a minute or two, became lost in music of his own invention.

He said at one point, "After a few sessions, I'm hearing things in a different way. I am feeling the nuances of each note in a more intense way. It's like when I was growing up—they'd say that you must chew each mouthful of rice seventy-two times to really taste the sweetness of the rice. There's something to that. Sometimes in classical music that's lost. This has taught me to be more appreciative of each note."

Hong deftly related all this back to the Brahms he had played that morning. He launched into a free rendition of the grand chromatic line that soars through the orchestra at the beginning of the First Symphony, giving each note a slightly different color and weight. He stopped at the topmost B flat, letting the note float out over the canyon.

To spend time with a musician like Hong is to realize that the effect of a conductor on an orchestra is easily overstated: the L.A. Philharmonic is the sum of a hundred distinct personalities. Salonen knows this as well as anyone; as a youth, he was skeptical of his future profession. "I had no great desires of becoming a conductor," he says. "In fact, I thought conductors were disgusting. I very much disliked this image of a conductor like Herbert von Karajan, riding a Harley-Davidson on an LP cover, conducting *Ein Heldenleben*. I thought that was really bad. I still do, actually. I thought that conductors get so much attention for almost no reason and the really important guy, i.e., the composer, is the worst-paid one and the one who always stays in the worst hotel and is kicked on the head by everybody else, and I thought that was rotten. I still do, actually."

For several years, Salonen had been making semipublic noises about leaving the Philharmonic. He had set himself various goals—to move into the new hall, to find an artistic vision befitting Gehry's space, to elevate the orchestra's playing, to cultivate its financial health. "Bit by bit," he told me, "all this started to become reality." He had thought of stepping away after the opening of Disney Hall, but he couldn't yet give up the heady experience of conducting in that space. "I thought, This is too much fun. It felt like the harvesting time. There also was a new level to the relationship with the orchestra. I quite often felt as though they were reading my mind—they would do something just as I was vaguely thinking of it. A lot of warmth and good feeling on both sides." Still, even when he was on a break, he sensed the obligations of the job pressing on him.

In the spring of 2006, while Minimalist Jukebox was going on in L.A., Salonen was in Paris, leading the world premiere of the opera *Adriana Mater*, by his old schoolmate Kaija Saariaho. In Paris, Salonen started making sketches for a Piano Concerto, which the New York Philharmonic had commissioned from him. Work proceeded in fits and starts over the summer and through the fall, and the score was finally finished over Christmas. As he reluctantly stole away from his family into his studio, he felt more acutely the need to give up the directorship of the orchestra.

The concerto was written for the pianist Yefim Bronfman, one of Salonen's closest friends and a leading interpreter of Rachmaninov. Salonen was determined to confront the legacy of the virtuoso Romantic concerto, and he indulged in cascading double octaves, wide-spanning chords, and, at the end of the second movement, a certifiable Big Tune. At the same time, the musical language of the piece feels very up to date; there are bopping rhythms, trickily shifting beats, alarms and noises, malfunctioning machine patterns, and a fabulously eerie section that Salonen characterizes as "Synthetic Folk Music with Artificial Birds." In a lively program note, he connects that last episode to a "post-biological culture where the cybernetic systems suddenly develop an existential need of folklore." In all, it's a plausible reinvention of the Romantic concerto, and Salonen's most assured work to date.

Bronfman had to learn the solo part in a few weeks, and initially he complained about its punishing difficulty. (Subconscious feelings of guilt may have produced a cryptic dream that the composer reported having one night, in which Bronfman was falsely accused of the murder of the actress Helen Mirren.) Salonen conducted the premiere himself, appearing with the New York Philharmonic for the first time since 1986. The performance took place on February 1, 2007, and the audience responded with more wholehearted enthusiasm than is normal for a New York subscription-series premiere. An elderly couple was observed holding hands during the slow movement.

Afterward, Salonen was more confident about his choice to step down. "I felt that this is the way to go," he later told me. "Now I'm ready for the next project." He had long talked of writing an opera. He was also planning a piece for chorus and orchestra, possibly based on Joseph Brodsky's final poetry collection, *So Forth*. Some lines from the Brodsky poem "New Life" seemed relevant: "Ultimately, one's unbound / curiosity about these empty zones, / about these objectless vistas, / is what art seems to be all about."

• • •

The Philharmonic players were keenly interested in the question of who might come next. "We're cresting a wave—it's just amazing," Meredith Snow, a member of the viola section, told me in January 2007. "The transition from Salonen scares us. But it feels like our management is really looking out for that."

I asked Snow and David Allen Moore, a double-bass player, which conductors had made a good impression. The list of names was relatively short. "There's such a vacuum," Snow said. "We're so desperate for the quality of honesty. At least in this orchestra, there's no baggage of people prejudging conductors. It's, like, 'Please be good.' We'll participate if you show us what you want, emotionally and musically."

Dudamel's name was the first one they mentioned. "He was great," Snow said. "He has it all. This orchestra was on fire with him."

Moore added, "It's not just about a mythical being on the podium who by his own will makes everything somehow happen. It's not so much about the cult of personality of the maestro anymore. Esa-Pekka clearly has a strong personality and all that, but with him it definitely feels more collaborative."

Borda had observed how other orchestras underwent protracted searches for new music directors, replete with internal politicking for one conductor or another, speculation and second-guessing in the press, hurt feelings as renowned musicians were reported to have "not gone over well" with the players, and so on—all the result of the empowerment of musicians as adjudicators in recent decades. She decided to do a "stealth search," gathering evaluations and reviewing them with the Artistic Liaison Committee. The musicians would have a say, only they wouldn't quite know it.

Some players were already chattering about Dudamel's future with the orchestra after his very first rehearsal as guest conductor, in 2005, at the Hollywood Bowl. "I was tempted to go for him right then," Borda says. "But I wouldn't do that." Instead, over the next year and a half, she regularly traveled to hear Dudamel conduct, getting to know him and his wife, Eloísa, and commandeering his schedule with various projects. Somehow, she managed to do this without attracting undue notice from music-industry professionals. "I'm quite short," she joked.

All this wouldn't have mattered if Dudamel hadn't won over the players when he returned to conduct at the beginning of 2007, in a program of Kodály, Rachmaninov, and Bartók. Halfway through the first piece, Salonen, who was sitting in the audience, leaned over to his wife and whispered, "This is the man." The contract was signed at the end of March in Lucerne, where Dudamel was on tour. "We did it about two in the morning someplace," Borda told me, relishing the cloak-and-dagger aspect of the operation. "I don't think anybody knew, even with the crème de la crème of the European managers dancing attendance."

Dudamel's contract was for five years. "Someday he may go on to be the music director of the Berlin Philharmonic," Borda told me. "But I'm not going to worry about that. We have a tradition of people starting young, staying for a long time, and then going on to the next thing. Part of what we do here is we're nimble."

The new director was born in Barquisimeto, Venezuela, in 1981. His father played trombone in a salsa band. He studied music from an early age, learning the basics of notation and theory before he took up an instrument, the violin, at the age of ten. He showed an interest in composition, and, at one of his early conducting gigs, at the age of fifteen, he led his own Trombone Concerto. Conducting quickly took over, and by his late teens he was leading ninety concerts a year with the Simón Bolívar Youth Orchestra, the chief ensemble in Venezuela's youth-ensemble system. Venezuela has a music-education system unmatched by any in the world; since the seventies, the composer José Antonio Abreu has been building up an organization called the National System of Youth and Children's Orchestras of Venezuela, or El Sistema. There are now 250,000 students in the system. Abreu has managed to maintain support for his system through various regimes, including that of Hugo Chávez.

Having won notice at the Bamberg competition in 2004, Dudamel found himself in the tricky position of being hailed as a savior of classical music. It only added to the furor that he was a non-Caucasian face in an industry suffering from the appearance of elitism. Deutsche Grammophon recorded him leading Beethoven's Fifth and Seventh Symphonies with the youth orchestra. My first reaction to the disc was skeptical; the interpretations were expertly handled, but there was nothing obviously extraordinary about them.

What the recording didn't reveal was the electricity that crackles around Dudamel in performance. Just before his Philharmonic appointment was announced, he conducted a program with the Chicago Symphony that included Mahler's First Symphony, and I stopped over on my way to L.A. to hear it. The conductor made smart choices throughout, managed tempo changes fluidly, shaped phrases with an idiomatic hand. At every turn, though, the players responded with unusual intensity, until the performance became an event. As Salonen told me, "He lets music be what it is, but somehow puts it on fire in some mysterious way." Dudamel did not seem to be outside the music, imposing his ideas on it; instead, he appeared captive to it. During the coda of the Mahler, he jumped around with a boyish, Bernstein-like glee that would have appeared a bit ridiculous if you weren't also hearing the regal roar of the orchestra in front of him.

A thunderous ovation greeted Dudamel at Chicago's Orchestra Hall. More than a few people in the hall—including members of the orchestra—believed that he could be their next conductor. In fact, he was about to fly to Los Angeles. Late the following day, he looked around the Disney stage and conferred with Borda in her office. The story had broken in the *Los Angeles Times* that morning, and people were already congratulating him; several of the guards offered greetings in Spanish.

Dudamel is a warm, exuberant man, and he responded to every well-wisher with a torrent of phrases along the lines of "It is wonderful," "This is so special," and "I am so happy for this big opportunity." His English was not yet fluent, but he expressed himself gracefully, wittily, and, when necessary, with artful vagueness. He deflected questions about Chávez, apologizing for being "politically disconnected." When I asked him about his intentions with the Philharmonic, he said that he needed to gain more experience with the orchestra and its repertory before he could think about programming. He said that he had long admired Salonen. When he was eleven, his mother bought him the conductor's recording of Stravinsky's *Rite* and Symphony in Three Movements, and he was amazed to find such a "*very young* conductor" leading a major orchestra. "'Oh, my God, who is this guy?' From that time he was an idol for me." When Dudamel repeated that anecdote at the press conference, Salonen looked suitably embarrassed.

Most of L.A.'s television stations sent reporters and cameras, their coverage revealing that after fifteen years the local announcers still can't pronounce the music director's name ("Eessa-peeka," "Salanon"). The orchestra's press office fielded calls from *The Tonight Show* and Al Jazeera.

Dudamel appeared healthily detached from the attention. At the press conference, when Salonen introduced him with an uncharacteristically florid fanfare—"We are interested in the future. We are not trying to re-create the glories of the past, like so many other symphony orchestras"— Dudamel got a laugh by advancing to the microphone, pausing for a long moment, and saying, "So-o-o-o . . ." The art of understatement isn't dead at Walt Disney Concert Hall.

Afterward, Salonen sat in his office, a cool, quiet space within Disney Hall's curving walls. He was looking for words that would express in a not too sentimental or clichéd way the idea that he had decided to take the plunge, follow his dream, reject the beaten path. "I'm approaching fifty," he told me. "And, going by the sort of ten-year chunks by which we measure our lives, even if I behave, the number of decades available is sadly limited. Bill Viola sent me an e-mail this morning saying that there is an old Bulgarian proverb: If you decide to kill yourself by drowning, don't do it in shallow waters."

Several times in the preceding weeks, Salonen had touched on the theme of growing older. At his Apple Store event, he had said, "At this point, my feeling is that somebody will conduct concerts, no question, but only I can write my music, for better or worse. And we're not getting younger, necessarily." In a radio interview, he proposed that people in their thirties and forties might be rediscovering classical music because "you realize that your time is not unlimited, that there might be an end to all this, and that life is too short to be wasted on things that are not quality."

That morning, Salonen had surprised his colleagues by showing up in a cerulean sports jacket. He habitually dresses in a black T-shirt and black jeans, and no one could recall him wearing color. This was an inside joke for the orchestra, he explained to Smith. At his first rehearsal as music director, everyone had dressed in black in homage to him, and, in those shoe-gazing days, he had to have the joke pointed out.

Salonen described what had happened that Saturday after he told the orchestra he was leaving. Drained by the experience, he sat in his office alone. (Ben Hong reported that the speech had been "really heartfelt, one of the few times he's been emotional.") Borda stopped by, and they shared some vodka. Then she went off to attend to business. As he was preparing to leave, his assistant buzzed him, saying that a small group of the musicians were outside the door. He invited them in and chatted for a while. There was another buzz: more musicians had arrived, fortified by a trip to a nearby bar.

"It became like a sort of mini-party," Salonen said. "I don't know what goes on in other orchestras, but it really felt extremely personal and extremely unique." Well into the evening, he finally went home to his wife and children, one more free man in California.

7

GREAT SOUL

SEARCHING FOR SCHUBERT

What was he like? You hear different things. In public, Franz Schubert usually presented himself as an amiable bohemian, wearing a face suitable for the master of the art of song. But from time to time he showed a more savage side of his character. If a colorful tale is to be believed, he got drunk one night in a tavern and began verbally abusing a group of Viennese musicians who had asked him to write a piece. Suddenly, a mighty artistic imagination was venting its wrath on a mediocre world:

> You consider yourselves artists? Blowers and fiddlers is what you all are! I am an artist! I am Schubert, Franz Schubert, whom the whole world knows and talks about! Maker of great and beautiful things that you can't begin to understand! . . . Cantatas and quartets, operas and symphonies! For I am not just a Ländler composer, as the idiotic newspapers say and idiots repeat—I am Schubert! Franz Schubert! Don't you know it! And when the word "art" is used, it refers to *me*, not to you worms and insects who long for solos that I will never write . . . Crawling, nibbling worms who should be squashed under my foot—the foot of a man reaching for the stars—*sublimi feriam sidera vertice*, translate that for them!

This tirade was written down long after the fact by Eduard von Bauernfeld, a friend given to suspiciously detailed anecdotes. It may be partly or entirely fictional: such are the problems for anyone trying to grasp the poorly documented, excruciatingly short-lived phenomenon that was Schubert. Yet something here rings true, despite the melodramatic flourishes. It is the tone of confidence, of youthful certainty, that Schubert sustained right up to his early death. You can also hear it in a little rhyme by the playwright Franz Grillparzer, seemingly written as a kind of memento of the composer's personality:

> I am Schubert, Schubert's my name,
> Can't prevent it, can't complain.
> If you like the path I took,
> Very well then, do the same!

The same peremptory voice crops up in Schubert's infrequent personal writings. "Their world-system is human / Mine I know to be divine," he proclaims in one poem. In another, he seeks to become a "pure, powerful being." Once, in the middle of the night, he scrawled in a notebook, "Enviable Nero, you who had the courage to destroy a loathsome people with strings and song!!"

As with the protean Mozart, impressions of Schubert's character have varied widely over time. Many of the composer's friends were intent on remembering him as a lovable tippler who scribbled in a somnambulistic trance. This is the image that became standard in the nineteenth century, particularly in Victorian Britain. Even Robert Schumann, who promoted Schubert's greatness, liked to picture him as a "guileless child romping among giants"—the kind of metaphor so often applied to Mozart in the same period. The twentieth century, inevitably, has been preoccupied instead with disclosing Schubert's darkness and complexity. In recent decades there has been talk of the syphilitic Schubert, the hedonistic Schubert, the dissident Schubert, the homosexual Schubert. You can measure the change in the composer's image by listening to movie soundtracks. Where Richard Tauber once sang ditsy operetta arrangements of Schubert in *Blossom Time*, Woody Allen's *Crimes and Misdemeanors* used the vacillating harmonies of the String Quartet in G Major to symbolize the moral slide of a doctor who arranges the murder of his mistress, and Roman Polanski's *Death and the Maiden* employed the Schubert quartet of that title as accompaniment to torture.

In part, the image of Schubert has proved unstable simply because the historical record is so weak. We know a fair amount about his movements and activities in any given year, much less about his private life and inner world. Most extant arrangements of the biographical material seem to leave out something essential. Proponents of the cutesy Schubert (there are still some, especially in Austria) have trouble explaining his propensity for texts like "Freiwilliges Versinken" ("Voluntary Oblivion") and "Ich schleiche bang und still herum" ("I Creep Around, Anxious and Silent"). Fans of the dark side don't know what to do with documents incontrovertibly demonstrating that he had a jolly time in coffeehouses. In short, a lot of the ambivalence emanates from Schubert himself. I have been making my way through dozens of books and articles about Schubert, and I still have difficulty in imagining who this man was.

The man is not quite there; the music is another thing altogether. Its presence—its immediacy—is tremendous. It often inspires a kind of unsafe love in its listeners. I am certainly one of the victims. I remember my first encounters with Schubert's works like teenage crushes. Most of all, I remember playing through the first movement of the great Piano Sonata in B-flat and physically trembling as the main theme stole back onto the page, one octave higher, like a handsome ghost of itself. The ferment in Schubert biography and scholarship has come about because people love the music so, even if the cryptic data of his life have led biographers to radically different conclusions. And it has also come about because the music, so rich in its understanding of emotion, sends out profoundly mixed messages. Schubert indeed wrote melodies of unaffected beauty, childlike in their innocence. He was also capable of rhythmic and harmonic violence that would not be equaled until Wagner. And he could play the entire gamut of emotion as one ambiguous chord, dissolving differences between agony and joy.

What was he like? It's safe to hazard a few guesses. He was friendly, up to a point; rude, when pressed; very shy or very arrogant, or probably both at once. He was colossally ambitious. He made a career and religion of music; he was a voracious reader who constantly tested the musical capability of texts. He could not grovel in front of potential patrons, yet he worked tolerably hard at self-promotion. His leisure hours were often drunkenly aimless. He formed intense friendships with men; he worshipped women, but from afar. He theorized love more than he experienced it. He was prone both to euphoria and to paralyzing melancholy, but he steadied himself with work. He was more a watcher of life than a participant in it: he had little time for anything unrelated to his art. There were no limits whatsoever to his musical imagination.

...

Schubert was born in 1797, in Vienna, and died in that city in 1828. Over a period of about seventeen years he wrote a thousand works. No other composer in history managed to do quite so much in so short a span. A favorite means of measuring Schubert's achievement is to imagine how his fellow giants of the repertory might be remembered if they, too, had died at the age of thirty-one. Verdi, composer of *Nabucco?* Beethoven, composer of numerous piano sonatas and one Symphony in C? Johann Sebastian Bach, the distinguished writer of organ music? Mozart would remain Mozart, even without *The Magic Flute.* But Schubert could have died at the age of eighteen, after writing "Der Erlkönig" and two hundred other lieder, and he would still have left intact his reputation as an epoch-making composer of song.

Vienna now celebrates Schubert as its most faithful child. Although composers flocked to the imperial capital in the eighteenth and nineteenth centuries, Schubert was the only major one before Schoenberg to be native to the city. Yet he had a hard time making his name, because, ironically, his devotion to Viennese Classical tradition made him a somewhat unfashionable figure. Around 1820, sonatas, quartets, and symphonies in the manner of Haydn, Mozart, and Beethoven were no longer in high demand; the rage was for dance tunes, Italian opera (not always the most artful kind), and the virtuosity of Paganini. Biedermeier kitsch was coming to the fore. Schubert's first song publication came, unpromisingly, in the *Pictorial Pocket-Book for Friends of Interesting Regional, Natural, and Artistic Curiosities of the Austrian Monarchy.*

He was picked to sing in the Court Chapel choir, now the Vienna Boys' Choir, and several years later began studying with none other than Antonio Salieri, who, more than twenty years after Mozart's death, retained the position of Kapellmeister. Salieri drilled his student in the older Italian styles and apparently tried to discourage a growing interest in Beethoven and other Germanic repertory. While Schubert might have found that regimen frustrating, he grew fond of his teacher, who, notwithstanding the portrait offered in *Amadeus,* was exceptionally generous to his charges. And the grounding in Italian style is apparent in everything Schubert wrote, especially in his sunnier moods: limpid melodies, buoyant rhythms, and sparkling modulations provide a welcome contrast to the bouts of anxious creeping. The old-fashioned schooling also evidently prompted a taste for arcane musical games. The scholar Brian Newbould has discovered a perfect musical palindrome—nineteen bars repeated in mirror formation—in Schubert's melodrama *Die Zauberharfe*.

Schubert found his mature musical personality at the age of seventeen— specifically, in the last months of 1814. His most celebrated breakthrough was the song "Gretchen am Spinnrade," from Goethe's *Faust*. The propulsive, repetitive piano accompaniment, an archetypal feat of tone painting, depicts the mechanical whirl of Gretchen's spinning-wheel as she sings of her jittery passion. The wavelike rise and fall of the vocal line points ahead to the mournful climax of the "Unfinished" Symphony. "Nachtgesang," a second major Goethe setting, reveals Schubert's ability to muse upon simple harmonies and transform them into painterly objects. Songs dominated this period, but September of 1814 also brought his first characteristic instrumental work—the String Quartet in B-flat, with its telltale blend of melting melody and errant harmony. In such passages Schubert seems to speak the language of Goethe's *Sorrows of Young Werther*, which remained popular for decades after its publication in 1774. When Werther complains of an "inner, unfathomable turmoil that threatens to burst the confines of my breast and choke me," he does not throw himself into some world-changing crusade. Instead, he finds temporary solace in a winter walk: "I wander about in the dread nocturnal setting of this unfriendly season."

The years 1816 to 1822 were a time of exploration. In his songwriting, Schubert was sometimes self-consciously classical, sometimes boldly experimental. When Rossini conquered Vienna, in 1816, Schubert joined the admiring crowds and appropriated some of Rossini's trademark devices, adding a contemporary flair to the Italianate side of his personality. Seeking a fortune in the mainstream market, he made various attempts at opera, most of them undermined by idiotic librettos and theatrical inexperience. Instrumental forms regained importance from 1822 to 1828: Schubert wrote his two mature symphonies and embarked on a tour de force of chamber and piano music, with Beethoven as his model. He also invented an entirely new form: the epic song cycle. *Die schöne Müllerin* tells of a young man's desperate love for a beautiful miller girl, and *Winterreise* is the winter journey of an even more battered soul. A further cycle, on poems of Heinrich Heine, got under way in 1828. (The so-called *Schwanengesang* cycle, which includes the six Heine songs, is a publisher's creation.)

Beethoven died in 1827. In the close confines of Vienna, Schubert and Beethoven had had almost no contact. The older biographies portray

Schubert as a terrified admirer, fleeing rooms to avoid confronting his hero. More likely, he was too proud to show the obsequiousness that his admiration would have demanded. John Reed suggests that Schubert saw Beethoven's death as an opening: music's throne was empty, and he was the "legitimate heir." He scheduled his first and only public concert on the anniversary of Beethoven's death; he produced songs on poems Beethoven had intended to set; he wrote his C-Major String Quintet in fulfillment of another Beethoven project; he prepared an edition of three piano sonatas, a favorite grouping of Beethoven's youth. And, at the end, he began a D-major symphony that scholars have identified as a sort of Tombeau de Beethoven, complete with a central elegy in B minor. (There have been several attempts to complete the work; Peter Gülke's version of the slow movement—austere, archaic, yet devastating—is notably successful.) Even when he realized he wouldn't make it, he kept to the program. "Beethoven does not lie here," he mumbled on his deathbed, apparently requesting that he be buried near the Master. So he was.

There is, of course, more to the story than this. Schubert was the last of the Viennese Classical masters, but he was also in many ways the first Romantic, subjecting music to what Charles Rosen calls, in *The Romantic Generation*, the "disorder of experience." Both as man and musician, Schubert was prey to storms of emotion. Moodiness is inherent in his style: certain of his earliest works, notably the Fantasia in G Minor (1811), show a nervous motion from one tonality to another, a habit of incessant modulation that would remain one of his principal signatures. And his urge to picture torrents of feeling led him to an obsessive study of poetry: he was—and remains—among the most literary of composers. The poetry and the poets who were part of his life in turn raise some fiendishly difficult questions about aesthetics, politics, psychology, and sexuality. Some of the most important research of recent years—that by Susan Youens, Richard Kramer, and David Gramit—has focused on the relationship between Schubert and the poets who furnished texts for his more than six hundred songs.

Schubert lived in an uneasy, transitional time. As he came to maturity, the egalitarian hopes of the Napoleonic period had faded, and monarchies across Europe celebrated Restoration with repression. Prince Metternich's regime in Austria was nothing short of a police state. Some members of artistic circles still agitated for revolution, but most accepted the decorous conservatism of the Biedermeier period. Schubert had arrived on the scene just after the high Romantic period in literature—the age of Goethe, Schiller, Kleist, and Hölderlin. Music had yet to unleash the full Romantic welter of feeling, although Beethoven certainly made a start. So Schubert was caught in what turned out to be a productive paradox: he helped inaugurate musical Romanticism yet joined a literary scene that was moving on to other concerns.

From the start, Schubert sought a seamless integration of poetry and music. In 1816, with his friend Josef Spaun, he drew up a plan for eight volumes of songs inspired by major poets, beginning with Goethe. Unfortunately, the plan relied on the hope that Goethe himself would promote it. Spaun mailed off a collection of Schubert songs; Goethe, whose multifarious genius grew curiously feeble when it approached the realm of music, did not respond. Despite that setback, Schubert pushed toward his greatest innovation, the song cycle. He was probably heartened by—but by no means dependent on—the example of Beethoven's interrelated *Distant Beloved* songs. Richard Kramer, in his book *Distant Cycles*, argues that the song-cycle category should include not only the famous *Die schöne Müllerin* and *Winterreise* but also a cycle on poems by the philosopher Friedrich Schlegel. And the pianist Graham Johnson, the mastermind of a complete edition of Schubert songs on the Hyperion label, proposes a cycle for the semi-deranged erotomanic poet Ernst Schulze. (Volumes 18 and 27 of the Hyperion edition, sung by Peter Schreier and Matthias Goerne, give gripping hints of what these might have been like.) Months before his death, Schubert began setting Heine, who was well reviewed but not yet renowned: the composer's literary instincts had become razor-sharp.

Schubert's love of poetry is inseparable from the close-knit friendships that dominated his social life from 1814 until his death. Spaun, a fellow student at the Court Chapel, had drawn him into a group called the Bildung Circle, which consisted of young men from various artistic professions, dedicated to *Bildung* (the great German pastime of intellectual self-improvement), literary readings, aesthetic debate, and friendship. At first glance, these young men look like a band of poetry-reciting layabouts out of *La Bohème*, their own poetry innocuous and sentimental, but in fact they were serious and sometimes daring in their pursuits. Most poetry came Schubert's way through books and manuscripts exchanged in the circle; he had no money to buy books of his own. In terms of literary accomplishment, the most impressive member of the circle was a poet named Johann Mayrhofer, who also became arguably the most significant influence on Schubert's mind.

Mayrhofer, about whom much is learned in Susan Youens's book *Schubert's Poets and the Making of Lieder*, was a man of terminal contradictions. He was steeped in the world of ancient Greece; his politics tended toward revolutionary liberalism; yet he worked as a censor for the Metternich regime. He was reclusive, morose, misogynistic, self-critical, and in all likelihood homosexual. He killed himself in 1836. His poems are full of disjointed, dreamlike images that look beyond Romanticism to the nightmare Symbolism of Georg Trakl. At the same time, however, he championed art as an impersonal, light-suffusing instrument of order, against the Romantic grain. Schubert was closest to this bizarre character from 1816 to 1820; they shared an apartment for eighteen months. During this time, Schubert's songs concentrated heavily on mythological subjects, not only by way of Mayrhofer's own poetry but also by way of Schiller's and Goethe's. The forty-seven Mayrhofer settings themselves have a restless quality that mirrors the character of the poet.

The song "Auf der Donau," for example, is a weird scene on the Danube that begins with conventional Romantic images of waves, forests, and castles and ends with visions of doom (*Untergang*). Schubert's music matches the poem's trajectory from idyll to disaster: as Youens observes, the song ends in a jarringly different key from the one in which it began, and *Untergang* arrives in ice-cold tones at the bottom of the keyboard. Other Mayrhofer poems, however, contain suggestions that Schubert does not readily take up. "Uraniens Flucht" is an ode to the mythological figure of Urania—not the Muse of Astronomy but the goddess Aphrodite under another name. Graham Johnson argues that the poem's cryptic scenario, in which a genderless "loving pair" praises the goddess, makes sense only as code for homoerotic love. (Johnson leaves out the clincher, though: the citation of Urania in Plato's *Symposium* as a protectress of love between men.) More remains to be uncovered in Mayrhofer's obscure erotic zone: the implications of his libretto for Schubert's unfinished opera *Adrast*, which would have contained one of the few same-sex love arias in opera, and a peculiarly sentimentalized scene of self-castration in the poem "Atys" (based on Catullus).

There was a break between Schubert and Mayrhofer in 1820. The composer moved to another apartment and ceased working from Mayrhofer's manuscripts. In the next two years, Schubert's life veered toward crisis. He was present at the scene of a disturbance involving Johann Senn, an activist in pro-democratic, anticlerical student politics; Metternich's police placed Senn in lengthy confinement and briefly questioned Schubert. Schubert seems to have made a mute protest against Senn's arrest by publishing songs on two Senn poems in 1823. In that same collection, he set "Die Liebe hat gelogen" ("Love has lied") by the German poet August von Platen, who was also a political dissident and—incidentally or not—was as close to an outspoken homosexual as the era would permit. (Platen, like Mayrhofer, used the unhappy ancient Greek figure Adrastus as code: in his diaries, one of his amours goes by that name.) Meanwhile, Franz von Schober, the dashing bad boy of the circle, apparently led Schubert on adventures in low life. By the end of this "wild period," in 1822, Schubert had contracted syphilis.

All of this raises questions about Schubert's own sexual identity. The issue came to the fore of Schubert scholarship in 1989, when Maynard Solomon, a keen biographer of Mozart and Beethoven, published a subversive essay titled "Franz Schubert and the Peacocks of Benvenuto Cellini," suggesting that Schubert was homosexual and was part of a gay subculture. Solomon's thesis was based not only on the Mayrhofer friendship but also on unexplained oddities in the documentary record, notably an entry in the diary of Eduard von Bauernfeld—the same friend who recorded Schubert's foot-stamping tirade—saying that "Schubert [is] half-sick (he needs 'young peacocks,' like Benvenuto Cellini)." Peacocks, Solomon noticed, are in Cellini's autobiography not so subtle code for young men he has seduced. Also significant in this respect were some euphemistic-sounding accounts of Schubert's attitude toward women (phrases such as a "dominating aversion for the daughters of Eve" and "indifferent to the charms of the fair sex").

The musicological furor over Solomon's article was unenlightening. It told more about anxieties over sexuality at both ends of the spectrum than anything in Schubert's nature. Conservative elements shouted down the "homosexual Schubert" as a categorical impossibility. The Canadian musicologist Rita Steblin exposed some flaws in Solomon's research, but her careful recounting of the archival record gave way to manifestations of bigotry; in a letter to the editors of *The New York Review of Books*, she likened gay-friendly musicology to Nazism, describing both of them as "fashionable political ideologies." At the opposite extreme, Susan McClary listened to the Andante of the "Unfinished" and heard an "open, flexible sense of self," a supposedly gay voice evident in specific musical procedures. This argument depended on stereotypes of Schubert's "gentleness" that many episodes in his music deny; it also depended on stereotypes of homosexuality itself.

Some fair-minded scholars have had trouble accepting Solomon's conclusions. The argument is indeed speculative, although Solomon succeeds in showing that presumptions of a heterosexual Schubert are no less speculative, and that no reliable evidence for *any* romantic relationship exists—not even for Schubert's often-mentioned attachment to the soprano Therese Grob. Those who have tried to rebut Solomon's article—among them Elizabeth McKay, in a 1996 biography—have simply dreamed up new fantasies of heterosexual affairs in the conditional tense: "If Schubert fell in love with the 'bewitching Sophie' . . . it would not be surprising," and so on. In between the protectively cheery anecdotes, his friends admitted the unresolved mysteries of his nature. "Schubert is much praised, but they say he conceals himself," goes an entry in Beethoven's conversation books for 1823. All signs suggest that Schubert hung back from commitment to anyone or anything, yet his syphilitic condition after 1822 indicates that he somewhere found a physical outlet for his sexuality. To paraphrase Bob Dylan, something's going on here, but we don't know what it is.

We know at least that Schubert emerged a changed man. He devoted himself again to Classical forms: first to piano sonatas, then to chamber music and the symphony. In 1824 he wrote the A-Minor and "Death and the Maiden" Quartets in swift succession; and just before beginning work on "Death and the Maiden," he had turned to Mayrhofer's poetry for the last time. He chose poems that speak of self-purification, recognition of the inaccessibility of Love, and wakefulness in a sleeping world. The most remarkable of the group is "Auflösung" ("Dissolution"), in which Mayrhofer shouts in his most visionary voice, "Go under, world, and never more disturb / These sweet, ethereal choirs." The images resonate with a murky poem that the composer himself had written during his previous illness-ridden year, titled "My Prayer": this also speaks of *Untergang*, self-abnegation, self-transformation. "Kill it, kill me with it," Schubert wrote of his life up to that time.

It is difficult to describe the nearly Wagnerian music that Schubert brings to "Auflösung": dark rolling chords on the piano, whiplash changes of key, incongruously grand phrases on the word "sweet," a slide back down to banging low notes and stammerings of "Go under," and a tenuous resolution at the end. (Brigitte Fassbaender delivers a hair-raising rendition of this song in the Hyperion series.) "Auflösung" is, I think, a great early feat of Romantic confession, but Schubert would not write more songs like it. He would not write a "history of my feelings," to use the phrase that Count Platen applied to his amazingly frank diaries. Although Schubert was now verifiably doomed, caught in the supreme Romantic predicament, he would bury emotion more deeply in music. The "Death and the Maiden" Quartet is a pure Classical composition, written according to the old rules.

The feelings, suddenly, are ours.

We are back where traditional musicologists like to have us—with "the music itself." History holds traces of a powerful personality, but it seems as if the life has been raided, robbed, emptied by a ruthless devotion to art. The music, again, has an uncommonly immediate presence. Schubert is somehow more with us than most of the bust-on-the-piano classics. Contemporary composers look to him as a colleague and search his scores for new paths. Various compositions of recent decades have taken off from Schubertian sources: Luciano Berio's *Rendering*, John Harbison's *November 19, 1828* (the date, of course, of Schubert's death), Edison Denisov's *Lazarus*, and Georg Friedrich Haas's *Torso*, to name a few. Meanwhile, Schubert himself seems to be still composing: different editors' realizations of his numerous unfinished pieces arrive every few years.

At the end of the line, at the limits of what music can express, are the masterpieces that appeared between 1823 and 1828: the last three quartets, the two piano trios, the String Quintet, the last eight or so piano sonatas, the Ninth Symphony, and the song cycles. In his final years, Schubert writes with greater detachment, greater economy of means, but also with an increasing command of the bigger forms. All his youthful innovations are mobilized as a means of controlling large structures. He uses his eccentric modulations and equivocal chords to create subtle changes of color across a sprawling vista. He opens up space by distributing figures through

far-flung registers of the piano, or by spreading a filigreed texture of sound
through the strings. In that space, one voice might cry out, like the amazing second cello line in the String Quintet, or instruments might repeat a
rhythm relentlessly to give a sense of traveling motion.

In some ways, the late works are highly conservative in form. In other
ways, they enter uncharted regions. The G-Major Quartet of 1826 is perhaps the most "advanced" of all: the abrupt, wrenching gestures of its
opening bars look past the nineteenth century to the twentieth. The ven-
turesomeness of the harmony does not come by way of dissonance—the
usual index of progressive musical thinking. Schubert is able to exploit
tensions in the tonal system without resorting to the chromatic congestion
that had begun in Beethoven and would end in Schoenberg. Instead, he
follows circuitous new paths from one warmly familiar chord to another;
in the quartet, as in other pieces, he touches on the whole-tone scale,
which would become the foundation of Claude Debussy's post-tonal language many decades later. At the same time, Schubert's unearthly harmonies have a historical basis. Lurking in the opening section of the quartet
is the lamento bass—the somber stepwise descent familiar from Dido's
Lament, the "Crucifixus" of the B-Minor Mass, and the overture of *Don
Giovanni.*

"It's sigh, it's nostalgia," György Ligeti said of the lamenting figure, at
the outset of a virtuoso analysis of the G-Major Quartet at the New England Conservatory, in 1993. The old pattern is woven through the first
bars of Schubert's work like a slender thread. A soft G-major chord leads
by way of a rapid crescendo to lashing G minor, which in turn subsides to
reassuring D major, the companion chord of G. That chord then blackens
to D minor before giving way to A major, with a diminished seventh and
a dominant seventh on D ensuing. From these chords you can extract the
chromatic fourth (G down to D, step by step). In the next section—a more
subdued episode, with tremolos buzzing softly all around—the lamenting
fall recurs, except that it now appears plainly in the cello, assuming its
traditional bass function. But the harmonization is different: around the
note F-natural there materializes not a D-minor triad but a trembling
chord of F major, foreign to the home key. "A total shock," Ligeti said of
this moment. "You cannot understand [it] in the tonal context." Musical
language is almost torn apart by memories of its past as well as by premonitions of its future.

The song cycles, too, blend convention and revolution. Their tales of unhappy love, set in archetypal, not quite real places like the Mill, the Village, and the Inn, shift from a Romantic here-and-now to an interior plane. *Winterreise* casts a very cool gaze on despair: it has something in common with Wallace Stevens's "mind of winter," contemplating "nothing that is not there and the nothing that is," and even more with the skeletal lyricism of Samuel Beckett, who nursed a deep love for Schubert's work and for *Winterreise* in particular. Indeed, the cycle unfolds like a Beckett play, in a landscape as vivid as it is vague. A young man who has been spurned by his beloved goes walking in and around the village where she lives, apparently fading into nonexistence in the process. Feet crunch in snow, ice cracks over a river, a post horn blows, a leaf flutters down from a tree, a crow circles in the air, dogs bark, clouds scurry across the sky, and, in the "Leiermann" epilogue, an ancient organ-grinder enters, playing a tune for no one. To an uncanny degree, you hear those sounds in Schubert's piano writing, down to the rattling of the chains that hold the barking dogs. Yet there is something abstract about the aimless journey, which keeps circling back to the same places and the same motifs, the walking rhythm entering time and again. By the end, the young man seems to have merged with the figure of the hurdy-gurdy man, as if he has grown old in an hour.

The six Heine songs of 1828 take up where *Winterreise* left off, in a world of self-alienation and derangement. Schubert's powers of suggestion now extend to the musicalizing of literary abstractions. In "Der Doppelgänger," the narrator sees his "double" and feels he has become a ghost himself, watching his own ridiculous life. Setting the scene, Schubert writes an acutely unnerving progression in B minor in which each chord has been lobotomized by the surgical removal of one essential note. These chords draw a picture of a walking corpse.

Listeners often have the idea that Schubert in his late period is looking into the face of death. The String Quintet and Sonata in B-flat, both of which were finished in September of 1828, do sound like a conscious farewell and summing up. The sequence of events of the Quintet's Adagio—a halting, nearly unbearably wistful principal theme; a vehement central section; a return to the first theme, enfeebled but ever more lovely; the briefest flash again of anger; then a passage into silence—might show an awareness, a defiance, and then an acceptance of death. But this is the story

Schubert told from the beginning: the going-forth of beautiful melody, a crack-up or collapse, a recovery of peace. The B-flat sonata, so vast and calm and mysterious, refines this story to an extreme of subtlety. Its principal theme bestows grace for seven measures. Then a trill rumbles ominously in the bass. Then the theme resumes, as if nothing has happened.

It remains to mention the Great C-Major Symphony, which both the New York Philharmonic and the Cleveland Orchestra played in New York on the occasion of the young man's two-hundredth birthday, on January 31, 1997. We call it the Ninth, but Schubert probably considered it his First—his first "grand symphony," his first utterance worthy of Beethoven's mantle. Sketched during an 1825 trip through the Austrian Alps, it seems to document the overcoming of morbidity, of all Romantic fascination with death. The force of the effort is both exhilarating and frightening. In the finale, the composer returns to a scene of innocence—a huge rustic dance, heralded by fanfares. By the end, the ceremony borders on violence: in a clear reminiscence of the hellish climax of *Don Giovanni*, the note C is repeatedly slammed down in the bass regions of the orchestra while a wild sequence of chords pivots around it. For all the world, it sounds like the stamping of a man reaching for the stars.

8

EMOTIONAL LANDSCAPES

BJÖRK'S SAGA

I first met Björk in the lobby of the Hotel Borg, a funky Art Deco palace in the center of the Icelandic capital of Reykjavík. The Borg opened in 1930, the dream project of a noted wrestler who hosted swank parties for American military officers and the odd movie star. Eventually, the wrestler died and the hotel fell on hard times. In the early 1980s, it became the gathering spot for a group of aggressively bohemian teenagers, who theorized punk-rock anarchy at the hotel bar. One of the gang was Björk Guðmundsdóttir, the daughter of an electrician and a feminist activist. She sang in a band called Kukl, which means "black magic," and she outraged older Icelanders with her antics. Parents shuddered when the singer bared her midriff on television while visibly pregnant. Even in her late thirties, she still looked as though she could fall in with a group of fashionable delinquents. She walked through the door of the Borg wearing a ladybug cap and white shoes with red pompoms on the toes.

It was a pale, mild morning in January 2004. The day before, an ice storm had rendered the city impassable, but some shift in the Gulf Stream had warmed the air overnight. We took a taxi into the suburbs, where Björk was working on a new album. She held in her hands a program for the play *The Master and Margarita*, which she had seen the night before. She read Mikhail Bulgakov's novel, on which the play was based, when she was young, and it remains one of her favorite books. "The book is very popular with Icelanders," she said. "It has a very Nordic feeling to it, even though it is Russian. It ridicules bureaucracy, it has black magic and Arctic magic realism. You could say it is Alice in Wonderland for the Arctic grown-up." I nodded, and glanced at a snowcapped mountain ridge in the distance. "Of course," she added, "you have to watch for the Nordic cliché. 'Hello! I am a Viking! My name is Björk!' A friend of mine says that when record-company executives come to Iceland they ask the bands if they believe in elves, and whoever says yes gets signed up."

Björk is probably the most famous Icelander since Leif Eriksson, who voyaged to America a thousand years ago. Vigdís Finnbogadóttir, who served as the country's president from 1980 to 1996, once compared her to the women of the national sagas, like Brynhild and Aud the Deep-Minded. Björk has spent much time abroad in part to escape this monumentalizing attention, which makes her uneasy. Instead, she has ended up with a global sort of fame: as the creator of eight solo albums, involving British, American, Indian, Iranian, Brazilian, Danish, Turkish, and Inuit musicians; as a sometime actress, who in 2000 won the best-actress prize in Cannes for her performance in the film *Dancer in the Dark*; and, more recently, as a denizen of the New York art-world circles frequented by her partner, Matthew Barney. Her appearance at the opening ceremonies of the 2004 Athens Olympics, singing an ornate new song called "Oceania," confirmed her status as the ultimate musical cosmopolitan, acquainted with both Karlheinz Stockhausen and the Wu-Tang Clan. Though she now spends much of her time in New York, she keeps coming back to Iceland, where she lives for several months of the year. The relative simplicity of the place is reassuring to her. Once, she translated a local news headline for my benefit: TIRE TRACKS IN FOOTBALL FIELD. A look of pleasure crossed her face as she studied photographic evidence of the catastrophe. "This is so Iceland," she said.

In my talks with Björk, which began in Reykjavík and continued in New York, London, and Salvador, Brazil, she mentioned the "Nordic idea" several times, although she was never too specific about it. Some sort of Nordic idea is plainly at the heart of her album *Medúlla*, which appeared in the summer of 2004. The moment you try to put this idea into words, however, the glacier of cliché begins to advance. Ásmundur Jónsson, the visionary manager of the Icelandic record label Bad Taste, once said that her earliest solo recordings made him think of a solitary figure standing in an open space; but there is nothing inherently northern in that. Whatever is Nordic in Björk's music is filtered through her own creative personality, which is all-devouring by nature, taking in dance music, avant-garde electronic music, twentieth-century composition, contemporary R&B, jazz, hip-hop, and almost everything else under the winter sun.

When it becomes known that you have met Björk, people tend to ask, with an insinuating grin, "What's she like?" She is expected to be a cyclone of elfin zaniness; she is, after all, the woman who showed up at the 2001 Academy Awards with what looked to be a swan carcass draped around her body. She does have her zany moments—I won't soon forget the image of her dancing down a street in Salvador shouting "Bring the noise!"—but it is not the first word that comes to mind. She is warm, watchful, sharp-witted, restless, often serious, seldom solemn, innocent but never naïve, honest and direct in a way that invites confidences, shockingly easy to talk to on almost any subject but herself. Teresa Stratas once said that Lotte Lenya was "an earth sprite, a Lulu, at once vulnerable and strong, soft and hard-edged, child-like and world-weary." Much the same could be said of Björk, except that she is rather nicer than Lulu—and far from being weary of the world.

Early work on *Medúlla*, whose name describes the inner part of an animal or plant structure and, more appositely, the lower part of the human brain, was done at Greenhouse Studios, which belongs to the producer Valgeir Sigurðsson. Valgeir, a mellow, soft-spoken guy in his early thirties, had been working with Björk since 1998, when the two collaborated on the soundtrack for *Dancer in the Dark*. The studio is at the end of a cul-de-sac in the suburbs of Reykjavík. From the outside, it looks like an ordinary home, which it partly is: Valgeir lives with his family on one side. The main recording console is in a long room with cathedral-style windows and gleaming beech floors. Downstairs is a small performance space, with an adjoining kitchenette. The place is cool, spare, and abnormally neat, Valgeir's T-shirt-and-torn-jeans style notwithstanding. By the time we went upstairs, the midwinter day was already ending. An hour later, a full moon was hanging uncomfortably close. The white-capped mountains glowed in the distance.

Björk sat down to listen to sketches and partly finished versions of the songs that she wanted to put on the album. She had written many of them at the end of the previous year, during a trip to Gomera, in the Canary Islands. "I am at the point where I can let it out for other people, hear them through other people's ears," she said. "There is a point where you are very secretive, but then you become confident enough that you can hear criticism, and not become discouraged." I nodded sympathetically, as if I, too, were an Icelandic pop star who has erased boundaries between genres. Björk often uses the second person to close the distance between herself and others.

She'd laid down the initial vocal tracks in a spontaneous rush, standing over the mixing board with a handheld mike—"a big old 1950s thing," she said—while electronic mockups of the harmonies and beats played on Valgeir's computer. "The album is about voices," she said. "I want to get away from instruments and electronics, which was the world of my last album, *Vespertine*. I want to see what can be done with the entire emotional range of the human voice—a single voice, a chorus, trained voices, pop voices, folk voices, strange voices. Not just melodies but everything else, every noise that a throat makes." She mentioned as possible collaborators the avant-garde rock vocalist Mike Patton, the Inuit throat-singer Tanya Tagaq, the "human beatboxes" Dokaka and Rahzel, and the R&B superstar Beyoncé. "The last album was very introverted," she said. "It was avoiding eye contact. This one is a little more earthy, but, you know, not exactly simple." She stopped to answer a phone call about school fees for her older child, Sindri, who is of college age.

Björk started playing the tracks and commenting on each. Some were full-fledged four- or five-minute songs, with verses and a chorus; others were briefer, more atmospheric, more elusive. Most immediately gripping was a song called "Who Is It," which Björk had started working on during the *Vespertine* sessions. This version began with two minutes or so of vaguely medieval-sounding choral writing, a misty mass of overlapping lines. Then big bass notes began to growl, and in a matter of seconds the song transformed itself before one's ears into the kind of quirkily ebullient anthem that Björk specialized in earlier in her career: "Who is it that never lets you down? / Who is it that gave you back your crown?" I thought of *The Master and Margarita*, of the midnight carnival erupting in a Nordic place. As it was, "Who Is It" was something between a pop song and a choral meditation by Arvo Pärt. Remixed with a few more heavy beats, it could rule every dance floor in the world.

Not yet satisfied with her creation, Björk sat down at a keyboard and worked out new vocal lines to add to the swell of sound at the beginning of the song. At least half the time I was with Björk, she was hunched over a keyboard or a computer, building her synthesis one piece at a time. She seldom sits absolutely still, and is constantly crossing or uncrossing her legs, squatting in a chair in various yoga-like positions, or getting up to twirl her body this way or that. Yet her gaze stays fixed on whatever is engaging her attention; her body seems distracted but her mind is not.

At around 6:00 p.m. the next day, sixteen singers arrived at the studio to record the choral parts that Björk and Valgeir had been working on for several months. In the past, Valgeir told me, they had printed out string and orchestral arrangements directly from the computer, using the Sibelius music-notation program, but in this case they engaged a copyist to produce clean vocal parts. Most of the singers were members of a group called Schola Cantorum, which has appeared on several recordings of the music of the furiously original Icelandic composer Jón Leifs. Björk heard the Leifs recordings and liked the chorus's sound. In recent years, she had worked with professional choruses and also with a group of large-voiced Inuit women, who came along on her *Vespertine* tour. (She found them while on a vacation in Greenland, by putting up ads in a supermarket.) These singers, she hoped, would be classical in technique but flexible in their approach. "I want a little bit of a pagan edge, a bit of Slavic," she said.

The session was on the late side because most of the singers have day jobs. They congregated in the kitchen, looking nervous but game. Valgeir placed the vocal parts in piles, and the singers picked them up in a shuffling line. If you had walked in off the street, you might have thought that this was a gathering of procrastinating Christmas carolers, not a major-label recording session. Björk offered bowls of chocolate-covered almonds and raisins. Valgeir's son practiced in-line skating in the hall. After an initial run-through, five Domino's pizzas arrived, and the singers began devouring them. Valgeir hovered in the background, chatting about Brian Eno and keeping an eye on the pizza situation. Fifteen minutes later, there was no trace that the pizzas had ever existed.

To convey her ideas to the singers, Björk sang, danced, conducted, gestured, talked, and joked. She is noted for using extravagant metaphors when she talks about music. "I say, 'Like marzipan,' and they say, 'Oh, you mean dolcissimo,'" she told me. Since Valgeir was upstairs at the mixing board, Björk also took care of some technical matters, fiddling for a while with a malfunctioning Wurlitzer piano and unplugging some unused headphones that were lying on the floor. She was unfailingly, elaborately polite. In several months of recording, I never heard her raise her voice or deliver anything like a firm command. Criticisms were prefaced with phrases like "the only thing I would say is . . ." and "the one thing I'm not so crazy about is . . ." If one of her collaborators sought specific guidance, she might say, "Whatever hits your fancy. I just like to hear whatever you do with it."

Yet Björk does put forward some specific instructions. Most of the parts for the Icelandic singers consisted of wordless vocalise, but she asked them to apply different syllables to the notes—"hoo" instead of "aah," for instance—and had to rein them in when they started inventing faux-African mumbo-jumbo. In some cases, she changed the parts on the spot, either to clarify a texture or to make it richer. She got very excited when the basses kicked in with Mephistophelian tones; she was depending on them to take the place of the big, low electronic beats that had moored so many of her songs in the past. She assigned them to sing along in the middle section of "Where Is the Line," an aggressive song in which Björk lays down the law for someone who has been abusing her patience. "More of a rock feel," she said happily. Valgeir looked on with a quizzical smile, scratching the stubble on his face. "We've been talking about the choral arrangement for so long," he said. "It's such a relief it's actually happening."

Later, in the upstairs recording room, I noticed something remarkable about Björk's voice. The singers were in a circle, with a microphone positioned in front of each. Björk was usually in the center of the circle or on the outside, with no microphone within reach. Yet whenever she was singing or talking her voice was at the center of the sound. You could pick it out in a second from the Icelandic chatter: the dusky timbre, deep in the mezzo-soprano range; the tremor in it, which occasionally takes on the rasp of a pubescent boy's voice; the way it slices through the sonic haze, as if a few extra frequencies in a given range are being twanged to life. It carries without effort, like those Mongolian voices that can be heard across the steppe. Somehow, the mere fact of her voice became a creative magnet, pulling the music in the right direction.

On the day I was to leave Iceland, Björk decided that I should see something of Reykjavík's art scene. Jóga, one of her oldest friends, is married to the actor and artist Jón Gnarr, who was having an opening that afternoon. We drove in another taxi—if Iceland has limousines, Björk does not use them—to an old Lutheran church in the center of town. The show was titled *INRI*, and it consisted of a series of photographs of G.I. Joe and Ken dolls acting out the Stations of the Cross. The resulting evocation of Christ's last days was unconventional—only four of the attendees of the Last Supper wear clothes, and the best-dressed one, in khakis and a sweater-vest, is Satan—but if any conservative Christians were scandalized they did not make themselves known. The mood of the piece was whimsical rather than provocative. "Judas looks like a rave kid," Björk said, giggling approvingly.

In the church, everyone seemed to know Björk, but no one made a fuss over her. I had a hard time telling whether the people who greeted her were relatives, old friends, fans, or simply extroverted strangers. At one point, a blond boy walked up to Björk and said "Hi, Björk!" Björk said "Hi!" in return, whereupon the kid casually sauntered away. Two older teens were dressed in tattered, oddly festooned military-style greatcoats; they looked like stylish deserters from the final Army of the Tsar. Outside the church, a television reporter was interviewing Gnarr. On a nearby lake, swans made a noise that sounded like an anarchist brass band, or so it seemed in this context. The snow and ice melted in the weak glare of the sun. I said goodbye to Björk and took a cab to the airport.

My incoming flight had landed after dark, and I had seen nothing of the landscape around the city. Now I stared in wonder at the miles of blackish lava, at the volcanic boulders that had dropped from the sky, at the conical peak of Mount Keilir, in the distance. I had gone from a fashionable modern place into a charcoal sketch of an unfinished world.

For a long time, there was nothing where Iceland now is. The volcanoes of the island began rising from the Atlantic twenty million years ago—a geological pause for breath. The island was undisturbed by what the Icelandic novelist Halldór Laxness called "the tyranny of mankind" until about A.D. 870, when Norse and Celtic farmers began to settle it. They brought with them the lore of the Germanic tribes, which became the basis of an oral and written tradition that changed little in the following nine centuries. The stories of gods, heroes, Vikings, and ordinary Icelanders were expounded in *rímur*, or extended chanted tales. When they are read today, they are uncannily familiar, for they have burrowed their way into modern mythologies of Western culture; Wagner used them as the principal source of the *Ring* cycle, and J.R.R. Tolkien put them at the core of *The Lord of the Rings*. Wagner's Ring of Fire and Tolkien's Mount Doom come straight out of the Icelandic landscape. No wonder I felt a chill when I saw Mount Keilir looming over the plain.

Until the early twentieth century, the Icelanders lived out of sight and mind, more a rumor than a fact. Laxness changed this by winning the Nobel Prize, in 1955, for his novel *Independent People*, which tells of a sheepherder named Bjartur, who holds on to his parcel of land in the face of mounting natural and supernatural obstacles. The book is notable for, among other things, its ambivalent relationship with the Nordic idea; it paints an epic portrait of a hardy, solitary soul, yet it undercuts that mythology with slow-burning deadpan humor and blindsiding blasts of emotion. If Bjartur suffers in isolation, the novel suggests, it is because he chose to. Laxness's mixture of dignity and irony seems central to the national character.

Modern Icelandic music begins with Jón Leifs, who lived from 1899 to 1968, and whose 1961 work *Hekla* helped bring Björk and her chorus together. While in Reykjavík, I had lunch with Árni Heimir Ingólfsson, a young Harvard-educated musicologist who is writing a biography of Leifs. "He was a tremendously complex personality," Árni told me. "To some, he was witty, charming, and sophisticated; to others a paranoid megalomaniac." Despite his drastic individuality, Leifs based his music on a close study of Icelandic folk music: his lurching rhythms follow the patterns of the *rímur* chant, and his craggy, medieval-sounding melodies imitate a song style called *tvísöngur*. The composer spent much of his early career studying in Germany, and remained there throughout the Third Reich. Unfortunately, his messianic belief in Icelandic tradition blended all too well with Nazi philosophy, which prized Iceland as the locus of an uncontaminated Aryan culture. Yet his roiling dissonances and percussive effects caused some to label him a "degenerate." The fact that he had married a Jewish German pianist did not help his position. He and his wife escaped to Sweden in 1944.

Hekla, which is named after Iceland's largest active volcano, has been described as the loudest piece of music ever written. It requires nineteen percussionists, who play a fantastic battery of instruments, including anvils, stones, sirens, bells, ships' chains, a sort of tree-hammer, shotguns, and cannons. During a break in Björk's choral recording sessions, I asked one of the Schola Cantorum singers about their recording of *Hekla*, on the BIS label. "That was totally crazy," he told me. "Leifs knew that a lot of what he wrote couldn't really be sung, but he wrote it down anyway. Björk is very easy to work with by comparison, although the music is surprisingly similar sometimes." Björk herself loves Leifs's music. "I think he almost animated eruptions and lava in sound," she said. Yet this composer lived out the tragedy of Laxness's "independent man," who fails to see that his pride is the source of his suffering. It seemed to me that Björk has been working her entire career to correct this mythology—still to maintain independence, to seek the new and the strange, but also to make compromises when necessary, to live in reality, to accept imperfection.

Björk listens avidly to choral music, which plays a dominant role in Iceland's music culture. If one in ten inhabitants seems to play in a rock band, one in five sings in a choir. While working on *Medúlla*, Björk was listening to several CDs of choral songs by Reykjavík's Hamrahlid Choir, which she herself once sang in. It is somberly beautiful music that sets you on the edge of paralyzing sadness, or, perhaps, pulls you back gently from the brink. Later on, she reconvened the entire Schola Cantorum to record a choral arrangement of Jórunn Viðar's song "Vökuró" ("Vigil"), a simple, elegiac setting of a poem by Jakobína Sigurðardóttir:

> *Far away wakes the great world,*
> *mad with grim enchantment,*
> *disquieted,*
> *fearful of night and day.*
> *Your eyes,*
> *fearless and serene,*
> *smile bright at me.*

For decades, Viðar was the only female member of the Icelandic Composers' Society. She was eighty-six when *Medúlla* was made, and her song became the still center of the album. It is one of the most purely entrancing recordings that Björk has made.

Björk, like a lot of her countrymen, had a complicated family background; the idea of the nuclear family has never really taken root in Iceland. Her parents divorced when she was two, and she grew up in several households at once. Her mother, whose second marriage was to a rock musician, cultivated a hippie, communelike atmosphere. Her father, who went on to become the head of the Icelandic electricians' union, kept a more orderly, conservative household. Björk's working method, a mixture of elaborate preparation and last-minute improvisation, perhaps reflects this divided upbringing. Her most substantial family inheritance may have been from her grandmothers, who could remember the timeless rural world of Laxness's novels and preserved the romance of the landscape. From them Björk heard Icelandic folk songs, which she calls "old-woman melodies."

Starting at the age of five, Björk attended the Tónmenntaskóli, a music school in Reykjavík. She took theory and history classes, sang in school choirs, and mastered the flute well enough to play an atonal Finnish concerto whose name she has now forgotten. In 1980, at the age of fifteen, she wrote a piece called *Glora*, which is the only extant recording of her as a flutist (Björk included the track on her 2002 boxed set, *Family Tree*); the playing is pristine, the music a bit like the beginning of the second part of *The Rite of Spring*. Under the guidance of a teacher named Stefan Edelstein, she explored the more radical corners of the classical repertory, gravitating toward Stockhausen, Messiaen, and John Cage. Stockhausen remains one of Björk's heroes; she interviewed the composer in 1996 for the magazine *Dazed & Confused*, defining him as a man "obsessed with the marriage between mystery and science." Early on, she made her own attempts at avant-garde experimentation. She made beats from a tape of her grandfather snoring and played drums to the sound of a popcorn machine.

As she headed toward her teenage years, Björk had shaken off her classical upbringing. She was frustrated by its obsession with the past—"all this retro, constant Beethoven and Bach bollocks," as she later said in her Stockhausen interview. With her stepfather's encouragement, she started singing pop songs, and in 1977 she recorded an album of covers that sold respectably well as a novelty item. She formed a self-consciously "difficult" band with other conservatory alums, then appeared with a succession of riotous punk outfits, the most famous of which was Kukl. (There was a Kukl side project with the enticing name Elgar Sisters.) Kukl signed with Crass Records, the English anarchist label, which preached an anti-bourgeois, anticommercial code. But Björk was skeptical of punk's purist ideology: she immediately rebelled against the rebellion.

Björk found fame abruptly, almost accidentally. In 1986, shortly before Reagan and Gorbachev arrived in Reykjavík for their nuclear summit, Björk and her comrades formed a collective organization called Bad Taste, whose manifesto announced, "Bad Taste will use every imaginable and unimaginable method, e.g. inoculation, extermination, tasteless advertisements and announcements, distribution and sale of common junk and excrement." Principally, this assault took the form of a Bad Taste band, called the Sugarcubes, who aimed to send up the kind of bouncy clichés that passed for Icelandic pop. A song called "Birthday" became a surprise hit in Britain, and within a few months the band was an international phenomenon. The alternately charming and irritating synthetic jangle of the Sugarcubes was really an expression of the sensibility of Einar Örn, a poetic prankster who later released one of the freakiest rap albums in history. Björk, however, inevitably stepped forward as the band's most conspicuous personality. The band ran its course after three albums.

By 1990, Björk was striking out on her own. That summer, she went on a long bicycle tour of remote parts of Iceland, stopping in tiny village churches and playing for an hour or two on the organ or harmonium. From this adventure emerged "Anchor Song," which has a meandering melodic purity that is very Björkian. Around this time, she made a record of jazz standards, *Gling-Gló*, which suggests that she could have had a major career as a jazz singer. Most important, she delved into electronic pop, which traced its technique, if not its content, to Stockhausen's pioneering synthesizer compositions of the early 1950s. She started out listening to Brian Eno and Kraftwerk, then moved on to dance music and rap. She used to take her boom box out into the Icelandic countryside to listen to Public Enemy's *Fear of a Black Planet* at proper volume. It remains one of her favorite records; the voluptuous menace of tracks like "Welcome to the Terrordome"—beats and samples stacked up in a droning roar, like Stockhausen stuck on A-B repeat—echoes through all her work.

In 1992, Björk moved to England, where she could experience electronic music at its most creatively intense. The whomping beats of techno dominated the London and Manchester dance floors, while ambient bleeps and clicks wafted through sweaty rooms in Sheffield. With new digital technologies, electronic artists could cover up the fuzz of synthesizers and manufacture hyperreal, crystalline soundscapes. Björk was especially attracted to Massive Attack, which fused the languid pacing of reggae with the sonic depth of hip-hop. Like disco in the seventies, the new digital music often became a backdrop for strong female voices like Björk's, which could burn like candles in a dark room. At this stage, Björk left much of the work to her producers, who included, to name the most significant among dozens, Graham Massey, Nellee Hooper, Tricky, and Mark Bell.

In 1993, Björk made a phenomenal solo entrance, singing "Human Behavior" on the album *Debut*. Over a cheesy, funky timpani riff, which was sampled from the Antônio Carlos Jobim–Quincy Jones soundtrack album *The Adventurers*, she sang gleefully from an alien point of view, assessing the risk of getting close to the human species. It was a career-defining move: Björk positioned herself as a figure outside convention—as a member of another species, even—while implicating the listener in the conspiracy. The songs on *Debut* and its follow-up, *Post*, show Björk at large in the world, falling in and out of love with Venus-like boys, dancing at druggy parties, circulating through the neon glamour of nineties London. Behind the travelogue of the Icelander abroad was a sneakily imposing thesis about technology and music. She had delivered her manifesto in 1992, when she met up with Massey to record the track "Modern Things." Machines, she sang over a gently burbling electronic stream, have always existed, waiting for their time in the sun. Technology, in other words, need not be a sleek, soulless force; it can embrace nature, teem with life.

Indeed, *Debut* and *Post* lack the emotional detachment of many British electronic records of the period—the cooler-than-thou stance of Tricky, for example, with whom Björk had a short romance in 1995. From the outset, Björk wanted to bring traditional instruments into the mix; her first idea was to have a brass band playing over severe electronic beats. In the event, she relied on flute, harp, accordion, and harmonium. Talvin Singh supplied Indian string arrangements; the Brazilian arranger Eumir Deodato came out of retirement to endow techno stompers like "Hyper-ballad" with a Nelson Riddle lushness. The intermeshing of acoustic and electronic textures succeeded not only because the production avoided the usual clichés but because the songs were stocked with historical cues. Several of them lean on a stately tango rhythm, which supplies a hint of between-the-wars cabaret. The gently rocking chords of "Isobel" are cousins of Gershwin's chords for "Summertime."

The intermittent nostalgia of Björk's musical material is tempered by the urgent optimism of her verbal imagery, which seems always charged with the sense that the next moment or meeting could transform everything. She likes to exclaim in breathy terms of some visceral but elusive "it": "I've Seen It All," "It's in Our Hands," "It's Not Up to You." Her lyrics, which are sometimes composed with the help of the poet Sjón, are a kind of poetry of possibility. She is unafraid of the darker byways of emotion, but she has no time for modernist-style alienation. On "Who Is It," she sings, in a definitive statement of her emotional philosophy, "I carry my joy on the left / Carry my pain on the right."

Like the greatest opera singers, Björk combines precision of pitch with force of feeling, and any diva will tell you how hard it is to have one without sacrificing the other. If you throw a lot of emotion into your voice, you will easily lose control of the pitch. If you focus on the pitch, you will find it difficult to convey emotion. Something tremendous must be happening in the brain when a singer is able to escape that double bind, and Björk's new album is like a CAT scan of the process.

"Everyone loves Maria Callas," Björk told me, "because she doesn't get locked up in a technique box. She keeps her *rrrr*"—she gestured toward her chest. "The unity of emotion and word and tone. Especially, the purity of expression. Every genre has these mechanical clichés that get implanted in the voices and start to hide the power of words." She sang a bit of rock and roll around the words "I don't know nothing" and made a bit of bel canto from the words "I know everything." Björk manages to sound as if she knows everything and nothing at once.

In February 2004, Björk went to Salvador, the capital of the Bahia province of Brazil, to watch Matthew Barney create a high-tech, avant-garde float for Carnaval. Salvador's Carnaval is not as flamboyant as Rio de Janeiro's; the emphasis is more on the energy of Brazilian music and dance, especially the African-accented music of the Bahia region. Gilberto Gil and Caetano Veloso, leaders of the Tropicália musical revolution of the sixties and seventies, both come from Bahia, and both were in attendance as Barney's float made its entrance. Barney's musical consultant was the downtown New York musician Arto Lindsay, who spent his childhood in Brazil. Björk wasn't directly involved in the float project, but the Nordic idea was manifest in the person of Valgeir, who was in charge of electronic samples.

Björk settled herself apart from the action, renting a house in the old hippie community of Arembepe, about an hour up the coast. She was having a hard time adjusting to the warm weather and had come down with the flu. The other Icelanders had instituted a minor social revolution at the Brazilian house. They released a supposedly bad-mannered dog from its kennel, and the animal now happily roamed free with a tennis ball. They invited the house's domestic staff—a gardener, a cook, and a cleaning lady—to sit down at the dinner table with them.

Valgeir had set up a makeshift studio in a ten-by-ten-foot spare bedroom. An old air conditioner rattled ineffectively in the window. When Björk was feeling better, she played me the results of her sessions with Tanya Tagaq, the Inuit throat-singer. The Inuit tribes in northern Canada have a long-cherished game in which two female singers sit face-to-face and make all manner of rapid, breathy noises, in an attempt to make each other smile. Björk fell in love with this kind of vocal horseplay at the time of *Vespertine*; it recalled the sensuous avant-gardism of Meredith Monk, whom she had long admired. On *Medúlla*, Tagaq's artful hyperventilations fill up the middle spaces that, on earlier albums, were occupied by the electronic swirl.

Bahia was ready to muscle its way into the already crowded sound-world of the record. Björk had been listening in on Lindsay's rehearsals with a group of Afro-Brazilian drummers, who were to play alongside the float. They came from two Bahian groups, Cortejo Afro and Ilê Aiyê. They played rollicking, ever-shifting beats with a martial tinge. Björk thought of putting them on "Mouth's Cradle," another of the choral-powered songs on the album. Later, the drummers were recorded, and they gave the music a grainy texture and a forward drive. But they weighed on Björk's conscience; they violated the strictly vocal concept that she had set up, and they seemed too obvious a move for a tourist from the north. "I don't want to be colonial, culinary," she told me. "My brain says no, but my heart says yes."

The climactic night of Carnaval arrived. Barney's creation was to make its appearance in the parade of floats as it moved along the oceanfront of Salvador. Björk ventured out in a small van with various Icelanders and friends of Barney's. About a mile from the beach, a Brazilian security detail—nine men in charcoal-gray suits, sunglasses, and earpiece headphones—drove up in a second van to supervise the celebrity visitor. Björk wanted to walk the rest of the way through the crowd, but the security people vetoed the idea. They formed a V-shaped wedge in front, and the crowd parted. Björk sang along to Madonna's "Like a Prayer" on the radio and talked again about *The Master and Margarita*, which Johann, her Pilates instructor, had just read. "When I was young," she said, "I was surrounded by friends who were always having these drunken passionate arguments all around me. I sometimes feel as if I read a lot of important books just by listening to their arguments."

Brazilian paparazzi had got wind of the approaching convoy; they swarmed around the van as we disembarked. Indeed, the entire expedition had been arranged with the understanding that if Björk allowed herself to be photographed on this occasion then she would otherwise be left alone. "Robert Altman should make a movie about the paparazzi," Björk said, registering the tension of the situation. "About this little world of people who lurk in the bushes for five days, hardly sleeping or eating, waiting like hunters for the prey, for Lady Diana or whoever. They hate each other, and they hate the prey. It is all about the moment of the kill. It would be a very interesting movie, yes?" She said all this without bitterness, as if she were observing a phenomenon that had nothing to do with her, which, indeed, it really didn't. "Actually, most people here don't know who I am. They just know that I'm famous for some reason."

A little later, we were on a balcony high above the street, facing the old lighthouse of Barra. Barney's float came into view. In the lead was a big industrial tractor decorated with tree trunks on which phallic candles had been mounted. It was pulling a long trailer bed with high walls the color of rust, on top of which Arto Lindsay's musicians and Valgeir were playing. Björk explained that Valgeir was sampling the sounds of wheels crunching over various wood implements that had great significance in the Afro-Brazilian candomblé religion. She began to sing her own version of a candomblé hymn.

Valgeir, dressed in a lab technician's coat, was hunched over his laptop. Barney was directing the action from the street. Björk waved at them while the paparazzi snapped away and the security men warded off an overzealous journalist who had begun yelling at Björk in frustration. An hour later, Björk succeeded in shaking off all but two of the security people and worked her way into the crowds that were following the floats. For fifteen minutes or so, before the photographers picked up her trail, she danced along the Avenida Oceanica with a couple of friends. I thought of Bulgakov's Margarita, flying on her broom above the dead lights of Moscow: "Invisible and free! Invisible and free!"

In 1998, Björk moved from London back to Reykjavík. It was the beginning of a period of retrenchment, a retreat from the gregarious, promiscuous spirit of *Debut* and *Post*. Her albums of the next few years, *Homogenic* and *Vespertine*, turn progressively inward. A certain harshness enters the music. "The album represented some kind of doomsday," Björk said of *Homogenic* in an extended interview with Ásmundur Jónsson, the record producer, that appeared with her *Live Box* collection. "Some kind of explosion had to take place, some kind of death." At the same time, *Homogenic* evoked reassuringly familiar Icelandic landscapes, whether the sonic meadows of "Jóga"—written in honor of the woman I met at the art show in Reykjavík—or the seismic cracking of "Pluto," which seems like Björk's answer to Leifs's *Hekla*. By this time, Mark Bell had become Björk's electronic guru, and he gave the production a rough metallic sheen.

Vespertine, released at the end of the summer of 2001, was a homecoming of a different kind—a swerve toward a more intimate, chamber-music style of performance, without any of the heavy beats that had made her earlier music amenable to clubgoers. Matmos, an electronic duo then based in San Francisco, wrapped several songs in a bewitching sonic filigree, a gentle overlay of murmurs and rustles and clicks. *Vespertine* was Björk's most ambitious work to date; it made clear what was already implicit in the previous albums—that she was not simply a singer with great taste in collaborators but a full-fledged composer with a singular command of melody, harmony, rhythm, and texture. The tone of *Vespertine* is established by the first sound you hear: a half-diminished seventh, a Romantic chord of brooding ambiguity. "There lies my passion hidden," Björk sings, drawing the chord around her like a blanket. The harmonic adventurousness climaxes on the song "An Echo, a Stain," in which a chorus dwells at length on a huge, soft, luminous cluster of tones.

While intellectual types celebrated Björk's latest turn—a prospectus for an academic anthology solicited papers on such topics as "cyborg/nature dichotomy," "grammatical and syntactic deterritorialization," and, most appropriately, "anti- and hyper-pop"—some longtime fans voiced discontent. *Vespertine* was not unlike Radiohead's pop-averse *Kid A*, which had come out the previous year. (Thom Yorke joined Björk in a duet on *Selmasongs*, the companion record to *Dancer in the Dark*.) But Björk avoided the appearance of writing against her audience, of launching a polemic against mainstream popular music. She manages to stand apart from the crowd while not holding herself aloof from it. In private, she can wax critical about a lot of the music that's going on around her, but her catholicity of taste is real and automatic. I didn't hear anything cynical or calculated, for example, in the way she talked about collaborating with Beyoncé. When I asked what she liked about Beyoncé, she answered, with a slightly disbelieving look, "This is an album about voices, and she's got the most amazing voice."

Although Björk disavowed the classical world at an early age, she never entirely detached from it. She has a good working knowledge of the twentieth-century repertory, and is happy to discuss the pros and cons of Morton Feldman, Sofia Gubaidulina, and Steve Reich. ("Minimalism is my abyss!" she says, meaning that she does not like it.) She has experimented from time to time with a direct pop-classical fusion: one version of her song "Cover Me" incorporates the dance of the shepherds from Messiaen's *La Nativité du Seigneur*. Her most daring venture was to sing excerpts from Schoenberg's *Pierrot lunaire* at the Verbier Festival, in Switzerland, in 1996. She sallied into high atonal Schoenberg at the invitation of the conductor Kent Nagano. "It was an amazing experience for me," she recalled. "The songs left so much to the imagination of the singer—you know, they were originally written for a cabaret singer or an untrained singer like me. Kent Nagano wanted to make a recording of it, but I really felt like I would be invading the territory of people who sing this for a lifetime."

Medúlla, the successor to *Vespertine*, performs a typical Björkian maneuver, moving forward and looking backward at once. "Who Is It" and "Triumph of a Heart" are reassuring for those who cherish the big-time sensuality of Björk's early work. Yet, with contrapuntal layerings of choral parts and tricky harmonies throughout, the record is perhaps Björk's most "classical" and "composed" to date. The short interludes are not so much songs as studies in vocal texture, in the manner of Meredith Monk. But they are crucial to Björk's conception of the album, forging the links among its diverse vocal styles, from Inuit throat-singing to African-American beatboxing, with the "old-woman melodies" of Iceland still at the core. I had the sense that *Medúlla* was the realization of something that Björk had first imagined when she was still very young. "Sometimes after a long time you end up back where you started," she told me while riding in the van in Brazil.

After a while, the effort to find a place for Björk in the geography of popular, classical, art, folk, Icelandic, or non-Icelandic music seems fussy. What's most precious in her work is the glimpse that it affords, in flashing moments, of a future world in which the ideologies, teleologies, style wars, and subdivisions that have so defined music in the past hundred years slip away. Music is restored to its original bliss, free both of the fear of pretension that limits popular music and of the fear of vulgarity that limits classical music. The creative artist once more moves along an unbroken continuum, from folk to art and back again. So far, though, this utopia has only one inhabitant.

Two months after her trip to Brazil, Björk went to London to oversee the mixing of *Medúlla*. She settled into Olympic Studios, in Barnes, a quiet neighborhood south of the Thames. First, Mark Bell came in to co-produce four of the songs, and he worked his ambient magic on them, processing the voices in ways that sometimes rendered them unrecognizable. The mixing itself was handled by another éminence grise of English electronica, Mark (Spike) Stent, who has worked with Björk since the time of *Post*. The control room overlooked a not very glamorous English back garden. Adjoining the studio was a converted greenhouse, which had warmed to a boil on this sunny day. Björk sat on a swivel chair behind a ten-foot-wide mixing console. Two candles were burning in front of six speakers on top of the board.

The songs had rapidly evolved since I had last heard them, in a studio in downtown Manhattan the previous month. The session with Beyoncé had fallen victim to scheduling problems, but the beatbox crew—Rahzel and Dokaka—had reported for duty and heated up the sound. If the Icelandic choral singers and Tagaq demonstrated the voice's power to imitate nature, the beatboxers showed its power to imitate technology. A "human beatbox" is a hip-hop performer who mimics beats, turntable scratches, and other electronic effects when the equipment itself isn't available. Rahzel is considered the heavyweight of the art, and provides much of the album's bass end. Dokaka, a Japanese-born beatboxer, lets loose rapid-fire noises in the middle range. You could also now hear Mike Patton growling incisively beneath the opening line of "Where Is the Line." "Yeah, now it's got some balls," Björk said when Patton's voice butted in.

"Who Is It" had become a trouble spot. Björk's idea of having the grand, brash anthem emerge from a mist of Icelandic choral harmony wasn't panning out. The "long version" of the song sat uncomfortably with the music around it. The minor-key radiance of "Vökuró" was sufficient to anchor the album in the Nordic idea. Instead, "Who Is It" wound down with what sounds like tones of a wheezy old organ: it's actually a sample of Björk's voice played on a keyboard. The Afro-Brazilian drummers also fell to the wayside, hopefully to see the light of day on one of Björk's archival collections, although you can still hear a ghost of their rhythms in the beatboxing on "Mouth's Cradle." There was even talk of cutting the track "Desired Constellation," on the ground that its softly chiming electronic production, by the Frenchman Olivier Alary, was too *Vespertine*-like in mood. "It doesn't fit into the concept," Björk said. "But you cannot always be locked into the concept. You have to kick your way out of it sometimes." The fact that everyone who heard it went into a trance swayed Björk toward including it after all.

On "Mouth's Cradle," Björk was unhappy with the recorded quality of the Icelandic singers. "The chorus should be more in the middle of the mix, not in the background," she told Spike. "More earthy, more scruffy." She drew three diagrams to illustrate what she wanted. The first one was a box with a line straight across the middle. "This is the convention," she said. "Voices this much, beats this much. Now here"—she drew a second diagram, with a thin band labeled "Björk" at the bottom—"this is *Vespertine*, where I was whispering, not taking up too much space in the mix. Finally"—she made a box with a broad ellipse in the middle—"this is what we want now. The voices taking the place of guitars, drums, et cetera." Spike studied the diagram with a baffled look. It was cogent in itself, but he seemed unsure how to convert it into sound. "I'm just a little worried," she added. "I'm not trying to be negative. The one thing I'm not so crazy about . . ."

Recordings were mobilized to back up her diagram. Björk mentioned Ariel Ramírez's *Misa Criolla*, an Andean folk-song setting of the Mass, in which the chorus has a raw, penetrating edge. Mark Bell downloaded the music from the Internet, but in that version the chorus sounded tame. Eventually, someone found the original recording at Björk's flat. This was played and discussed. Björk brought her iBook laptop into the studio in order to play other music files from her MP3 library. A whirlwind tour of modern and ancient music followed: a track or two from Meredith Monk's *Dolmen Music*; the Hamrahlid Choir singing the doleful Christmas carol "Maríukvæði"; the veteran avant-garde vocalist Joan La Barbara and the former Soft Machine drummer Robert Wyatt singing pieces by John Cage. The really dizzying moment came when Björk followed thirty seconds of Justin Timberlake singing "Rock Your Body" with thirty seconds of Stockhausen's *Stimmung*.

"It's very simple," Björk said. "A little Justin, a little Karlheinz. But not world music. And not pop, and not avant-garde, and not classical, and not church music. Don't you see? Kind of—" She gave out a soft roar, with her hand held out in a stylized gesture.

"Slavic?" Spike asked.

"Exactly," Björk said. "'Slavic' is the word. But wi' a li'l bit of David Beckham." David Beckham's allegedly troubled marriage to Victoria (Posh Spice) Beckham was all over the British tabloids at the time, and Björk professed to find the story riveting.

"Right," Spike said, light dawning in his face. "I think I'm getting the vibe. All these things have a really natural sound in the vocal. A single voice in a natural room, like an old hall or a cathedral."

"No church!" Björk shouted.

"Right, no church," Spike said. He turned to one of his assistants and said, "Order me a TC 6000." The TC 6000, Valgeir told me, is a reverb device that allowed Spike to add spatial effects to the voices without upsetting the balance.

Björk played the entire exchange for laughs, but, as usual, she was driving at something serious and specific. Afterward, she talked more about her "Slavic" idea. "I use words like 'pagan' sometimes," she said. "But these are things I say just to get something across, not because I have a picture in my head. But there is a feeling. A feeling I carry around in me, and that I really want to put at the center of this album. Kind of like folk music, but without any folk attached."

She asked me for a definition of the word "iconoclastic." Remembering lessons from Greek Orthodox Sunday school, I said that it was a radical

movement within the Church to end the use of icons, any visual represen-
tation of Jesus. Björk looked a little disappointed. "OK," she said. "Someone told me it meant not only smashing icons but also forming new ones
to take their place. Making your own icons to replace the old."

There were a few more major changes in the weeks to come. Björk
recorded a throaty song called "Submarine," with Robert Wyatt, at his
home. She worked out a piano-vocal version of "Oceania," the Olympic song,
with the young New York–based composer Nico Muhly; then she decided
once again to stick with the concept and use electronically tweaked choral
voices. There was some last-minute polishing by Mark Bell. But, for the
most part, *Medúlla* was complete, and Björk seemed cautiously elated
with her work.

On the last night I was in London, Matthew Barney came to the studio. He sat down with headphones to hear what Björk had done. Isadora,
their daughter, played with wooden blocks representing the animals of
Noah's Ark. Mark Bell cranked up music on the speakers, to compete
against the sound of a hard spring rain drumming on the roof. Björk began
dancing slowly around the room with her child in her arms. "The pleasure
is all mine," the composer sang, "to finally let go."

9

SYMPHONY OF MILLIONS

CLASSICAL MUSIC IN CHINA

In the spring of 2008, Chen Qigang, a Chinese composer who was supervising the music program for the opening ceremony of the Beijing Olympics, received a National Spirit Achievers Award at a press event in Beijing. He was one of ten artists and businesspeople to receive the prize, which came courtesy of the Chinese magazine *Life* and of Mercedes-AMG, the high-performance-vehicle division of Mercedes-Benz. The award ceremony, typical of modern China in its mixture of nationalist bombast, materialist excess, and cultural bizarrerie, took place in the 798 art zone—a cavernous factory complex that has been converted into exhibition space. Four AMG vehicles were on display, surrounded by models clad in silver-lamé outfits, in presumably inadvertent homage to *Goldfinger*. Projected on the walls and the ceiling of the factory were the words "Will," "Power," and "Dream," with Chinese characters to match. "We believe that Mercedes-AMG will infuse powerful new vigor into China's national car culture," Klaus Maier, the head of Mercedes-Benz China, said. Chen stood to one side, a quizzical expression on his face. Before the ceremony began, he had said to me, "I have no idea what is happening."

While classical musicians around the world yearn for a glint of media attention, their counterparts in China have no trouble drawing the spotlight. Western classical music is big business, or, at least, official business. Chen Qigang, a mild-mannered man whose works elegantly synthesize Western-modernist and traditional Chinese elements, had been reminded of this the previous year, when he moved from Paris, where he had resided since 1984, back to Beijing, where he had lived during the Cultural Revolution. In a conversation at his Beijing apartment, he recalled the world of his youth as a repressive, barbaric place, where classical music was forbidden. Then, in Paris, he had grown accustomed to a culture in which the same small cohort of connoisseurs attended new-music concerts night after night. On a visit to Beijing in 2007, Chen was summoned to meet the film director Zhang Yimou, who made *Hero* and *House of Flying Daggers*, and who was in charge of the Olympic ceremonies. Zhang inquired if Chen had any "free time" in 2008. The next day, the composer met with Olympic officials, who asked him to cancel future plans. Chen agreed, and accepted an offer to run the music program, not only because he felt official pressure but because he relished the challenge of directing a retinue of fifty composers, from both classical and popular genres, to entertain a global audience. In America, he noted, no classical composer would be given such a task.

"For the past fifteen or twenty years, classical music has been very à la mode in China," Chen told me, in French. "The halls are full. There are many students. There might also be some difficulties. But there is a very powerful phenomenon at work in the education system. When I visited my old primary school, I found that, out of a class of forty students, thirty-six were studying piano. This points to the future."

Western musicians, administrators, and critics who visit China have lately come away murmuring observations along the lines of "classical music is exploding" and "the future of classical music lies in China." Between thirty million and a hundred million children are said to be learning piano, violin, or both, depending on which source you consult. When the New York Philharmonic came to Beijing in February 2008, the Associated Press offered this summary of a press conference given by Lorin Maazel: "Facing dwindling popularity in the West, classical music could find its savior among China's large population that is increasingly interested in other cultures, the music director of the New York Philharmonic said."

After a visit to Beijing, I had some doubts about China's putative lock on the musical future. Concert halls may be full and conservatories mobbed, but classical music is hobbled by commercial and political pressures. The creative climate, with its system of punishments and rewards, still resembles that of the late-period Soviet Union, which heavily influenced the development of China's musical institutions. At the same time, the sonic landscape of Beijing is as chaotically rich as that of any Western city: nights of experimental fare, indie-rock shows soaked in hipster attitude, pop idols cavorting on HD monitors in malls, retirees singing Peking opera in parks. In the *Li Chi*, or *Book of Rites*, it is written, "The music of a well-ruled state is peaceful and joyous . . . that of a country in confusion is full of resentment . . . and that of a dying country is mournful and pensive." All three kinds of music, together with others that might well have confounded Confucian scholars, intersect in the People's Republic.

The most outwardly impressive symbol of China's musical ambition is the National Center for the Performing Arts, a colossal, low-slung, titanium-clad dome west of Tiananmen Square. Representations of the well-ruled state surround it: the Great Hall of the People is next door, and Zhongnanhai, the Party-leadership compound, lies across the avenue. An inscription above the center's entrance bears the signature of Jiang Zemin, who was China's president from 1993 to 2003, and who made a show of admiring classical music. (After the death of Deng Xiaoping, Jiang told the press that he had consoled himself by listening to Mozart's Requiem through the night.) The president of the center, which Beijingers call the Egg, is a local potentate named Chen Ping, who has developed deluxe shopping malls in the eastern part of the city. The complex was originally scheduled to open in 2004, but Paul Andreu, the architect, had to reevaluate the design after another of his projects, a terminal at Charles de Gaulle International Airport, partially collapsed. When the building finally opened, at the end of 2007, Chen Ping described it as a "concrete example of China's rising soft power and comprehensive national strength."

As architecture, the building may live up to its pompous billing, but, as a place for music, the Egg is problematic. There are two main halls: the opera house, which seats 2,400, and the concert hall, which seats 2,000. The concert hall has reasonably clear acoustics but lacks warmth. In the top gallery of the opera house, where the sound should be best, the orchestra comes across as tinny and colorless. There is little evidence that musical considerations played a role in the design. No serious acoustician would have approved the halls' pockets of extra space, where sound bounces around and gets lost.

The performances themselves suffered in comparison with what you hear on even a so-so night in New York, London, Paris, or Berlin. They showed the inevitable limitations of a classical culture that is less than a

century old and has been periodically roiled by political upheaval. China's
music-education system may yield notable soloists, but it has yet to develop the breadth of talent and the collaborative mentality that make for
great orchestras. Strings are generally polished; winds and brass threaten
to puncture the ears. On my first visit to the Egg, I saw a production of
Turandot featuring the orchestra and the chorus of the Shanghai Opera
House. The trumpets let out a piercing flubbed note in the first bar, and
many misadventures followed; at times, it sounded as though a civic orchestra had been augmented by members of a college marching band. Yet
the raucousness was oddly compelling. The idea of the production was
to reclaim Puccini's Italianized, Romanticized fantasy of imperial China;
Chen Xinyi, the director, emulated the values of traditional Chinese theater, and the composer Hao Weiya supplied a fluid if somewhat watery
ending for the opera, which Puccini left unfinished at his death. In that
sense, the rawness of the sound added to the effect, though it wasn't an
experience I'd want to repeat.

Near-capacity crowds attended *Turandot* and other events I saw at the
Egg. This was noteworthy, considering the cost of the tickets; for a seat in
the uppermost gallery of the opera house, I paid 480 yuan—about seventy
dollars. That price is considerably higher than for an equivalent seat at the
Metropolitan Opera, and vertiginously high when you consider that a low-
level white-collar worker at a Chinese firm earns only about four hundred
dollars a month. But not everyone has to pay to get in. Large blocks of
tickets are set aside for politicians, diplomats, CEOs, and corporate clients;
some fail to show up, resulting in rows of empty seats at allegedly sold-out
events, and others make an early exit to attend another function or to escape boredom. One Beijing composer told me scornfully that much of the
audience was "scouting real estate," and that it would disappear once its
curiosity had been satisfied.

It was encouraging, however, to see so many young people in the
house—many more than you see in most American concert halls or opera
houses. At a performance by the China National Symphony Orchestra,
under the direction of Michel Plasson, I watched as a cluster of teenagers,
outfitted with bejeweled BlackBerrys, A.P.C. jeans, and other tokens of
new wealth, grew excited by the orchestra's noisily energetic rendition of
Berlioz's *Symphonie Fantastique*, leaving aside their text-messaging to applaud each movement. In general, listeners behaved more informally than

I was used to: some older people, following the looser etiquette of Peking opera, talked among themselves, pointed at the stage, or read newspapers. The hubbub was distracting at times—ushers largely failed to prevent the taking of pictures and videos—but it was refreshing in comparison with the self-conscious solemnity that encroaches on Western concert halls. The music wasn't taken for granted; Berlioz still had shock value.

The youthfulness of the audience at the Egg reflects the real wonder of the Chinese classical scene: the staggering number of people who are currently studying music, whether in schools or with private tutors. The Sichuan Conservatory, in Chengdu, is said to have more than ten thousand students; Juilliard, by contrast, has eight hundred. An American high-school student who practices piano several hours a day is apt to be pegged something of a freak; in China, such a routine is commonplace.

The violist Qi Yue, a young professor at Renmin University, explained to me the various factors that are driving the surge in music lessons. For one thing, students who demonstrate musical gifts can get away with scoring fewer points on the *gaokao*, China's college-admissions test, not unlike athletes in the United States. Also, the conservatory system has a history of fostering pop stars, who prompt legions of imitators. Cui Jian, the founder of Chinese rock, played trumpet in the Beijing Symphony in the 1980s before embarking on a pop career. The Sichuan Conservatory produced the pop singer Li Yuchun, who, in 2005, entered as a contestant on *Super Girl*, a Chinese version of *American Idol*, and won the competition with a hip-hop-flavored, gender-bending style. (With hundreds of millions of votes cast in the form of text messages, *Super Girl* has been called China's largest democratic election. Perhaps for this reason, the show was canceled after the 2006 season.)

Qi took me on a tour of the Central Conservatory, China's flagship music school, in the company of his former teacher, the violist Wing Ho. Familiar airs wafted out of the practice rooms—Chopin from the pianists, Rossini from the singers, Tchaikovsky from the violinists. When I looked in on a composition class, though, it turned out to be a lesson in pop-music arranging. A shaggy-haired, T-shirt-clad student named Zhang Tianye was leaning over a computer terminal, working on a mix of drums, guitar, piano, and bass. When I asked him what music he likes, he said he listened "mostly to pop, sometimes classical." Another student, Qu Dawei, sat down at the piano to execute a half-Romantic, half-jazzy solo somewhat in the manner of Gershwin. In other words, attending a conservatory in China doesn't automatically equate with interest in classical music. Yet the intermingling of genres may have the healthy effect of integrating European tradition into the wider culture.

Like most serious Chinese musicians, Qi Yue politely rejected the notion of China as a classical paradise, although he predicted that it would become a major market in twenty or thirty years. Long Yu, China's most prominent conductor, felt much the same way. "On the outside, newspapers are saying that China is the largest musical country in the world, or that millions of kids are learning piano," he told me. "I'm not that optimistic. The thing is, I do my best to serve the people who really need fine arts and classical music. I do not have the duty to make everyone like it." A German-trained musician who operates with a kind of bulldozer charm, Long Yu directs the Beijing Music Festival, has built the China Philharmonic into China's finest orchestra, and holds posts in Guangzhou and Shanghai. To maintain political connections, he serves on the Chinese People's Political Consultative Conference. Yet he keeps a certain distance from the notion of classical music as "official culture"; he has sought funding from private sources and tried to keep ticket prices down. Notably, he had yet to appear at the Egg.

For a musician on Long Yu's level, politics is unavoidable. Since the Tiananmen Square protests of 1989, the Party has discouraged dissent not just by clamping down on rebellious voices but by handsomely rewarding those who play it safe. Richard Kraus, in his book *The Party and the Arty in China*, writes, "By 1992, the Party had given up trying to purge all dissident voices and opted instead for the strategy of urging all arts organizations to strive to earn more money." Those who work within the system may be expected to reach a stage where they can win prizes, obtain sinecures, hold illustrious posts, and be well paid for teaching. Artists end up censoring themselves—a habit ingrained in Chinese history. Behind the industrious façade is a fair degree of political anxiety. Reviews often read like press releases; indeed, I was told that concert organizations routinely pay journalists to provide favorable coverage. Critics feel pressure to deliver positive judgments, and, if they don't, they may be reprimanded or hounded by colleagues. One critic I talked to got fed up and quit writing about music altogether.

"If you are not free yourself, how can you interpret music freely?" the former music critic told me. We met in the lobby of the Grand Hyatt Beijing, above Oriental Plaza, the gaudiest of Chen Ping's malls. Businesspeople negotiated deals at neighboring tables while Norah Jones cooed on the speakers. "It's very sad," the critic went on. "Freedom is the biggest thing and it affects everything. People are scared, and they act in a way that scares others. I'm not just talking about music; I'm talking about many professions. There is a lot more to say, and sometimes I don't know where to begin. Many things are stuck in my head."

Western music formally arrived in China in 1601, when the Jesuit missionary Matteo Ricci presented a clavichord to Wanli, the longest-ruling of the Ming emperors. As Sheila Melvin and Jindong Cai relate, in their absorbing book *Rhapsody in Red: How Western Classical Music Became Chinese*, the emperor's eunuchs experimented with the instrument for a little while and then set it aside. It stayed undisturbed in a box for several decades, until Chongzhen, the last of the Ming rulers, discovered it and sought out a German Jesuit priest to explain its workings. Of succeeding emperors, Kangxi and Qianlong showed the most enthusiasm for Western music; the latter, who ruled China for the better part of the eighteenth century, at one point assembled a full-scale chamber orchestra, with the eunuchs dressed in European suits and wigs.

Only in the nineteenth century did Western music really spread beyond the walls of the imperial palaces, often in the form of military and municipal bands. The first true orchestra was the Shanghai Municipal Orchestra (later the Shanghai Symphony), which began playing in 1919, under the direction of an expatriate Italian virtuoso named Mario Paci. At first, the orchestra had only foreign players and stayed within the bounds of Shanghai's colonial settlements, but Paci eventually reached out to the Chinese population. In 1927, Xiao Youmei, a German-trained pianist and composer, founded the Shanghai Conservatory, the first Western-style music school on Chinese soil. The growth of the Shanghai music scene profited from a lively community of adventurers, exiles, and, with the rise of Nazism, German-Jewish refugees; on the faculty of the Shanghai Conservatory were associates of Schoenberg and Berg.

Mao Zedong, on assuming power, in 1949, initially encouraged the imported music, although he kept it within strict ideological bounds. In the library of the Central Conservatory, I looked at back issues of *People's Music*, a house journal whose first issue appeared in 1950, the year that the conservatory was founded. There were lyrics for songs called "We Are Busy Producing" and "The Little Song of Handing In Your Grains." Each article, my companions pointed out, began with an automatic spasm of revolutionary rhetoric: "Our musical workers must develop people's musical activities with limitless zeal." Nonetheless, composers made fitful attempts to modernize their art, especially during the Hundred Flowers period, when Mao permitted them to "apply appropriate foreign principles and use foreign musical instruments."

The onset of the Cultural Revolution, in 1966, effectively shut down the Central Conservatory. Western classical music was pushed out, along with most of the native traditions from the imperial era. To replace the extant repertory, Jiang Qing, otherwise known as Madame Mao, commissioned a group of eight "model" scores on revolutionary topics. The most famous of these was the ballet *Red Detachment of Women*, which has a kitschily charming score in a light-classical vein, with an array of native Chinese sounds. Composers had to work within the often peculiar stylistic boundaries that Jiang Qing set up; on one occasion, she extolled Aaron Copland's film score for *The Red Pony*, and another time she outlawed the tuba.

The operatic bass Hao Jiang Tian, who, while I was in Beijing, was singing the role of Timur in *Turandot*, described to me what it was like to study music amid the insanity of the Cultural Revolution. His first musical performances were as an accordionist and singer in the Mao Zedong Thought Propaganda Team of the Beijing Boiler Factory. (He relates these experiences in an engaging memoir, *Along the Roaring River*.) Tian's father and mother worked for the People's Liberation Army Zhongzheng Song and Dance Ensemble, as conductor and composer, respectively, but they came under suspicion and eventually had to leave Beijing. One day, Tian's father said that the family had to get rid of its record collection. With a shudder, Tian remembers the childish glee that he felt as he smashed the albums.

With the winding down of the Cultural Revolution, in the early seventies, Western music again crept into Chinese life. When Henry Kissinger first visited China, in 1971, in advance of Richard Nixon's history-making tour, Zhou Enlai suggested that the Central Philharmonic—the orchestra now known as the China National Symphony—play a work by Beethoven in honor of Kissinger's German heritage. Jiang Qing and her comrades proceeded to review Beethoven's symphonies for ideological errors. The *Eroica* was rejected because of its association with the imperialist figure of Napoleon; the Fifth fell short because it was said to be fatalistic. The Sixth Symphony, with its wholesome evocations of birds and babbling brooks, passed muster. When the Philadelphia Orchestra toured China in 1973, it originally planned to play the Fifth, but after Jiang Qing's views were made known the orchestra had to scramble to find parts for the Sixth.

In the wake of Mao's death and the fall of Jiang Qing, classical musicians emerged from hiding. When the Central Conservatory reopened, in 1978, eighteen thousand people applied for a hundred places. Present in that first class was a group of composers who define contemporary Chinese music today: Tan Dun, Chen Yi, Zhou Long, Chen Qigang, and Guo Wenjing. Under the guidance of various visiting mentors—among them the expatriate modernist Chou Wen-chung, who had gone to America in 1946 and later taken a position at Columbia University—these composers Westernized themselves at high speed, consuming serialism, chance procedures, and other novelties. In so doing, they came up with fresh and vital combinations of sounds, especially when they added to the mix the clear-cut melodies and jangling timbres of traditional Chinese music. Almost all the students had been forced to perform manual labor or study folk music in the countryside during the Cultural Revolution, and they arrived at the school with a strong grasp of Chinese heritage.

A diaspora followed. Chen Qigang went to Paris to study with Messiaen. Tan Dun, Chen Yi, and Zhou Long traveled to New York to work with Chou Wen-chung; all three took up residence in the city. Tan quickly gravitated to New York's downtown scene, particularly to the world of John Cage. By combining Cage's chance processes and natural noises with plush Romantic melodies, Tan concocted a kind of crowd-pleasing avant-gardism. In 2008, at the Egg, he demonstrated that sensibility with a concert of "Organic Music," with the China Youth Symphony; in *Paper Concerto* and *Water Concerto*, the Japanese percussionist Haruka Fujii crinkled paper and swished water in amplified bowls and other receptacles. In a further feat of packaging, Tan relates this music to shamanistic rituals of Hunan province, where he grew up. With such deft gestures of fusion, Tan has satisfied a Western craving for authentic-seeming, folklore-based music.

Many of the '78 composers have worked to reconcile avant-garde and populist values. "In the West, our situation as composers is very sad," Chen Qigang told me. "In the 1950s, we lost command of the field, not just because popular composers took over but because we ceded the terrain. We 'developed' to the point where we no longer knew anything about the art of writing melody. We had a kind of nonexistence in musical life." Nodding to his Olympics experience, he added, "Now I understand how hard it is to compose a cheery little song." No composer has embraced that challenge as eagerly as Tan Dun, whose submission to the Olympic ceremony was a radically bathetic pop ballad titled "One World, One Dream." Conceived in league with the songwriter and producer David Foster, Tan's song has been recorded by Andrea Bocelli, the platinum-selling crossover tenor, and Zhang Liangying, another competitor from the 2005 *Super Girl* contest. "You are me and I am you," they sing together, in English. Unfortunately, they don't go on to say, "I am the walrus."

After spending several days in the monumental environs of Tiananmen Square, I was relieved to receive an invitation to brunch at the home of Hao Jiang Tian, the singer who smashed his family's records, and his wife, the geneticist and pianist Martha Liao. They live in a Swiss-designed building with a superior ventilation system, which keeps Beijing's acrid air at bay. Tian and Liao also invited Guo Wenjing, who, of the composers of the 1978 generation, is the one least known in the West, principally because he never studied abroad. In some ways, he is the most interesting of all, because he has achieved a substantial degree of independence within the sometimes stifling atmosphere of Chinese music. There is a whiff of danger in his work.

Guo makes an unassuming first impression. He looks like a perpetual graduate student, his squarish face set off by heavy-rimmed glasses and a serrated edge of jet-black hair. But a certain wildness in his personality soon emerges. He comes from Chongqing, in Sichuan province. His conversation has a slightly percussive edge, accentuated with sweeping gestures and abrupt exclamations.

At the core of Guo's work is an encyclopedic knowledge of Chinese traditional music. In the 1980s, he collected folk songs in the mountains around the upper Yangtze River. His hero was Béla Bartók, who showed how a composer could immerse himself in folk materials while retaining a potent individual personality. Guo was also drawn to Dmitri Shostakovich, the master of the Soviet symphony; Guo's mature works, with their martial rhythms, flashes of biting wit, and explosive climaxes, have much in common with Shostakovich's, even if the musical material is drastically different. The eternally ambiguous Shostakovich might also have been a model for Guo while he traversed treacherous political terrain; although there are "official" pieces in Guo's catalogue, such as an overture celebrating the reabsorption of Hong Kong into China, he has also set to music the poetry of Xi Chuan, a bold and enigmatic writer who had ties to the 1989 student protests.

For a time, Guo chaired the composition department at the Central Conservatory. He stepped down because, he said curtly, "I didn't like it. I'm not good at multitasking." A few nights before, I had heard a choral symphony by Tang Jianping, the conservatory's current composition chair. With the help of members of the Inner Mongolian Song and Dance Ensemble, the symphony told of the life and times of Genghis Khan. It strongly resembled the pseudo-folkloristic pieces that Soviet composers dutifully produced in honor of non-Russian nationalities. This is the kind of assignment that Guo is now generally able to avoid. He still teaches, although he is discouraged by the tendency among younger Chinese composers to copy European trends in order to establish their academic bona fides. "Say there is a young composer who writes in the style of one of Jiang Qing's revolutionary operas," he said. "Today, others would criticize him because he does not sound like Luciano Berio. But I would say, 'Look, he had the guts to do something that everyone criticizes him for. There must be something good about him.'"

In fact, Guo is carrying on, with greater subtlety, a musical idea that dominated the revolutionary years: melding Western technique with Chinese tradition. Theater pieces such as *Wolf Cub Village* and *Poet Li Bai*, and symphonic pieces like *Chou Kong Shan* (*Sorrowful, Desolate Mountain*) and *Suspended Ancient Coffins on the Cliffs in Sichuan*, confront listeners with gritty, grinding sonorities, battering assaults of percussion, exuberant bashings and roarings of gongs, and, in the operas, extreme vocal techniques representing extreme psychological states. If Guo strays at times on the wrong side of the divide between ritual grandeur and monotony, he invariably has a strong impact. Some lines from *Poet Li Bai*, which chronicles one of the great free spirits of Taoism, seem to sum him up: "Wild and free / Like my poetry / Would I stoop before men of power, / And deny myself a pleasant hour?"

At brunch, Guo was in a sunny mood, but at one point I managed to annoy him. Speaking of the music of Chen Qigang, I said that its refined, free-floating timbres suggested an affinity between modern Chinese composition and the sound-world of Debussy and Messiaen. Guo swept his arms wide, nearly upsetting the tableware, and proclaimed, "This view shows that foreigners don't understand China. Music here has nothing to do with France. Opposite direction. Different taste." Then he smiled, his argument made. He held up two stubby fingers in the air, as if about to give a blessing. "I am anti-fashion. I look down on the trend. I want to escape the whole question of sounding like the West or sounding like the East. Non-European composers always have to have their cultural identity, their symbols. In Germany or France, they have real freedom. They absolutely have the freedom to write what they want. Of course"—his eyes lit up—"if they are so free, why do they end up sounding the same?"

If Guo Wenjing is a composer with one foot in the official world and one foot outside, the sound artist, critic, and impresario Yan Jun lives an almost entirely independent existence. "It is very boring, very dangerous to life, dangerous to young people's heart and mind," Yan said of the academic and professional music worlds. "You go to school, you lose your soul. You learn how to join the official system. It's not about music." Although avant-gardists in every major city take a similar line, it has an extra edge coming from an artist in China. Thanks to the Internet, such musicians are less isolated than they were in the eighties and nineties, when the idea of a Chinese avant-garde was still far-fetched. Well before I met Yan Jun, I had listened to a couple of hours of his music on his various websites and blogs.

Yan Jun, who was born in Langzhou in 1973, is the genial, laid-back leader of Beijing's modestly scaled but thriving experimental-music scene. Specializing in creating electronic soundscapes from the noises and voices of the city, he releases recordings on two labels and presents music once a week at a bar called 2 Kolegas, on the grounds of a drive-in movie theater. The night I went there, the bill included Li Zenghui, a twenty-four-year-old saxophonist in a bebop getup, who delivered a breathy, growling solo, and a Japanese-Korean duo called 10, whose female lead singer alternately sang and shrieked into a microphone while sporting oversized heart-shaped sunglasses.

In his mission to cultivate a "downtown" scene comparable to New York's or Berlin's, Yan has been almost too successful. If the bar and everyone in it had been plopped down in Brooklyn, nothing would have seemed amiss. Out of a crowd of some twenty people, fewer than half were Chinese. Another night, I went to see a flock of indie-rock bands at the alternative club D-22, and found myself engulfed by moshing mobs of American college kids on their semester abroad. Yet the expatriate presence is having a dynamic effect on native musicians. The city is still cheap by Western standards, and, like Berlin after the fall of the Wall, it has become a mecca for artists in search of low rent and new audiences. The expat community includes the young American composer Eli Marshall, who leads the Beijing New Music Ensemble, and Michael Pettis, a former Wall Street investment banker, who founded D-22 in 2006.

The pride of Beijing's underground—No Beijing, Yan Jun calls it—is an indie-rock wunderkind named Zhang Shouwang, who also goes by the name Jeffray Zhang. Pettis saw him one day in the Houhai district wearing a Velvet Underground T-shirt and struck up a conversation. Zhang turned out to be a fast-fingered guitarist with a wide-open musical mind. Pettis gave Zhang a vintage Gibson SG electric guitar and promoted his bands and side projects, which include Carsick Cars, a locally popular group that has opened for Sonic Youth. The first night I went to D-22, Zhang, who was then twenty-two, performed a solo piece that featured minimalist patterns over steady drones, moving purposefully from clean, simple harmonies into duskier, more chromatic regions. In time-honored Led Zeppelin fashion, Zhang played the guitar strings with a violin bow, to which he diligently applied rosin beforehand.

Afterward, in hesitant but idiomatic English, Zhang spoke to me about his New York–centric interests, which range from alternative rock to minimalist composers like Steve Reich, Philip Glass, and Glenn Branca. In 2006, he went to New York to participate in a recording of Branca's *Hallucination City*, the electric-guitar symphony that played at Disney Hall at around the same time. Zhang was working on a piece for Marshall's Beijing New Music Ensemble. "I've never composed before, so it's going

slowly," Zhang said, sipping a beer at a back table in D-22. He'd looked at
an orchestration manual for clues on how to write for the instruments,
but, he said, the book told him only how to pass a test. Eventually, he
came up with *Xizhimen Traffic Lights*, a fluent, mellow study in slowly changing patterns, in the spirit of Reich.

Zhang's premiere took place after I left Beijing, but I later heard the
piece on the website of the BBC, which underwrote the concert. I also
checked Yan Jun's blog to find what sounds he had lately collected, and
listened to an audio portrait of Tiananmen Square during a moment of
silence in honor of victims of the Sichuan earthquake of May 2008. A
voice is heard saying on a loudspeaker, "It is now two twenty-eight p.m.,
Beijing time. All please stand to attention facing the flag for three minutes
of silence." This being Beijing, the silence was loud. Thousands of drivers
leaned on their horns to create a vast, dreamily dissonant harmony, a fundamental chord of the city.

The curious thing about the Chinese enthusiasm for Western classical
music is that the People's Republic, with its far-flung provinces and myriad ethnic groups, possesses a store of musical traditions that rival the
proudest products of Europe and go back much deeper in time. Holding
to core principles in the face of change, traditional Chinese music is more
"classical" than anything in the West.

In many of Beijing's public spaces, you see amateurs playing native
instruments, especially the dizi, or bamboo flute, and the erhu, or two-
stringed fiddle. They perform mostly for their own pleasure, not for money.
But it's surprisingly difficult to find professional performances in pure
classical style. In concert halls, the instruments are often deposited, as
a sonic spice, into Western-style arrangements, as in the Genghis Khan
symphony I heard at the Egg. Institutionalized "Chinese orchestras" imitate the layout of Western ensembles. Music intended for small spaces
has been beefed up, amplified, and transformed into spectacles suitable
for national television. A colleague reports that an alleged evening of authentic Chinese music in Shanghai ended with a chunk of Mahler's Second Symphony. Those who remain devoted to the ancient traditions often
struggle to show their relevance in the age of *Super Girl*. Some master
instrumentalists teach at the conservatories but seldom play in public.

Even Peking opera, which attracts sizable crowds, feels the pressure. When, in early 2008, the Ministry of Education introduced a new program to foster interest in Peking opera among the young, a poll found that more than 50 percent opposed the initiative as a waste of resources.

The project of revitalizing Chinese tradition has fallen to younger artists like Wu Na, who wields what some consider the aristocrat of instruments: the guqin, or seven-stringed zither. It is more than three thousand years old, and has a repertory that reaches back to the first millennium. Philosophers and poets from Confucius to Li Bai prided themselves on learning it. In the modern era, the guqin has become somewhat esoteric, though interest is growing again. With the support of an elderly Taiwanese couple, Wu runs a guqin school at a teahouse in Zhongshan Park, in Beijing. When I stopped by, two college students were seated at their instruments, imitating their instructor's moves. Wu herself wasn't there; she was in New York, on a fellowship from the Asian Cultural Council. After I returned home, I visited her at her temporary apartment, in Chelsea. When I walked in, she was listening to a recording of Liu Shaochun, one of the players who helped to preserve guqin tradition through the tumult of the revolution. It is music of intimate address and subtle power that is able to suggest immense spaces; skittering figures and arching melodies give way to sustained, slowly decaying tones and long, meditative pauses.

"Liu Shaochun came from a wealthy family," Wu told me. "He grew up playing guqin, practicing calligraphy, writing poetry." Then the empire fell. "In the end, he had only his guqin. But he was still very powerful. He taught the 'give up'—you can give up everything and become very free."

Despite her fastidious attention to guqin technique, Wu also loves avant-garde music and jazz. She is friends with Yan Jun and goes almost every week to 2 Kolegas. There is a vague likeness between the art of guqin and Western experimental music: the scores indicate tunings, fingerings, and articulations but fail to specify rhythms, resulting in markedly different interpretations by performers of competing schools. Wu plays in the "old times" style, as she calls it, but she has also explored a kind of cool, modal jazz approach; either way, she shows profound sensitivity to her instrument.

Wu Na spoke of developing a cross-cultural exchange that would bring traditional Chinese masters to New York and jazz and blues musicians to Beijing. She noted that audiences in Beijing have little grasp of African-

American music in its classic, early-twentieth-century forms. And I realized that, while I had gone around Beijing looking for "authentic" Chinese music, she had been doing the same in New York, searching, with little success, for old-time jazz and blues.

On a day when the center of Beijing was overrun by Olympic hullabaloo—in front of the Gate of Heavenly Peace, President Hu Jintao was lighting the Olympic torch, to the accompaniment of Hollywoodish fanfares—I went for a walk in the august sprawl of the Temple of Heaven, and saw a sign pointing to the "Divine Music Administration." No such place was listed in my guidebook, but I followed the arrows all the same. After going around in circles for a while, I came upon a series of buildings where court musicians of the Ming dynasty once rehearsed. The buildings had recently been renovated, most of the rooms filled with exhibitions on Chinese musical history. One could bang replicas of ancient bronze bells and strum on a guqin. A young attendant was standing by. When I asked a question, she proceeded to play the guqin with expert grace. She seemed grateful for the attention; in the past hour, I had been the museum's only visitor.

Then I heard music—not recorded music but the real thing, a slow, grand, impeccably austere procession of sonorities. It emanated from behind the closed doors of a hall in the center of the complex. I cracked open the door, but an attendant shooed me away. "Not allowed," she said. I walked over to the box office and asked if a public performance was scheduled; the man behind the counter shook his head vigorously and said, "No music." Just when I was preparing to give up, I saw a van approaching. Twenty or so well-dressed Chinese tourists piled out. Guessing that they were headed into the hall, I slipped into their midst, and made it through the doors.

A half-hour performance ensued, with a full complement of Chinese instruments, and players dressed in vivid courtly garb. It was a sound at once rigid and brilliant, an eruption of color within a strict frame. It was the most memorable musical experience of my trip. At the time, I didn't quite know what I was hearing, but I later surmised that I had witnessed a re-creation of *zhonghe shaoyue*, the music that resounded at the temple while the emperor made sacrifices to heaven. Confucius, in the Analects, calls it *yayue*—"elegant music"—and laments that the people are discarding it in favor of vernacular tunes. Now it is a ghost in a phantom museum.

I walked for another hour in the temple park, thrilled to have had an aural glimpse of what I took to be the true music of China. A little later, I heard a plaintive melody coming from an unseen bamboo flute, and went in search of its source, hoping for another revelation. After making my way through a maze of pine trees, I found a man of great age and haunted visage, playing the theme from *The Godfather*.

10

SONG OF THE EARTH

THE ARCTIC SOUND OF JOHN LUTHER ADAMS

When I took a trip to the Alaskan interior several years ago, I didn't get to see the aurora borealis, but I did manage to hear it. At the Museum of the North, on the grounds of the University of Alaska in Fairbanks, the composer John Luther Adams has created a sound-and-light installation called *The Place Where You Go to Listen*—a kind of infinite musical work that is controlled by natural events occurring in real time. The title refers to Naalagiagvik, a place on the coast of the Arctic Ocean where, according to legend, a spiritually attuned Inupiaq woman went to hear the voices of birds, whales, and unseen things around her. In keeping with that idea, the mechanism of *The Place* translates raw data into music: information from seismological, meteorological, and geomagnetic stations in various parts of Alaska is fed into a computer and transformed into a luminous field of electronic sound.

The Place occupies a small white-walled room on the museum's second floor. You sit on a bench before five glass panels, which change color according to the time of day and the season. What you notice first is a dense, organlike sonority, which Adams has named the Day Choir. Its notes follow the contour of the natural harmonic series—the rainbow of overtones that emanate from a vibrating string—and have the brightness of music in a major key. In overcast weather, the harmonies are relatively narrow in range; when the sun comes out, they stretch across four octaves. After the sun goes down, a moodier set of chords, the Night Choir, moves to the forefront. The moon is audible as a narrow sliver of noise. Pulsating patterns in the bass, which Adams calls Earth Drums, are activated by small earthquakes and other seismic events around Alaska. And shimmering sounds in the highest registers—the Aurora Bells—are tied to the fluctuations in the magnetic field that cause the Northern Lights.

The first day I was there, *The Place* was subdued, though it still cast a spell. Checking the Alaskan data stations on my laptop, I saw that geomagnetic activity was negligible. Some minor seismic episodes in the region had set off the bass frequencies, but it was a rather opaque ripple of beats, suggestive of a dance party in an underground crypt. Clouds covered the sky, so the Day Choir was muted. After a few minutes, there was a noticeable change: the solar harmonies acquired extra radiance, with upper intervals oscillating in an almost melodic fashion. Certain that the sun had come out, I left *The Place*, and looked out the windows of the lobby. The Alaska Range was glistening on the far side of the Tanana Valley.

When I arrived the next day, just before noon, *The Place* was jumping. A mild earthquake in the Alaska Range, measuring 2.99 on the Richter scale, was causing the Earth Drums to pound more loudly and go deeper in register. (If a major earthquake were to hit Fairbanks, *The Place*, if it survived, would throb to the frequency 24.27 Hz, an abyssal tone that Adams associates with the rotation of the earth.) Even more spectacular were the high sounds coming down from speakers on the ceiling. On the website of the University of Alaska's Geophysical Institute, aurora activity was rated 5 on a scale from 0 to 9, or "active." This was sufficient to make the Aurora Bells come alive. The Day and Night Choirs follow the equal-tempered tuning used by most Western instruments, but the Bells are filtered through a different harmonic prism, one determined by various series of prime numbers. I had the impression of a carillon ringing miles above the earth.

On the two days I visited *The Place*, various tourists came and went. Some, armed with cameras and guidebooks, stood against the back wall, looking alarmed, and left quickly. Others were entranced. One young woman assumed a yoga position and meditated; she took *The Place* to be a specimen of ambient music, the kind of thing you can bliss out to, and she wasn't entirely mistaken. At the same time, it is a forbiddingly complex creation that contains a probably unresolvable philosophical contradiction. On the one hand, it lacks a will of its own; it is at the mercy of its data streams, the humors of the earth. On the other hand, it is a deeply personal work, whose material reflects Adams's long-standing preoccupation with multiple systems of tuning, his fascination with slow-motion formal processes, his love of foggy masses of sound in which many events are playing out at independent tempos.

The Place, which opened on the spring equinox in 2006, confirmed Adams's status as one of the most original musical thinkers of the new century. He has become a standard-bearer of American experimental music, of the tradition of solitary sonic tinkering that began on the West Coast almost a century ago and gained new strength after the Second World War, when John Cage and Morton Feldman created supreme abstractions in musical form. Talking about his work, Adams admits that it can sound strange, that it lacks familiar reference points, that it's not exactly popular—by a twist of fate, he is sometimes confused with John Coolidge Adams, the creator of *Nixon in China* and the most widely performed of living American composers—and yet he'll also say that it's got something, or, at least, "It's not nothing."

Above all, Adams strives to create musical counterparts to the geography, ecology, and native culture of Alaska, where he moved in 1978, when he was twenty-five. He does this not merely by giving his compositions evocative titles—his catalogue includes *Earth and the Great Weather, In the White Silence, Strange and Sacred Noise, Dark Waves*—but by literally anchoring the work in the landscapes that have inspired it.

"My music is going inexorably from being about place to becoming place," Adams said of his installation. "I have a vivid memory of flying out of Alaska early one morning on my way to Oberlin, where I taught for a couple of fall semesters. It was a glorious early-fall day. Winter was coming in. I love winter, and I didn't want to go. As we crested the central peaks of the Alaska Range, I looked down at Mount Hayes, and all at once I was overcome by the intense love that I have for this place—an almost erotic feeling about those mountains. Over the next fifteen minutes, I found myself furiously sketching, and when I came up for air I realized, There it is. I knew that I wanted to hear the unheard, that I wanted to somehow transpose the music that is just beyond the reach of our ears into audible vibrations. I knew that it had to be its own space. And I knew that it had to be real—that I couldn't fake this, that nothing could be recorded. It had to have the ring of truth.

"Actually, my original conception for *The Place* was truly grandiose. I thought that it might be a piece that could be realized at any location on the earth, and that each location would have its unique sonic signature. That idea—tuning the whole world—stayed with me for a long time. But at some point I realized that I was tuning it so that this place, this room, on this hill, looking out over the Alaska Range, was the sweetest-sounding spot on earth."

Adams blends in well with the proudly scruffy characters who populate the diners and bars of Fairbanks. Tall and rail-thin, his handsomely weathered face framed by a short beard, he bears a certain resemblance to Clint Eastwood, and speaks in a similarly soft, husky voice. He's not unworldly—he travels frequently to New York, Los Angeles, Amsterdam, and other cultural capitals—but he is happiest when he goes on extended camping trips into the wilderness, especially to the Arctic National Wildlife Refuge. He exudes a regular-guy coolness that is somewhat unusual in contemporary composers.

He lives on a hill outside Fairbanks, in a sparsely furnished, light-filled split-level house, much of which he designed and built himself. He shares it with his second wife, Cynthia Adams, who has been the mainstay of his occasionally precarious existence since the late 1970s. Cindy, as spirited as her husband is soft-spoken, runs GrantStation, an Internet business that advises nonprofit organizations across the country. To many locals, the Adamses are best known for serving on the board of the Alaska Goldpanners, Fairbanks's amateur baseball team. When they go shopping at Fred Meyer, the all-purpose store in town, they are peppered with questions about the state of the team.

Like many Alaskans, Adams migrated to the state from a very different world. He was born in Meridian, Mississippi, in 1953; his father worked for AT&T, first as an accountant and later in upper management, and the family moved often when he was a child. Much of his adolescence was spent in Millburn, New Jersey, where he developed a passion for rock and roll. He was the drummer in several bands, one of which, Pocket Fuzz, had the honor of opening for the Beach Boys at a local New Jersey show.

Frank Zappa caused a sudden change of perspective. In the liner notes to Zappa's 1966 album *Freak Out!* Adams noticed a quotation: "'The present-day composer refuses to die!'—Edgard Varèse." Adams went hunting for information about this mystery figure, whose name he pronounced "Var-EE-zee." A friend, the composer Richard Einhorn, found a Varèse disc in a Greenwich Village record shop, and the two braved the sonic hailstorms of *Poème électronique*. Adams was soon devouring the music of the postwar European and American avant-garde: Karlheinz Stockhausen, Iannis Xenakis, György Ligeti, and, most important, John Cage.

"Once I discovered that stuff, I rapidly lost interest in the backbeat and the three chords," Adams said. "I was still in bands, but they kept getting weirder and weirder. In the last band, a trio called Sloth, we were trying to work with open-form scores and graphic notation."

In 1969, the family moved again, to Macon, Georgia. Adams enrolled in Westminster Academy, an elite boarding school, from which he failed to graduate. "I was your classic problem kid," he said. "My grades were OK; it was my behavior that was the problem." At the age of sixteen, he fell in love with a young woman named Margrit von Braun—the younger daughter of Wernher von Braun, the godfather of the American space program. Not too surprisingly, the German émigré and the American teenager didn't get along. In 1969, Adams says, he was impressed more by the Miracle Mets than by the first moon landing. Nonetheless, he and Margrit married, and for several years he coexisted uneasily with her powerful father.

In 1971, Adams moved to Los Angeles to study music at CalArts. One teacher there, the composer James Tenney, became a significant mentor, his unruly imagination as compelling as his rigorous methods. Likewise, beneath the dreamlike surfaces of Adams's work are mathematical schemes controlling the interrelationship of rhythms and the unfolding of melodic patterns. At CalArts, the novice composer also familiarized himself with the oddball heroes of the American avant-garde: Harry Partch, who adopted a hobo lifestyle during the Great Depression; Conlon Nancarrow, who spent the better part of his career writing pieces for player piano in Mexico City; and Lou Harrison, who sought musical truth in the Indonesian gamelan tradition. Adams calls them "composers who burned down the house and started over." Harrison became another musical and spiritual guide, advising Adams to avoid the "competitive careerism of the metropolis."

Adams's most crucial encounter was with Morton Feldman, the loquacious New Yorker whose music has an otherworldly quietude and breadth.

On a Columbia LP he heard Feldman's *Piece for Four Pianos*, in which four pianists play through the same music at different rates, floating around one another like the arms of a Calder mobile. That work galvanized Adams, teaching him that music could break free of European tradition while retaining a sensuous allure. One of his first characteristic pieces, for three percussion players, bears the Feldmanesque title *Always Very Soft*, although the seamlessness of the construction—accelerating and decelerating patterns overlap to create a single, ever-evolving sonority—hints at a distinct sensibility.

When *Always Very Soft* had its first performance, at CalArts, in 1973, Wernher von Braun was in attendance. Afterward, Adams went with his wife and in-laws to a showing of *Planet of the Apes*. The young composer found himself in a euphoric mood, bouncing around and making jokes. Wernher testily asked what was wrong with him. "Dad, he just launched a rocket," Margrit explained.

Southern California also brought Adams in contact with the environmental movement. He became obsessed with the plight of the California condor, which was facing extinction. Several expeditions into Los Padres National Forest, where the last wild California condors lived, led him to make his first attempt at "nature music"—a cycle of pieces titled *songbirdsongs*. Messiaen had been taking inspiration from birdsong for decades. With "the self-consciousness of the self-styled young iconoclast," Adams says, he went out of his way to avoid Messiaen's influence, and his own personality emerged in the unhurried pacing of events and the wide-open sense of space.

By the mid-seventies, Adams was working with the Wilderness Society and other conservation groups. At the time, one of their major projects was lobbying for the Alaska Lands Act, whose purpose was to protect large tracts of the state from oil drilling and industrial development. Adams first went to Alaska in 1975, and returned in 1977 to spend a summer in the Arctic. His marriage to Margrit von Braun unraveled that year. Around that time, he met Cindy, who was also an environmental activist. They fell in love during the long battle for passage of the Alaska Lands Act, which President Carter signed into law in 1980.

What Adams needed most, after a turbulent decade, was solitude. During the first decade of his relationship with Cindy, he lived in a rudimentary cabin in the woods outside Fairbanks, a mile from the nearest road. "It was my Thoreau fantasy—cutting wood and carrying water," he told me. The fantasy subsided when Cindy suggested in a non-roundabout way that he should either join her full-time—by now the couple had a son, Sage—or go his own way. In 1989, he moved out of the woods, and has never returned to his old cabin.

Adams embraced his new life in Fairbanks, but he still struggled to find his way as a composer. The eighties were, he now says, "lost years": he made various attempts to write orchestral pieces that would reach a wider audience, and, though he was pleased with the work, he didn't feel that it was entirely his. At times, he wondered whether he would make more headway in New York or Los Angeles. In this same period, not incidentally, John Adams, of Berkeley, California, found fame with *Nixon in China*. The two composers had known each other since 1976; they moved in the same circles, and one week they stayed together at Lou Harrison's house. All the same, the phenomenal success of the Californian Adams pushed the Alaskan Adams to differentiate himself, not only by using his middle name but by finding territory he could call his own.

"In a way, that experience challenged me to reevaluate my whole relationship to the idea of success," he says. "Maybe it confirmed my outsider resolve—'No, I'm not moving from Alaska; this is who I am, this is where I belong, this is what I'm supposed to be doing'—but most of all it helped my sense of humor. For me, finally, it's kind of worked out. John is always very gracious. We occasionally exchange e-mails about the latest incidents of mistaken identity. Recently, someone thought he was me. Very sweet."

By the 1990s, Adams had begun to carve out a singular body of work, which can be sampled on recordings on the New World, New Albion, Cold Blue, Mode, and Cantaloupe labels. First came a conceptual Alaskan opera titled *Earth and the Great Weather*, much of which is given over to the chanting of place-names and descriptive phrases from the native Inupiaq and Gwich'in languages, both in the original and in translation. One section describes various stages of the seasons: "The time of new sunshine," "The time when polar bears bring out their young," "The time of the small wind," "The time of eagles." The music runs from pure, ethereal sonorities for strings—tuned in a scheme similar to that of the Aurora Bells in *The Place*—to viscerally pummeling movements for quartets of drums.

In the next decade, Adams further explored the new sonic terrain that he had mapped out in his opera. *In the White Silence*, a seventy-five-minute piece for harp, celesta, vibraphones, and strings, is derived from the seven notes of the C-major scale; in a striking feat of metaphor, the composer equates the consuming whiteness of midwinter Alaska with the white keys of the piano. *Strange and Sacred Noise*, another seventy-five-minute cycle, evokes the violence of changing seasons: four percussionists deploy drums, gongs, bells, sirens, and mallet percussion to summon up an alternately beguiling and frightening tableau of musical noises, most of which were inspired by a trip that Adams took up the Yukon River in spring, when the ice was collapsing. Whether unabashedly sweet or unremittingly harsh—*Clouds of Forgetting, Clouds of Unknowing*, a memorial to the composer's father, manages to be both at once—Adams's major works have the appearance of being beyond style; they transcend the squabbles of contemporary classical music, the unending arguments over the relative value of tonal and atonal languages.

The sense of vastness, separateness, and solitude is even more pronounced in Adams's recent electronic compositions. The 2005 installation *Veils*, which has appeared in several venues in America and Europe, uses a "virtual choir" of ninety polyphonic voices and goes on for six hours. *The Place Where You Go to Listen* could last decades. Both Cage and Feldman talked about making music that you can live with, much as you can live with visual art; *Veils* and *The Place* execute that idea with uncommon vigor. Adams is an avid art-viewer, and is particularly keen on the second generation of American abstract painters: Frank Stella, Ellsworth Kelly, Jasper Johns, and Joan Mitchell. There are more art books than music books on the shelves of his studio, a neat one-room cabin that faces south, toward the Alaska Range.

Adams says, "I remember thinking, To hell with classical music. I'm going into the art world; I'm going to do installations. But I was really just interested in working with new media. And it doesn't matter what I think I'm doing. The work has a life of its own, and I'm just along for the ride. Richard Serra talks about the point at which all your influences are assimilated and then your work can come out of the work."

Although Adams is content to write for electronics, small ensembles, and percussion groups, he still longs to write for larger forces, and, above all, for orchestra. For most of the eighties, he was the timpanist for the Fairbanks Symphony, which, at the time, was led by the conductor, composer, and environmental activist Gordon Wright. During Adams's cabin-in-the-forest period, Wright was living nearby, and the two became close friends, often trekking into the wilderness together. Once, they drove into the Alaska Range while listening to Bruckner's Eighth Symphony, music that has the weight of mountains. "This may be where our musical worlds meet," Adams said to him.

Wright died in 2007, near Anchorage, at the age of seventy-two; he was found one night on the deck of his cabin. A few days later, the Anchorage Symphony played the premiere of Adams's *Dark Waves*, a thirteen-minute work for orchestra and electronics, which the composer dedicated to Wright. One of the most arresting American orchestral compositions of recent years, it suggests a huge entity, of indeterminate shape, that approaches slowly, exerts apocalyptic force, and then recedes. Every instrument is, in one way or another, playing with the simple interval of the perfect fifth—the basic building block of harmony—but at the climax the lines coalesce into roaring dissonances, with all twelve notes of the chromatic scale sounding together.

Adams has been contemplating a large-scale piece in the vein of *Dark Waves*. It might bring him into a Brucknerian or even Wagnerian realm. Wagner's *Parsifal* is one of three opera scores in Adams's library; the others are Mussorgsky's *Boris Godunov* and Debussy's *Pelléas et Mélisande*. He speaks with awe—and a little envy—of the resources Wagner had at his command. A few years ago, Adams went to see *Die Walküre* at the Metropolitan Opera, and departed with his mind full of fresh longings.

"I thought, This couldn't be repeated," Adams told me. "Wagner kind of caught the perfect wave. But I did wonder what kind of opportunities exist for us, right now." He sat still for a moment, his blue-gray eyes drifting. I sensed some wordless, high-tech, back-to-the-earth *Parsifal* waiting to be born.

Knowing of Adams's love for Alaska's remotest places, I asked him to take me to one of them. His favorite place on earth is the Brooks Range, the northernmost extension of the Rocky Mountains, but that area was inaccessible when I visited. Instead, we went south, to Lake Louise. Snowy weather blocked most of the mountains as we drove, although looming white shapes occasionally pierced the flurries. "Aw, that's nothing," Adams would say, slipping into the role of the hardened Alaskan lifer. "Foothills. The big guys aren't coming out."

Lake Louise is framed by several of North America's grandest mountain ranges: the Alaska, the Chugach, the Wrangell–St. Elias, and the Talkeetna. The native word for this kind of place is *chiiviteenlii*, or "pointed mountains scattered all around." The lake was covered with ice four feet thick, and, after spending the night at a local lodge, we went for a walk on it. The sun was burning faintly through the mist above. Periodically, a curtain of snow descended and the shores and islands of the lake disappeared from view. I noticed that Adams was listening closely to this seemingly featureless expanse, and kept pulling information from it: the fluttering of a flock of snow buntings, the low whistle of wind through a stand of gaunt spruce, the sinister whine of a pair of snowmobiles. He also noted the curiously musical noises that our feet were making. Tapping the crust of snow atop the ice, under which the wind had carved little tunnels, he compared the sounds to those of xylophones or marimbas. Meanwhile, a dog had wandered out on the ice and was howling to itself. "He has some fantasy he's a wolf," Adams said. He yelled at the dog to go home.

Adams recalled the Yukon River trip that led him to write *Strange and Sacred Noise* and other tone poems of natural upheaval. "When the ice breakup comes, it makes incredible sounds," he said. "It's symphonic. There's candle ice, which is crystals hanging down like chandeliers. They chime together in the wind. Or whirlpools open up along the shore or out in the middle of the river, and water goes swirling through them. Or sizzle ice, which makes a sound like the effervescent popping you hear when you pour water over ice cubes. I have literally hundreds of hours of field recordings that I made back in the *Earth and the Great Weather* period, in the early nineties. I keep thinking that maybe one day I could work with some of that material—maybe try to transcribe it, completely remove it from the original reality, extract the music in it."

We were standing on a tiny island, where cormorants had built a network of nests. Adams had discovered these nests on a trip to the lake a few weeks earlier. One of the nests had slid off the ridge onto the lake, and we carried it back to land.

"All along, I've had this obsessive, delusional idea that I could somehow be outside culture, which is, of course, patently absurd," he said. "But

I could at least hold the illusion of being outside culture, where culture is put in proper perspective. That's why I am so concerned with the landscape. Barry Lopez"—the author of the epic travelogue *Arctic Dreams*—"says that landscape is the culture that contains all human cultures, all forms and artifacts and culture and language. Maybe it's just a hippy-dippy sixties-seventies thing, but, to tell the truth, I was never such a good hippie."

Adams is well aware of the naïveté, sentimentality, and outright foolishness that can attach to fantasies of dropping out of society in search of "the real." But that same naïveté can lead to work of uncompromising power, especially when it is wedded to artistic craft. In this regard, Adams cites another of his heroes, the Alaskan poet John Haines, who, after the Second World War, took up residence in a one-room cabin he built off the Richardson Highway, south of Fairbanks, and stayed there for some twenty years, living off the land in time-honored fashion. Not long before Adams moved to Alaska, he read Haines's first book, *Winter News*, falling in love with poems such as "Listening in October":

> There are silences so deep
> you can hear
> the journeys of the soul,
> enormous footsteps
> downward in a freezing earth.

In a collection of writings titled *Winter Music*, Adams mentions, among other reasons for moving to the state, the richness of its silences. He writes, "Much of Alaska is still filled with silence, and one of the most persuasive arguments for the preservation of the original landscape here may be its spiritual value as a great reservoir of silence."

One evening, in Fairbanks, we went to see Haines at his home. He was then eighty-three years old, and had recently endured a near-fatal bout of pneumonia, but he still welcomed visitors, especially those who brought a good bottle of whisky—in this case, a seventeen-year-old Highland Park single malt. Haines was at work on several reminiscences to supplement his memoir *The Stars, the Snows, the Fire*, an elegant account of his long years in isolation. He described for us a surreal episode that took place in

1966, shortly after *Winter News* was published. One day, he looked out his window and saw a small group of people ascending the path toward the cabin. On opening the door, he found himself face-to-face with the Russian poet Yevgeny Yevtushenko, who had with him a professor from Queens, a photographer, and a reporter from *Life* magazine. Yevtushenko had been told that an unsung American bard was living in the area. Haines served the party blueberry wine that he had made in his backyard.

Adams asked Haines to recite one or two of his poems. Haines chanted several of them in a courtly, melancholy voice, somewhat in the manner of William Butler Yeats delivering "The Lake Isle of Innisfree." He ended with "Return to Richardson, Spring 1981," which looks back fondly and sadly on the homestead period, when his life was "like a boat set loose," and evenings were spent reading books since forgotten:

> *In this restless air I know*
> *On this ground I can never forget*
> *Where will I set my foot*
> *With so much passion again.*

After a pause, Adams said, "That hurts." We talked for a few more minutes, Adams gave Haines the whisky, and we said goodbye.

On our way to Lake Louise, we passed Haines's old homestead. The highway now cuts close to the house, ruining its splendid isolation. Alaska's "great reservoir of silence" is ebbing away; even in the farthest reaches of the Brooks Range, Adams commented, you will sooner or later hear the drone of a snow machine or the hum of a small plane. Adams spoke also of the scary pace of climate change, of how the thaw now comes as much as a month earlier than it did when he moved to the state. He talked about various future projects—an outdoor percussion piece for the Banff Centre, in Alberta, Canada, an installation in Venice—and explained why his work was becoming more global in focus.

"I tried to run away," Adams said. "I hid for quite a while. I had a rich life; I had incredible experiences, a very slow development of a certain musical world. I wouldn't trade it for anything. But I can't live there anymore. Because, in a sense, it doesn't exist anymore. A piece like *In the White Silence* is almost—I didn't realize this at the time—almost an elegy for a place that has disappeared."

11

VERDI'S GRIP

OPERA AS POPULAR ART

According to *The Guinness Book of Records*, Vincent La Selva, a native of Cleveland, Ohio, is the only man ever to have conducted all twenty-eight operas of Giuseppe Verdi in chronological order. La Selva runs a company called New York Grand Opera, which, in the years leading up to the hundredth anniversary of Verdi's death, in 2001, presented the composer's entire canon, on an outdoor stage in Central Park, free of charge. The cycle began in 1994, with a boisterous rendition of *Oberto*, and ended seven years later, with *Aida*, *Otello*, and *Falstaff*. I saw the *Otello* on a sticky night in July. Several thousand people were on hand, and several hundred others were trying to get in. A policeman was shouting, "No more seats! No opera!" There was a lot of pushing and pleading, as at a rock show. "My name has to be on the list," said a youngish man in an Atari shirt. Many people ended up camping out on the grass, listening to the music as it wafted over the loudspeakers. Verdi has not lost the mass appeal that brought forth hundreds of thousands of mourners on the day of his funeral, in 1901.

During the Verdi anniversary season, I saw nine productions of the composer's operas, in the major New York houses and at two venerable Italian theaters. Perhaps surprisingly, the Central Park *Otello* is the one that has stayed longest in my mind. It was by no means the best-sung Verdi of the season; needless to say, the Metropolitan Opera and the Teatro alla Scala of Milan fielded far starrier casts. Nor were the acoustics satisfactory. The singers had microphones clipped to their costumes, and every few minutes one of them would let out a mechanical squawk or disappear from the mix. During the Homage Chorus, in Act II, the mandolin was deafening and the chorus was inaudible. But the production had a fine, pearly-voiced Desdemona in Judith Von Houser, and an idiomatic conductor in La Selva. This was Verdi 101, stripped of directorial brainstorms and conductorial ego trips. By the end, I had forgotten about the tackiness of the scenery and fallen under Verdi's spell.

The appeal of Italian opera is difficult to put into words, but it has something to do with the activation of primal feelings. Operatic characters have a way of laying themselves bare, and they are never more uninhibited than at the climax of a Verdi tragedy. *Otello* is a crescendo of anger; yet the ultimate moment of the opera, during which Central Park fell silent, is a surpassingly lyrical one. When Otello kills Desdemona, the act is framed by two repetitions of the "bacio" motif—a nine-bar theme that first appears in Act I, when husband and wife trade kisses (*"un bacio . . . un bacio . . . ancora un bacio"*). It is an enchanting object, but from the outset it has carried a tinge of sadness, its ecstatic phrases pinned on a chromatic descending bass. By the end, it has become a token of Otello's insanity. His love for Desdemona was, he says, a "mirage"—not because she betrayed him but because he never saw her as a real person. His note-for-note recapitulation of the love music marks the point at which he chooses the mirage over life itself. All the orchestra can offer, by way of a final statement, is three soft, black chords. "Fall down the steps," Verdi writes. Edward Perretti, the tenor singing Otello, followed the instruction exactly. Everyone shuddered.

Vincent La Selva's *Otello* was an unexpectedly haunting experience, because it put the drama first. It had no star singers, and, unlike so many modern productions, it made no attempt to deconstruct or recontextualize the story. In this sense, it gave an approximate sense of how generations of operagoers—especially those outside Milan, New York, London, and other capitals—got to know the composer. These days, millions see Verdi each year around the world, yet for a number of years the business of staging the operas has been suffering through an apparent crisis. Devotees ask where the great Verdi singers have gone, and when they are not lamenting the dearth of right-sounding voices they are deploring the excess of wrongheaded directors. We love Verdi more than ever, but we struggle to understand him: the glib irony of our age is at odds with his raging sincerity. One prominent director has been quoted as saying, "Nobody comes to Verdi for the plots." More likely, people come to Verdi because he meant every word.

• • •

In the nineteenth century, German musicians often described their art in idealistic terms, as a lofty pursuit above the crowd. E.T.A. Hoffmann, in an essay on Beethoven, asked the public, "What if it is entirely *your* fault that the composer's language is clear to the initiated but not to you?" Verdi, despite his reclusive habits and porcupine personality, saw no shame in the pursuit of public adoration. "The box office is the proper thermometer of success," he remarked. He also said, "You have to be wall-eyed, with one eye on the public and one on art." He would probably have endorsed Leopold Mozart's instruction to his son, that "in your work you think not only of the musical cognoscenti but also of the listeners who are unmusical." But the real model was Shakespeare, who succeeded in thrilling both the groundlings and the connoisseurs. Even if Verdi had never written *Macbeth*, *Otello*, and *Falstaff* the comparison would have been made.

For a glimpse of Verdi's two-faced nature, one need only look at his catchiest tune, "La donna è mobile," which has sold vast quantities of pasta in television commercials. It appears at the beginning of Act III of *Rigoletto*. More than a pretty melody, it is packed with double meanings, some of them quite ugly. The irony of the aria is hinted at in the opening bars, as the players stop and start again, like actors clearing their throats. The first line translates as "Women are fickle," but the sentiment is less than straightforward, being the rationalization of a fickle Duke who uses women for amusement. Gilda, who has fallen for the Duke, overhears the song, grasps its meaning, and is plunged into despair. Rigoletto, her father, plots revenge, forgetting for a while that he himself facilitated the Duke's adventures and was cursed by one of his victims. At the end of the night, an assassin hauls out a sack that is supposed to contain the Duke's corpse. Just as Rigoletto bends over it, a familiar tenor is heard singing a familiar air offstage—"La donna è mobile." So whose is the body in the bag? *Maledizione!* A chirpy ditty becomes the knife-edge of the curse that cuts Rigoletto down.

In old age, Verdi was hailed as a man of the people, a self-taught peasant genius. Modern biographers have pointed out the many ways in which this image departed from the facts. His father, a small-time innkeeper and landowner, was, if not rich, prosperous enough to be able to give his son a thorough musical education, and the young man had the help of many aristocratic friends. In later years, as the composer amassed profits from his operas, he filled rather too well the role of the hard-hearted land-lord. Yet the peasant image retains a conceptual truth. Verdi had a funda-mentally earthy nature, a preference for action over theory. His ear for popular melody was inborn. As with Mozart, his ability to produce hum-mable tunes—"La donna è mobile," the Anvil Chorus from *Il trovatore*, the Triumphal March from *Aida*, and dozens of others—was so fecund that he could use them as background decor, as bait for unsuspecting ears.

Verdi was born in 1813, outside the town of Busseto, in the province of Parma. In his youth, he seemed destined to become Busseto's musical director, following his teacher, but clerical elements had their favorite and put roadblocks in his way. Others loudly backed Verdi's cause. As Mary Jane Phillips-Matz recounts, in her epic biography of the composer, there were fights in the streets, shouting matches, libelous sonnets, obscene songs, and a near-brawl in church. The uproar was out of proportion to the unobjectionable church compositions and student pieces that consti-tuted what we know of Verdi's output at the time, but music was serious business in Italian towns. Eventually, the clerics gave in and offered Verdi the job, but his attention soon moved elsewhere. His talent drew the inter-est of the manager of La Scala, and also of two leading singers, the bari-tone Giorgio Ronconi and the soprano Giuseppina Strepponi. In 1839, La Scala staged Verdi's first opera, *Oberto*, with considerable success. After a traumatic period that saw the failure of a comic opera, *Un giorno di regno*, and the sudden deaths of his wife and two of his children, Verdi scored an outright hit with the blood-and-thunder biblical drama *Nabucco*, in 1842. From then on he was the de facto chief of Italian opera.

Throughout the 1840s, Verdi worked hard to maintain his position. In those ten years he produced thirteen operas—among them *I lombardi*, *Ernani*, *Attila*, and *Macbeth*—and captivated the public with one spine-tingling tale after another. John Rosselli, the author of the best short life of Verdi, says of these works, "The dominant mood is of heroic, slightly crazed grandeur, interspersed with lightning discharges of energy." Stage by stage, Verdi asserted his personality; the measured splendor of Rossini and Donizetti gives way to hurtling scenes, hotly expressive vocal writing, an increasingly feisty orchestra, choruses of brutish force, and endings that arrive with guillotine speed. Verdi was speaking straight to the crowd, and he became not only a popular icon but also something of a national symbol, notably in the years leading up to the revolutions of 1848 and the short-lived Roman Republic of 1849. After one of the first performances of *Macbeth*, in Florence, a giddy crowd unhitched horses from the composer's carriage and pulled him back to his hotel. Certain choruses served as cues for patriotic displays. *La battaglia di Legnano*, the most blatantly nationalist of Verdi's operas, had its premiere in Rome two weeks before the proclamation of the republic, and the ovations were all but indistinguishable from the demonstrations.

Yet Verdi's role in the Risorgimento has been exaggerated. On at least two occasions in 1848 he was, in fact, criticized for choosing exotic subjects that seemed remote from the concerns of the day. Just as the revolution crested, he turned inward, expanding the psychological dimension of his art. Between 1847 and 1849, he lived mainly in Paris, where he carried on an affair with Strepponi—his devoted, often thankless companion for more than four decades thereafter—and absorbed new theatrical ideas. He emerged with a taste for more intimate scenarios, especially those in which private passions went against the social grain. (Parochial disapproval of his arrangement with Strepponi, whom he did not marry until 1859, may have heightened that interest.) In *Luisa Miller*, a soldier's daughter and a count's son fall in love and run afoul of the social order; in *Stiffelio*, a Protestant minister decides to forgive his errant wife after reading the biblical verse "He that is without sin among you, let him first cast a stone at her." These operas set the stage for *Rigoletto*, *Il trovatore*, and *La traviata*, the trifecta of 1851–53, in which the passions are not only romantic but familial: Rigoletto tries to shield his daughter from the Duke; the Gypsy Azucena broods over the loss of her infant son; and the courtesan Violetta ("La traviata" means "the wayward woman") forsakes her lover at the behest of his status-conscious father. The escalation of emotion goes hand in hand with a change in the musical line; in *Traviata*, Verdi deemphasizes bel-canto finery, instead favoring a more direct, impulsive style of delivery.

As the 1850s gave way to the '60s, Verdi edged back into the political sphere, but he no longer dealt in obvious symbols of Italian glory. Instead, struck by the sprawling historical spectacles of French grand opera, he produced a series of works—*Les Vêpres siciliennes*, *Simon Boccanegra*, *Un ballo in maschera*, *La forza del destino*, and *Don Carlos*—in which stately tableaux are shot through with a deepening pessimism. Fate is now hammered out by earthly monsters of authority, the worst of them being the

Grand Inquisitor, in *Don Carlos*. The opera tells of love and intolerance in Philip II's Spain, and the supremely pitiless Inquisitor lets us see the wholesale corruption of Christian teachings by the politics of power: when Philip asks how he can justify the killing of his son—the rebel prince Carlos—the Inquisitor replies, in an icy, nearly monotone line, "God sacrificed his own to save us all." The orchestra plays a string of major triads around that pronouncement (B major, G major, E major, C major), but the sequence defies harmonic logic and produces a sulphurous atmosphere. Throughout his later operas, Verdi grew ever more daring in his musical language, not so much by introducing dissonances as by treating simple chords with cavalier freedom, as if he were throwing dice.

Following *Aida*'s triumph, at a gala premiere in Cairo, Verdi seemed prepared to retire from opera. In 1873, he produced a string quartet, the following year a Requiem that sounded like a summing up. But, in a benevolent conspiracy, the publisher Giulio Ricordi and the composer and author Arrigo Boito brought the old man back into the game, using Shakespeare as the lure. *Otello* and *Falstaff*, based on finely crafted librettos by Boito, consolidate with unwavering skill everything that has come before: bel canto, Romantic theater, French grand opera, morsels of Wagnerian leitmotif-work and orchestration. The economy of the writing becomes severe: melodies that another composer might have milked for an evening appear for a few seconds and then are gone. The seventy-something Verdi seems almost to be taunting his colleagues. *Falstaff* ends with a virtuoso fugue on the line "All the world's a joke."

In his last years, Verdi began to be dismissed as a dated figure. Younger Italian intellectuals flocked to Wagner, who preached the synthesis of the arts and set about obliterating the conventions that underpinned Verdi's art to the end. For some years the Verdi operas were widely dismissed as creaky vehicles for star singers, although the most famous works—*Rigoletto, Trovatore, Traviata, Aida*—never ceased to please the general public. Only with the rise of neoclassical modernism in the 1920s and '30s did the composer's intellectual reputation begin to recover. Leonard Bernstein once suggested that Stravinsky had derived the four-note fate motive of his opera-oratorio *Oedipus Rex* from "Pietà ti prenda del mio dolor" in *Aida*—the slave girl's plea for mercy. Bernstein ironically summarized the fashionable attitude of his youth by calling *Aida* "that cheap, low, sentimental melodrama, the splashiest and flashiest of all the Verdi operas."

Yet, he acknowledged, Verdi was an august poet of "pity and power," of the individual's struggle with fate.

The downfall of German culture under the aegis of the Wagner-loving Hitler may have hastened the Verdi revival after 1945: here was one national hero who had an instinctive distrust of authority and no history of demonizing large groups of people. ("A fine civilization we have, with all its unhappiness," he said in 1896, condemning colonialism in Africa and India.) An extraordinary postwar vocal cohort—Zinka Milanov, Maria Callas, Leontyne Price, Giulietta Simionato, Carlo Bergonzi, Richard Tucker, Leonard Warren, and Tito Gobbi, to name a few—demonstrated that Verdi runs as deep as any singer dares to plunge. The early operas returned to circulation; *Don Carlos* was finally heard in something close to its original version. (Andrew Porter, my peerless predecessor at *The New Yorker*, found some discarded portions of the score in the library of the Palais Garnier in 1970.) Now Verdi seems more popular than ever; during the anniversary year of 2001, some four hundred productions of his operas were mounted around the world. Whether we have preserved the Verdi style is another matter.

Verdi's writing for voice is a camera that zooms in on a person's soul. Consider the moment in Act II of *La traviata* when Violetta, the wayward woman, leaves her lover, Alfredo. Alfredo believes that she is merely going into the garden, but he will soon receive a letter from her saying that she is gone forever. "I will always be here, near you, among the flowers," Violetta says to him. "Love me, Alfredo, as much as I love you. Goodbye!" *Amami, Alfredo, quant'io t'amo.* When a great soprano unfurls these phrases—I am listening to Callas live at La Scala, in 1955—you hear so much you can hardly take it all in. You hear what Alfredo hears, the frantic talk of an overwrought lover: "I love you even though I am going into the garden." You hear what Violetta cannot bring herself to say out loud: "I am leaving you, but will always love you." And you hear premonitions of her deathbed plea, at the end of the opera: "Remember the one who loved you so."

This matrix of meaning is contained in a simple tune that you already know even if you have never seen an opera: a twice-heard phrase that curves steeply down the notes of the F-major scale, followed by a reach up to a high B-flat and a more gradual, winding descent to the lower F. Be-

neath the voice, strings play throbbing tremolo chords. Verdi's operas often pivot on such curt, charged phrases, which singers are expected to
make into epiphanies. The composer hounded his librettists to find the
right words for these passages; he wanted banner headlines of emotion.
When Francesco Piave, his favorite collaborator before Boito, was working
on *Macbeth*, Verdi issued this command: "USE FEW WORDS . . . FEW
WORDS . . . FEW BUT SIGNIFICANT." So significant was "Amami,
Alfredo" in Verdi's mind that he made the melody the main theme of the
opera's prelude, even though its only appearance in the opera proper is in
these eighteen bars of Act II. There is no more impressive demonstration
of Verdi's lightning art: the audience hardly knows what hit it.

Callas's execution of "Amami, Alfredo" on the 1955 set is among the
most stunning pieces of Verdi singing on record. In the tense passage
leading up to the outburst, the soprano adopts a breathless, fretful tone,
communicating Violetta's initially panicked response to the situation—
vocal babbling, the Verdi scholar Julian Budden calls it. Then, with the
trembling of the strings, she seems to flip a switch, her voice burning
hugely from within. When she reaches up to the A and the B-flat, she
claws at the notes, practically tears them off the page, although her tone
retains a desperate beauty. Her delivery is so unnervingly vehement—
here is what Björk, in her discussion of Callas, called the "*rrrr*"—that it
risks anticlimax. Where can the opera possibly go from here? When you
listen again, you understand: Violetta's spirit is broken, and from now on
she will sing as if she were already dead.

Such fearless pushing to the limit is exactly what Verdi demanded
from his singers. John Rosselli quotes a letter that Verdi wrote to the librettist Salvadore Cammarano on the subject of casting the role of Lady
Macbeth:

> Tadolini is a fine figure of a woman, and I should like Lady Mac-
> beth to look ugly and evil. Tadolini sings to perfection; and I would
> rather that Lady didn't sing at all. Tadolini has a wonderful voice,
> clear, limpid, and strong; and I would rather that Lady's voice were
> rough, hollow, stifled. Tadolini's voice has something angelic in it.
> Lady's should have something devilish.

Even if Verdi was overstating for effect, he was declaring his preference
for dramatically committed singers over technically finished ones—or,

ideally, for well-trained singers who are willing to sacrifice beauty in the name of drama. Callas, experienced in Wagner as well as Donizetti, had no trouble blindsiding her audience with an abrupt surge of tone.

If a crisis in Verdi singing now exists, the reason may be that vocal training is far more professionalized, routinized, and specialized than it was fifty or a hundred years ago. To study archival recordings is to realize how idiosyncratic and free-spirited the art used to be. On the EMI label there is a classic compilation titled *Les Introuvables du chant Verdien*, which is almost guaranteed to transform even the huskiest young fan into a tiresome old opera queen who complains that no one can sing Verdi anymore. At the same time, these recordings demonstrate that there never was a single Verdi style. Frida Leider delivers penetrating Verdi in German; Francesco Tamagno, the original Otello, sings in what sounds like a slight French accent (presumably an Italian dialect); Nellie Melba croons mercilessly. What the golden-age singers had in common was a way of seeming to reach the limit and then pushing over it. Caruso would swell his voice tremendously at moments where it ought to have given out; Rosa Ponselle would sustain a line over supernatural spans of time, so that the music acquired the steady glow of moonlight. Their feats seem physically unrepeatable: no one has lungs like that now.

Yet the crisis is not simply the result of some obscure genetic decline. The sense of freedom that you find on the old recordings is related to the fact that the stars of a century ago generally did not have to contend with star conductors. Even as these recordings were being made, Mahler and Toscanini were imposing new forms of discipline, and, although the rise of the international maestro undoubtedly led to sizable improvements in the opera house, it may also have contributed to the decline of Italian style. Conductors of the past few decades have tended to resist the constant adjustments of tempo—*ritenuto*, *rallentando*, *stretto*, and other ways of varying the pace—that Italian singing requires. Ironically, as Verdi's intellectual stock rose, conductors sought to highlight the symphonic unity of his scores, to the detriment of vocal individuality.

In 2001, I stopped in at La Scala to see how Verdi was faring in the opera capital. I found the Neapolitan maestro Riccardo Muti—who had led the company since 1986—conducting *Un ballo* with a fiery diligence that seemed more appropriate to, say, Stravinsky's *Oedipus*. In the middle of the formation was the young tenor Salvatore Licitra, who sang with a certain authentic swagger. When Licitra tried to linger over a possible epiphany, you could feel Muti tugging him onward, like a parent marching a child past a candy store. The performance was engrossing, but it felt like a succession of vocal highlights inserted into an orchestral narrative.

Despite the parlous state of Verdi performance, gifted singers are still able to create memorable portrayals under the right conditions. In 2006, the Romanian diva Angela Gheorghiu sang *La traviata* at the Met, and when she arrived at "Amami, Alfredo" she chose not to indulge in a vocal explosion à la Callas—perhaps because such an explosion didn't really lie within her abilities. Instead, as the strings launched into their tremolo, she assumed a cool façade, proceeding toward her lover in statuesque fashion, painting the vocal line in sustained, majestic strokes. Instead of baring all, this Violetta raised her defenses against the world, to protect her shattered heart. Gheorghiu was not a perfect Violetta for the Met— she often sounded underpowered against the full orchestra—but she succeeded in placing her imprint on the role. Peter G. Davis, writing in *New York* magazine, characterized Gheorghiu aptly as "a dark-haired, impeccably gowned lady of the camellias with a sad cameo face, dangerous fragility, and an air that commands attention without hogging the scene."

Three years later, the American singer Sondra Radvanovsky came to the Met to undertake the taxing role of Leonora, in *Trovatore*. She brought to bear a richly colored, lightly tremulous soprano, reminiscent of Old World voices of yore. The high notes didn't always fall squarely on pitch, but they sailed through the house, and, more important, they were joined together in a strongly flowing musical line. She sounded weaker in the lower register, where some of Leonora's most wrenching music lies. "Tacea la notte placida," the aria in which Leonora unveils her doomed passion for the troubadour Manrico, flickered out rather than smoldered in the bottom range. Yet, in all, Radvanovsky had more oomph than several others who had lately tried the part. She sang "D'amor sull'ali rosee," her second big aria, at a daringly slow tempo, embodying a woman lost in a dreamworld of unattainable love. The conductor, Gianandrea Noseda, encouraged rather than curtailed her exploration of the part.

The age of legends always seems distant, and yet it has a way of catching up to you as time goes by. Although I'm a relatively young operagoer, in the early 1990s I was able to hear one portrayal that has already passed into operatic history: the Otello of Plácido Domingo, who whipped up storms of rage and anguish in his superbly flexible, colorful voice, and ended on a devastating whisper of "*bacio.*" To imagine what Verdi might have thought of Domingo's achievement is to enter into the realm of the counterfactual, but everything we know of the composer's opinions on singing and acting suggests that Domingo would have satisfied him thoroughly.

If singers and conductors tend to be too studious in their approach to Verdi, today's directors too often treat the composer with a license bordering on contempt. In 2001, the critic Matthew Gurewitsch asked several leading directors to articulate their visions of Verdi, and he received some eyebrow-raising replies. Francesca Zambello, who once set *Aida* in a nuclear-winter landscape, said, "If I have to think of a work of Verdi that moved me on stage, that's going to be pretty hard." Christopher Alden, who created a *Rigoletto* with bouts of transvestism and public sex, said, "You have to throw cold water on an audience. You have to wake them up, poke holes into the operas so that the inner life will flow out." Mark Lamos, whose *Rigoletto* also featured a graphic orgy, said, "To be blunt, I find Verdi's operas about as stageworthy as his Requiem."

With their outlandish coincidences and hyperventilating exits, Verdi's plots do seem silly at first glance. *Il trovatore* is the most notorious example, possessing a plot so improbable that it inspired two great parodies—Gilbert and Sullivan's *The Pirates of Penzance* and the Marx Brothers' *A Night at the Opera*. The short version is this: a Spanish Gypsy tries to avenge her mother's death at the hands of a count by throwing the count's infant son, Manrico, into the fire, but, in her excitement, she grabs the wrong baby and incinerates her own son instead. Actually, this all happens before the curtain rises; the opera ends with the count's other son ordering Manrico's execution without knowing of the family connection. The tragedy of Leonora is that she does not go back to sleep when she hears this particular troubadour playing outside her window.

Then again, most entertainment appears silly when it is viewed from a distance. Nothing in Verdi is any more implausible than the events of the average Shakespeare play, or, for that matter, of the average Hollywood action picture. The difference is that the conventions of the latter are widely accepted these days, so that if, say, Matt Damon rides a unicycle the wrong way down the Autobahn and kills a squad of Uzbek thugs with a package of Twizzlers, the audience cheers rather than guffaws. The loopier things get, the better. Opera is no different. Verdi didn't seize on the lurid matter of *Trovatore* because he found it believable; rather, he relished the extremity of the situation, which required his characters to behave in extreme ways. His beloved maledictions, vendettas, and forces of destiny *add* plausibility rather than take it away; they make the violent accents of operatic singing seem like a natural reaction under the circumstances.

In other words, stories that seem ridiculous are on a deeper level truthful. The same cannot be said of the scenarios that many modern directors have devised. They tend to display precisely the faults they have assigned to Verdi: the work is too often stilted and cryptic, as if obeying some extraterrestrial social code. In 2000, the Met put on a *Trovatore* so monumentally opaque that the director, Graham Vick, later removed his name from it, in the spirit of the "Allen Smithee" movies that periodically come out of Hollywood. That affair was mild in comparison with what regularly appears on European stages. For some reason, *Un ballo in maschera* seems especially prone to manhandling. In 2001, the Spanish director Calixto Bieto placed the opera in Franco's Spain, leading off with a scene of conspirators sitting on toilets. A 2008 staging in Erfurt featured the ruins of the World Trade Center, a cast of Elvis impersonators, naked elderly people in Mickey Mouse masks, and a woman dressed as Hitler.

Director-dominated opera is known as Regietheater, or director-theater, and it is telling that the word exists only in German. Regietheater came into fashion partly as a way of evading the unsavory side of the legacy of Wagner, in particular the sick stagecraft of Nazism. When the Bayreuth Festival reopened, in 1951, Wieland Wagner, the composer's grandson, unveiled a *Parsifal* in which all the old medieval clutter had been cleared away, leaving a play of light and bodies on an almost empty stage. In the same theater, in 1976, Patrice Chéreau introduced a radical reimagining of the *Ring*; the curtain rose on what appeared to be a hydroelectric dam, setting in motion a critique of industrial civilization. In my European travels, I have seen a *Tristan* in which most of the action unfolded inside a pulsating pink cube; a *Ring* whose Wotan expressed his desperation by feeding papers into a shredder; and a *Parsifal* where the climactic transfiguration of the Grail Temple was accompanied by film footage of decomposing rabbits. Somehow, Wagner retains his identity even when all hell is breaking loose onstage. His music can serve as a hypnotic soundtrack for any set of images, from Valkyries in traditional getups to the Vietnam air raid of *Apocalypse Now*.

Verdi, on the other hand, is minutely site-specific. His arching phrases imply a certain mode of address, his rhythms a certain way of stalking to and fro. Indeed, for the later operas, Verdi's publisher created staging manuals that indicate exactly how the scenic action should follow the music. Verdi characters are defined by and against their social worlds, and if Violetta is singing against a featureless brick wall her insoluble dilemma probably won't come through. Above all, Verdi's art of dramatic irony depends for its effect on a veneer of ordinariness. In the climactic masked-ball scene of *Un ballo*, in the long minutes before Riccardo is fatally stabbed, dance music heightens the suspense, and, in one of the composer's most ferocious strokes, it keeps playing for a little while *after* the attack; as the staging manual explains, news of the murder has yet to reach musicians in other parts of the palace. Such nuances probably won't register if the opera has been moved to Iraq or outer space. Too many productions are masked balls from the outset, so you never know when anyone is putting on a disguise.

Yet the Regietheater approach to Verdi has intelligent defenders. The eminent opera scholar Philip Gossett, in his book *Divas and Scholars*, notes that Verdi seldom hesitated to move his operas from one era to another when the censors raised objections. *Rigoletto* migrated from the court of King Francis I to that of the Gonzagas in Mantua; *Un ballo*, from late-eighteenth-century Sweden to late-seventeenth-century Boston, with an aborted stopover in twelfth-century Florence. Realism in the conventional sense bored this composer; he once said, "Copying the truth may be a good thing, but *inventing the truth* is better, much better." If we are so concerned with Verdi's intentions, why are we hung up on realistic values that didn't concern him? Gossett further points out that the "traditional" approach, which these days comes freighted with opulent decor, can sabotage the rapid scene changes to which Verdi was accustomed. The composer might have exploded in frustration if he had known that Franco Zeffirelli's *Traviata* at the Met would require a break of several minutes between the two scenes of Act II, where, in a masterly transition, Violetta's break with Alfredo gives way to a frolicsome party.

Gossett chides several music critics, the present writer among them, for advocating an excessively slavish devotion to the libretto. In the original version of this essay, published in *The New Yorker* in 2001, I over-stated the case against radical direction, failing to admit that a drastic change of setting can sometimes bring potent insights. Gossett cites Jonathan Miller's 1982 production of *Rigoletto* at the English National Opera, which relocated the work to New York, with Mafia dons taking the place of Renaissance dukes. In a preamble to the production, Miller observes that Verdi's opera is itself guilty of anachronisms: the waltzing strains of "La donna è mobile" bear no resemblance to dances of the Renaissance period. In a way, such music makes *more* sense in Miller's ingenious Mafia scenario. Even more important, the Mafia's social code is not far removed from that of the Gonzagas: we have no trouble believing that a strongman is mortally afraid of exposing his daughter to his bosses, or that a hit job has gone horribly, grotesquely awry. During the protracted debate with the censors over the scenario of *Rigoletto*, Verdi commented that the action might take place in any number of places and periods so long as the Duke's underlings live in fear of their ruler. Miller's conception certainly passes that test.

The German director Peter Konwitschny made an even bolder intervention in a 2004 staging of *Don Carlos* at the Vienna State Opera—a presentation without cuts, in the form that the composer first offered the work to the Paris Opéra. (TDK released a DVD of one of the Vienna performances, with Bertrand de Billy conducting.) For the most part, the performers appear in period costumes, albeit within cold minimalist walls, but several times the historical boundaries are exploded. Konwitschny's most arresting gesture comes in the second scene of Act III, when Philip presides over a burning of heretics. Suddenly, we are in the present day, and at the Vienna State Opera; the king and his entourage are attending a gala premiere. In-house television cameras take us to the palatial staircase of the Staatsoper lobby, where a slick TV host is jabbering in several languages ("*Guten Abend, Europa!* Good evening, ladies and gentlemen! . . . *Bonsoir, mesdames et messieurs!* . . . And here he is, the Grand Inquisitor!"). When the heretics are dragged in, their muted screams mingle with the march music and celebratory chorus that greet Philip as he walks down the red carpet toward the stage. The auto-da-fé becomes a modern media spectacle, heightening Verdi's critique of the iconography of political and religious power. This is no condescending attempt at bringing Verdi "up to date"; rather, Konwitschny shows the degree to which we are still living in Verdi's world.

Reflexive traditionalists and reflexive radicals may see themselves as sworn enemies, but they are both making the same mistake, applying a universal template to the scores. The crucial thing is to be responsive rather than reductive, to let the work dictate the staging. Andrew Porter has it right when he says, on the topic of producing Verdi, that "one needs to be totally pragmatic." Nothing should be ruled out, but directors should respect the dramatic trajectory of the music and keep in mind Verdi's own staging ideas. And let it be remembered that on any given night many people will be seeing the opera for the first time. Gossett notices that opera-goers, as a rule, show much less of a spirit of adventure than the audiences for Shakespeare plays and other theater classics. But most playgoers have been exposed to Shakespeare from grade school onward; they know how it's supposed to go, and are open to different approaches. Those seeing *Trovatore* for the first time will be intoxicated by the old-fashioned crazi-ness of the plot; they want to see hysteria, bizarre occurrences, a mother accidentally throwing her baby on the fire. On at least some nights, they should have it.

In the spring of 2001, I went to the old port city of Genoa to see a produc-tion of *Giovanna d'Arco* (*Joan of Arc*), a lesser but still absorbing work from Verdi's early years. The staging was by the German filmmaker Werner Herzog, who, despite his visual flair, struggled to bring the opera to life. I remember the trip less for the performance itself than for scenes I wit-nessed in the streets outside. The Associazione Nazionale Alpini, an orga-nization of veterans of the Alpine military corps, was holding its annual convention that weekend, and Genoa was thronged with small bands of men of all ages, each group from a different part of Italy. As they marched to and fro, they periodically burst into song, accompanying themselves on beat-up brass instruments. I was struck by the fact that these amateurs were employing essentially the same musical language that runs through the Verdi canon. The raw matter of *Traviata* and *Trovatore* was filling the air. Some of the tunes were, in fact, Verdi's own: at one point I heard the strains of "Va pensiero," the famous chorus from *Nabucco*. I tried to cross the avenue to see who was playing it, but I found my path blocked by a large truck, on top of which a woman in Alpine costume was dancing.

"Va pensiero"—the lamentation of the Hebrews by the waters of Babylon—has a tangled history. According to a long-standing legend, the chorus sparked a patriotic riot at the premiere of *Nabucco*, with Italian operagoers relating the Hebrews' plight to their own situation under Austrian rule. That legend was apparently a retroactive invention; the scholar Roger Parker has found no evidence that "Va pensiero" received special attention on opening night. Yet, as Philip Gossett points out, the police had decided to keep an eye on *Nabucco*, fearing an "inappropriate reaction" to the biblical plot. Even if no overt demonstration occurred, the crowd may have been seething all the same. Over the following decades, "Va pensiero" increasingly dominated the Italian psyche, to the point where it became something like an alternative national anthem. Beyond that, it has become a song of solidarity in foreign lands. When the Metropolitan Opera opened its season in September 2001, eleven days after the destruction of the World Trade Center, the chorus began by singing "Va pensiero" in honor of the victims of the attack. The scene was utterly different from the one I had witnessed in Genoa some months before, but the link between music and public was just as strong.

The greatness of Verdi is a simple thing. Solitary by nature, he found a way of speaking to limitless crowds, and his method was to sink himself completely into his characters. He never composed music for music's sake; every phrase helps to tell a story. The most astounding scenes in his work are those in which all the voices come together in a visceral mass—like a human wave that could carry anything before it. The voices at the end of *Simon Boccanegra*, crying out in grief; the voices at the end of *Un ballo*, overcome by the spiritual magnificence of a dying man; and, of course, the voices of "Va pensiero," remembering, in a unison line, the destruction of Jerusalem. In the modern world, we seldom find ourselves in the grip of a single emotion, and this is what Verdi restores to us—the sense of belonging.

12

ALMOST FAMOUS

ON THE ROAD WITH THE ST. LAWRENCE QUARTET

At the beginning of the 1990s, the Emerson String Quartet, well on its way to becoming the most celebrated American chamber group, was auditioning younger ensembles for a training program at the Hartt School of Music, in Connecticut. Piles of performance tapes came in, and the members of the Emerson decided to listen to them while driving between destinations on a European tour. One tape, from a young Toronto quartet, juxtaposed the expected Beethoven with a contemporary Canadian work in which the players were required to yell at the top of their lungs. The screaming began just as the Emersons were negotiating a difficult stretch of Alpine road. "We'd heard this perfectly good Beethoven, and we were saying, 'Very nice,' when the screaming started, and we almost lost control of the car," the violinist Philip Setzer recalled. "We could all have died right then and there. Of course, we had to meet the crazy kids who sent in the tape."

By the beginning of the following decade, the members of the St. Lawrence String Quartet—Geoff Nuttall, Barry Shiffman, Lesley Robertson, and Marina Hoover—had gained a firm foothold in the world of American chamber music. They were the ensemble-in-residence at Stanford University, and they regularly trained younger quartets themselves. Yet they had not lost their contrarian streak; they had a way of catching audiences off guard. Their playing retained a certain jumpy freedom, as if the dinner-party conversation of chamber music were about to break down into altercation, demonstration, or confession. "They've got something," David Finckel, the cellist of the Emerson, told me. "Performers either have something or they don't, and the St. Lawrence does. I'm not sure what it is. Partly, it's the ability to play the most familiar music as if it were new and unusual. Everything the quartet does becomes contemporary music. Listening, I forget that I do the same thing for a living."

There are at least a hundred full-time professional string quartets in North America, plus an untold number of amateurs. To make a living in this field, you have to be willing to play almost anywhere and at any time. Even a group as famous as the Emerson follows the same exhausting routine: fly into a strange town, rent a car, test out the hall, play the concert, go to the postconcert reception, get a few hours' sleep, return to the airport, and fly to the next date. The Lawrences have played in international culture capitals, and they have also won the acclaim of Canadian fishing villages, Uruguayan mountain towns, and Kansas City public schools. Perhaps their most unusual appearance was in Vietnam, at the Hanoi Opera House, a replica of the Palais Garnier, in Paris. The wealthier patrons were seated in the auditorium, but a crowd of thousands watched a telecast of the concert outside, many of them leaning on their scooters.

One of my earliest assignments as a New York music critic was to cover the Lawrences' New York debut, in 1992, in the Young Concert Artists series at the 92nd Street Y. I was struck by the intelligent passion that the group brought to performances of Mozart's "Dissonant" Quartet, Alban Berg's Quartet Opus 3, and Beethoven's Quartet in C-sharp Minor. Although in the subsequent ten years they made quick advances in the music business—signing with the powerhouse agency Columbia Artists Management, Inc., or CAMI; winning a recording contract with EMI— they never returned to New York in a flashy way. So, in the spring of 2001, I decided to follow them on tour for a week or so, to get a sense of what life was like for a gifted but overlooked classical ensemble. In recent years, the Lawrences have moved to the front rank of their profession, appearing regularly at Lincoln Center and Carnegie Hall, and they have undergone two changes of personnel, with Shiffman and Hoover ceding their places to Scott St. John and Christopher Costanza. Yet their approach to making music remains essentially the same. If the score asks them to scream, they happily do so.

When I joined the St. Lawrence Quartet on the road, the group was scheduled to play two concerts in El Paso, Texas, and one in Joplin, Missouri. There were the usual travel hassles. A sandstorm delayed flights out of Dallas–Fort Worth, and when the members of the quartet got to the hotel, at midnight, the reception desk had no record of their reservations. It was one of those sleepy, lost-in-time places—call it the Vista Grande—where guests can be a confusing novelty. When I arrived, I was handed a cryptic message that said, "Barry: Call Alex." Still, the vista was grand. You could look out over basketball courts, medical facilities, and pueblo-style suburbs to the brown expanse of the Rio Grande, with Juárez stretching out on the other side.

The next day, at around noon, the Lawrences gathered in the lobby. If you had been told that they were musicians, but not of the classical kind, you might have guessed that they were a veteran indie-rock band, some well-traveled cousin to Yo La Tengo. Nuttall, the athletic first violinist, found a YMCA and had been lifting weights. Shiffman, the second violinist, and Robertson, the violist, had been practicing. Hoover, the cellist, was with her husband, Richard Bernstein, and their seven-month-old baby, Benjamin. Hoover often looks harried: traveling with a baby is hard enough, but a baby and a cello together can spell real trouble. Flight attendants have tried to bar her cello from planes, even though she always buys a seat for it. The attendants apparently have a vision of the instrument flying around the cabin and causing a crash. Hoover is the most organized of the Lawrences—she is the one who knows when the next plane leaves—and she has a way of barreling past human annoyances as if they simply were not there.

Kwang-Wu Kim, the artistic director of El Paso Pro-Musica, was waiting for the quartet in the lobby. He was, in classical-music parlance, the "presenter." The Lawrences have had all kinds of experiences with presenters: some good, some bad, some indifferent. They have worked with a music-loving radiologist who goes over programming minutiae while on break from the hospital; a philosophy professor who has a seventy-person concert hall in his home; and an eclectic Florida promoter who puts on chamber music one night and Steve Lawrence and Eydie Gorme the next. Presenters who usually have to deal with disorderly pop acts are pleased by their demeanor. One impresario found them refreshing after a run-in with a well-known folk-music personality, who had disappeared from her hotel after noticing that an instance of "improper land management" was visible from her window.

The Lawrences thought highly of Kwang-Wu Kim. "He's a genius," they said to me beforehand. A pianist, professor, and all-around explainer, Kim has degrees in philosophy from Yale and in music from Peabody. He had attracted a Who's Who of American chamber players to El Paso, and also ventured into the city's schools, retrieving out-of-tune pianos from janitorial closets and introducing kids to the classics.

Kim and the Lawrences traded complaints about the unhelpfulness of CAMI. "The people there sent me the wrong programs, and then they told me that they didn't understand the need for sending copies of the program notes in advance," Kim said. The Lawrences collectively rolled their eyes: management's aloofness from their daily lives had been a long-running problem. The subject of audience turnout came up. "We're not sure if this is going to be our biggest audience of the year," Kim said. "Somehow, we forgot that this weekend is Passover. Also, Matchbox Twenty is playing tonight at the University of Texas, which means that the students probably won't show up. And we couldn't get an article into the local paper. They told us that they were concerned about already giving too much attention to classical music, which is pretty funny, because they don't pay any attention to classical music at all."

More than three hundred people attended the two concerts, most of them well-to-do and middle-aged. At one point, Kim gave a talk, revealing his flair for persuasion. He was a blast of positive energy, flattering the audience with a sense that this series was no less important than the East Coast world from which he came. "I was the laughingstock of the Peabody conservatory when I announced that I was going to El Paso," he said. "They were horrified. Their basic attitude was 'Another one bites the dust.' Well, we need to stop making value judgments about place. There is absolutely no difference in real musical value between a concert in Carnegie Hall and a concert at the Fox Fine Arts Center in El Paso. Music is a universal act of human conversation, and an identical act of conversation is happening in each place. Haydn didn't write his quartets for New York City, and they are equally at home in El Paso."

Some old-school musicians disdain the idea of addressing the audience, but the Lawrences find it natural to talk about what they're up to. They have a gift for describing musical abstractions in down-to-earth terms. Nuttall warned the El Paso crowd that a contemporary piece— Jonathan Berger's *Miracles and Mud*—would appear on the first half of the program. "We like to put the modern work second, just before inter-mission," he said. "That way, you can't come late and miss it, and you can't leave at intermission and skip it." There was knowing laughter from the crowd. He explained the idea behind Berger's work, which has to do with the Israeli-Palestinian conflict, and played the two recurring folk themes that represent the warring peoples. This demonstration seemed to make Berger's tangy, Bartókian dissonances more palatable. Three-fourths of the quartet are generally gung-ho for contemporary works; Robertson tends to be skeptical, at least initially. "The viola part is often more interesting in the modern pieces," she told me, "but sometimes I'm happier droning on one note in a Haydn quartet, because I know exactly where that note belongs, logically and emotionally."

Nuttall then talked about Haydn's "Quinten," or "Fifths," Quartet, which opened the concert. "I have most of the hard licks," he said. "I'd happily play Haydn all the time, but the others get bored with repeating the same simple figures." He did a run of notes in his sweet-toned, Heifetz-like style. When he plays, he has a habit of kicking one leg back and half getting out of his chair. His hair tends to change length and color; in El Paso, it was cropped short, with blond highlights. "He looks like some dude from the beach," a man at the back of the room whispered. Nuttall's looks are a plus when he is addressing youngsters in educational programs, but the Pro-Musica regulars were a little suspicious. Still, his way of explicating details seemed to win them over. "In the final move-ment," he went on, "Haydn does this thing to the solo line which is actu-ally pretty cool. He puts in this weird fingering so you end up having to slide from one note to another, and suddenly you're playing in Gypsy style—portamento. It's as if Haydn were telling conservatory-trained vio-linists to forget their training and loosen up."

Nuttall is the St. Lawrence's "secret weapon," as the rest of the group admits. An opera maven and pop-music fan, he executes his solo lines with an airy, vocal freedom, revealing a vibrant personality that is lacking in many better-known soloists. "He has a way of generating intensity in all of us, with his revved-up excitement at whatever he's playing," Hoover told me. Something about him harks back to the unregulated virtuosos of a century ago; his phrasing often upsets the central pulse of a movement, and the others either follow his lead or scramble to restore rhythmic order. As a result, despite the discipline of the quartet's rehearsal process, many passages sound almost improvised. "They play with un-self-conscious joy," says the composer Osvaldo Golijov, whose work *The Dreams and Prayers of Isaac the Blind*, for quartet and klezmer clarinet, is a St. Lawrence specialty. "They can excite people who show up at chamber-music concerts by a fluke. I saw this happen with a group of Argentine soccer players."

The St. Lawrence's spontaneity had a bracing effect on Tchaikovsky's Third Quartet, which was the centerpiece of the El Paso concerts. Tchaikovsky and Schumann are two composers whom the Lawrences have investigated thoroughly; they had recorded two Schumann quartets for EMI, and were preparing to release a disc of Tchaikovsky. Both composers have been accused of writing unidiomatic chamber music, but the Tchaikovsky roared to life. In rehearsal, the players concentrated on clarifying its three-against-two cross-rhythms. In performance, they threw everything back up in the air, flirting with disaster in the opening movement. In the funeral-march Andante, Nuttall's solos sobbed in the middle distance, sounding like 78-rpm records of turn-of-the-century divas; Shiffman's obsessive, one-note patterns gnawed at the fabric of the harmony. The finale played a bit like a drunken wake.

Cocktail-party chatter is the last thing you might want to engage in after such a performance, but the postconcert reception is a fact of life on the chamber circuit, and the Lawrences go at it gamely. The El Paso crowd turned out to be more interesting than most. The players were buttonholed in the lobby by the Reverend Paul Green, who congratulated them on raising the cultural temper of the town, and by J. O. Stewart, Jr., who underwrote the concert. Stewart was an impressive man with a hawk-like face and a handsome pair of cowboy boots; he had recently sold his company, El Paso Disposal, for $140 million. "I worked in the trash business for thirty years," he said, "so I may be a trashy guy, but that was a fine concert, and I liked the new thing, too. Maybe I can get used to that stuff. Like I always say, you can only play with one tennis racquet at a time."

There was a late-night dinner at the home of Charles and Ellen Lacy, in the hills above El Paso. Nuttall, who lived in Texas when he was a child, stayed the longest, drinking wine with a group of reformed good old boys. "I like those guys," he said, as we drove back to the Vista Grande. "They know how to kick back. They're not stuffy, even though they have some weird-ass politics. But I wish there had been a few more young people. Where were the University of Texas students? At Matchbox Twenty, I guess. Kind of kills me that there's ten thousand people seeing them and a hundred people seeing us. I don't see why the difference should be that dramatic. I mean, Rob Thomas is a good singer and all, but we're—we've got the deeper songs."

After the second concert, which happened the following afternoon, the Lawrences left for Joplin. In travel mode, they go their separate ways, not worrying if the others are on schedule. In the vastness of the Dallas–Fort Worth Airport, I noticed that Nuttall had wandered off. "Where's Geoff?" I asked. "We never ask that question," the others replied. It was well after midnight when we reached Joplin. It's a midsize town in the southwestern corner of the state, not far from the country-and-western playground of Branson. Shiffman caught sight of a poster for Shoji Tabuchi, a Liberace-style fiddler who plays in Branson. The poster read, "Shoji: Need We Say More?" "This is great!" the violinist said, jumping up and down in a fit of ironic glee. "We should have this kind of marketing. 'The St. Lawrence String Quartet: Need We Say More?'"

Joplin offered a recapitulation of themes already developed in El Paso. This series was also called Pro Musica, and it, too, had a decisive person-ality at the center. Cynthia Schwab, a Manhattan native, has been work-ing to create a musical oasis in Joplin for twenty years. "The three things in life that mean the most to me are God, hockey, and music," she said. In her garage, a New York Rangers banner hung next to a poster for the Leipzig Chamber Orchestra. Schwab had approached the St. Lawrence with a surprising proposal: for the twentieth anniversary of her series, she wanted the group to play an all-contemporary program.

The Joplin concert took place in a fine old church at the center of town. The star attraction was the Third Quartet of R. Murray Schafer, a Cana-dian avant-garde composer who has specialized in dismantling the stan-dard concert experience and bringing music into the wider environment. The Schafer quartet has long been one of the St. Lawrence's favorites. It begins with the cellist playing alone onstage, somewhat despondently. One by one, the others enter—from behind the stage and from the back of the hall. War erupts between the violins, with savage accusations traded back and forth. In the second movement, all hell breaks loose: the Lawrences reprise their yelling act, screaming gibberish in tandem with fast-moving dissonant lines. It's a spellbinding spectacle, and it is also a hilarious send-up of the emotional infantilism of certain ultramodern composers. Then, in the final movement, the mood turns solemn, as the quartet plays a prayerful unison melody in ghostly quarter tones. At the end, the music disappears over the horizon of audibility, leaving a mystical silence.

The citizens of Joplin had a mixed reaction to this astonishing piece. A third of them didn't buy it, and they expressed their dismay by leaving at intermission, trudging in stony silence to the church parking lot. There were approving yelps, however, from a group of younger people in the back rows. They turned out to be music students, some of whom had worked with the Lawrences in their quartet-training program at Stanford, and they had driven three hours from Kansas City to see their mentors play. Four of them belonged to a quartet called the Yurodivy, which is Russian for "holy fool." The leader of the Yurodivys was Francisco Herrera, a large fellow in a purple sash. "Did you hear the intonation in the third move-ment?" he asked. "Incredible. There's no kitsch in their playing. They ab-solutely believe in what they're doing."

At the inevitable postconcert dinner, Cynthia Schwab made it clear that the Yurodivy crew could not be accommodated. The mood turned glum. Nuttall, in particular, looked crestfallen. He poked at his dessert unenthusiastically. "I'm sorry your young friends weren't able to come," Schwab eventually said, after conversation glided to a halt. "I had to get you over here, and I have responsibilities to my board members." Nuttall shook his head and replied, "You should be bringing more young people like them to your concerts. They are the audience of the future."

It was now close to midnight, and the Lawrences had to catch a 7:00 flight the next morning. They piled into their rented Dodge Caravan and drove off. From this tour, each of them had earned, after expenses, a low four-figure sum that wouldn't have covered the hotel bill for Maurizio Pollini's piano. As I headed to my motel room, I thought of the Yurodivys, driving back to Kansas City in the dark, and of Cynthia Schwab's recep-tion, and of the many ways in which classical music entangles itself in a web of money and status. And I realized that the four musicians of the St. Lawrence deserve fame not simply for the quality of their music-making but for the joy they take in the act of connection.

13

EDGES OF POP

KIKI AND HERB, CECIL TAYLOR AND SONIC YOUTH,

SINATRA, KURT COBAIN

KIKI AND HERB, 2003

It is said of many show-business legends that they lose touch with the ordinary world and become cartoons of their former selves. Kiki DuRane, a sixty-something lounge singer who tours ad nauseam with a doleful accompanist named Herb, has gone in the opposite direction; she is a fictional creation who has acquired the grit of the real. Kiki and Herb are the invention of the writer-performer Justin Bond and the pianist Kenny Mellman, who have long been fixtures at downtown New York venues like Flamingo East, PS 122, and Fez. They have refined their act into an Off-Broadway show, *Kiki & Herb: Coup de Théâtre*, which recently opened at the Cherry Lane. It is a slashingly funny, psychically unsettling entertainment—part cabaret, part rock and roll, part Victorian melodrama—to which the category of camp does not apply. Camp implies knowingness and detachment; Bond's Kiki is anarchic and atavistic, in the grip of forces beyond her control. She is almost militant in her decrepitude. Reminiscing airily about her old friend Grace Kelly, barking obscenely at childhood foes, drifting into a sullen stupor, snapping back to life with yawps of vicious glee, Kiki is a beacon of insanity in a world that may finally be coming around to her point of view.

The conceit of the show is that Kiki, a self-described "boozy chanteusie," is aiming to attract new listeners by singing contemporary hits. "It is both thrilling and humbling that so many young people have, as it were, 'tuned in to our sound,'" she says, with the overenunciation of the early-evening alcoholic. Thus begins a scorched-earth advance across decades of pop music, from Bob Merrill's "Make Yourself Comfortable" to Kylie Minogue's "Can't Get You out of My Head." Kiki's flailing stabs at modern trends call to mind such classic miscalculations as Mae West's renditions of Beatles songs and Ethel Merman's disco album, but the genius of Kiki is that her entire career seems to consist of bungled crossover projects: a bossa-nova album (*Kiki and Herb: Don't Blame It on Kiki and Herb*, 1964), a spoken-word record (*Kiki and Herb: Whitey on the Moon*, 1972), a belated disco effort (*Kiki and Herb: One Last Chance to Blow*, 1983). The songstress hurls herself at this material with such dire enthusiasm that she takes full possession of it. Lately, she has taken an interest in rap, which she calls "the folk music of today." In past shows, she has sung Wu-Tang Clan and Snoop Doggy Dogg, adding jazz vocalise to such lyrics as "All my niggaz and my bitches / Throw your motherfuckin' hands in the air!" This time, she takes on Eminem, whose self-pitying hysteria suits her beautifully.

Between the songs come autobiographical vignettes. Bond has mapped out the life of Kiki in loving detail, and each show adds a few new twists to the familiar downward spiral. The singer was born during the Great Depression, overshadowed by tragedy from the start. "A lot of people jumped out of windows when the stock market collapsed in 1929," she recalls, "but not all of them died. My father was such a man." She was given the diagnosis of "retard" and placed in a children's institution in western Pennsylvania. There she met Herb, a foundling of indeterminate origin. When Herb fell victim to a predatory delinquent named Danny, Kiki was there to comfort him, and a great friendship was born. (The Danny episode inspires one of the show's set pieces, a dramatic monologue built around the song "I'm Ugly and I Don't Know Why," by an obscure band called Butt Trumpet, with adornments from the inspirational Christian poem "Footprints.") The duo's musical career developed only in fits and starts. There was a prolonged interruption when Kiki had to serve a jail sentence for the attempted murder of her first husband, an abusive boxer named Ruby. "I wasn't trying to kill him," Kiki explains, "only trying to get his attention."

Throughout the evening, the chanteuse looks back ruefully to the year 1967, when her life turned momentarily posh. A flashback sequence re-creates the scene: Kiki and Herb are playing at the Grand Casino, in Monte Carlo, at the invitation of Princess Grace. They are making what should have been their triumphant comeback album, *Kiki and Herb: It's Not Unusual.* Kiki has Aristotle Onassis as a lover, Maria Callas as a rival. Fortune has raised her up, but now a terrible tragedy lays her low. During a Mediterranean cruise, she leaves her seven-year-old daughter, Coco, alone on deck while she goes below to satisfy her carnal needs. "Ladies and gentlemen," she says, head cast down, "where the hell can a kid go on the deck of a boat?" At this juncture, the performance begins to waver between black comedy and something like genuine pathos. Kiki's failures as a singer pale next to her failures as a mother. The watery death of Coco haunts her. She has lost touch with her two other children, who claim not to know her, even though she sends them all her press clippings. She takes refuge in another glass of Canadian Club and ginger ale—the piano is equipped with a drink holder—and the drink begins to take its toll. She digresses, and digresses again—"Where was I, ladeezh n genlmn?"—and then stops, staring fixedly at nothing.

Just when it seems that the comic spirit of the evening has been swallowed up in melancholy, the original, rampaging Kiki returns, her extreme jazz vocals now fueled by rage at herself and the world. She turns for solace to her fans, who have always stood by her side, albeit in dwindling numbers. What the world needs, she says, is more love, for "without love . . . there is only rape."

Kiki & Herb is a comedy, at least on the surface, but the performers are serious people who smuggle into their act a fair degree of theatrical and musical sophistication. Bond, who is forty, is a native of Hagerstown, Maryland. He studied classical acting in London, but he developed a distaste for that aspect of theater which involved working with directors. He moved to San Francisco in 1988 and threw himself into street theater, avant-garde noise, and conceptual cabaret. One night, while trying to think of an innovative birthday present for a friend, he drew age marks on his face and assumed the Kiki persona. He is resigned to being labeled a "drag queen," although, after meeting him offstage, you want to find a mellower label for his particular brand of gender vagueness. Bond is simply a svelte person who looks stylish in women's clothes, especially swinging-sixties outfits, like the ones Faye Dunaway wore in *The Thomas Crown Affair.*

Mellman, who is thirty-four, has the innocent face, diffident air, and slightly bewildered expression of someone who has spent long hours at the piano since childhood. He studied composition at the University of California at Berkeley, but became disenchanted with the music department when he was told that Erik Satie's seldom heard *Socrate* was too boring to warrant a performance. He switched to San Francisco State to study poetry, and sought a new medium for his musical curiosity. He found it when he met Bond, and began accompanying the singer in such hard-to-reconstruct nightclub evenings as *Dixie McCall's Patterns for Living*. Kiki made her public debut one night in 1993, when, at the end of a Gay Pride weekend, Bond and Mellman felt too exhausted to do their usual program. "You're Herb, I'm Kiki," Bond said, before they went onstage, and a fading star was born.

The early Kiki and Herb shows were distinctly messier than the one at the Cherry Lane. They were fueled by the energy and anger of AIDS activism—the in-your-face tactics of ACT UP and Queer Nation. Bond and Mellman used to heighten the naturalism of the show by drinking copiously onstage. When I first saw them, in the late nineties, Kiki would climb on top of café tables and order the customers to lick her legs. If you tried to move your drink out of the way, she might grab it out of your hand. Another night, she threw a tray of steak knives, fortunately causing no harm. When Bond was asked to perform at Madonna's birthday party, he got into a scuffle with the R&B artist D'Angelo. Kiki and Herb emerged as much from the spit-spewing, scenery-chewing mentality of punk rock as from the cabaret tradition. It's not much of a contradiction, when you consider how many of the original New York punk rockers came out of the avant-garde art scene, the gay underground, and other bohemias.

In the end, *Kiki & Herb* is more political than its premise suggests. We should have expected no less from a woman who alleges to have been engaged to the radical black presidential candidate Dick Gregory. The politics surfaces not just in Kiki's commentary on current affairs—summing up George W. Bush's approach to homeland security, she advises, "Whatever you do, don't go out and don't stay in"—but also in her obsession with the figure of the abandoned, abused, or socially outcast child. The stories return relentlessly to this theme—a young gay boy raped by his classmates, a girl cast aside by her mother and placed in an institution. Of course, whenever Kiki is beginning to break your heart with these tales, she has to blurt out something stunningly grotesque. "If you weren't abused as a child," she declares, "you must have been an ugly kid." The unshockable downtown crowd never fails to gasp at that one.

Only an academic paper in gender studies could do justice to the complexities of Kikiness. (In fact, an NYU graduate student has written a thesis on the subject.) The show also makes interesting points about music—about how songs are sung and about what they mean. This is where poor Herb comes to the fore. Kenny Mellman's job is to make sense on the piano of his partner's daft repertoire, and those who feel that modern pop songs have too much technology and too little music will enjoy his Luddite solutions. Rachmaninovian bass octaves give symphonic heft to a song like Radiohead's "Exit Music (for a Film)." To suggest the saturated textures of hip-hop production, he attacks the instrument in a dissonant frenzy, substituting cluster chords for synthetic beats. He gets a big, bellowing sound out of the piano. Herb, as Kiki portrays him, is a damaged child seeking refuge in music, and the piano is the vehicle of his revenge.

The high points of the show are the medleys, which are carefully constructed simulations of music losing its mind. One song morphs into the next before you really notice what's going on. In Kiki and Herb's beloved Christmas medleys, "We Wish You a Merry Christmas" becomes the Velvet Underground's "Heroin"; "Rudolph the Red-Nosed Reindeer" becomes Nirvana's "Smells Like Teen Spirit." The showstopper in the current show begins with "Whitey on the Moon," Gil Scott-Heron's protest song about moon landings and racial injustice. After a minute or two, Scott-Heron's spoken-word anthem has mutated into latter-day rap—Eminem's "Lose Yourself," with its inspiring chorus, "You better lose yourself in the music, the moment / you own it, you better never let it go." A second later, Kiki shrieks, "And you may ask yourself, 'What is that beautiful house?'" and we are in the middle of Talking Heads' "Once in a Lifetime." The transitions are seamless because Mellman translates all the songs into his own peculiar musical voice, which might be described as John Cage cocktail lounge.

When I asked Mellman about the Eminem medley, he said that he had spent a weekend working on it and that the theme of it was appropriation. Kiki singing Eminem is ridiculous; but no less ridiculous than Eminem, a white kid, mimicking black culture, or Talking Heads incorporating African beats into their SoHo art rock. Every singer, even Gil Scott-Heron, is pretending in one way or another—putting on drag—and Kiki does the service of bulldozing all the façades of authenticity. There's something liberating about the way the songs break free of categories and come together in a midnight carnival. The music becomes as androgynous as the performer: it is always changing shape and identity. This is probably why fellow musicians find Kiki and Herb so compelling. Everyone from Lou Reed to the Pet Shop Boys has attended their shows. Among the rock memorabilia that Bond has accumulated is Edie Sedgwick's leopard-skin pillbox hat; he wears it while singing Bob Dylan's "Leopard-Skin Pill-Box Hat."

Bond and Mellman are in the curious position of being celebrities' celebrities—famous to the famous but little known outside the downtown scene. For years, they have contemplated taking their act out of lounges and into legitimate theaters; with some trepidation, they are now doing it. If they find wider fame, it will be richly deserved, but their longtime fans don't want them to wander too far from their punk-drag roots, when they scared the daylights out of unsuspecting customers. Once, during a show in San Francisco, Bond went to an open window and began shouting to people on the street outside: "Just don't get too comfortable out there!" ·

SONIC YOUTH AND CECIL TAYLOR, 1998

Picture music as a map, and musical genres as continents—classical music as Europe, jazz as America, rock as Asia. Each genre has its distinct culture of playing and listening. Between the genres are the cold oceans of taste, which can be cruel to musicians who try to cross over. There are always brave souls willing to make the attempt: Aretha Franklin sings "Nessun dorma" at the Grammys; Paul McCartney writes a symphony; violinists perform on British TV in punk regalia or lingerie. Such exploits get the kind of giddy attention that used to greet early aeronautical feats like Charles Lindbergh's solo flight and the maiden voyage of the Hindenburg.

There is another route between genres. It's the avant-garde path—a kind of icy Northern Passage that you can traverse on foot. Practitioners of free jazz, underground rock, and avant-garde classical music are, in fact, closer to one another than they are to their less radical colleagues. Listeners, too, can make unexpected connections in this territory. As I discovered in my college years, it is easy to go from the orchestral hurly-burly of Xenakis and Penderecki to the free-jazz piano of Cecil Taylor and the dissonant rock of Sonic Youth. For lack of a better term, call it the art of noise.

"Noise" is a tricky word that quickly slides into the pejorative. Often, it's the word we use to describe a new kind of music that we don't understand. Variations on the put-down "That's just noise" were heard at the premiere of Stravinsky's *Rite of Spring*, during Dylan's first tours with a band, and on street corners when kids started blasting rap. But "noise" can also accurately describe an acoustical phenomenon, and it needn't be negative. Human ears are attracted to certain euphonious chords based on the overtone series; when musicians pile on too many extraneous tones, the ear "maxes out." This is the reason that free jazz, experimental rock, and experimental classical music seem to be speaking the same language: from the perspective of the panicking ear, they are. It's a question not of volume but of density. There is, however, pleasure to be had in the kind of harmonic density that shatters into noise. The pleasure comes in the control of chaos, in the movement back and forth across the border of what is comprehensible.

Cecil Taylor is a master of this kind of music—perhaps *the* master. Since he first made his mark, in 1956, with the hard-hitting post-bop album *Jazz Advance*, he has built up a large catalogue of recordings, yet he remains well off the grid of pop culture. When you first see him, you have the impression of a crazy man pounding a piano to pieces. The cascade of tones saturates the ears. But once you get over the dynamism of his hands and fingers, you feel the dynamism of his mind. At the beginning of one of his improvisations, a short run of notes spatters across the lower or middle range of the piano. It's seldom couched in traditional jazz scales: it may be a rising-and-falling chromatic pattern, or an angular figure running around a minor triad, or some more abstract sequence of intervals. The development of these ideas shows a voracious intelligence; they are thrown into different octaves, turned upside down, smashed apart, mutated into song. In an appearance at the 1998 Texaco Jazz Festival, Taylor fell into an unusually lyrical mood: his Hammerklavier sound suddenly faded in the latter part of the set. Some young jazz types left in apparent boredom. But it was in that long, soft epilogue that you could hear the symmetrical beauty of his melodies most clearly.

Taylor is viewed with suspicion by many people in the jazz world, and perhaps with good reason: he comes off more as a self-willed improvising composer than as a jazz democrat. Still, pianists like Matthew Shipp and Marilyn Crispell have followed his lead in importing modern classical harmonies to jazz. The radical saxophonist John Zorn has made a move in the opposite direction, building up a catalogue of works for classical chamber groups and orchestra. Roscoe Mitchell and Anthony Braxton are two other jazz people who have blurred the line between improvisation and formal composition. They have replicated, to a disorienting degree, the fragmented sound world of serialism, which ordinarily relies on laborious contrapuntal procedures. And because of the relative spontaneity of the approach, jazz atonality sounds rather more sensuous to the ear. This, of course, is not what Schoenberg had in mind when he introduced the twelve-tone system. He said that it would ensure the supremacy of German music for another hundred years; he did not think that it would generate cool chords for jazz.

Can rock also go free and atonal? This possibility opened up in the late sixties. The Beatles cited Stockhausen as a model and hired an orchestra to play ad libitum on "A Day in the Life." The Byrds modeled their hyped-up guitar work in "Eight Miles High" on space-age Coltrane. The Velvet Underground placed surreally pretty fragments of pop amid firestorms of overlapping guitars. And Frank Zappa borrowed abrasive harmonies from Edgard Varèse. Many seekers of avant-rock gravitated to New York; they rumbled behind punk in the seventies, and pooled resources at the end of the decade in a movement called No Wave. After crossing paths on various occasions in the late seventies, the core members of Sonic Youth—Thurston Moore, Kim Gordon, and Lee Ranaldo—came together in 1981, at a nine-day event called Noise Fest. Steve Shelley joined as the drummer in 1985. It's a measure of Sonic Youth's oblique relationship with rock-and-roll-as-usual that the band has been stable and prolific for nearly twenty years.

Sonic Youth's guitars don't twist and shout—they chime and blend. The strings are retuned to unusual pitch collections, melodies are honed to roughly hummable fragments, harmonies slide out of sync and accumulate in dreamy clusters. More often than not the songs fall into an A-B-A structure in which the B section is pure anarchy. That pattern isn't a Sonic Youth invention; Led Zeppelin had foisted it on a mass public with

"Whole Lotta Love." But Sonic Youth give their noise an arty sheen. There's no druggy delirium or macho stadium swell; instead, there's a bemused, straight-faced exhibition of extremities. Moore and Ranaldo sometimes lay their guitars down on the stage and poke at them with blunt instruments. (That technique originated with the experimental collective AMM, whose 1966 work "After Rapidly Circling the Plaza" is the *Don Giovanni*, the *Kind of Blue*, of noise.) Gordon, with her electric bass slung over her dress, adds a hint of rock glamour, although her voice—at once fierce and fatigued—drips with downtown disaffection.

The no longer youthful members of Sonic Youth have set aside the old rock-and-roll mission to broadcast breaking news about youth culture. Instead, they have more of a jazz mentality: they invite you to check in from time to time on an act that stays aggressively in place. It wasn't always so. Not long ago they were being acclaimed as prophets of grunge. They'd signed with Geffen Records in 1990 and had persuaded the label to sign their opening act, Nirvana. Their records from that period were jittery, marred by self-conscious attempts at punk-pop hits. Sonic Youth are back on track with a new record, *A Thousand Leaves*, which is loose, spacious, psychedelic. The band even shows a hint of classical hauteur on a recent series of independently released EPs, which are designed to look like fifties-era avant-garde artifacts. These discs carry the legend "Musical Perspectives"; they're printed in Dutch, French, and Esperanto, and have songs titled "Anagrama," "Improvisation Ajoutée," and "Stil." Modernist intellectuality is being mocked and also slyly appropriated. Sonic Youth are now writing, in the best sense, classical music.

FRANK SINATRA, 1998

People always assumed that Frank Sinatra's voice was a projection of his personality—that the voice and the man were one and the same. In fact, there was a long, quiet struggle between them. The trumped-up legend doesn't jive with the underlying steadiness of Sinatra's musicianship. We should remember his startling intelligence as a singer—the way he husbanded his good but not necessarily great voice into something joyful and profound. We should remember his phenomenal breath control—the way he spun out long, luxurious phrases without seeming to stop for air. (He used to swim laps underwater, thinking about lyrics all the while.) We should remember his vocal courage—the way he saved his voice at mid-career by making virtues of the cracks that had appeared in his technique. We should remember his love of language—the way he dramatized words, brought dry polysyllables to life. (No other singer could make so much of the word "unphotographable.") And we should remember his love of complex orchestral arrangements, his instinct for matching his voice to the instruments, his graciousness toward his regular players. The sweetest moment in Gay Talese's classic *Esquire* profile, "Frank Sinatra Has a Cold," is the singer's greeting to Vincent DeRosa, the great L.A. studio horn player: "Vicenzo, how's your little girl?"

To some extent, yes, the voice was the man. Sinatra's "swingin'" songs act out in musical terms his Vegas persona. But the flip sides of those songs—desolate torchers like "In the Wee Small Hours," "It's a Lonesome Old Town," and "September of My Years"—seem to come from nowhere. The source of that low, lonely thrum hasn't been identified by Sinatra's multiplying biographers; it may not have to be, because it was a musical effect, an expression of the baritone art. The voice was veering in the opposite direction from the legend: Sinatra was a lean young man who grew wealthy and stout, but it's his younger voice that sounds plump and it's his older voice that sounds thin and hungry. He knew all along— or at least until his effortful last years—that his voice was all that counted in the end. Now the voice is the only real thing we have left: the bright, sad man on the record player.

KURT COBAIN, 1994

When Kurt Cobain, the lead singer of the band Nirvana, killed himself on April 5 with a shotgun blast to the head, major media outlets gave the story wide play and warmed to its significance. Dan Rather, on the CBS network, led off hesitantly, his face full of dim amazement as he read aloud phrases like "the Seattle sound" and "Smells Like Teen Spirit." But ABC ventured bravely into interpretation, explaining the phenomenon of grunge music to "people over thirty" and obtaining one man-in-the-street reaction. "When you reach that kind of fame and you're still miserable, there's something wrong," a long-haired stoner-looking dude observed.

And NBC's correspondent ambitiously invoked "the violence, the drugs, and the diminished opportunities of an entire generation," with Tom Brokaw, the network anchor, appending a regretful smirk. This was only the evening of the first day: the newsstands were soon heavy with fresh musings on the latest lost generation, the twilit twentysomethings, the new unhappiness.

From the outset of his career, the desperately individualistic Cobain was caught in a great media babble about grunge style and twentysomething discontent. His adamantly personal songs became exhibits in the nation's ongoing symposium on generational identity—a fruitless project blending the principles of sociology and astrology. He was loudly and publicly tormented by his notoriety, his influence, his importance. Everything written about him and his wife, Courtney Love, seemed to wound him in some way.

Yet he chose a way of death guaranteed to bring down a hailstorm of prying analytical chatter far in excess of anything he had experienced while he was alive. This is the paradoxical allure of suicide: to leave the chattering world behind and yet to stage-manage the exit so that one is talked about in the right way. This was also the paradox of Cobain's pop-star career—his choice both to reject the mainstream and to attempt to redirect it. He thought he could take the road less traveled and then persuade everyone to follow him. It's amazing he got as far as he did.

MTV, the video clubhouse that brought the Nirvanamania to fever pitch, identified the band with a problematic category called "alternative." Alternative culture proposes that the establishment is reprehensible but that our substitute establishment can coexist with it, on the same commercial playing field. It differs from sixties notions of counterculture insofar as no one took it seriously even at the beginning; it sold out as a matter of principle. MTV seized on the "alternative" label as a way of laterally diversifying its offerings, much as soft-drink companies seek to invent new flavors.

Alternative music in the 1990s claimed descent from the punk-rock movement that crisscrossed America in the seventies and eighties. The claim rang false because punk in its pure form disavowed commercial success, a disavowal that united an otherwise motley array of youth subcultures: high-school misfits, skateboard kids, hardcore skinheads, doped-out postcollegiate slackers. Punk's obsession was autonomy—independent labels, clubs installed in suburban garages and warehouses, flyers and fanzines photocopied at temp jobs after hours. Some of the music was vulgar and dumb, some of it ruggedly inventive; rock finally had a viable avant-garde. In the eighties, this do-it-yourself network solidified into indie rock, anchored in college radio stations and alternative newspapers. Dumbness persisted, but there were always scattered bands picking out weird, rich chords and giving no thought to a major-label future.

Nirvana, who enjoyed local celebrity on the indie scenes of Aberdeen, Olympia, and Seattle, Washington, before blundering into the mainstream, were perfectly poised between the margin and the center. The band didn't have to dilute itself to make the transition, because its brand of grunge rock already drew more on the thunderous tread of hard rock and heavy metal than on the clean, fast, matter-of-fact attack of punk or hardcore. Where punk and indie bands generally made vocals secondary to the disordered clamor of guitars, Nirvana depended on Cobain's resonantly snarling voice, an instrument full of commercial potential from the start. But the singer was resolutely punk in spirit. He undermined his own publicity campaigns and used his commercial clout to support lesser-known bands; he was planning to start his own label, Exploitation Records, and distribute the records himself while on tour.

The songs on Nirvana's breakthrough second album, *Nevermind*, walked a difficult line between punk form and pop content. For the most part, they triumphed, and more than that they struck a nerve, not only with kids but with people in their twenties or older who recognized the mixture of components that went into the music. Dave Grohl, the dead-on drummer who kept Nirvana on an even keel, had a pragmatic view of the album's appeal: "The songs were catchy and they were simple, just like an ABC song when you were a kid." Cobain was a close, direct presence, everyone's friendless friend. The songs, despite their sometimes messy roar, were cunningly fashioned, switching in midstream from meditation to melee.

It was in the fall of 1991 that Nirvana took hold of the nation's youth and began selling records in the millions. It's best not to analyze this sudden popularity too closely; as Michael Azerrad points out in his book *Come As You Are: The Story of Nirvana*, the kind of instantaneous word-of-mouth sensation that lifted the band to the top of the charts also buoyed the careers of such differently talented personalities as Peter Frampton and Vanilla Ice. Adolescents are an omnipotent commercial force precisely because their tastes are so mercurial. In the deep dusk of the Reagan-Bush era, some segments of the youth demographic undoubtedly identified with Cobain's punkish worldview, his sympathies and discontents, and, yes, the diminished opportunities of an entire generation. Others just got off on the crushing power of the sound.

Cobain was at once irritated and intrigued by the randomness of his new audience. He lashed out at the "jock numbskulls, frat boys, and metal kids" (in Azerrad's words) who jammed clubs and arenas for his post-*Nevermind* tours. But he also liked the idea of bending their minds toward his own punk ideals and left-leaning politics: "I wanted to fool people at first. I wanted people to think that we were no different than Guns n' Roses. Because that way they would listen to the music first, accept us, and then maybe start listening to a few things that we had to say." After the initial period of fame, he let loose with social messages, not as heavy-handed or as earnest as R.E.M.'s or U2's, but carefully aimed. He was happy to discover that high schools were divided between Nirvana kids and Guns n' Roses kids.

The zeal for subversion was well meant but naïve. By condemning racists, sexists, and homophobes in his audiences, he may have promoted the cause of politically correct language in certain high-school cliques, but he did not and could not attack the deep-seated prejudices simmering beneath that language. When he declared himself "gay in spirit," as he did in an interview with the gay weekly *The Advocate*, he made a political toy out of fragile identity. And his renunciations of masculine aggression sounded hollow alongside a stage show that dealt in equipment-smashing mayhem.

The attempt to carry out social engineering through rock lyrics is a dubious one. Rock and roll has never been and will never be a vehicle for social amelioration, despite many fond hopes. Music is robbed of its intentions and associations as it goes out into the great wide open; like a rumor passed through a crowd, it emerges utterly changed. Pop songs become the property of their fans and are marked with the circumstances of their consumption, not their creation. An unsought listenership can brand the music indelibly, as the Beatles discovered when Charles Manson embraced "Helter Skelter." Or as Cobain discovered when a recording of "Smells Like Teen Spirit" was played at a Guns n' Roses show in Madison Square Garden while women in the audience were ogled on giant video screens.

...

In his suicide note, Cobain gestured toward all these crises, his lack of passion, and his disconnectedness from the broad rock audience. The story underneath is simpler and sadder: he was trying to get off drugs and found himself helpless without their support. He leaned on drugs long before he became famous, and the malevolent media circus of his last few years can't be entirely blamed for his bad end. Even when he started out, he looked tired and haggard. The rest of the story lies between him and his dealer.

Killing himself as and when he did, Cobain at least managed to deliver a final jolt to the rock world he loved and loathed. Rock stars are glamorized for dying young, but they aren't supposed to kill themselves on purpose. Greil Marcus's invaluable compendium "Rock Death in the 1970s" records 116 untimely demises, only a handful of suicides among them. A transcendent drug-induced descent is the preferred exit. Certainly, the shotgun blast casts a different light on Cobain's career; the lyrics all sound like suicide notes now. ("What else could I write / I don't have the right / What else should I be / All apologies.") He made his death unrhapsodizable.

The rage we feel at suicides may be motivated by love, but it is the love that comes of possession, not compassion. It is the urge of the crowd to repossess the defective individual. The most mordant words on the subject are still John Donne's, in defense of righteous suicide: "No detestation nor dehortation against this sin of desperation (when it is a sin) can be too earnest. But yet since it may be without infidelity, it cannot be greater than that." This sin cannot be greater than our own urge to rationalize and allegorize the recently dead, especially those who were somehow faithful to themselves.

14

LEARNING THE SCORE

THE CRISIS IN MUSIC EDUCATION

The first day I went out to Malcolm X Shabazz High School, in Newark, New Jersey, the corridors of the school were empty. When I told the guard at the entrance that I had an appointment to see Hassan Ralph Williams, the director of the Malcolm X Shabazz marching band, I was informed that the teachers and students were "at the memorial." The memorial was for Dawud Roberts, a sixteen-year-old Shabazz football player, who, a few days before, on February 9, 2005, had suffered a fatal stab wound on Johnson Avenue, a few hundred feet from the school. Some students enjoy Williams's class, which meets for three hours every afternoon, because they love playing music; others see it more pragmatically, as a way to get through the day unscathed.

A tall, suave, mellow-voiced man with a mustache and a gleaming shaved pate, Williams is a native of Ozark, Alabama. He served in the army for twenty-one years, leading marching bands in the 82nd Airborne Division and in the 25th Infantry. He then played jazz in New York, Philadelphia, and elsewhere with musicians such as Walter Bishop, Jr., and Woody Shaw. He got into teaching almost by accident, looking for work that would keep him busy between gigs. According to Donald Gatling, a longtime teacher at Shabazz, the school had a lackluster band when Williams arrived, in 1988. Now the Malcolm X Shabazz marching band is considered one of the better ones in the state, in demand for its pealing brass, explosive drum line, and manic energy.

The band room is decorated with the faces of jazz masters. Duke Ellington holds the place of honor, above the center of the blackboard. There are also placards stating the virtues of discipline, decorum, respect, and attention. One of them says, "The future belongs to those who prepare for it." A corner of the blackboard is posted with some student essays on the topic of Mozart's Requiem. "Mozart died while trying to complete this piece about Death," one student wrote. "How ironic." In front of the blackboard are five computers, each equipped with the Sibelius composing program and various tools for teaching notation. Williams encourages the students to learn musical notation at the computer, and to write their own music.

When I walked in, the Shabazz band was rehearsing John Philip Sousa's *The Stars and Stripes Forever*. The kids were making a happy noise, but details were getting lost. "Listen downward," Williams kept saying, trying to get the upper lines in sync with the lower ones. He wanted the players to bring out Sousa's dance rhythms, such as the habanera, and the songful, Italianate shape of his melodies. "A long time ago, before electricity and TV and radio, people used to dance to this," Williams said. Two clarinetists responded by jumping out of their seats and dancing around, half gleefully and half sardonically.

Members of the Shabazz band, who range in age from eight to eighteen, work hard. They not only practice from 4:00 to 7:00 p.m. each school day but also play most weekends, either at football games or at public events. In the summer, they go on the road to band camp. Williams does more than beat time; he teaches music history, social history, and black history. (Ninety-five percent of Shabazz students are African-American.) Sometimes he interrupts his usual attitude of jazz cool with a military bark. "This ain't gonna roll," he might roar when there is too much noise in the room. "This isn't happening. You may look around and see a chair coming at your head!" But the drill-sergeant routines last only a few minutes, and the kids aren't afraid to talk back. If Williams asks, "Who's got the melody?" a girl might answer, "You do!" If he drops the name Wynton Marsalis, a few might shout out, "Who dat?" (They know.)

Later in the rehearsal, the piccolo players were struggling with the twirling solos that accompany Sousa's most famous tune, the one to which the words "Three cheers for the red-white-and-blue" are sung, or, as Williams prefers to render it, "Be kind to our four-legged friends." Jihad Moore, a tall junior with a crooked smile who wore a blue-and-white basketball jersey with the number 24, was amusing himself by making an imaginary pistol out of his piccolo, holding one end of it with his thumb and gesturing toward the floor, gangsta-style. Williams was trying to get him to concentrate. He'd been telling Jihad that if he got to a certain level with the flute, or mastered a more unusual instrument like the oboe, he might be able to get into college on a scholarship. He sat Jihad next to another player, Kahliah Jordan, and had both students type their parts into the computers, using the Sibelius software. He figured that it would help them grasp the parts and memorize them.

"Put a trill on that first A-flat," he said, leaning over their shoulders.

Jihad frowned at his part and asked, "Do we have to write grandioso?"

"No, skip the grandioso."

Williams offered a new incentive. "I'll take y'all to the International Buffet if you get this solo. Just the piccolos, at the International Buffet. But only if you all get it. If you all get this, we can wipe out any band on the planet."

"I'll wipe out any piccolo players," Jihad answered enthusiastically.

The standout player in the band was a senior named Vernon Jones. A slender young man with bright eyes and wide cheekbones, Vernon was getting a brilliant singing sound out of his trumpet—which Williams had bought for him—and, whenever the others took breaks, he kept working away at tricky leaps and rapid runs. He was also a composer, and wrote music and made arrangements on the computers. Like many bands, Shabazz spices up its repertory with Top 40 songs, and Williams often relied on Vernon to find suitable songs and make idiomatic arrangements. Vernon needed only thirty minutes to knock out an arrangement of "I Believe I Can Fly"—a pungent, slightly weird orchestration, amped up by drums and brass, dense with jazzy harmonies. Vernon had been in Williams's band since he was seven; he had been accepted at Rutgers, and his acceptance letter was taped to the blackboard.

Toward the end of the rehearsal, Williams stepped back and listened with his arms folded. He asked another of the trumpet players, a round-faced, wide-eyed eight-year-old named Keyshawn Mayo, to take over. Earlier in the day, Keyshawn had been offended that he had been demoted to a secondary part. "I can play first trumpet," he said. "I'm the best person my age." Now his face lit up, and he ran to the front. His small voice filled the room as he snapped his fingers: "And a five! And a six! And a seven and an eight!"

• • •

When President George W. Bush signed into law the No Child Left Behind Act, in 2002, he probably did not intend it to have a debilitating effect on arts education in the United States. The law rewards schools that meet certain testing standards in core subjects—reading, math, the sciences—and punishes those that fall short. By 2006, 71 percent of school districts had narrowed their elementary-school curricula in order to make up the difference, and the arts had repeatedly been deemed expendable. In California, between 1999 and 2004, the number of students enrolled in music courses fell by nearly half, from 1.1 million to 589,000. Music education had been disappearing from schools for decades, but No Child Left Behind transformed a slow decline into a precipitate fall.

Advocates have issued studies, pamphlets, and talking points that marshal alarming statistics on the diminishment of music programs and argue passionately for their preservation. But there is something maddeningly vague at the heart of the literature. Why must music be taught? The answer seems obvious in the case of Vernon Jones: he's a natural musician, and, for him, the Shabazz band is the first step in what may turn out to be a major classical or jazz career. For most students, though, the usefulness of music class is much less clear. Anyone who has loved music from an early age feels certain that it has a unique and irreplaceable value, but it is difficult to translate that conviction into hard sociological data. Whenever advocates try to build a case for music on utilitarian grounds, they run up against fundamental uncertainties about the ultimate purpose of an art whose appeal is, as Plato anxiously observed, illogical and irrational.

The Mozart Effect has often been cited by proponents of music in schools. In 1993, researchers claimed that a group of thirty-six undergraduates who had been subjected to ten minutes of Mozart's Sonata for Two Pianos performed better than average on the abstract-and-spatial-reasoning section of the IQ test. Subsequent studies failed to reproduce this result. Nonetheless, the Mozart Effect inspired several books, a ream of newspaper articles, the pseudo-educational *Baby Mozart* video, and a shadowy-sounding organization called the Music Intelligence Neural Development Institute. People love the idea that they might be able to make their kids smarter by switching on Mozart once a day; it's seen as a shortcut to Parents' Weekend at Harvard. But kids aren't likely to fall in love with music that is administered to them like vitamins.

Other studies suggest that music students score higher on proficiency tests, or that their math grades go up with each year of study, or that they are less likely to get in trouble with the law. But none of this pro-music science has stemmed the cuts in music programs. To the contrary, music invariably presents itself as the most tempting target. In California, the decline in visual-arts courses was minimal compared with that of music classes, and enrollments in theater and dance went up. According to the advocacy group Music for All, which in 2004 issued a dire report on the California crisis called "The Sound of Silence," music programs "represented single, relatively significant, politically expedient targets for cuts."

Part of the problem is that American music education has largely evolved out of classical-music culture, whose standoffish mentality long ago became self-defeating. Another problem is that music education lacks a powerful lobby. When politicians speak up for it, striking things happen. When Mike Huckabee was governor of Arkansas, he not only professed a love for music, as Bill Clinton often did, but devised legislation to bolster it. In 2005, Huckabee signed a law requiring every child in grades one through six to receive at least forty minutes a week of instruction in music and other arts. "In the true spirit of No Child Left Behind," Huckabee explained, "leaving the arts out is beyond neglect and is virtual abuse of a child."

Although Huckabee has had a few imitators—in 2006, Arnold Schwarzenegger announced a plan to rescue music and arts education in California—the national outlook remains grim. Public funding for anything related to the arts has been contentious since the 1880s, when the progressive patron Jeannette Thurber failed to persuade Congress to fund a national conservatory. For practitioners of classical music, jazz, folk music, and other tradition-minded disciplines that lack mainstream commercial appeal, the situation looks particularly bleak. How can they engage listeners who have heard almost nothing about the history and practice of the art in school? One alternative has increasingly become the norm: they can do the teaching themselves.

Around the same time I started going out to Malcolm X Shabazz in Newark, I met up in Brooklyn with a twenty-seven-year-old pianist named Soheil Nasseri, who had been visiting school assemblies around the city in an effort to incite interest in classical music. Nasseri's trick was to start the session by talking about hip-hop. At Fort Hamilton School in Bay Ridge, he caught the attention of the crowd by mentioning that he was a friend of the impresario Damon Dash, whose name drew respectful nods. Nasseri then invited a student named Jovan Parish onstage, gave him a hip-hop handshake, and had him rap over some minor-key piano chords. (There was a line about "my vocabulary skills are ill.") It was up to the children to decide what this had to do with Beethoven's Sonata in F-sharp, which Nasseri played next. Afterward, students offered a string of questions about Beethoven and the piano: "What do you do when you make mistakes?" "What's the name of the piece that goes 'buh-buh-buh-BUH'?" "Why don't you compose yourself?" "When you play someone else's music, aren't you stealing?"

These days, virtually every orchestra, opera house, chamber-music series, and jazz organization has an education department. Musicians are sent into schools to teach the basics and, in theory, to encourage an interest that will survive the rigors of adolescence, in the course of which any kid with a liking for classical music discovers that it's considered stuffy, sissified, and terminally uncool. The effectiveness of "outreach" depends on the charisma of the person reaching out. Nasseri certainly has a knack for talking to kids. So, too, does David Robertson, the conductor of the St. Louis Symphony, whose guileless manner recalls the style of the late, great Fred Rogers. Michael Tilson Thomas, at the San Francisco Symphony, is a natural teacher, stirring memories of his longtime mentor, Leonard Bernstein.

Wynton Marsalis, the artistic director of Jazz at Lincoln Center, has a similar gift for discussing music in a sophisticated yet unaffected way. One day I watched Marsalis take command of an unruly crowd of schoolkids at the Apollo Theatre, in Harlem. He launched into a lecture on connections between jazz and modern art, the thesis of which was that jazz was a form of modernism, and he backed it up with pictures, performances, and a never-ending stream of talk. He dropped the names Jackson Pollock and Piet Mondrian, gave a shout-out to Frank Gehry, and supplied a lovely definition of the word "cosmopolitan" ("It means you fit in wherever you go"). He administered discipline ("I'm old school—no talking"), explained the blues as a kind of emotional vaccination ("The blues gives you a little to keep it away"), and interrupted an explication of the African practice of call-and-response to acknowledge a sneeze ("Bless you—call-and-response!"). One of the teachers in the audience said to a colleague, "They ain't gettin' it. I couldn't appreciate this when I was their age." But, on the subway afterward, there was a positive buzz among the kids. One quoted a Marsalis aphorism to his friend: "You gotta have heat in everything you do."

Many orchestra administrators cling to the idea that a smattering of Young People's Concerts will indoctrinate children into the wonders of classical music. Sarah Johnson, when she was running education programs at the Philadelphia Orchestra, became skeptical of that approach. "Many people say, 'Wow, we can bring twenty-six hundred students into the hall,' and feel like it's a great thing," Johnson told me. "This may have worked in the age of Bernstein, when classical musicians were celebrities on radio and early television. Today, those kids need to meet the musicians, find out how they got into music, what else they do when they're not playing. It has to be more up close and one-on-one. People have this picture of musicians as not quite human. We need to humanize them. We want to get to the point where we are cultural partners at certain schools, practically giving them a new music-faculty member."

The writer and consultant Joseph Horowitz, the author of *Classical Music in America: A History of Its Rise and Fall*, has long urged orchestras to reinvent themselves as miniature conservatories and cultural centers. With orchestras such as the Brooklyn Philharmonic, the New Jersey Symphony, and the Pacific Symphony, Horowitz has devised cross-disciplinary festivals that can be translated into curricula for area schools. "The orchestra should be, first and foremost, an educational institution," Horowitz told me. "It should know how to explain to an audience what the art means and where it came from. Orchestras can feed the humanities programs at high schools. You can do Mozart and have the drama department put on *Amadeus*. You can do Dvořák and get American-history classes and African-American studies involved. Dvořák is the greatest gift, because there is no better way to link American and European musical traditions."

Not every orchestra is prepared to undertake such an approach. When Horowitz was working with the New Jersey Symphony, he made contact with Hassan Williams and the students of Malcolm X Shabazz. He invited them to events at the hall and visited the school with members of the orchestra. (It was Horowitz who suggested that I observe Williams's class.) On the occasion of a New Jersey Sibelius festival, Vernon Jones was inspired to write a Sibelius-like piece for band. Unfortunately, the initiative met resistance from a member of the administration, who did not enjoy having the students on the premises. One day, when they left the hall, he was heard to say, "Never again." That man is no longer with the orchestra, but his spirit persists at more than one classical institution.

On Westminster Street, in the West End section of Providence, Rhode Island, there are diners, corner markets, auto-repair stores, and, at number 1392, the Providence String Quartet. People often do a double take at the surreal sight of a chamber group playing Beethoven behind a storefront in a lower-income neighborhood. Although the quartet performs at colleges and museums, its main mission is to teach. It is the heart of a nonprofit organization, Community MusicWorks, which does more than bring music to young people; it is an authentically revolutionary outfit in which the distinction between performing and teaching disappears.

The core members of Community MusicWorks, which was founded in 1997, are Jesse Holstein and Jessie Montgomery, violinists; Sebastian Ruth, violist; and Sara Stalnaker, cellist. They were trained for conventional careers at Juilliard, Oberlin, and Brown University, but they chose a different definition of success. Ruth, a man with an elegant face and a mellifluous voice, is their ringleader. He grew up in Ithaca, the son of two ex-hippie parents, who sent him to the Alternative Community School. Instead of going to a conservatory, he went to Brown and studied the philosophy of education. He read the work of Paulo Freire, the author of *Pedagogy of the Oppressed*, and Maxine Greene, who wrote *Releasing the Imagination*. Greene has argued that arts education can be not only a leisure pursuit or subculture for gifted children but an instigator of social change. Ruth decided to put these ideas into practice, by playing in a group that was part of the street life of a city.

"We want people to see the quartet where they wouldn't expect to," Ruth said. "We're here on the street, we're in the community center, we're in the soup kitchen, we're in the nursing home, or the 'assisted-living center,' I should say. We're over at the Rhode Island School of Design, or an indie-rock club, or City Hall. We kind of feel like there should be an office with a string quartet in City Hall. They've got a lot of offices there for things you might not think are strictly necessary."

Ruth dislikes the word "outreach," which makes it sound as if he and the other musicians were extending their hands to unlucky souls drowning at sea. "We are already living in the place that other people reach out to," he said, with a mildly pugnacious look. He also resists the idea that his program's primary purpose is to scout out and nourish exceptional talent. "We're not searching for genius, for 'diamonds in the rough,'" he said. "We're relating music-making to the community."

I sat in the back of the Westminster office to see how the idea of Community MusicWorks played out. The students, who are between seven and eighteen years old and come from Dominican, Haitian, Liberian, and Cambodian backgrounds, walked in one by one, their parents hovering at the door for a minute or two with smiles on their faces. The Providence players bantered with them for a while. Then Holstein shouted, "Let's do it!" and the children sat down to play. The Providence musicians corrected mistakes and suggested improvements, but accuracy wasn't their primary concern. "You're worrying too much," Jessie Montgomery told Tae Ortiz, a violinist. "Even if you make mistakes, you'll find people don't care." Afterward, about five boys and ten girls sat down for a spaghetti dinner. There was an extended discussion of a young man who appeared on a motorcycle in a Britney Spears video; hip-hop selections played on the Community MusicWorks computer. Everyone stopped eating to sing along to Ciara's "1, 2 Step."

At one point, Carolina Jimenez, a young cellist, turned to me and happily announced, "I got into Classical!" I told her that I also got into classical when I was her age, but it turned out that she was talking about Providence Classical High School, a local public school. Ruth suggested that perhaps getting into one kind of "classical" helped Carolina get into the other Classical, and she rolled her eyes.

Ruth and his colleagues regularly go with the kids and their families to concerts by local orchestras, where they are faced with such questions as "Why are we the only black people in the audience?" Some of the older students meet up on Friday nights or on weekend retreats in a program called Phase 2, where they delve into deeper emotional and social issues. For this smaller group of students, the musicians of the Providence Quartet become, in effect, full-time counselors, even part-time foster parents. In 2006, there were 132 people on the waiting list for Community Music-Works, and news of the program had begun to spread around the country. A fellowship program was established for young professional musicians, who sit in with the group and learn its unusual methods, in order to apply them elsewhere.

One evening, the Providence players gave a concert at the West End Community Center, a mile or so from their studio. They use this space at least once or twice a week to teach larger groups. The concert took place on the center's basketball court: a piano was wheeled out, a rug was placed in the middle of the floor, and strings of Christmas lights provided a bit of atmosphere. About two hundred people showed up—parents, older and younger siblings, friends, and supporters of the quartet. Sitting in with them was Jonathan Biss, a meticulous and poetic young pianist who knew Heath Marlow, Community MusicWorks' director of development, from music camp.

This being a classical-music concert, there was a certain amount of concern about decorum. "Sit like a lady," one parent said to her preteen daughter. "Ladies don't sit like that." Before the first piece, Ruth got up to encourage the crowd to stay silent during the performance, but he avoided taking a hallway-monitor tone. "Sometimes we get excited by this kind of music, but mostly we stay quiet," he said. "If it makes you want to get up and dance, well, just *think* about getting up and dancing." There was some giggling, a shout of "Cut it out!" and much changing of seats, but I have witnessed noisier and more disrespectful audiences on Sunday afternoons at Carnegie Hall. There was no dancing.

The Providence opened the concert with the first movement of Beethoven's *Serioso* Quartet. Tae Ortiz, now less nervous, played Boccherini's Minuet, accompanied by Biss. Jovanne Jean-François and Carolina Jimenez played the Adagio from Vivaldi's Concerto in G Minor for two cellos. Vanessa Centeno and Ruth Desrosiers, violinists, performed Schumann's "The Two Grenadiers." The main event was Brahms's Piano Quintet in F Minor, a craggy monument of the chamber repertory, which Biss and the Providence delivered at a level that would have satisfied most chamber-music audiences. A couple of lanky teenage boys tapped their feet to the driving rhythms of the Scherzo. "That was bangin'," one of them said afterward. "I wanna play on the piano someday," an eight-year-old behind me told his mother.

After the concert, as people stood around and talked and the younger children resumed running around the room, Ruth Desrosiers's brother David—a stout young man in a Shady University T-shirt—gravitated toward the piano on which Biss had just hammered out the coda of the Brahms. David is one of Sebastian Ruth's viola students, but he has also taught himself some piano. He approached the instrument somewhat stealthily, but Biss noticed him, and watched with curiosity as the boy launched into a bluesy melody apparently of his own invention, with a strong bass line and a snaking melody. It turned out to be a West End variation on Beethoven's *Für Elise*.

The philosopher John Dewey, in his 1934 book, *Art as Experience*, lamented the American habit of putting art on a "remote pedestal." He wrote, "When an art product once attains classic status, it somehow becomes isolated from the human conditions under which it was brought into being and from the human consequences it engenders in actual life-experience." Dewey's book was widely read, but the argument never really sank in. To this day, the arts in America, when pressed, define themselves in opposition to society. Perhaps the most intractable problem with contemporary music education is that so many teachers have been trained in the monastic culture of the music conservatory, where mastery of technique is the dominant topic and where discussion of music's social or political or spiritual meaning is often discouraged. The Canadian scholar Paul Woodford, in a book-length essay on the relationship between Dewey's ideas and music education, writes, "In my own experience, few music education majors entering their senior year can distinguish Marxism from capitalism, capitalism from democracy, the political Left from Right, or the modern from the postmodern." They are, in cultural terms, idiot savants.

Releasing the Imagination, the Maxine Greene book that so impressed Ruth, proposes that the arts must be incorporated into democratic culture not for their own sake but for the sake of democracy itself. She believes that children can gain deeper understanding of the world by looking at it from the peculiar vantage point of a work of art. She writes, "To tap into imagination is to become able to break with what is supposedly fixed and finished, objectively and independently real." Children learn to notice surprising details that undermine a popular stereotype; they grow tolerant of difference, attuned to idiosyncrasy. They also can experience a shock of perception that shows them alternative possibilities within their own lives, whether or not those possibilities or those lives have an obvious relationship with the artwork in question. Thus, Greene argues, even the oldest art forms can become vehicles of democratic thinking. Because they have transcended time, they can become part of any time.

But why Brahms? Isn't it simply a self-indulgent fantasy to think that German chamber music could change the world of a girl whose mother is living on food stamps?

Ruth paused, his rueful smile indicating that he had answered this question many times.

"I don't know how it works," he said. "I guess, in the beginning, it is something I want to do for myself. Because there's something so bleak about a performing career these days. I don't mean just in terms of the prospects of getting a job. I also mean what you feel once you get the job. You are in this tight, closed-off world. You are playing generally at very expensive concerts for people who can afford it, and who are already steeped in it. You fight the feeling that it's not real. We get wonderful collaborators like Jonathan Biss because other people are fighting that feeling, too. They want to tap into a much more visceral sense of emotional connection.

"Here I'm feeding off all this energy around me, this rebellious energy, and I'm playing for people who usually don't know this music at all. We're out here making it up as we go along, because we're not teachers in the conventional sense and not performers in the conventional sense. Hopefully, we're not just scattering experiences here and there, hopefully we're creating continuity from one to the other. But I really don't know what effect we're having. Certainly, we're happy. It's as if we'd never left college. We're posting signs, organizing things at the last minute, putting on performances in any space available.

"But what does it do? I don't know if it changes anything right in a single moment in anyone's life. But it might change how someone thinks. Maxine Greene talks about the arts creating openings, this mysterious clearing in people's lives, so they walk out of the forest and can breathe. Maybe, at that moment, music becomes a huge part of their lives. Or maybe they use the clearing to see themselves in a new light, and go on to do something different. It could be any kind of music, could be any other art form."

Ruth looked out at Westminster Street, which was empty of people.

"Of course, it's all full of contradictions," he went on. "Let me tell you a story about Vanessa Centeno, who's been with us for many years. Her mom works various jobs, day and night. She doesn't want her daughter to have the same existence. There was an article about us in the paper, in which she was quoted as saying that she loves our program because classical music is 'for people who have class.' It was funny that she said that, when my whole thing has been about trying to undo these stereotypes, deconstruct the idea that this music has 'class,' and make the point that music can be made anywhere by anyone at any time.

"Vanessa's mom and I had such different ideas in mind. I was trying to get out of the world that she was trying to get into. But, in the end, we're going in the same direction." He stretched out his arm toward the door and the street. "We are both moving toward Violin."

15

VOICE OF THE CENTURY

MARIAN ANDERSON

On Easter Sunday 1939, the contralto Marian Anderson sang on the steps of the Lincoln Memorial. The Daughters of the American Revolution had refused to let her appear at Constitution Hall, Washington's largest concert venue, because of the color of her skin. In response, Eleanor Roosevelt, the First Lady, resigned from the DAR, and President Roosevelt gave permission for a concert on the Mall. Seventy-five thousand people gathered to watch Anderson perform. Harold Ickes, the secretary of the interior, introduced her with the words "In this great auditorium under the sky, all of us are free."

The impact was immediate and immense; one newsreel carried the legend "Nation's Capital Gets Lesson in Tolerance." But Anderson herself made no obvious statement. She presented, as she had done countless times before, a mixture of classical selections—"O mio Fernando," from Donizetti's *La favorita*, and Schubert's "Ave Maria"—and African-American spirituals. Perhaps there was a hint of defiance in her rendition of "My Country, 'Tis of Thee"; perhaps a message of solidarity when she changed the line "Of thee I sing" to "Of thee we sing." Principally, though, her protest came in the unfurling of her voice—that gently awesome instrument, vast in range and warm in tone. In her early years, Anderson was known as "the colored contralto," but, by the late thirties, she was *the* contralto, the preeminent representative of her voice type. Toscanini said that she was the kind of singer who comes along once every hundred years; Sibelius welcomed her to his home, saying, "My roof is too low for you." There was no rational reason for a serious concert venue to refuse entry to such a phenomenon. No clearer demonstration of prejudice could be found.

One person who appreciated the significance of the occasion was the ten-year-old Martin Luther King, Jr. Five years later, King entered a speaking contest on the topic "The Negro and the Constitution," and he mentioned Anderson's performance in his oration: "She sang as never before, with tears in her eyes. When the words of 'America' and 'Nobody Knows de Trouble I Seen' rang out over that great gathering, there was a hush on the sea of uplifted faces, black and white, and a new baptism of liberty, equality, and fraternity. That was a touching tribute, but Miss Anderson may not as yet spend the night in any good hotel in America." When, two decades later, King stood on the Lincoln Memorial steps to deliver his "I Have a Dream" speech, he surely had Anderson in mind. In his improvised peroration, he recited the first verse of "My Country, 'Tis of Thee," then imagined freedom ringing from every mountainside in the land.

Ickes, in 1939, bestowed on Anderson a word that put her in the company of Bach and Beethoven: "Genius, like justice, is blind . . . Genius draws no color line." With the massive stone image of Lincoln gazing out over her, with a host of distinguished white men seated at her feet— senators, cabinet members, Supreme Court justices—and with a bank of microphones arrayed in front of her, Anderson attained something greater than fame: for an instant, she became a figure of quasi-political power. In Richard Powers's novel *The Time of Our Singing*, a magisterial fantasia on race and music, the concert becomes nothing less than the evocation of a new America—"a nation that, for a few measures, in song at least, is everything it claims to be." Fittingly, when Barack Obama became the first African-American president of the United States, in January 2009, "My Country, 'Tis of Thee" floated out over the Mall once more, from the mouth of Aretha Franklin to a crowd of two million.

Anderson was born in 1897, in a poor section of Philadelphia. Her father died when she was young; her mother worked in a tobacco factory, did laundry, and, for some years, scrubbed floors at Wanamaker's department store. Her musical gifts were evident early, but she had an arduously difficult time finding voice teachers who were willing to take on someone of her race and economic background. A core of self-confidence, rarely visible behind her reserved façade, allowed her to endure a series of potentially crushing disappointments. The sharpest setback is described in her autobiography, *My Lord, What a Morning*: when she applied to a Philadelphia music school, in 1914, a young woman at the reception desk made her wait while everyone behind her in line was served. Finally, the woman said, "We don't take colored."

Anderson received positive notices throughout the 1920s—her first *New York Times* review, in 1925, registered "a voice of unusual compass, color, and dramatic capacity"—but she needed time to master the finer points of style and diction in foreign-language songs. A notable aspect of her story—related in Allan Keiler's biography, *Marian Anderson: A Singer's Journey*—is that she found real recognition only when she began an extended European residency, in 1930, giving numerous recitals with piano accompaniment. German critics received her respectfully, and with little condescension. In Finland and the Soviet Union, there were near-riots of enthusiasm. In 1935, she sang in Salzburg, eliciting from Toscanini his voice-of-the-century plaudit, which the impresario Sol Hurok promptly spread through the press. During a series of American tours in the late thirties, she performed in sold-out halls night after night and found herself one of the better-paid entertainers of her time. (In 1938, she earned nearly a quarter of a million dollars, which, adjusted for inflation, comes to $3.7 million.) The American critics capitulated. Howard Taubman, of the *Times*, who later ghostwrote her memoir, called her the "mistress of all she surveyed."

What did she sound like in her prime? A slew of recordings made between 1936 and 1939 give an indication, although her voice plainly possessed the kind of incandescence that no machine can capture fully. The discs certainly demonstrate her ability to produce a deep-hued timbre in all parts of her range, from the lowest tones of the female voice well up into the soprano zone. When she sings Schubert's "Erlkönig"—in which a child, his father, and the headless horseman speak in turn—you seem to be hearing three singers, yet there are no obvious vocal breaks between them. She is fastidious but seldom stiff, with caressing little slides from note to note and a delicately trembling tone adding human warmth. Perhaps Anderson's most famous performance was of Brahms's *Alto Rhapsody*, which she first recorded in 1939, with Eugene Ormandy conducting the Philadelphia Orchestra. (It can be heard on a Pearl CD that collects some of her finest early recordings.) In the Goethe poem on which Brahms's work is based, an embittered soul wanders the desert, eliciting a prayer for his redemption: "If there is on your psaltery, O father of Love, one sound acceptable to his ear, refresh his heart with it." Anderson effortlessly issues the healing tone, but, before that, she mobilizes the lowest register of her voice to evoke the dark night of the soul.

Anderson was a musician of a pure, inward kind, to whom grand gestures did not come naturally. The historic drama at the Lincoln Memorial was not something she sought, and, in fact, she contemplated canceling the concert at the last minute. Throughout her life, she preferred not to make a scene. As Raymond Arsenault writes, in *The Sound of Freedom: Marian Anderson, the Lincoln Memorial, and the Concert That Awakened America*, her negotiation of Jim Crow America displayed a "spirit of pragmatism" that could be interpreted as "quiescence." Although she refused to sing in halls that employed "horizontal segregation"—that is, with whites in the orchestra seats and blacks in the galleries—for many years she did accept vertical segregation, with whites on one side of the aisle and blacks on the other. She usually took her meals in her hotel room, in order not to cause complications in restaurants. "I always bear in mind that my mission is to leave behind me the kind of impression that will make it easier for those who follow," she explained in her memoir.

On occasion, she extracted a certain dignity from the ugliness of segregation: when the Nassau Inn, in Princeton, New Jersey, refused to give her a room, she spent the night at the home of Albert Einstein. Usually, though, the humiliation was intense. In Birmingham, Alabama, during the Second World War, she had to stand outside a train-station waiting room while her accompanist, the German pianist Franz Rupp, went to fetch a sandwich for her. Sitting inside was a group of German prisoners of war.

By the time Anderson's career entered its final phase, in the fifties and sixties, such obstacles had begun to disappear. Segregated halls were no longer on her schedule. She broke a momentous barrier in 1955, when she became the first black soloist to appear at the Metropolitan Opera, as Ulrica, in *Un ballo in maschera*. By then, her voice was past its prime, the pitch unstable and the vibrato distracting. She went on singing for ten more years, less because she couldn't leave the spotlight than because audiences wouldn't let her go. They cherished not only what she was but also what she had been. And she might have achieved even more if the world of opera had been open to her earlier. To hear her assume soprano arias such as "Casta diva" or "Pace, pace, mio Dio" (transposed down a step) is to realize that she was capable of singing almost anything. If, as Toscanini said, such a voice arrives once a century, no successor is in sight.

What has changed since Anderson made her lonely ascent, basking in ecstatic applause and then eating alone in second-class hotels? Certainly, she made it easier for the black singers who came after her, especially the women. Leontyne Price enjoyed the operatic triumphs that were denied to Anderson, and after Price came such female stars as Shirley Verrett, Grace Bumbry, Jessye Norman, and Kathleen Battle—although the flameout of Battle's career might indicate the difficulties that await a black diva who doesn't go out of her way to avoid making a scene. Opportunities for black males have been markedly more limited, despite the pioneering work of Roland Hayes, Paul Robeson, Todd Duncan, and George Shirley, among others. African-American conductors are hard to find; the most prominent is James DePreist, who happens to be Marian Anderson's nephew. According to statistics compiled by the League of American Orchestras, only 2 percent of orchestral players are black. African-American composers are scattered across college faculties, but they seldom receive high-profile premieres. The black contingent of the classical audience is, in most places, minuscule.

To a great extent, this racial divide stemmed directly from prejudice. Racism hardly disappeared from classical institutions after Anderson reached the apex of her fame. Consider the twisting career of the singer-songwriter Nina Simone, who originally aspired to become a concert pianist. Anderson was a hero to Simone and her family; one of her uncles knew the singer well. But when she failed to win a place at the Curtis Institute of Music, for what she surmised were racial reasons, she turned instead to playing and singing in clubs. In her autobiography, *I Put a Spell on You*, Simone wrote, "My music was dedicated to a purpose more important than classical music's pursuit of excellence; it was dedicated to the fight for freedom and the historical destiny of my people." Miles Davis used harsher language when he explained why he gave up studying trumpet at Juilliard: "No white symphony orchestra was going to hire a little black motherfucker like me." He went on to mock a teacher who stated that "the reason black people played the blues was because they were poor and had to pick cotton." Davis, the son of a successful dentist, lost confidence in the school soon afterward.

There is another, less baleful explanation for the absence of African-Americans from classical music: beginning with jazz, black musicians invented their own forms of high art, and the talent that might have dominated instrumental music and contemporary composition migrated elsewhere. Perhaps Simone would have made a fine concert pianist, and Davis surely would have been a sensational first trumpeter in a major orchestra, but it's difficult to imagine that they would have found as much creative fulfillment along those paths. Instead, they used their classical training to add new dimensions to jazz and pop. Davis, an admirer of Stockhausen, made a point of criticizing the "ghetto mentality" that prevented some black musicians from investigating classical music. Simone, for her part, never forgot the music of her youth. "Bach made me dedicate my life to music," she wrote in her memoir.

In May 1965, in the tense months that fell between the killing of Malcolm X and the Watts riots in Los Angeles, Simone made a recording of "Strange Fruit," the anti-lynching ballad immortalized by Billie Holiday in 1939. (As it happens, Holiday's original recording was set down eleven days after Anderson's Easter Sunday concert on the Mall.) The ghosts of classical tradition hang over Simone's radically reworked version: the piano accompaniment becomes a spare lament in the Baroque manner, and there is a strong reminiscence of Schubert's "Der Doppelgänger"—a song that Anderson sang in memorably ashen style. At the climax—"For the sun to rot, for the leaves to drop"—Simone let her immaculately true-toned voice deliquesce into an agonizing slow glissando, traversing the lamenting interval of the fourth. Schubert's song is about recurring nightmares, identical tragedies being acted out from life to life; Simone, in a gorgeous fury, tells much the same story.

Sadly, African-American classical musicians today seem almost as lonely as ever. They are accustomed to being viewed as walking paradoxes. William Eddins, the music director of the Edmonton Symphony, has addressed the situation on his blog, Sticks and Drones. In the black community, Eddins writes, classical music is "looked on with intense suspicion," as "one of the last true bastions of segregation in America." Eddins sees it differently: "If you sat me down and asked me to describe one truly racist incident that has happened to me in this business, I'd most likely stare at you blankly. I can't think of a one." The problem is one of perception; African-Americans think that classical music is for other people, he says, and the almost total absence of music education in public schools prevents a different story from being told. "People tend to support and listen to the music that they hear from a young age," Eddins writes.

The irony is that classical music has become a far more heterogeneous culture than it was when Anderson sang on the Mall. The most-talked-about conductor of the moment is Gustavo Dudamel; the superstar pianist is Lang Lang; the most famous of all classical musicians is Yo-Yo Ma. (When people talk about the "whiteness" of this world, they tend to count Asians as white.) No longer a European patrimony, classical music is a polyglot business with a global audience. Why does it still somehow seem inherently unlikely that a black person should compose an opera for the Met, or become the music director of the Philadelphia Orchestra? Unlikelier things have happened, such as the election of a half-Kansan, half-Kenyan as president of the United States. Incidentally, President Obama apparently has a taste for classical music; in 2005, he narrated a performance of Aaron Copland's *Lincoln Portrait*. The conductor was William Eddins, who noted afterward that his soloist was well prepared. A few carefully staged recitals at the White House could break the stalemate that Eddins describes.

Anderson died in 1993, at the age of ninety-six. The obituaries singled out the Lincoln Memorial concert as the zenith of her career, but her autobiography leaves the impression that other experiences gave her a deeper satisfaction. For Anderson, Easter Sunday 1939 may have been an ambiguous triumph—marking a major advance in civil rights but, on a private level, intruding on her dream of a purely musical life. An artist became a symbol. Her happiest memories, one gathers, were of those international tours in the thirties, when the European critics declared her a singer to watch, and the Finns went wild, and Toscanini blubbered his praise, and she became nothing less—and nothing more—than one of the great voices of her time.

16

THE MUSIC MOUNTAIN

INSIDE THE MARLBORO RETREAT

Mitsuko Uchida, a pianist of piercing intelligence and consoling warmth, could comfortably pass her summers flying from one festival to another, staying in luxury hotels and private villas. Instead, she stays on the campus of Marlboro College, a small liberal-arts institution in southern Vermont. Since 1951, the college has hosted Marlboro Music, an outwardly low-key summer gathering that functions variously as a chamber-music festival, a sort of finishing school for gifted young performers, and a summit for the musical intelligentsia. Uchida and the pianist Richard Goode serve as Marlboro's co-directors, alternating the lead role from year to year; in the summer of 2008, when I visited three times, Uchida was in residence from late June until early August. She plays a variety of roles in the Marlboro world—high priest, den mother, provocateur, jester, and arbiter of style.

Marlboro is a singular phenomenon. The great Austrian-born pianist Rudolf Serkin, Marlboro's co-founder and longtime leader, once declared that he wished to "create a community, almost utopian," where artists could forget about commerce and escape into a purely musical realm. Marlboro has been compared to a kibbutz, a hippie commune, Shangri-la, a cult (but "a good cult"), Princeton's Institute for Advanced Study, and George Orwell's Animal Farm, where "all animals are equal, but some animals are more equal than others." On certain lazy days, it becomes a highbrow summer camp, where brainy musicians go swimming in the local pond.

At Marlboro, Uchida follows a set routine. Between 9:30 and 10:00 in the morning, she arrives at the campus coffee shop, where breakfast is served to those who have missed the morning buffet in the dining hall. Young musicians slouch on blue and purple couches around the room, and she stops to chat with them. Aside from her Peggy Guggenheim sunglasses—a bright blue model with pointy edges, patterned after a Venetian Carnival mask—she dresses simply, often wearing sweatpants and a sweatshirt emblazoned with the name Marlboro. One day, "House of the Rising Sun" was playing on the coffee-shop stereo; this gave way to a Scott Joplin rag. Uchida shimmied to the music as she approached the counter to place her order. Her favorite dish is the Egg McMarlboro, a sandwich made with a fried egg, local tomato, Vermont Cheddar, and bacon. Most patrons are served on paper plates, but Uchida's dish was carried out on a wooden tray, with a cappuccino in a china cup.

Matan Porat, an Israeli-born composer and pianist with an impressively tangled, Beethoven-like mane, sat down across from Uchida and noticed the cappuccino. "Nice!" he said. "I didn't know they were doing it."

"Actually, they are not," she said. "But they do it for me. I must allow myself a few small luxuries." She smiled sweetly and took a sip.

The oboist James Austin Smith, who had graduated from the Yale School of Music the previous spring, flopped down on the adjacent couch, propping sandaled feet on the table. Oboists, with their limited chamber repertory, have less reason to be intimidated by the pianist than others who may dream of performing with her; in any case, Smith and Uchida had struck up a playful rapport. Smith announced that he was adding some ornaments, or unwritten musical elaborations, to his part in a Haydn symphony that the musicians were presenting informally that night.

"Cheeky James!" Uchida exclaimed, in mock horror. "No illegal ornaments! I forbid it!"

Uchida speaks a language that can only be described as Uchida. In 1961, when she was twelve, her father, a Japanese diplomat, was appointed ambassador to Austria, and she spent her adolescence in Vienna, becoming fluent in German. In her early twenties, she moved to London, which remains her home, and she acquired a kind of Japanese-Austrian-British accent. (In 2009, Queen Elizabeth II named her Dame Commander of the Order of the British Empire.) Her many summers at Marlboro have added to her repertory a sizable American vocabulary, which she is always seeking to expand. "What is 'ditzy'?" she asked at one point. "Not so bright? Talkative but not so bright? OK! Gotcha!"

Her speech falls into a pattern of soaring phrases followed by rat-a-tat bursts. At breakfast, she holds everyone transfixed with a barrage of stories, epigrams, snap judgments, and gossip. On an overhyped instrumentalist: "For the Germans, the greatest thing since Karajan. Karajan, of course, was the greatest thing since Hitler." On a veteran singer: "She has nothing in her brain, but she is a fantastic coach." On a celebrated conductor: "Obviously, he has charisma. But I don't want charisma. I want something other than charisma." On prodigies: "Do you want yourself to be operated on by a genius twenty-year-old heart surgeon? Do you want to go to the theater and see a teenager play King Lear?" Such comments are often punctuated by a wildly oscillating laugh that sounds like a flock of songbirds ready to be transcribed by Olivier Messiaen. When she is preparing to throw one of her verbal darts, she narrows her eyes and purses her lips. When she has words of praise, she opens her eyes wide, raises one hand to her heart, and draws in her breath sharply.

It was the last week of June. The Marlboro population—thirteen pianists, forty-three string players, sixteen wind and brass players, and nine singers, along with a staff of administrators, coaches, schedulers, librarians, recording engineers, piano technicians, receptionists, interns, cooks, babysitters, and a lifeguard—had been in residence for a week. They had settled into dorm rooms, apartments, and cabins. Some were surprised to find themselves reverting to a collegiate lifestyle, sharing a bathroom and hanging out late at night. But all of them knew that a successful term at Marlboro can practically assure one's career. More than a hundred alumni hold jobs in eight leading American orchestras, twenty-two in the Metropolitan Opera Orchestra alone. The most venerable of American string quartets, the Guarneri, which retired in 2009, formed at Marlboro in 1964. The Emerson, Juilliard, Orion, and St. Lawrence Quartets also have Marlboro connections, and Murray Perahia, Joshua Bell, and Hilary Hahn received early guidance there. Peter Serkin, Rudolf's son, made his debut at Marlboro in 1958, at the age of eleven, and went on to have a major career.

Uchida keeps returning because she cherishes the chance to immerse herself in music in a way that no other institution permits. "I was here when I was very young, in 1974," she told me. "I had a wonderful time, but I didn't quite understand. When I came back, in 1992"—Serkin had died the previous year, and Uchida became an unofficial adviser, with an official appointment following in 1999—"then I understood. I got hooked. In Marlboro, you get a different way of not only looking at the world but also of looking at life. If you spend weeks together, day in and day out, eating the meals together, chatting and sitting around and drinking the beer together and God knows what, you begin to get a basic outline of what it really means to be a musician, as opposed to flying from one city to the next and rehearsing the 'Archduke' Trio for half an hour and then already walking onstage. Ultimately, Marlboro is about the concept of time. We have time to rehearse, time simply to think. But never quite enough time. Time slows down and time accelerates."

After breakfast, Uchida practices in her apartment for several hours, going through her repertory for the coming season. Those spells of exploration have become vital to her evolution. When she first made her name, in the 1980s, as a Mozart specialist, she was noted chiefly for her fluid phrasing and her lustrous tone. Over the years, her repertory has broadened— at one Carnegie Hall recital, she paired pieces by Bach with the elegantly cryptic works of the contemporary Hungarian composer György Kurtág— and her performances have taken on philosophical depth. In late sonatas of Beethoven and Schubert, she conjures up a fractured, even chaotic emotional landscape without committing anything like an excessive gesture. Mozart remains her home ground. On the same night that James Smith inserted his cheeky ornaments into Haydn's Symphony No. 96, Uchida joined a small Marlboro orchestra to read through Mozart's Concerto No. 12 in A. The instrumental playing, with a few inexact entries, wasn't quite perfect, but it had other advantages: the music-making was mellow, naturally flowing, affectionately human. Only a few dozen people heard the performance, and in its intimacy it probably came closer to Mozart's own concerts than what we normally experience in a modern hall.

For decades, a sign has stood beside the road through the Marlboro campus: CAUTION: MUSICIANS AT PLAY. Performers are liberated from tight schedules; managers, agents, and publicity people do not watch from the wings. Works of Beethoven, Schubert, and Brahms melt into a landscape that resembles the pastoral settings from which those composers drew inspiration; when Uchida and a group of players rehearse a Dvořák quintet in a hut on a hillside, it mixes with fugues of birdsong and the ostinato of insects. Wireless Internet aside, participants are effectively isolated in a premodern existence where one walks around all day and eats meals at long tables in a community that includes both toddlers and octogenarians. Above all, as Uchida says, Marlboro causes a stretching out and slowing down of time. One musician after another says the same thing: from September to May, when they sit down to play in an antiseptic postwar performing-arts center after an hour or two of rehearsal, they close their eyes and think of Marlboro.

Rudolf Serkin—or Mr. Serkin, as older Marlboro people still reverently call him—haunts the campus where he spent the last forty summers of his life. Marlboro's split personality, its refusal to decide between Teutonic solemnity and all-American anarchy, reflects Serkin's character. A musician of manic dedication, he practiced scales for hours on end and, in ensemble rehearsals, fretted over details until his collaborators were ready to crawl out of their skins. At other times, he behaved like a madcap schoolboy. He was famous for staging pranks; Arnold Steinhardt, the first violinist of the Guarneri Quartet, remembers the time a cherry bomb exploded under the hood of his car. Yet woe betide an unproven musician who presumed to treat him as an equal. The story is told of a young player who, while turning pages for Serkin, chimed in about a particular passage: "Rudi, what if you tried it this way . . . ?" Serkin thanked him with a tight-lipped smile. A little later, a roar of anger was heard behind a closed door.

The violinist and violist Philipp Naegele came to Marlboro during the first summer and returned some fifty times. "What do I remember about Serkin?" he said. "Oh, the immense vitality. He had a real farm on a dirt road, with a peach orchard, horses, chickens, whatever one has. And he would go back and forth between the mud and the cows and the children and dogs and Beethoven. His vitality was inseparable from his physical groundedness. He was a great hiker, always going up in the mountains. Like Gustav Mahler. He looked a bit like Mahler, too. He had hands twice as wide and twice as heavy as anybody else's hands, and he could play softer than anybody else, because he didn't have to push. He ran a house that was absolutely impeccable, in terms of the decor, the art, the books, the food. But he had a sense of humor that was more than down to earth."

Serkin was born in 1903 in Bohemia, to a family of impoverished Eastern European Jews. As Stephen Lehmann and Marion Faber recount, in a biography of the pianist, Serkin first displayed talent when he heard one of his sisters at the piano. "It's all wrong," the boy said, bursting into tears. At the age of nine, he went to study in Vienna, where he fell under the influence of Eugenie Schwarzwald, a pedagogue and social activist. Through Schwarzwald, Serkin encountered Adolf Loos, Oskar Kokoschka, Karl Popper, and Arnold Schoenberg, with whom he studied composition. Schwarzwald's summertime gatherings of luminaries in mountain retreats influenced Marlboro, as did Schoenberg's Society for Private Musical Performances, which tried to break free of commercial concert culture.

The dominant force in Serkin's life was the German violinist Adolf Busch, a brilliant player who detested virtuoso showmanship and devoted himself in almost monkish fashion to the heights of the German chamber and solo repertory. Serkin met Busch in 1920, when he was still in his teens, and adopted the violinist's belief system. "It's the philosophy of *Werktreue*, of being absolutely faithful to the score," Richard Goode, who came to Marlboro when he was fifteen, says. "People may discuss the limitations of that approach today, but back then their idealism was so important." (Goode carries on the tradition in sovereign performances of Bach, Mozart, Beethoven, and Schubert.) Serkin joined Busch's household and, in 1935, married the violinist's daughter, Irene. The two men appeared as a duo across Europe, setting standards for chamber-music performance. Busch also led the Busch Quartet, whose sinewy recordings of Beethoven and Schubert mesmerized the young Mitsuko Uchida.

When Hitler came to power, Serkin's German career ended swiftly, and Busch, who was not Jewish, responded by canceling all his German engagements. He paid a price for this rare act of solidarity: when he tried to establish himself in the United States, where he moved in 1939, he made little headway, his slightly astringent tone failing to please audiences accustomed to the sweet tones of Heifetz and Kreisler. In 1940, Busch suffered a heart attack, which further limited his public career. He moved to the small Vermont town of Guilford, with his daughter and son-in-law living in the house next door. The surroundings reminded the émigrés of Switzerland and the Vienna Woods.

The idea arose that Busch and his brother, the cellist Herman, should join several other refugees—the French flutist Marcel Moyse; Moyse's son, Louis; and Louis's wife, the violinist Blanche Honegger Moyse—in running a summer music school at Marlboro College, which had started up in 1946, on the site of a nearby dairy farm. At first, Serkin had no intention of being closely involved. Busch provided Marlboro's core philosophy: the concept of master musicians guiding neophytes, the emphasis on rehearsal and conversation over performance and publicity. (Busch complained that New York musicians were obsessed with "covering everything and just getting the notes right . . . A love of music was rarely present.") After Busch's death, in 1952, Serkin took over, and remained Marlboro's director until his death.

In the early years, turmoil reigned on the business end, with Serkin donating much of his concert income to keep the operation afloat. (Anointed by Toscanini, Serkin fared much better in America than Busch did.) Naegele remembered that some prospective students walked into the dining hall—formerly a cow barn—and then walked out, unable to believe that a ragtag group of beer-drinking, pipe-smoking foreigners had anything to offer. But young musicians soon understood what they had to gain by attending, and Marlboro's renown grew from year to year. The cellist Pablo Casals began visiting in 1960, his fame attracting international press. The Columbia label issued best-selling recordings in the Music from Marlboro series. When Casals turned ninety-one, in 1967, the *Bell Telephone Hour* devoted a national broadcast to his activities at Marlboro.

"When Casals came, the balance shifted, and not always for the best," Goode told me. "The personality cult around him was so immense." Naegele, too, experienced a degree of alienation. "Casals could do anything he pleased," Naegele said. "He had the whole place in his hand. And there was something overloaded, driven, almost hysterical, about the playing in that period. The 'Marlboro bustle,' the critic Michael Steinberg called it. We were in danger of becoming an orthodoxy. Marlboro almost suffocated on its success."

After a certain point, Serkin, innately suspicious of publicity, started to shun inquiries from the outside world. When *The New Yorker* proposed to write at length about him and the festival, he said no. A kind of retrenchment happened—a return to the quiet informality of early years. This wariness persists. Marlboro-ites ruefully recall what happened when Lang Lang, the Chinese superstar, dropped by a few years back. "You know, this place could be really famous!" Lang Lang reportedly said. It would rather not.

• • •

Yo-Yo Ma and Emanuel Ax are two of the hundreds of musicians who have made the pilgrimage. On August 3, 1973, they played their first concert together, in a Marlboro performance of Brahms's Piano Quartet in C Minor. They recalled their experiences over coffee at Café Ronda, near Lincoln Center.

"We had met at the Juilliard cafeteria," Ax said. "We ended up being roommates at Marlboro, although you were never in the room. You were always with Jill."

"I met Jill, my wife, at Marlboro," Ma explained.

"Do you remember the dress rehearsal of the Brahms, when Mr. Serkin came? He had this thing—whatever was printed in the music, that's how you play. If, say, the upper register has a note that is very difficult, and it would be easier to play that one note with your left hand, you *don't* do it." Ax mentioned Beethoven's "Hammerklavier" Sonata, which begins with a rapid leap in the left hand. The easy way out is to split the leap between the hands. "Somebody did that in an audition. That was it."

"Zank you very much!" Ma said, in the Serkin accent. *"Zank you very much for findink ze time!"*

"That guy could have played like Horowitz, and he would not have gotten in," Ax went on. "So, in the Brahms, there is a horrible spot in the last movement, where I couldn't stretch my hand wide enough to play this one chord. So I rolled it. 'Ach!' Serkin said. 'There is no arpeggiando on that chord.' 'I know, Mr. Serkin, but my hand isn't big enough.' And he said, 'Don't worry! In the concert, it will grow a little bit.'"

"He said your hand will grow?" Ma asked.

"A little bit, yes. What happened was, I played the chord, and I also played every note in between. And that was OK. He was happy with that."

As Ax idolized Serkin—that summer, he spoke only briefly with the great man, unable to find the courage to have an extended conversation—Ma stood in awe of Pablo Casals, who had performed for Queen Victoria in his youth and remained active into his nineties.

"I played for Casals in a class," Ma said. "He kept saying, 'I can't hear you! I can't hear you!' That was the feedback. But it was great, especially when he conducted the orchestra in—I think it was Beethoven's Fourth. Because here's this guy who had to use an oxygen thing backstage, who needed two people to walk him out. You think he is about to see death.

And then the music starts." Ma impersonated an ancient, shrunken man coming to life, growing in stature, raising his arms high in the air and roaring vague commands: *"Nooooo! . . . Beethoven! . . . M-u-u-usic! . . . Crescendo!"* Ma went on, "I wasn't so sure that I wanted to have a musical career at that time. I wasn't sure that music was all it was cracked up to be. But to see a guy like that, way past retirement age, getting it up for Beethoven's Fourth—where does this energy come from? And I realized there was something very potent at work."

Each senior figure had a distinctive approach. Moyse, the master of the French school of flute playing, had his students read through opera arias so that they learned to imitate the human voice. The Polish-born pianist Mieczysław Horszowski said little, sometimes merely pointing and smiling at a passage in a score. Felix Galimir, the hyper-cultivated Viennese violinist, coached players in the psychology of chamber music, where, as Ax says, "no one leads and no one follows." Alexander Schneider, of the Budapest Quartet, was a Russian-accented volcano, exhorting and berating his charges. And Isidore Cohen, the longtime violinist of the Beaux Arts Trio, encouraged independence. Ma said, "He'd look at you, smoking a cigarette, and say, 'What do you think? Should there be a decrescendo?' He'd force you to make choices."

"Maybe there were some at Marlboro who used the idea of chamber music like a club—a club to beat people with," Ax added. He assumed the tone of an unctuously disapproving elder: "'I know he plays the instrument well, but he doesn't know about *cha-a-a-mber* music.' But in the end there was no orthodoxy."

"There couldn't be," Ma said. "Because you were seeing all these different characters with their different approaches being passionate in different ways."

Uchida and Goode admire what Busch and Serkin created and have no wish to alter the formula. But they have put their imprint on the institution. "When I first came back, in '92, every second word was 'Rudi never did that,' 'Mr. Serkin never did that,'" Uchida told me. "Nobody says things like that anymore. Richard and I really work very hard on that. The place is more open—yeah, sure. I always keep my antennae going. I watch out for the ones who need more care. The ones who are very gifted but not, you know, whiz kids. That's why I go to the coffee shop all the time. I sniff around. I always know who is going out with whom—Richard has no idea! And, look, Richard and I, we are both oddballs. But we have careers. And that is what I say to the kids—if *I* can have a career, anyone can have a career."

In the old days, with various male egos competing for the upper hand, there was something almost macho about Marlboro. Uchida, both as a personality and as a performer, projects authority without demanding it. The mezzo-soprano Rebecca Ringle recalled what Uchida said after rehearsing the Mozart A-Major Concerto: "She said of one passage, 'It's happy but it's powerful. It's the way women can be now—happy, good, beautiful, powerful.' And I almost cried when I heard that, because that's what she is. She's so elfin but really powerful and definitely feminine and totally intelligent."

The Uchida summers and the Goode summers are said to have discrete identities. Goode tends to bring about a looser, more libertine atmosphere. "He's such an incredibly sweet man, off in his own world," one musician said to me. "He thinks of music instead of himself. He's so funny in rehearsal. Sometimes he'll say, 'Let's do that again,' not because the passage needs work but simply because he loves it and wants to hear it one more time. Mitsuko is more intense. She is always watching, always listening. When she says, 'Ben Beilman is *quite good,*' everyone notices." (Beilman, a spookily mature nineteen-year-old violinist, was studying at the Curtis Institute, in Philadelphia.) "Together, the two of them are the perfect substitute parents."

Most young musicians who are accepted at Marlboro spend two or three consecutive summers there. Over the winter, hundreds audition for the small number of spots that open up annually. When I asked Goode to define what qualities he and Uchida were looking for, he said, "A certain technical excellence is a prerequisite. But you also listen for urgency, emotional reality. Maybe that is the primary thing in the end. I guess you could call it 'musicality.' You can often hear it right away. There's a story that when Murray Perahia auditioned for Marlboro he played the C-Minor Impromptu of Schubert, which begins with fortissimo Gs." Goode imitated the sound. "And right after that Horszowski supposedly turned to Serkin and said, 'Let's take him.'" Uchida puts it in her pithy way: "As a rule, the imaginative ones are lacking the technique and the ones that have good technique haven't got a clue. But there are exceptions to the rule, and we try to snap them up."

Marlboro is designed so that the youth contingent receives guidance from several generations of older musicians: "seniors," veterans who have been coming to Marlboro for years, and "junior seniors," established younger players who serve as intermediaries between the generations. Anthony Checchia, Frank Salomon, and Philip Maneval serve as Marlboro's administrators, binding the group together. They are keepers of Marlboro's traditions—for example, the rule that all members of the community should take turns waiting on tables in the dining hall. Salomon says, "One of the great things is to see somebody who's here for the first time, a nineteen- or twenty-one-year-old kid, looking up to see Mitsuko Uchida or Arnold Steinhardt, or someone else they've idolized for ten or fifteen years, asking, 'What would you like to drink?'"

In 2008, the repertory at Marlboro included 221 works by 70 composers. In a given week, there may be more than two hundred rehearsals, in studios, classrooms, and common spaces around the campus, all activity coordinated on a color-coded schedule board. The Central European golden age predominates—Haydn, Mozart, Beethoven, Schubert, Schumann, Dvořák, Brahms—although a fair amount of contemporary music and offbeat fare figures in the mix. One or two composers are usually in residence; the summer I was there, the German composer Jörg Widmann coached his *Hunt Quartet*, in which players are asked to swish the air with their bows. For the first three weeks, Marlboro participants do nothing but rehearse; in July, they begin putting on weekend concerts for a paying public, in a 630-seat hall. As rehearsals progress, senior members meet on Thursday evenings to devise a schedule for those groups that feel ready to perform. Although everyone insists that the rehearsals matter more than the performances, a competitive edge seeps in.

One muggy Saturday, I spent a day watching one rehearsal after another. The common room of the Happy Valley dormitory, a drab space with triangular eaves and a carpet purplish gray in color, was a hub of activity. In the morning, three musicians in their late twenties and early thirties—the violinist Viviane Hagner, the cellist Priscilla Lee, and the pianist Jonathan Biss, whom I knew from Community MusicWorks, in Providence—were preparing Beethoven's Piano Trio Opus 1 No. 2. Biss, who first came to Marlboro when he was sixteen, talked more than the others, although he couched his ideas in politely tentative fashion. "I was

thinking of playing a slightly faster grace note. You hate it? Any feeling?";
"You can make a crescendo and I will blithely ignore you and go on my
merry way." They worked on a repeating phrase, so that it initially had a
sunny sound and later darkened. Lee drew a smiley face over the first instance. This led to a digression on the topic of messages that musicians
write on their parts to remind themselves when they need to give a cue to
other players ("ME!" or "Q") or when they need to fold out a hidden extra
page ("Open the stupid page, motherfucker!" is an extreme example).

In the New Presser building, four wind players—the flutist Joshua
Smith, the oboist Jaren Philleo, the clarinettist Romie de Guise-Langlois,
and the bassoonist William Winstead—were wrestling with Elliott Carter's *Eight Etudes and a Fantasy,* a taxing 1950 work in a more or less atonal
idiom. Winstead and Smith hold lead positions with the Cincinnati and
Cleveland Orchestras, while Guise-Langlois has been a member of Juilliard and Carnegie Hall's elite Academy program and Philleo plays in the
Louisiana Philharmonic. The mood in the room was tense; the musicians
felt frustrated by the score, which, they thought, wasn't giving them quite
enough information. Winstead puzzled over a stream of eighth notes that
were divided into groups of five and seven. Inevitably, such phrases break
down into subsidiary units of two and three, but the bassoonist couldn't
decide where those breaks should fall.

"How about in the last half of seventy-eight I play three plus two plus
two," Winstead said. "No, wait—what if it were two plus two plus three?"

The players tried again but weren't convinced. They passed around a
miniature score so they could see how the parts intermeshed. They started
in once more, then broke down, amid exclamations of "Argh!" and "Shit!"

Winstead reflected on how the slow pace at Marlboro had made him
look afresh at music that he thought he knew well. He spoke about playing the Carter on the concert circuit: "You're not asking, 'What's it all about?'
You're just trying to stay together and get through it. I've never delved into
these kinds of details before."

Smith attempted to rally the others. "When in doubt, the theme is in
the flute," he said.

Back at Happy Valley, Uchida had arrived for a pair of rehearsals, and
was fussing with a recalcitrant dehumidifier. "You jiggle and whack and
kick, and it works," she said. She is particular about the health of her instruments and has had a dehumidifier installed in every room with a piano. Her first rehearsal was of Schubert's Piano Trio in E-flat. Joining her

were Soovin Kim, a thirty-three-year-old violinist whose subtle expressivity suits Uchida's style, and David Soyer, an eighty-six-year-old chamber-music legend, who played cello in the Guarneri Quartet for most of its existence. Soyer, a bearish man who enjoyed playing the role of the village curmudgeon, was famous for claiming insistently that pianists always play too loudly when they join chamber groups. He was also possessive of his music stand, which carried the notice "David Soyer's PERSONAL stand. HANDS OFF!"

The three musicians had reached the slow movement of the Schubert, which opens with one of the most extraordinary inventions in chamber music: softly marching chords on the piano, a plaintive cello melody featuring a repeated trill. Soyer, grunting softly as he played, brought to bear a nobly restrained tone and rhythmically incisive phrasing. He lavished attention on a pair of trills that lead into the hushed coda, wistfully prolonging the second as it precipitated a shift from C major to C minor. Kim executed everything with unfailing precision—so much so that the older players actually encouraged him to be *less* precise at times. "A little more Wiener schmaltz," Soyer suggested at one point, demonstrating a slide from note to note, like a carelessly dragging foot. "You can't play sloppy!" Uchida said, teasingly.

Kim protested that he could indeed play sloppy, and tried again, laying on a modicum of schmaltz. Uchida received only a single citation for being too loud. In accompanimental passages, she achieved the feat of almost disappearing, so that the piano became a nimbus floating around the string voices.

When Soyer and Kim left, the young soprano Charlotte Dobbs entered, ready to work with Uchida on Schoenberg's *The Book of the Hanging Gardens*, a song cycle on poems by the German Symbolist Stefan George. Uchida had never played the songs and was making a close study not only of the music but also of George's poetry. Dobbs, a sunny-tempered woman with a rapid-fire manner of speech, held her own; a recent graduate of Yale, she majored in English and wrote her thesis on Shakespeare and Joyce. With Dobbs, Uchida was noticeably more free-spirited than with the two male players, indulging in giggles, literary digressions, and moments of self-criticism.

"Schoenberg's music is echt Viennese," Uchida said. "When you get to 'Schnäbel kräuseln,' I hear a sort of Viennese nasal sound. No? And not '*klagend*' but '*kl-a-aa-gend*.'" She prompted Dobbs to bring out the rhythms more strongly, to accent certain consonants, to clarify the diction in places. Uchida also emphasized the differences between German and other languages. "You are singing it almost as if it were French," the pianist said. "French is very quick and even. '*Le président de la République a annoncé aujourd'hui dah-dah-dah-dah-dah.*' Japanese is kind of similar." She sang a fragment of a Japanese folk song, with a slight grimace. "German is more flowing, up and down."

Dobbs ventured a few suggestions. "I think I can bring more excitement to the tone when I sing '*reichsten Lade*,'" she said. "Try to do something silky. Put more dazzle in the voice. Can we try a slightly more flowing tempo?"

"Yes, I am maybe too slow," Uchida replied.

The duo arrived at the climax of the cycle, a violently expressive song that, as Dobbs observed, communicates "every possible emotion you could feel in love with someone, except for satisfaction." Beneath the word "*wahr*," or "true," there is a strangely shuddering whole-note chord consisting of a B-major triad with C-sharps attached; Schoenberg has marked it with a crescendo, which is technically an impossibility for a sustained chord, but with a coaxing of the pedal Uchida made it resonate through the bar.

By the end of the afternoon, sunshine had given way to a downpour. An SUV was summoned to transport Uchida back to her apartment. Dobbs and I rode with her. "The pure major becomes *so nasty*," she said, of that B-majorish chord. "I love it. So dark, so beautiful. This is fun, yeah? But *bloody* hard."

Marlboro's hoariest tradition is the paper-napkin-ball war that erupts most nights during dinner. History does not record whether Mr. Serkin originated the practice, but he was a lusty participant from the beginning. One night, when Queen Elisabeth of Belgium was passing through, the pianist Leon Fleisher had to raise an umbrella to shield her from bombardment. Uchida does not take part. "I am very good at *making*," she told me. "There is a technique. Pack in the corner, lightly, that is the idea. But I don't throw. If I start throwing, I will be *such* a target."

Other Marlboro rituals include an annual square dance; the International Dinner, at which the musicians cook up dishes from various cultures and afterward present comedy skits (Uchida impersonations are frequent); and pranks in the Serkin manner. The prizewinning prank of 2008 took the form of an extended fantasia on the sign attached to David Soyer's music stand in Happy Valley. One morning, people awoke to find that hundreds of objects across the campus had been festooned with signs declaring them to be Soyer's property. "It was something unbelievable," Uchida told me. "Everything had a sign. 'David Soyer's personal Baby Chair.' 'David Soyer's personal Water Jugs.' 'David Soyer's personal Exit Sign.' All the cars in the parking lot. Every chair in the dining hall. Ugly painting in the coffee shop: 'David Soyer's personal Ugly Painting.' It can't have been one person. I cannot imagine the man-hours it took. We still don't know who did it, although I have some ideas. Such secrets stay with me!"

Some newcomers roll their eyes at Marlboro's customs. Joshua Smith, the urbane Cleveland Orchestra flutist, initially squirmed at the prospect of the square dance. "Do we *have* to?" he asked at dinner one night. But he grew to love the magic-mountain mood. "I wish I could somehow package this feeling and bring it back home with me to Cleveland," he said. Others complained of hearing too many Serkin stories, or of being dragged on too many picnics, or of being inundated with Germanic repertory. One young musician jokingly scripted a mock infomercial: "Remember a time when only German music was considered important? When Poulenc was not allowed? At Marlboro, you can live that time again." But sooner or later the skeptics fell into reveries about playing Mozart while gazing at trees in the late-afternoon light. And Poulenc is indeed played, on occasion.

There is a conscious plan behind the quirky lore. Marlboro is a long-running experiment in altering the metabolism of city-based performers. When Serkin began inviting his colleagues to Vermont, he wanted them to lose their worldliness, to fall into a slower rhythm. Uchida agrees, and proposes that Marlboro's quaint habits have a specific musical application. "The kids have to become more naïve," she told me. "Because there is something very naïve about this music that they play, even the very greatest. What is it about? Mountains, trees, birds, young love, that kind of thing. Of course, there is quite a bit more to it than that, but you must grasp the simplicity of the surface."

After dinner, the musicians gravitate to the coffee shop, where they often remain until late in the night. The conversation has the typical tempo and jargon of Generations X and Y, although the references are idiosyncratic ("Your fiddle was made in 1717, too? Oh, my God, that's so weird").

There's discussion of disconcerting things that audience members say to performers after concerts ("I sometimes get suggestions for different things I could do with my hair," Rebecca Ringle said); of the familiar perils of traveling with instruments on planes ("They said I'd have to check my viola case, so I took the viola with me on the plane and cradled it in my lap the whole way, like a baby," the violist Kyle Armbrust recalled); and of the relative lack of scandal at Marlboro this summer ("Last summer was a summer of Sappho"). Instrumentalists talk about hearing "Der Doppelgänger" for the first time; singers learn how to name Mozart concertos by Köchel number; Uchida is urged to listen to Björk.

Uchida usually appears in the coffee shop on the early side, then heads off to bed, or, as she puts it, "sneaks away without anyone noticing." One night, I dropped by her apartment for a visit. "Here is one of the finest residences of Marlboro," she said with mock pride, after negotiating a sticky lock. "It even has a bathroom." It was a one-bedroom basement apartment with white cement walls, sparsely furnished and wanly lit. Uchida lived here alone, although her partner, the British diplomat Robert Cooper, joined her on the final weekend. The piano was piled high with music that Uchida was studying. On a bookshelf was some not particularly light summer reading: the *Inferno*, *Hamlet*, volumes of Yeats and Gerard Manley Hopkins, Stefan Zweig's autobiography (in German), W. G. Sebald's *Austerlitz*, and *501 Italian Verbs*. As we spoke, Uchida set out two more little luxuries she permits herself: first-flush Darjeeling tea and Marcolini chocolates.

In some ways, Uchida is even more high-minded than Serkin, who surprised people by praising Vladimir Horowitz, the arch-virtuoso and the un-Serkin. Uchida has few kind words for several leading virtuosos of today. Her remarks were off the record. "I talk only about people whom I love," she said. Her warmest words were for the Romanian pianist Radu Lupu, whom she calls "the most talented guy I have ever met." She tells of how she once tried to get Lupu to visit Marlboro. "I got very excited, describing how people do nothing but play music all day long. But he said no. His explanation was very funny. 'Mitsuko,' he said, 'I don't like music as much as you.'"

Her voice took on a confiding tone as she spoke of the composers with whom she spends her days. "Beethoven was the greatest altogether. Mozart was the greatest genius. And Schubert . . ." She drew in her breath, her eyes opening wide, her head tilting back. "He is the most beautiful. He is the one you will be listening to when you die." And then she spoke of a friend of hers who, on his deathbed, in a state of severe pain, was offered morphine and refused it. "He knew that he would die only once. He wanted to see what it felt like. That is some sort of a person, yes? It is a great pity that you can't come back to tell the tale."

The Marlboro summer customarily ends on a Sunday afternoon in August, with a festive performance of Beethoven's Choral Fantasy, for piano, chorus, and orchestra. Serkin used to bang it out at unbelievable volume, causing the piano, the floor, the walls, and, possibly, the Green Mountains to shake. Beethoven wrote the work in 1808, for a legendarily over-long benefit concert that also included the premieres of his Fifth and Sixth Symphonies. Composing in a hurry, he produced an uncharacteristically baggy piece that nonetheless surges with life. The main tune looks forward unmistakably to the "Ode to Joy," in the Ninth Symphony. The text celebrates the power of art to dispel the storm and stress of daily life. To quote from Philipp Naegele's translation:

> *When the magic sounds enchant*
> *And the word's solemnity speaks forth,*
> *Glorious things must come to be,*
> *Night and storms then turn to light.*

In a way, the Choral Fantasy is Beethoven's Ninth without the world-historical baggage—the perpetually unfulfilled promise of liberation. Instead, it is an anthem of music's celebration of itself. Hence, perhaps, Serkin's abiding love for the piece.

Goode told me, "Many people felt that Serkin playing the Choral Fantasy was a unique experience that could never be duplicated. After he died, the work was retired, and I thought that was the right decision. To my surprise, a few years later people said, 'You know, I think we have to have a Choral Fantasy.' We needed the catharsis."

It is never an especially polished affair. Serkin instituted the practice of inviting staff members, supporters, and musically inclined neighbors to sing in the chorus. Members of Marlboro's vocal program take the solos, guaranteeing that at least some of the singing will be at a high level, but there are always odd noises. In what had to be considered the final prank of the summer, one of the singers, the generally discerning tenor William Ferguson, decided that I should join the chorus. Trained as a pianist and an oboist, I have practically no singing experience, but I was herded into the baritone section for the final rehearsal. I stood in front of two excellent young singers, the baritone John Moore and the bass-baritone Jeremy Galyon, who encircled me with such stentorian tones that I could almost believe I was making them myself. "I heard you," Ferguson said afterward, a little ambiguously.

At the podium was the pianist and conductor Ignat Solzhenitsyn, who grew up in Cavendish, forty miles to the north of Marlboro. His father, the novelist, had died the week before, and he had just returned from the funeral, in Moscow. The orchestra was a mixture of Marlboro-ites junior and senior, with Arnold Steinhardt sitting uncomplainingly in the back row and Soovin Kim serving as concertmaster. (Steinhardt wore a sign on his back: PROPERTY OF DAVID SOYER.) In trading Beethoven's ideas back and forth, the musicians were recapitulating in musical terms ties that had formed over the summer. Uchida smiled or wiggled her eyebrows when different players took up the principal melody, as if resuming conversations that she had begun over Eggs McMarlboro at the coffee shop.

"It's great," Rebecca Ringle said to me during a break in the rehearsal. "You know everyone. Romie gets the theme, then James gets the theme."

The hall was packed for the performance, with many longtime friends of Marlboro in the crowd. Uchida assumed concert mode, unleashing the full strength of her mighty left hand in the portentous C-minor chords that open the piece. Throughout, she allowed herself a bit more Romantic flamboyance than is her custom. She also issued a smattering of wrong notes, as if in tribute to Serkin's philosophy of seeking the perfection beyond precision—the truth of the noblest, most honest effort. The great moment for the chorus comes in the insistently joyous setting of the line "When love and strength are wed": "*Und Kraft! Und Kraft! Und Kr-a-a-a-a-ft!*" I had the feeling of being carried along by an enormous wave, and, however approximate the sound coming from my throat, it added to the force of the mass. And I reflected on the fact that even the most exalted music-making comes from an accumulation of everyday labor, inextricable from human relationships.

"It was at least inspired," Uchida said afterward. "Not the cleanest, but bloody inspired."

On my way home, driving toward the interstate, I took a detour and stopped at a little white church in Guilford. Rudolf Serkin is buried in the churchyard there, a few feet away from Adolf Busch. The violinist's name is almost hidden by thick-growing bushes, which metaphorically suggest what Busch and Serkin achieved when they came to America. At a time when Hitler was dragging German music into the mire, these pure spirits succeeded in transplanting their tradition to Vermont. In a wider sense, Marlboro represents the migration of tradition across centuries and continents: a Japanese-born woman passing along her understanding of Mozart and Schoenberg to new generations of American kids. Marlboro is an enchanting place, but, in the end, there is nothing especially remarkable about it. The remarkable thing is the power of music to put down roots wherever it goes.

17

THE END OF SILENCE

JOHN CAGE

On August 29, 1952, David Tudor walked onto the stage of the Maverick
Concert Hall, near Woodstock, New York, sat down at the piano, and, for
four and a half minutes, made no sound. He was performing 4′33″, a conceptual work by John Cage. It has been called the "silent piece," but its
purpose is to make people listen. "There's no such thing as silence," Cage
said, recalling the premiere. "You could hear the wind stirring outside
during the first movement. During the second, raindrops began pattering
the roof, and during the third people themselves made all kinds of interesting sounds as they talked or walked out." Indeed, some listeners didn't
care for the experiment, although they saved their loudest protests for the
question-and-answer session afterward. Someone reportedly hollered, "Good
people of Woodstock, let's drive these people out of town!" Even Cage's
mother had her doubts. At a subsequent performance, she asked the composer Earle Brown, "Now, Earle, don't you think that John has gone too far
this time?"

In the summer of 2010, the pianist Pedja Muzijevic included 4′33″ in
a recital at Maverick, which is in a patch of woods a couple of miles outside Woodstock. I went up for the day, wanting to experience the piece in
its native habitat. The hall, made primarily of oak and pine, is rough-hewn
and barnlike. On pleasant summer evenings, the doors are left open, so
that patrons can listen from benches outside. Muzijevic, mindful of the
natural setting, chose not to use a mechanical timepiece; instead, he
counted off the seconds in his head. Technology intruded all the same, in
the form of a car stereo from somewhere nearby. A solitary bird in the
trees struggled to compete with the thumping bass. After a couple of

minutes, the stereo receded. There was no wind and no rain. The audience stayed perfectly still. For about a minute, we sat in deep, full silence. Muzijevic broke the spell savagely, with a blast of Wagner: Liszt's transcription of the Liebestod from *Tristan und Isolde*. Someone might as well have started up a chain saw. I might not have been the only listener who wished that the music of the forest had gone on a little longer.

Cage's mute manifesto has inspired reams of commentary. The composer and scholar Kyle Gann, in his 2010 book *No Such Thing as Silence: John Cage's* 4'33", defines the work as "an act of *framing*, of enclosing environmental and unintended sounds in a moment of attention in order to open the mind to the fact that all sounds are music." That last thought ruled Cage's life: he wanted to discard inherited structures, open doors to the exterior world, "let sounds be just sounds." Gann writes, "It begged for a new approach to listening, perhaps even a new understanding of music itself, a blurring of the conventional boundaries between art and life." On a simpler level, Cage had an itch to try new things. What would happen if you sat at a piano and did nothing? If you chose among an array of musical possibilities by flipping a coin and consulting the *I Ching*? If you made music from junkyard percussion, squads of radios, the scratching of pens, an amplified cactus? If you wrote music for dance—Merce Cunningham was Cage's longtime partner—in which dance and music went their separate ways? If you took at face value Erik Satie's conceit that his piano piece *Vexations* could be played 840 times in succession? Cage had an innocent, almost Boy Scout–like spirit of adventure. As he put it, "Art is a sort of experimental station in which one tries out living."

Many people, of course, won't hear of it. More than half a century after the work came into the world, 4'33" is still dismissed as "absolutely ridiculous," "stupid," "a gimmick," and the "emperor's new clothes"—to quote some sample putdowns that Gann extracted from an online comment board. Such judgments are especially common within classical music, where Cage, who died in 1992, remains an object of widespread scorn. In the visual arts, though, he long ago achieved monumental stature. He is considered a co-inventor of "happenings" and performance art; the Fluxus movement essentially arose from classes that Cage taught at the New School, in the late 1950s. (One exercise consisted of listening to a pin drop.) Cage emulated visual artists in turn, his chief idol being the master conceptualist Marcel Duchamp. The difference is that scorn for avant-garde art has almost entirely vanished. A *New York Times* editorial writer made an "emperor's new clothes" jab at Duchamp's *Nude Descending a Staircase* when it showed at the 69th Regiment Armory, in 1913. Jackson Pollock, too, was once widely mocked. Now the art market bows before them.

The simplest explanation for the resistance to avant-garde music is that human ears have a catlike vulnerability to unfamiliar sounds, and that when people feel trapped, as in a concert hall, they panic. In museums and galleries, we are free to move around, and turn away from what bewilders us. It's no surprise, then, that Cage has always gone over better in nontraditional spaces. In 2009, MACBA, in Barcelona, mounted a remarkable exhibition entitled The Anarchy of Silence, which traced Cage's career and his myriad connections to other arts. The day I was there, the crowd was notably youthful: high schoolers and college students dashed through galleries devoted to Cage's concepts and contraptions, their faces wavering between disbelief and delight. Like it or not, Cage will be with us a long time.

Morton Feldman, another avant-garde musician with an eye for the wider artistic landscape, once said, "John Cage was the first composer in the history of music who raised the question by implication that maybe music could be an art form rather than a music form." Feldman meant that, since the Middle Ages, even the most adventurous composers had labored within a craftsmanlike tradition. Cage held that an artist can work as freely with sound as with paint: he changed what it meant to be a composer, and every kid manipulating music on a laptop is in his debt. Not everything he did was laudable, or even tolerable. Even his strongest admirers may admit to sometimes feeling as Jeanne Reynal did when, in 1950, Cage recited his "Lecture on Nothing" at the Artists' Club: "John, I dearly love you, but I can't bear another minute." Yet the work remains inescapable, mesmerizing, and—as I've found over months of listening, mainly to Mode Records' comprehensive Cage edition—often unexpectedly touching. It encompasses some of the most violent sounds of the twentieth century, as well as some of the most gently beguiling. It confronts us with the elemental question of what music is, and confounds all easy answers.

Cage's high-school yearbook said of him, "Noted for: being radical." His radicalism was lifelong and unrelenting: he took the path of most resistance.

As much as any artist, he enjoyed receiving applause and recognition, but he had no need for wider public or institutional approval. The one time that I saw him up close, he was delivering the Charles Eliot Norton Lectures, at Harvard. Eminences of the faculty had gathered in Memorial Hall, possibly laboring under the illusion that in such august company Cage would finally drop his games and explain himself. Unease rippled through the room as Cage began reciting a string of mesostics—acrostics in which the organizing word runs down the middle instead of the side. The opening sounded like this: "Much of our of boredom toward talks in it misled him diplomatic skill to place to place but does it look at present most five Iranian fishermen cutbacks would not . . ." And it went on like that, for six lectures, the verbal material generated randomly from Thoreau, Wittgenstein, and *The New York Times*, among other sources. Later, when Cage was asked what he thought of being a Harvard professor, he commented that it was "not much different from not being a Harvard professor."

Carolyn Brown, a founding member of the Merce Cunningham Dance Company, offers a winning portrait of Cage in *Chance and Circumstance*, her 2007 memoir. "He was open, frank, ready to reveal all his most optimistic utopian schemes and dreams, willing to be a friend to any who sought him out," Brown writes. In the early days of the Cunningham company, Cage served, variously, as tour manager, publicist, fund-raiser, and bus driver; Brown recalls him behind the wheel, chattering away on innumerable subjects while taking detours in search of odd sights and out-of-the-way restaurants. He had a sunny disposition and a stubborn soul, and was prone to flashes of anger. When he learned, in 1953, that he had to give up a beloved home—his tenement on Monroe Street, on the Lower East Side—he was crestfallen, and Brown made matters worse by reminding him of the Zen Buddhist principle of nonattachment. "Don't you *ever* parrot my words back at me!" Cage roared. His indefatigable optimism carried him through periods of frustration. Gann writes, "He was a handbook on how to be a non-bitter composer in a democracy." The dance critic Jill Johnston called him a "cheerful existentialist."

Cage was born in Los Angeles in 1912. His father, a brilliant, intermittently successful inventor, devised one of the earliest functioning submarines; his mother covered the women's-club circuit for the *Los Angeles Times*. The art of publicity was hardly unknown in the Cage household, and the son inherited the ability to get his name in the papers, even when he was delivering an unpopular message. In 1928, he won the Southern California Oratorical Contest with a speech titled "Other People Think," which he delivered at the Hollywood Bowl:

> One of the greatest blessings that the United States could receive in the near future would be to have her industries halted, her business discontinued, her people speechless, a great pause in her world of affairs created . . . We should be hushed and silent, and we should have the opportunity to learn what other people think.

Cage's passion for silence, it seems, had political roots. He was a lonely, precocious child, mocked by classmates as a sissy. "People would lie in wait for me and beat me up," he said, in a rare comment on his personal life, shortly before his death. In 1935, when he was twenty-two, he married a young artist named Xenia Kashevaroff, but it soon became clear that he was more strongly attracted to men. His most sonically assaultive works might be understood, at least in part, as a sissy's revenge.

Cage dabbled in art and architecture before settling on music. He studied with Henry Cowell, the godfather of American experimental music, and then took lessons with none other than Arnold Schoenberg, the supreme modernist, first at USC and then at UCLA. Although Cage was not a disciple, rejecting most of the Germanic canon that Schoenberg held dear (Mozart and Grieg were the only classics he admitted to loving), he fulfilled Schoenberg's tenet that music should exercise a critical function, disturbing rather than comforting the listener. Cage was to the second half of the century what Schoenberg was to the first half: the angel of destruction, the agent of change. Some commentators later tried to dissociate Schoenberg from his most notorious student, claiming that the two had had little contact. But scraps of evidence suggest otherwise. When, in 1937, Schoenberg invited friends to his home for a run-through of his Fourth Quartet—the guest list included Otto Klemperer and the pianist Edward Steuermann—Cage seems to have been the only American pupil in attendance.

Schoenberg told Cage to immerse himself in harmony. Cage proceeded to ignore harmony for the next fifty years. He first made his name as a composer for percussion, following the example of Cowell and Edgard Varèse. He transformed the piano into a percussion instrument—the "prepared piano"—by inserting objects into its strings. He brought phono-graphs and radios into the concert hall. He famously declared, "I believe that the use of noise to make music will continue and increase until we reach a music produced through the aid of electrical instruments which will make available for musical purposes any and all sounds that can be heard." Yet most of his early music—from the mid-thirties to the end of the forties—speaks in a surprisingly subdued voice. *Music for Marcel Du-champ*, a prepared-piano work from 1947, never rises above mezzo-piano, offering exotic tendrils of melody, stop-and-start ostinatos, and, at the end, eighth-note patterns that drift upward into some vaguely Asian ether. "When the war came along, I decided to use only quiet sounds," Cage later said. "There seemed to be no truth, no good, in anything big in soci-ety. But quiet sounds were like loneliness, or love, or friendship."

Beneath the plinking of junkyard percussion and the chiming of the prepared piano was an unsettling new idea about the relation of music to time. Cage wanted sounds to follow one another in a free, artless se-quence, without harmonic glue. Works would be structured simply in terms of durations between events. Later in the forties, he laid out "gamuts"—gridlike arrays of preset sounds—trying to go from one to the next without consciously shaping the outcome. He read widely in South Asian and East Asian thought, his readings guided by the young Indian musician Gita Sarabhai and, later, by the Zen scholar D. T. Suzuki. Sarab-hai supplied him with a pivotal formulation of music's purpose: "to sober and quiet the mind, thus rendering it susceptible to divine influences." Cage also looked to Meister Eckhart and Thomas Aquinas, finding another motto in Aquinas's declaration that "art imitates nature in its manner of operation."

Audiences were initially unaware that a musical upheaval was taking place. More often than not, they found Cage's early work inoffensive, even charming. When he gave an all-percussion concert at the Museum of Modern Art in 1943, a year after he moved to New York, he received a wave of positive, if bemused, publicity. By the late forties, he had acquired a repu-tation as a serious new musical voice. After the premiere of his prepared-piano cycle *Sonatas and Interludes*, in 1949, the *Times* declared the work "haunting and lovely," and its composer "one of this country's finest."

Cage might easily have found a calling as a purveyor of delicate exoti-cism. Instead, he radicalized himself further. On a trip to Paris in 1949,

Cage encountered Pierre Boulez, whose handsomely brutal music made him feel quaint. In 1951, writing the closing movement of his Concerto for Prepared Piano, he finally let nature run its course, flipping coins and consulting the *I Ching* to determine which elements in his charts should come next. *Music of Changes*, a forty-three-minute piece for solo piano, was written entirely in this manner, the labor-intensive process consuming most of a year. As randomness took over, so did noise. *Imaginary Landscape No. 4* employs twelve radios, whose tuning, volume, and tone are governed by chance operations. *Imaginary Landscape No. 5* does much the same with forty-two phonograph records. *Williams Mix* is a collage of thousands of prerecorded tape fragments. *Water Music* asks a pianist not only to play his instrument but also to turn a radio on and off, shuffle cards, blow a duck whistle into a bowl of water, pour water from one receptacle into another, and slam the keyboard lid shut. *Black Mountain Piece*, which is considered the first true sixties-style "happening," involved piano playing, poetry recitation, record players, movie projectors, dancing, and, possibly, a barking dog. All this occurred in the eighteen or so months leading up to 4′33″, the still point in the sonic storm.

Did Cage love noise? Or did he merely make peace with it? Like many creative spirits, he was sensitive to intrusions of sound; years later, when he was living in the West Village, next door to John Lennon and Yoko Ono, he asked Lennon to stop using wall-mounted speakers. But he trained himself to find noise interesting rather than distracting. Once, in a radio discussion with Cage, Feldman complained about being subjected to the buzzing of radios at the beach. Never one to miss a good setup, Cage responded that in such a situation he'd say, "Well, they're just playing my piece." He also disliked Muzak, and in 1948 spoke of trying to sell a silent work to the Muzak company. Gann points out that in May 1952, three months before 4′33″, the Supreme Court took up a Muzak-related case, ruling against complainants who hoped to have piped-in music banned from public transport. There was no escaping the prosperous racket of postwar America. In a way, 4′33″ is a tombstone for silence. Kenneth Silverman, in his 2010 biography *Begin Again*, rightly emphasizes Cage's later obsession with Thoreau, who said, "Silence is the universal refuge."

Zen attitudes notwithstanding, Cage had a conservative, controlling side. It is a mistake to think of him as the guru of Anything Goes. He sometimes lost patience with performers who took his chance and conceptual pieces as invitations to do whatever they pleased. Even his most earnest devotees sometimes disappointed him. Carolyn Brown recounts how puzzled she was when, after she had laboriously followed Cage's instructions for one work, he reprimanded her for executing it "improperly." If the idea is to free oneself from conscious will, Brown wondered, how can the composer issue decrees of right and wrong?

Even a piece as open-ended as 4′33″ is, ultimately, an assertion of will. Lydia Goehr, in her book *The Imaginary Museum of Musical Works*, notes that Cage is still playing by traditional rules: "It is because of his specifications that people gather together, usually in a concert hall, to listen to the sounds of the hall for the allotted time period." If 4′33″ is supposed to explode the idea of a fixed repertory of formally constrained works, it has failed, by virtue of having become a modernist classic. You could argue that this was Cage's plan all along—his circuitous path to greatness. Richard Taruskin, in a cold-eyed 1993 essay reprinted in his collection *The Danger of Music*, proposes that Cage, no less than Schoenberg, participated in the Germanic cult of musical genius. Indeed, Taruskin writes, Cage brought the aesthetic of Western art "to its purest, scariest peak." Perhaps Cage's entire career was a colossal annexation of unclaimed territory. If, as he said, there is nothing that is not music, there is nothing that is not Cage.

Though Cage no doubt had one eye fixed on posterity, he delighted less in the spread of his influence than in the fracturing of the tidy musical order in which he came of age. Gann makes a persuasive case that 4′33″ effectively split open the musical scene of the mid-twentieth century. He writes, "Listening to or merely thinking about 4′33″ led composers to listen to phenomena that would have formerly been considered nonmusical"—sustained tones, repeating patterns, other murmurs of the mechanical world. Cage cleared the way for minimalism, even if he showed little sympathy for that movement when it came along. He also spurred the emergence of ambient music, sound art, and other forms of relating sound to particular spaces. (If you stand on the north end of the pedestrian island in Times Square between Forty-fifth and Forty-sixth Streets, you hear one such piece—Max Neuhaus's *Times Square*, a processing of resonances emanating from the subway tunnels below.) John Adams, in his memoir, *Hallelujah Junction*, describes how a reading of Cage's 1961 book *Silence* encouraged him to drop out of East Coast academia, pack his belongings into a VW Bug, and drive to California. The easiest way to pay tribute to Cage is to imagine how much duller the world would have been without him.

When Gann talks about 4′33″ in classes—he teaches composition and music theory at Bard College—a student invariably asks him, "You mean he got *paid* for that?" Kids, Cage was not in it for the money. The Maverick concert was a benefit; Cage earned nothing from the premiere of 4′33″ and little from anything else he was writing at the time. He had no publisher until the 1960s. After losing his loft on Monroe Street—the Vladeck Houses stand there now—he moved north of the city, to Stony Point, where several artists had formed a rural collective. From the mid-fifties until the late sixties, he lived in a two-room cabin measuring ten by twenty feet, paying $24.15 a month in rent. He wasn't far above the poverty level, and one year he received aid from the Musicians Emergency Fund. For years afterward, he counted every penny. I recently visited the collection of the John Cage Trust, at Bard, and had a look at his appointment books. Almost every page had a list like this one:

    .63 stamps
    1.29 turp.
    .25 comb
    1.17 fish
    3.40 shampoo
    2.36 groc
    5.10 beer
    6.00 Lucky

"I wanted to make poverty elegant," he once said.

By the end of the fifties, however, Cage's financial situation had improved, though not because of his music. After moving to Stony Point, he began collecting mushrooms during walks in the woods. Within a few years, he had mastered the mushroom literature and co-founded the New York Mycological Society. He supplied mushrooms to various elite restaurants, including the Four Seasons. In 1959, while working at the R.A.I. Studio of Musical Phonology, a pioneering electronic-music studio, in

Milan, he was invited on a game show called *Lascia o Raddoppia?*—a *Twenty One*–style program in which contestants were asked questions on a subject of their choice. Each week, Cage answered, with deadly accuracy, increasingly obscure questions about mushrooms. On his final appearance, he was asked to list "the twenty-four kinds of white-spore mushrooms listed in Atkinson." Cage named them all, in alphabetical order, and won eight thousand dollars. He used part of the money to purchase a VW bus for the Cunningham company. The following year, he appeared on the popular American game show *I've Got a Secret*: as he had done on *Lascia o Raddoppia?*, he performed *Water Walk*, a piece that employed, among other things, a rubber duck, a bathtub, and an electric mixer. Cage charmed the audience from the outset; when the host, Garry Moore, said that some viewers might laugh at him, the composer replied, in his sweet, reedy voice, "I consider laughter preferable to tears." (YouTube has the clip.) Radios were included in the score, but they could not be turned on, supposedly because of a union dispute. Instead, Cage hit them and knocked them on the floor.

As Cage's celebrity grew, his works became more anarchic and festive. For *Theatre Piece*, in 1960, Carolyn Brown put a tuba on her head, Cunningham slapped the strings of a piano with a dead fish, and David Tudor made tea. (This is when Brown was reprimanded for playing her part "improperly.") His lectures became performances, even a kind of surrealist standup comedy. In the midst of Cunningham's dance piece *How to Pass, Kick, Fall, and Run*, Cage sat at a table equipped with a microphone, a bottle of wine, and an ashtray, placidly reading aloud items such as this:

> [A] monk was walking along when he came to a lady who was sitting by the path weeping. "What's the matter?" he said. She said, sobbing, "I have lost my only child." He hit her over the head and said, "There, that'll give you something to cry about."

Later in the decade, Cage incited mass musical mayhem in huge venues such as the 69th Regiment Armory in New York and the Assembly Hall at the University of Illinois at Urbana-Champaign. At the Armory, for a piece titled *Variations VII*, Cage and his collaborators manipulated two long tablefuls of devices and dialed up sonic feeds from locations around the city, including the kitchen of Lüchow's Restaurant, the *Times* printing presses, the aviary at the zoo, a dog pound, a Con Ed power plant, a Sanitation Department depot, and Terry Riley's turtle tank. In Urbana-Champaign, six or seven thousand people materialized to hear *HPSCHD*, a five-hour multimedia onslaught involving harpsichords playing fragments of Mozart and other composers, fifty-one computer-generated tapes tuned to fifty-one different scales, and a mirror ball.

The carnival element persisted to the end. His five *Europeras* (1985–91) mash together centuries of operatic repertory. ("For two hundred years the Europeans have been sending us their operas," Cage explained. "Now I'm sending them back.") But in the music of Cage's last two decades you sense a paring down of elements and, often, a heightened expressivity, notwithstanding the composer's rejection of personal expression. The musicologist James Pritchett points out that even Cage's chanciest works have a personal stamp, because he took such care in selecting their components. The execution varies, yet the performances end up sounding more like one another than like any other piece by Cage or any other music in existence.

A case in point is *Ryoanji* (1983–85), which takes its name from the famous Zen temple and rock garden in Kyoto. Five solo instruments play a series of slow-moving, ever-sliding musical lines, their shapes derived from tracings of stones. A solo percussionist or ensemble supplies an irregular, halting pulse. The composer is not in full control of what the musicians play, yet he is the principal author of the spare, spacious, meditative music that emerges. Consider also the 1979 electronic composition *Roaratorio*, Cage's response to *Finnegans Wake*. A verbal component, which the composer recorded in a vaguely Irish brogue, consists of words and phrases drawn from Joyce's novel and arranged in mesostics. Around him swirls a collage of voices, noises, and musical fragments, based on sounds and places mentioned in the novel. Chance comes into play, but Cage has carefully followed the structure of the text. In the final section, the composer-reciter breaks into song, his folkish chant encircled by impressions of Anna Livia Plurabelle's plaintive final monologue—cries of seagulls, rumbling waters, an intimation of "peace and silence." It is an uncanny evocation of Joyce's world.

In his last years, Cage returned to his point of departure—the pointillistic sensibility of the early percussion and prepared-piano works. He released a series of scores that have come to be called "number pieces," their titles taken from the number of performers required (*Four*, *Seventy-four*, and so on). Within a given time bracket, players render notated material at their own pace—usually a single note or a short phrase. The result is music of overlapping drones and airy silences. "After all these years, I'm finally writing beautiful music," Cage drily commented.

Beautiful but dark. As he grew older, the cheerful existentialist had crises of doubt, intimations of apocalypse. Darkest of all was the installation *Lecture on the Weather*, which he created for the Bicentennial. Twelve vocalists recite or sing quotations from Thoreau against a backdrop of flashing images and the sounds of wind, rain, and thunder. The proportions of the three sections are about the same as in 4'33", but nature makes a crueler sound than it did on that August night in 1952. Attached to the piece is a politically tinged preface that echoes, perhaps consciously, Cage's teenage oration "Other People Think." It ends thus:

> We would do well to give up the notion that we alone can keep the world in line, that only we can solve its problems . . . Our political structures no longer fit the circumstances of our lives. Outside the bankrupt cities we live in Megalopolis which has no geographical limits. Wilderness is global park. I dedicate this work to the U.S.A. that it may become just another part of the world, no more, no less.

The last room of MACBA's Anarchy of Silence exhibition was taken up with a 2007 realization of *Lecture on the Weather*, with John Ashbery, Jasper Johns, and Merce Cunningham among the reciters. I sat for a long time in the gallery, listening to the grim swirl of sound and observing the reactions of visitors. Some poked their heads into the room, shrugged, and moved on. Others seemed transfixed. One young couple sat for a while in the opposite corner, their hands clenched together, their heads bent toward the floor. They looked like the last people on earth.

In July 1992, a mugger made his way into Cage's apartment, pretending to be a UPS man. After threatening violence, he took money from the composer's wallet. It was a weird premonition: on August 11, Cage suffered a stroke, and died the following day. I moved to New York a few weeks later,

and, as a fledgling music critic, attended various tributes to the late composer, the most memorable being the three-and-a-half-hour *Cagemusicir-*
cus, at Symphony Space. The afternoon began with Yoko Ono banging out
cluster chords on the piano and ended with a quietly intense performance
of Cage's early piece *Credo in Us*, for piano, two percussionists, and a performer operating a radio or a phonograph. In the final minutes, the hall
went dark and light fell on a spot in the middle of the stage. There the
audience saw a desk, a lamp, a glass of water, and an empty chair with a
gray coat draped over the back.

Cage's last home was in a top-floor loft at the corner of Eighteenth
Street and Sixth Avenue, in a cast-iron building that once housed the
B. Altman store. Cunningham remained in the apartment, and several
years ago I was invited there to dinner. Cunningham was, as so many had
reported, gentle, taciturn, elusive, and poetic in even his slightest gestures. The two men had their difficulties, but they were joined by a powerful physical and intellectual attraction. (Yet to be published is a birthday
mesostic in which Cage pays tribute to Cunningham's cock and ass.) I
listened avidly to Cunningham's stories of the avant-garde's pioneer days,
but I found myself distracted by noises floating up from the street below.
When the couple moved there, in 1979, Cage made his unconditional surrender to noise: certainly, on that corner, there was no such thing as silence. Yet, as I listened, the traffic, the honking, the beeping, the occasional
irate curses and drunken shouts seemed somehow changed, enhanced,
framed. I couldn't shake the impression that Cage was still composing the
sound of the city.

That block of Chelsea is not as dangerous, or as interesting, as it used
to be. When Cage and Cunningham arrived, the major store in the building was the Glassmasters Guild, which sold, among other things, stained-
glass models of Sopwith Camel and Piper Cherokee airplanes. Now there
is a Container Store. A Bed Bath & Beyond and a T.J.Maxx loom across
the street. At the beginning of 2010, the final glimmer of Cagean spirit
left the block when Laura Kuhn, the director of the John Cage Trust, removed the last of the couple's belongings from apartment 5B. At Christ-
mastime, she invited me over again. Several artist friends dropped in as
well. Christmas lights were strung up on the wall facing the kitchen.
Cunningham had liked the lights, and had let them hang year-round. On
July 26, 2009, at the age of ninety, he passed away beneath them.

Toward the end of his life, Cunningham wrote in his diary, "When one dies with this world in this meltdown, is one missing something grand that *will* happen?" He wondered whether people could learn to live less wastefully, whether traffic could die down, whether manufacturing could return to Kentucky towns, even whether "the Automat could return."

Cage and Cunningham's Manhattan is mostly gone. Real estate greed and political indifference have nearly driven bohemian culture out of Manhattan; "uptown" begins in Battery Park. Cage's urban collages are almost elegies now; with the mechanization of the radio business, even the piece for twelve radios has probably lost its random charm. But lamentation is not a Cagean mood. If he were alive, he would undoubtedly find a way to pull strange music from the high-end mall that Manhattan has become. He might even have been content to stay in that homogenized patch of lower midtown, where, after a long search, he found his Walden.

"I couldn't be happier than I am in this apartment, with the sounds from Sixth Avenue constantly surprising me, never once repeating themselves," Cage said late in life, in an interview with the filmmaker Elliot Caplan. "You know the story of the African prince who went to London, and they played a whole program of music for him, orchestral music, and he said, 'Why do you always play the same piece over and over?'" Cage laughed, his eyes glittering, his head tilting toward the window. "They never do that on Sixth Avenue."

PART III

18

I SAW THE LIGHT

FOLLOWING BOB DYLAN

America is no country for old men. Pop culture is a pedophile's delight. What to do with a well-worn, middle-aged songwriter who gravitates toward the melancholy and the absurd? If you look through what has been written about Bob Dylan in recent decades, you notice a persistent desire for the man to die off, so that his younger self can take its mythic place. When he had his famous motorcycle mishap in 1966, at the age of twenty-five, it was presumed that his career had come to a sudden end: rumors had him killed or maimed, like James Dean or Montgomery Clift. In 1978, after the fiasco of *Renaldo and Clara*, Dylan's four-hour art film, a writer for *The Village Voice* said, "I wish Bob Dylan died. Then Channel 5 would piece together an instant documentary on his life and times, the way they did with Hubert [Humphrey], Chaplin, and Adolf Hitler. Just the immutable facts." *Vanity Fair* was unhappy to find him still kicking in 1985: "My God, he sounds as if he could go on grinding out this crap *for ever.*" When Dylan was hospitalized with a chest infection in 1997, newspapers ran practice obituaries: "Bob Dylan, who helped transform pop music more than thirty years ago when he electrified folk music . . ."; "Bob Dylan, whose bittersweet love songs and politically tinged folk anthems made him an emblem of the 1960s counterculture . . ."

PUYALLUP, WASHINGTON. I'm at the 1998 Puyallup Fair, in this agricultural suburb of Tacoma, and among the attractions are Elmer, a 2,400-pound Red Holstein cow; a miniature haunted house ingeniously mounted on the back of a truck; bingo with Hoovers for prizes; and Bob Dylan. He is

announced, with cheesy gusto, as "Columbia recording artist Bob Dylan!"
He saunters from shadows in the back of the stage, indistinguishable at
first from the rest of the band (a well-honed group consisting of Tony
Garnier, Larry Campbell, Bucky Baxter, and David Kemper). He is dressed
in a gray-and-black Nashville getup and looks like a lopsided owl. As the
show gets under way, he tries a few cautious strutting and dancing moves,
Chuck Berry–style. He plays five numbers from his most recent album,
Time Out of Mind; several hits, among them "Don't Think Twice, It's Alright"
and "Masters of War"; and something more unexpected from his five-
hundred-song back catalogue—"You Ain't Goin' Nowhere." He ends with
"Forever Young." The crowd goes wild.

When I told people that I was going to follow Dylan on the road, I got
various bemused reactions. Some were surprised to hear that he still
played in public at all. It's easier, perhaps, to picture him in *Citizen Kane*–
like seclusion, glaring at the Bible and listening to the collected works of
Blind Willie McTell. Perhaps he does, but he also plays more than a hundred shows every year, crisscrossing the globe and meandering through
every corner of the American landscape: big-city stadiums, small-town
college gymnasiums, suburban fairgrounds, and rural ballfields.

In the fall of 1998, I went to ten Dylan concerts, including a six-day,
six-show stretch that took three thousand miles off the life of a rental car.
The crowds were more diverse than I'd expected: young urban record-
collector types, grizzled wackos, well-dressed ex-hippies, high-school kids
in Grateful Dead T-shirts. Deadheads are a big part of Dylan's audience,
and they created odd scenes as they descended on each venue: in Reno,
they streamed in a tie-dyed river through the Hilton casino. I asked some
of the younger fans how they had become interested in Dylan, since he
wasn't exactly omnipresent on MTV. Most had discovered him, they said,
while browsing through their parents' old LPs. One kid, who had been
listening to a 45-rpm single of "Hurricane," thought that he should come
and check out the man behind it. The younger fans didn't seem to be
bothered by the fact that Dylan was three times their age. A literate teenager asked me, "Do you have to be from Elizabethan England to appreciate Shakespeare?"

Before each show, for some reason, minor-key sonatas and concertos
by Mozart were played over the P.A. system. Male Dylanologists explained
lyrics to their girlfriends. "Every Dylan song contains *eight questions*," I

heard one saying. Bootleggers fumbled with their equipment: a common method of clandestine recording is to attach small microphones to the earpieces of glasses. (Thousands of tapes of Dylan shows are in circulation—the list stretches back to 1958.) Concession stands sold Dylan paraphernalia, including a bumper sticker that read "It's not dark yet, but it's getting there"—a line from *Time Out of Mind*.

A boozy group of Minnesotans who sat in front of me at a show in Minneapolis seemed to have the Dylan songbook pretty well memorized. The rowdiest of them was shouting out first lines of the songs at the top of his voice, and once, in his excitement, he crashed into the hard plastic seats. He got up again, blood dripping down his chin, and bellowed in my face, *"Once upon a time you dressed so fine! God said to Abraham, 'Kill me a son!'"* Other fans took a cooler view. Before a show in Portland, I chatted with a levelheaded twentysomething guy who played in a progressive funk group. "Last time I saw him, in '90, it was *brutal*," he told me. "I hope he doesn't fuck up the songs again. I hear he's better. Even when he's awful, he's sort of great—he's never just *mediocre*." In Dylan's vicinity, I noticed, everyone italicizes.

Dylan is said to make a mess of the songs. He does change them, and fans who come to hear live reenactments of favorite tracks tend to be disappointed. Dylan sometimes writes new melodies for old songs and he sometimes transposes one set of lyrics into the tune of another. He writes a little more each night: I kept hearing fresh bluesy bits of tunes in "Tangled Up in Blue," which was at the center of every set. As a performer, he is erratic: his voice has a way of thinning into a bleat, and every so often his guitar yelps wrong notes. But he has a saturnine ease onstage. Even from a hundred feet away, his squinting stare can give you a start. And he is musically in control. The band's pacing of each song—the unpredictable scampering to and fro over a loosely felt beat, the watch-and-wait atmosphere, the sudden knowing emphasis on one line or one note—is much the same as when Dylan plays solo. You can hear him thinking through the music bar by bar, tracing harmonies in winding figures. The basic structures of the songs remain unshakable. There may be wrong notes, but there is never a wrong chord.

In the verbal jungle of rock criticism, Dylan is seldom talked about in musical terms. His work is analyzed instead as poetry, punditry, or mystification. A book titled *The Bob Dylan Companion* goes so far as to call him "one of the least talented singers and guitarists around." But to hear Dylan live is to realize that he *is* a musician—of an eccentric and mesmerizing kind. It's hard to pin down what he does: he is a composer and a performer at once, and his shows cause his songs to mutate, so that no definitive or ideal version exists. Dylan's legacy will be the sum of thousands of performances, over many decades. The achievement is so large and so confusing that the impulse to ignore all that came after his partial disappearance in 1966 is understandable. It's simpler that way—and cheaper. You need only seven discs, instead of forty. But Columbia Records, after years of putting out bungled live recordings, is finally beginning to illustrate, in its *Bootleg Series*, the entire sweep of Dylan's performing career.

Don DeLillo, in his novel *Great Jones Street*, imagined a Dylanesque rock star and said of him, "Even if half-mad he is absorbed into the public's total madness; even if fully rational, a bureaucrat in hell, a secret genius of survival, he is sure to be destroyed by the public's contempt for survivors." But Dylan has survived without becoming a "survivor"—a professional star acting out the role of himself. He has a curious, sub-rosa place in pop culture, seeming to be everywhere and nowhere at once. He is historical enough to be the subject of university seminars, yet he wanders the land playing to tipsy crowds. The Dylan that people thought they knew—"the voice of a generation"—is going away. So I went searching for whatever might be taking its place. I went to the shows; I listened to the records; I patronized dusty Greenwich Village stores in search of bootlegs; I sought out the Dylanologists who are arguing over his legacy in print and on the Internet. Dylan himself may explain the songs best, just by singing them.

CONCORD, CALIFORNIA. The crowd is dominated by ex- and neo-hippies from Berkeley, twenty miles to the west. Dylan threatens to dampen their enthusiasm by opening with "Gotta Serve Somebody," the snarling gospel single that had horrified the counterculture in 1979. But he works his way back to the sing-along sixties anthem "Blowin' in the Wind." I was sitting near a teenage girl who had first heard Dylan in a class on the sixties and was there with her history teacher.

Dylan's looming presence in the culture of the sixties is for many a point in his favor: he wrote songs that "mattered," he "made a difference."

For others, particularly for those of us who grew up in later, less delirious decades, the sixties connection can be a stumbling block. Until my late twenties, when I started listening to Dylan in earnest, I had mentally shelved him as the archetypal radical leftover, reeking of politics and marijuana. I'd read a story that went something like this. He was born in Minnesota. He went to Greenwich Village. He wrote protest songs. He stopped writing protest songs. He took drugs, "went electric." He was booed. He fell off his motorcycle. He disappeared into a basement. He reappeared and sang country. He got divorced. He converted to Christianity. He converted back to something else. He croaked somewhere behind Stevie Wonder in "We Are the World." And so on. If you're not in the right age group, the collected bulletins of Dylan's progress read like alumni notes from a school you didn't attend.

The challenge for anyone who thinks Dylan is more than a lifestyle trendsetter is to define those qualities that have outlasted his boisterous tenure as the voice of a generation. So far, the informal discipline of Dylanology—founded around 1970, by a man named A. J. Weberman as he fished through Dylan's trash on MacDougal Street—has reached no consensus on the matter. At the moment, there are about a half-dozen luminaries in the field. The iconic rock critic Greil Marcus connects Dylan with a homegrown, folk-and-blues surrealism. Paul Williams, who founded the rock magazine *Crawdaddy!* in the sixties, celebrates Dylan as a tireless, generous performer who rewrites his songs at every show. The Dylan biographer Clinton Heylin pays heed to the gospel period and the biblical rants that followed in the eighties. Christopher Ricks, a renowned scholar of Milton, Tennyson, Eliot, and Beckett at Boston University, supplies a formalist reading—of Dylan as a pure poet, who thrives on word choice, rhythm, and structured rhyme. In the same spirit, Gordon Ball, a professor of English at the Virginia Military Institute, has nominated Dylan for a Nobel Prize in Literature.

Below the main authorities are the amateur Dylanologists: enthusiasts, editors of fanzines, caretakers of gigantically detailed Internet sites. There is no end to their productions. *The Cracked Bells*, for instance, is an unreadable book-length guide to Dylan's unreadable book-length poem *Tarantula*. The author, Robin Witting, writes, "*Tarantula* has six main themes: America, Viet Nam, Aretha, Mexico, Maria, and—the great panacea—Music." I didn't find much about music, but I enjoyed a note about geraniums: "Do geraniums stand for coolness? Insouciance? Moreover, the odour of death?" Aidan Day's *Jokerman*, a book on Dylan's lyrics, analyzes some lines from "Visions of Johanna," on *Blonde on Blonde*, and finds in them "a reduction of form to primal elements as—in an image that itself displaces Marcel Duchamp's rendering of the Mona Lisa in the painting *L.H.O.O.Q.* (1919)—even gender difference becomes confused and human contour and feature are erased." The text in question is "See the primitive wall-flower freeze / When the jelly-faced women all sneeze / Hear the one with the moustache say, 'Jeeze / I can't find my knees.'"

Despite everything that has been written about Dylan, not a great deal is known about him for certain. Heylin's chronology of Dylan's life, for example, is an archly self-canceling document, in that every piece of information points to a larger lack of information. Here are three consecutive entries for the year 1974:

> *Late April.* Dylan attends a concert by Buffy Sainte-Marie at the Bottom Line in New York. He is so impressed he returns the following two nights, and tells her he'd like to record her composition, "Until It's Time for You to Go."
> *May 6.* Dylan runs into Phil Ochs in front of the Chelsea Hotel and they decide to go for a drink together.
> *May 7.* Dylan visits Ochs at his apartment and agrees to perform at the "Friends of Chile" benefit Ochs has arranged at the Felt Forum. Tickets for the show had been selling very disappointingly.

What happened during the rest of the first week of May? Where *was* he going when he ran into Phil Ochs? Dylan's life story sometimes feels as if it has been pieced together from centuries-old manuscripts that were charred in a monastery fire. "Between January and June 1972 the only evidence he was in New York at all was a reading he attended by Russian poet Andrei Voznesensky at the Town Hall," Heylin writes in his attempt at a full-scale biography, *Bob Dylan: Behind the Shades*. A skeptical Englishman who is known for a history of American punk, Heylin is at least willing to admit what he doesn't know, and his book is the most reliable of several biographies.

The accumulated files of Dylanology, despite their gaps, give a rough sense of the man behind the cipher. A thumbnail sketch from a 1967 essay by Ellen Willis holds up well: "Friends describe [him] as shy and defensive, hyped up, careless of his health, a bit scared by fame, unmaterialistic but shrewd about money, a professional absorbed in his craft." Stubborn persistence is his main characteristic: although he has often vanished in a funk, he never fails to trudge back with some new twist on his obsessions. He is at odds with the modern world in many ways. "There's enough of everything," he said in a 1991 interview. "You name it, there's enough of it. There was too much of it with *electricity*, maybe, some people said that. Some people said the *lightbulb* was going too far." His eccentricity has an everyday quality—he's the weird neighbor you can never figure out. I heard an excellent anecdote from a friend who played on a Little League team with Dylan's kids in the late seventies, during the singer's gospel period. When a dog ran onto the field, my friend yelled, "Get that goddam dog off the field!" A familiar voice rasped from the parents' bench, "Ahhh, that was *what* kind of a dog?"

Joan Didion wrote of Joan Baez that she was a personality before she became a person, and the same could be said of Dylan. He was famous before he was twenty-one. World fame—not just celebrity but intellectual renown, plaudits from Allen Ginsberg, Frank O'Hara, and Philip Larkin— came to him by the age of twenty-five. The speed of his ascent required luck, but it was mostly a function of his energy. He skipped heedlessly from one genre to another: folk, blues, country, spirituals. He played at being a political activist, but his sharpest polemics, such as "The Lonesome Death of Hattie Carroll," were the character-driven ones. His early vocal style incorporated pieces of Woody Guthrie, Mississippi John Hurt, Hank Williams, and, not to be forgotten, Johnnie Ray, the flaky fifties crooner who smacked his consonants with unnerving ferocity. In the early sixties, Dylan sought to play rock and electric blues alongside his acoustic material: in high school, he'd hammered the piano à la Little Richard, and he longed to resume that kind of noisemaking. He originally planned to have his second album, *The Freewheelin' Bob Dylan*, be part electric and part acoustic, like the later *Bringing It All Back Home*. He signaled his intentions by covering "That's All Right, Mama," Elvis's debut single, at his first electric session, in October 1962. He was trying frantically to say everything at once.

But he soon discovered that you can be famous for only one thing at a time. The record business and the music press required a narrower genius. The electric songs from 1962 didn't fit the image that Columbia wanted to create—Dylan as folk oracle. He gained notice chiefly for his civil-rights and antiwar material, and Columbia advertised him accordingly:

> Bob Dylan has walked down many roads. For most of his 22 years he "rode freight trains for kicks and got beat up for laughs, cut grass for quarters and sang for dimes" . . . Bob does what a true folk singer is supposed to do—sing about the important ideas and events of the times . . . His new best-selling album (the first was *Bob Dylan*) is *The Freewheelin' Bob Dylan*. It features ten of Bob's own compositions, including the sensational hit, "Blowin' in the Wind." Also, songs on subjects ranging from love ("Girl From the North Country") to atomic fall-out ("A Hard Rain's A-Gonna Fall"). Hear it and you'll know why Bob Dylan is the voice of the times.

This ingenious ad copy, complete with Dylan's tall tales about his past, informed the press coverage. Dylan soon became annoyed at the generalizations, and found himself fighting his own publicity; he denied, for example, that "A Hard Rain's A-Gonna Fall" depicted a nuclear winter. Even so, he played along with the spirit of the marketing: he later claimed that the song had been a general reaction to the dread of the nuclear age, and to the Cuban Missile Crisis in particular. In a widely quoted statement, he said, "I wrote that when I didn't figure I'd have enough time left in life." "Hard Rain" had actually been written at least a month before the Cuban crisis began.

"Hard Rain" was a breakthrough in Dylan's songwriting, but for a different reason. It's a small epic, lasting seven minutes, and yet it lacks any trace of the blow-by-blow storytelling that sustains the picaresque ballads of the folk literature. How does Dylan keep us interested? One way is through repetition; another is through the changes that come between the first repetition and the last. Almost all of Dylan's songs have a structure of verse-refrain, verse-refrain, and the refrain is almost always a simple-seeming phrase that tolls like a bell: "Tangled up in blue," "You gotta serve somebody," "It's not dark yet, but it's getting there," "It's a hard rain's a-gonna fall."

The first lines of "Hard Rain"—"Oh, where have you been, my blue-eyed son? / And where have you been, my darling young one?"—are a nod to the old ballad "Lord Randal," which begins, "Oh, where ha' you been,

Lord Randal, my son? / Oh, where ha' you been, my handsome young man?"
Dylan breaks the symmetrical call-and-response of the original: his blue-
eyed son answers not with two lines but with five. The images—"twelve
misty mountains," "six crooked highways," and so forth—carry the flavor
of the book of Revelation, with its insistence on exact numbers of bizarre
objects ("I saw seven golden candlesticks"). The song hangs on a musical
trick of suspension: E and A chords seesaw hypnotically as the number of
answering phrases increases from five to seven and eventually to twelve.
In the chorus—"And it's a hard, and it's a hard . . ."—Dylan grasps for and
finally gets the resolution, which in each verse has moved a little farther
out of reach. Coming down the mountain of the song, he starts to sound
like a prophet.

Many myths of Dylan's sixties career lose credibility in the face of the
evidence gathered in Heylin's books and other Dylanological tomes. Dylan's
songwriting is said to have been transformed by a plunge into the drug
culture, but he had been using drugs on and off since his Minnesota days.
He was said to have been inspired by the Beatles to "go electric," but he
had sketched out his folk-rock sound as early as 1962. The first electric
shows reportedly provoked universal booing, but on the tape of his famous
appearance at the Newport Folk Festival, in 1965, it's difficult to hear
boos amid the applause. And D. A. Pennebaker, who filmed part of Dylan's
international tour in 1966, recalls that when confrontational scenes developed the ringleader didn't appear to be greatly bothered by them. "Dylan
was having the best time of his life," Pennebaker said at a symposium
on Dylan's unreleased tour movie *Eat the Document*, at the Museum of
Television and Radio in New York. "He was like a cricket jumping around
onstage."

Greil Marcus describes the 1965–66 tours differently—as a war against
dark reactionary forces. In his book *Invisible Republic* (later retitled *The
Old, Weird America*), he quotes Al Kooper's reason for not wanting to follow the tour into Texas: "Look what they did to JFK down there." Marcus
finds special significance in an exchange that took place between Dylan
and the audience in Manchester, England, in May 1966. The moment is
rendered as Dylan's ultimate encounter with the enemy:

As if he had been waiting . . . a person rises and shouts what he has
been silently rehearsing to himself all night. As over and over he

has imagined himself doing, he stands up, and stops time. He stops the show:

"JUDAS!"

Dylan stiffens against the flinch of his own body. "I don't believe you," he says, and the contempt in his voice is absolute. As one listens it turns the echo of the shouter's curse sour, you begin to hear the falseness in it, that loving rehearsal—and yet that same echo has already driven Dylan back. "YOU'RE A *LIAR!*" he screams hysterically.

When Columbia finally released a CD of the show in 1998—it had circulated for thirty years on bootlegs—neophytes may have skipped to the end in order to hear the "Judas!" dialogue. Not everyone will hear what Marcus heard. What you hear first is a lull, during which Dylan tunes his guitar. When the shout of "Judas!" comes, the crowd variously laughs, groans, and applauds. The voice from the back yammers on, and others join in. When Dylan responds, he is not screaming hysterically, or, indeed, screaming at all. He sounds tired and annoyed. It's as if he couldn't understand what the lads in the back were hollering and therefore supplied the kind of all-purpose non sequitur that he liked to dish out at press conferences.

Certainly, Dylan encountered a fair amount of venom on his 1966 tour, especially from British folk purists. But he doesn't seem to have faced a well-organized conspiracy. C. P. Lee, a British Dylanologist, took the trouble to write an entire book about the Manchester show, and in the wake of its publication, in 1998, a great discovery was made: the "Judas" shouter was no Pete Seeger–like elder statesman of folk but, it was claimed, a confused twenty-year-old university student named Keith Butler. Having landed in a job at a Toronto bank, Butler told the British press that his act was not premeditated. "I was very disappointed about what I was hearing," he said. "But I think what really sent me over the top was when he did those lovely songs—I think it was, er, there were two of them . . ."

Marcus may not provide a naturalistic account of what went down at the Manchester show, but he does something no less valuable: he captures the dementia that surrounded Dylan in the mid-sixties, when two disparate youth cultures—rock-and-rollers and folkies—jockeyed for control of his supposed message while older generations struggled to comprehend what was going on. Not since Wagner had a musician been subjected to such irrational, contradictory pressures. Small wonder that Dylan dropped out in the wake of his motorcycle accident, in the summer of 1966: he'd had enough of the messiah role. Instead, he hunkered down in West Saugerties, New York, with his formidable touring musicians—the Hawks, soon to be renamed the Band—and churned out dozens of achingly old-school numbers. Those songs, the Basement Tapes, are the main subject of Marcus's book; in them, he writes, "certain bedrock strains of American cultural language were retrieved and reinvented."

As the tour passed through California, I went to see Marcus, who lives in the Berkeley hills. "The funny thing is that I'm not a *Dylan person*," he told me, sipping a beer in his kitchen. "Many years went by when I didn't care about him at all." For Marcus, as for many of the original followers, the Dylan of the seventies and eighties was of little consequence. Marcus's *Rolling Stone* review of the 1970 album *Self Portrait*, a baffling detour in the direction of easy-listening pop, began with the words "What is this shit?" Only when Dylan started recording folk and blues covers in the nineties did Marcus become interested again. This critic is a connoisseur of the darkest, weirdest corners of American music—the shrapnel-voiced Dock Boggs and other comical-sinister backcountry singers who had been collected in Harry Smith's 1952 *Anthology of American Folk Music*—and he believes that Dylan belongs there, too. In a 1985 review, Marcus asked to hear "more Dock Boggs" in Dylan's aging voice, and that alchemy more or less happened. The writer seemed to get inside his subject's mind, and Dylan indicated as much by providing a blurb for the paperback of *Invisible Republic*.

Still, I felt that there must be something missing in a reading of Dylan that brushes over twenty years of his career. What if, as some think, he reached his peak not with the put-ons and put-downs of the sixties but with the chaotic love songs of the seventies? And what if, as Clinton Heylin suggests, he went even further in the eighties, when he fused the personal and the apocalyptic—"Love-sick Blues" and the book of Revelation? Lester Bangs wrote in 1981, "If people are going to dismiss or at best laugh at Dylan now as automatically as they once genuflected, then nobody is going to know if he ever makes a good album again. They're not listening now, which just might mean that they weren't really listening then either."

• • •

Back on the East Coast, I had tea with Christopher Ricks, the eminent close reader of canonical English poetry. We met in his sitting room in Cambridge, Massachusetts. "I don't teach Dylan," he told me. "It's just an *obsession*." Although he speaks in the clipped tones of a modern English don, he has a way of plunging into the passive-aggressive dynamic of Dylan's emotions. "The words constitute an *axis*," he said, early in our conversation. "They do not point in one direction." Dylan indulges heavily in irony, and he sometimes obtains ambiguity simply by repeating a phrase. "Think of 'Don't Think Twice, It's Alright,'" Ricks continued, intoning the refrain. "How many times can you tell somebody not to think twice? You can say 'It's all right' over and over. That's comforting—but not 'Don't think twice.' I'd start to think."

I was reminded of some similarly hazy lines from "Meet Me in the Morning," circa 1974:

> *Look at the sun, sinking like a ship*
> *Look at the sun, sinking like a ship*
> *Ain't that just like my heart, babe*
> *When you kissed my lips?*

This tangled metaphor—the sun like a ship, the heart like the sun—can spin in any direction. Is the heart glowing like a sunset? Or is it sinking out of sight? And is the ship going over the horizon, or is it just sinking? The less happy implication is that it is in the nature of ships, and of hearts, to sink.

When others have tried to read Dylan line by line, they have usually chased after outside references. (He mentioned the Bomb! T. S. Eliot! Joan Baez!) Talking about "The Lonesome Death of Hattie Carroll," Ricks begins not with the real-life case of William Zantzinger—a wealthy young Maryland farmer who, in 1963, caused the death of a black barmaid and got off with a six-month sentence—but with the rhythm of Zantzinger's name: a strong beat followed by a weak one. The whole song, he says, is dominated by that loping, tapering rhythm of the name, from which Dylan removed an unsingable "t":

> *William Zanzinger killed poor Hattie Carroll*
> *With a cane that he twirled round his diamond ring finger*
> *At a Baltimore hotel society gathering.*

It produces a feeling of helplessness, the way each line ends in a weak beat, and this seems to be the point: cry all you want, the gentle suffer. The dominant emotion is not political anger but a quavering sympathy for Hattie Carroll, whose race is never mentioned. This song certainly doesn't raise hopes for judicial reform, and it has not gone out of date, like the cardboard protest anthems of its era. (In 1991, William Zantzinger was found to have collected rent from tenants who had been living in extreme squalor in houses that he didn't own. This time, the judge handed out strongly an eighteen-month sentence, in a work-release program.)

"Now's the time for your tears," Dylan sings at the end. Ricks said to me, "He doesn't underscore it—say, 'Now *is* the time.' He doesn't exhort you. Maybe you should have cried before, when Hattie died." (Paul Williams thinks that the refrain for the preceding verses, "Now ain't the time for your tears," is actually sarcastic, and that Dylan is addressing "cause-chasing liberals who concern themselves with the issues and have no real empathy for people." Another axial moment.) Ricks went on to criticize some of Dylan's more recent performances of "Hattie Carroll": "He doesn't let it speak for itself. He sentimentalizes it, I'm afraid." Here I began to wonder whether the close reader had zoomed in too close. Ricks was fetishizing the details of a recording, denying the musician license to expand his songs in performance. I had just seen Dylan sing "Hattie Carroll," in Portland, and it was the best performance that I heard him give. He turned the accompaniment into a steady, sad waltz, and he played a lullaby-like solo at the center. You were reminded that the "hotel society gathering" was a Spinsters' Ball, whose dance went on before, during, and after the fatal attack on Hattie Carroll. This was an eerie twist on the meaning of the song, and not a sentimental one.

Ricks's readings are wonderfully perceptive, but they are, in the end, readings: they treat Dylan as a textual rather than musical phenomenon. They also tend to grant him an infallibility that runs counter to his shambolic creative process. Dylan himself declines the highbrow treatment—though you get the sense that he wouldn't mind picking up that Nobel Prize. Even in the sixties, he said of those who called him a poet, "Genius is a terrible word, a word they think will make me like them." He seems to prefer an audience of teenage Deadheads in a basketball arena. He may occasionally surprise the kids with moody masterworks, like "Hattie Carroll," "Visions of Johanna," and "Not Dark Yet," or he may teach them a

Stanley Brothers bluegrass hymn, but more often he gets them to jump up and down to "Tangled Up in Blue." This way, he packs in the crowds, and he also makes sure that he cannot be pinned down. Every night, whether he is in good or bad form, he says, in effect, "Think again."

DULUTH, MINNESOTA. Dylan was born here, in 1941, before moving with his family to the iron-ore town of Hibbing. He has never played in Duluth before. The city is moderately excited by his return. He is front-page news for two days running in the *Duluth News Tribune*. Storefronts downtown are adorned with WELCOME HOME, BOB signs. Duluthans are hoping that he will have something to say to the city: he did, after all, mention Duluth when he accepted the 1998 Grammy for Album of the Year. (WOW! DYLAN SAID 'DULUTH'! ran a local headline.) At the show, a fan tosses onto the stage a paper airplane on which he has written, "Please speak." It lands upside down. Dylan does not speak. The silence is a bit chilly; a few words would have made the audience ecstatic. Dylan's defense for this kind of criticism is that public speeches are a no-win situation. If he speaks a few words, people say he hasn't said enough. If he speaks at length, people think he's lost his mind. In the end, Minnesotans don't seem too miffed by the episode. I ask one local resident the following day whether he feels let down. "A little," he replies. "But in the paper it said he smiled a lot."

Discussion of Dylan often boils down to that: "Please speak. Tell us what it means." But does he need to? He had already given something away, during the ritual acoustic performance of "Tangled Up in Blue." This dense little tale, which may be about two couples, one couple, or one couple plus an interloper, seems autobiographical: it's easy to guess what Dylan might be thinking about when he sings, "When it all came crashing down, I became withdrawn / The only thing I knew how to do was keep on keeping on / Like a bird that flew . . ." See any number of ridiculous spectacles in Dylan's life. But the lines that he shouted out with extra emphasis came at the end:

> *Me, I'm still on the road, heading for another joint*
> *We always did feel the same, we just saw it from a different point*
> *Of view*
> *Tangled up in blue.*

Suddenly, the romance in question seemed to be the long, stormy one between Dylan and his audience. Dylan is over there and the rest of us are over here, and we're all seeing things from different points of view. And what is it that we're looking at? Perhaps the thing that comes between him and us—the music.

Night after night on this tour, "Tangled Up in Blue" brought the audience to life. The words had their bonding effect, but it was really the music that established a particular kind of intimacy between the singer and the crowd. Dylan's arrangement was itself an array of different musical points of view. The published version of the song is driven by sweetly chiming major chords, but in this version the singer kept slipping into a different scale—into the blues. Dismantling and rebuilding his own song, he bent notes down, inverted the melody, spread out the pitches of the chords, leaned on a single note while the chords changed around it, stressed the offbeats, laid triple rhythms on duple ones. As the rest of the band held on to straitlaced diatonic harmony and a one-two beat, the song tensed up: opposing scales met in bittersweet clashes, opposing pulses overlapped in a danceable bounce. The radio staple became a new animal.

As I went through my Dylan records and tapes, I realized that in many cases I was only half listening to the lyrics—that the music was giving the words their poetic aura. Often, Dylan's strongest verbal images occur toward the beginning of a song, and it falls to his musical sense to make something of the rest. In "Sad-Eyed Lady of the Lowlands," the eleven-minute ballad that closes *Blonde on Blonde*, Dylan fashions majestic metaphors to capture the object of his affection—"your eyes like smoke and your prayers like rhymes"—and then, in the second-to-last verse, he clouds over: "They wished you'd accepted the blame for the farm." What farm? What happened to it? Why would she be to blame for it? "Phony false alarm" is the rhyme in the next line, and it doesn't clear things up. The refrain makes another appearance—"My warehouse eyes, my Arabian drums / Should I leave them by your gate, / Or, sad-eyed lady, should I wait?"—and by this time you ought to be losing patience with it. What are "warehouse eyes," and how can one leave them? Dylanologists beat their heads against such questions. But the music makes you forget them. The melody of the refrain—a rising and descending arc, made up of consecutive notes of the D-major scale—is grand to begin with, but in the fifth verse Dylan makes it grander. As the band keeps playing the scale, he skates back up to the top D with each syllable. He sings on one note as the rest of the harmony moves around him: it's as if he's surveying the music from a summit. This is a trick as old as music. In Purcell's *Dido and Aeneas*, the soprano catches our hearts in the same way when she sings, "Remember me, remember me."

Like Hank Williams before him—or Schubert or Verdi, for that matter—Dylan sharpens the meaning of the lyrics in the mechanics of the music. Take "Mama, You Been on My Mind," which was long associated with Joan Baez and subsequently appeared in Dylan's own voice on the boxed set *The Bootleg Series, Vols. 1–3*. The song begins with a crabbed, cluttered image:

> *Perhaps it's the color of the sun cut flat*
> *And covering the crossroads I'm standing at . . .*

The harmony under these words moves from an E-major chord to a G-sharp seventh and on to C-sharp minor and an F-sharp seventh. It's an awkward series of changes, matching the baroque images on the page. Our eyes and ears go "Huh?" Then the singer seems to shrug off, with a self-deprecating grin, the attempt to poeticize his emotion—

> *Or maybe it's the weather or something like that*
> *But Mama, you been on my mind*

—and the harmony gets easier, too, going gently from E major to C-sharp minor and back to E. The meaning changes as the chords change.

Dozens of Dylan songs work in the same way. The disquieting gospel number "In the Garden" shows the agony of Jesus in Gethsemane by wandering through ten different chords, each one like a betrayal. "Idiot Wind," the centerpiece of *Blood on the Tracks*, channels its universal rage— "Someone's got it in for me, they're planting stories in the press"—into a single harmonic convulsion: each verse of the G-major song begins with grinding C minor, which is like a slap to the ear. More often, the chords are mysteriously simple. In "Knockin' on Heaven's Door," there are just four of them, but they are strung along in an unresolved, drooping sequence—a picture of the "long black cloud" that comes down on Billy the Kid.

This is not to say that the music is everything. Dylan does have a fearsome command of the English language. The neat click of the rhymes keeps you interested across all leaps of sense and changes of scene. John Lennon, not long before he died, satirized Dylan as a cynic who rhymed out of a lexicon, but I don't know of a dictionary that would have generated this couplet:

> *What can I say about Claudette?*
> *Ain't seen her since January,*
> *She could be respectably married or running*
> *a whorehouse in Buenos Aires.*

Dylan also has a knack for tricky enjambments—lines that seem complete in themselves but are subverted by what follows. These are effects for the ear, not for the eye, and Dylan sells them in performance. There's a tape of him singing "Simple Twist of Fate" in San Francisco in 1980, in which the meaning twirls almost word by word. It's a thoroughly rewritten version of the *Blood on the Tracks* song, and the last verse starts this way:

> *People tell me it's a crime*
> *To remember her for too long a time*
> *She should have caught me in my prime*
> *She would have stayed with me*
> *Instead of going back off to sea*
> *And leaving me*

Dylan slows down, and we may think that the story is at an end. But it's not.

> *To med-i-tate . . .*

A grin now steals into the voice, which had been appropriately elegiac before. Dylan's stress on "meditate" tells us that the title refrain is coming around for its final rhyme, but we can't quite guess how he'll make the leap. His voice fills with pride—pride is one of the great emotions that he can convey—and the tempo picks up again: "*Upon! A! Simple! Twist! Of! Fate!*"

Behind the wordplay are some deep musical resonances. The softly twanging bass line in "Simple Twist of Fate" takes the form of a *basso lamento*—the same kind of downward chromatic pattern that anchors

Dido's Lament. Admittedly, Dylan's tale of abandoned love doesn't have quite the same tragic weight as Purcell's. A man has a brief affair with a woman, and when she walks away he finds himself haunted by her, much as he tries to forget her. The music unfolds at a relaxed tempo, in a major key. Yet the lamento figure casts a creeping shadow, as it does in the opening bars of Schubert's String Quartet in G. And, as in the mighty Purcell aria, the words keep stressing the inscrutable fate that drives human affairs:

> *A saxophone someplace far off played*
> *As she was walking on by the arcade*
> *As the light burst through a beat-up shade*
> *Where he was waking up*
> *She dropped a coin into the cup*
> *Of a blind man at the gate*
> *And forgot about a simple twist of fate.*

A fascinating gender reversal has taken place across the centuries. In Purcell, it is the man who is called away, leaving Dido bereft: "Remember me, but ah! forget my fate." In Dylan's smaller-scale tragedy, the woman is the one who hits the road, and the man is left to contemplate the twisting and turning of fate.

Whether or not Dylan looked as far back as 1689—with him, you never know—the peculiar solidity of his lyrics comes in their easy give-and-take with older songs. He has said that the traditions of folk, blues, spirituals, and popular ballads are his real religion, and his habit of crossing genres may explain his habit of crossing religions. "I believe in Hank Williams singing 'I Saw the Light,'" he told the critic Jon Pareles. Dylan has a vise-like memory for lyrics of all sorts, and his favorite method as a songwriter is to take one line from an extant song and add one or a dozen lines of his own. "As I went out one morning," an old lyric says. "To breathe the air around Tom Paine's," Dylan adds. *Time Out of Mind* was a thrilling return to form because he picked up with a vengeance that magpie mode of composition. Old song: "She wrote me a letter and she wrote it so kind, / And in this letter these words you could find." Dylan rewrites the second line: "She put down in writing what was in her mind." Old song: "This train don't pull no gamblers, / Neither don't pull no midnight ramblers." Dylan says, "Some trains don't pull no gamblers, / No midnight ramblers, like they did before."

Everything on *Time Out of Mind* goes under one dreamy, archaic mood. The album manages to skip the twentieth century: trains discourage gambling, people ride in buggies, there's no air-conditioning ("It's too hot to sleep"), church bells ring, "gay" means "happy," the time of day is measured by the sun, lamps apparently run on gas (and are turned "down low"), and, most of the time, the singer is walking. He is almost ready to stray into the rustic wasteland of Schubert's *Winterreise*, which opens with the Dylanesque lines "I came here as a stranger / A stranger I depart." The wistfulness is intense: the singer is in love with a musical past that is gone forever. You picture him leaning late over his favorite records and songbooks, listening, writing, reading, writing. These are songs about the loneliness of listening: you could add to them "Blind Willie McTell," which was recorded in 1983 and appeared in the *Bootleg* boxed set as a kind of fanfare to *Time Out of Mind*. "I'm gazing out the window of the St. James Hotel," he sang. "And I know no one can sing the blues like Blind Willie McTell."

The melancholy could become crushing, but Dylan doesn't let it. The best songs on *Time Out of Mind* are inexplicably funny: there's a wicked glee in the performance as Dylan manipulates the tatters of his voice, the scatteredness of his inspiration, the paralysis that might arise from his obsession with history, the prevailing image of himself as a mumbling curmudgeon. And in one song—"Not Dark Yet"—all the flourishes of his songwriting come together: slow, stately chords, swinging like a pendulum between major and minor; creative tweakings of the past ("There's room enough in the heavens" becomes "There's not even room enough to be *anywhere*"); prickly aphorisms ("I can't even remember what it was I came here to get away from"; "Behind every beautiful thing there's been some kind of pain"); and glints of biblical revelation, not to mention what one Internet expert has identified as a quotation from the Talmud ("I was born here and I'll die here against my will"). If he can't sing some low notes, he gestures toward them with a slide, so that you feel them. And, as he did in "Sad-Eyed Lady," Dylan finds a way to augment the refrain. The line "It's not dark yet, but it's getting there" keeps creeping up, note by note, in the singer's now limited range. Like Skip James, the cracked genius among Delta blues singers, Dylan gives a circular form a dire sense of direction.

The sense of arrival in "Not Dark Yet" is enormous. Once again, as Christopher Ricks would point out, words turn on their axis and encompass their opposite. The song ends, "I don't even hear a murmur of a prayer /

It's not dark yet, but it's getting there." This couldn't be bleaker, could it? Bob Dylan stares into the face of death and decay. But as he sings "murmur of a prayer," he lifts the tune yet another step and does a graceful little turn at the top, creating an altogether new melody. And he slips in a triplet—a slight dancing rhythm that someone else picks up on guitar. As the song winds down, it's not the darkness that lingers but the freshly swaying motion in the music, and that theoretical possibility of a "murmur of a prayer." The man who worships Hank Williams is looking back at "I Saw the Light," a would-be uplifting gospel number that was really filled with terror. "I saw the light, I saw the light, / No more darkness, no more night," Hank insisted, in a melody that fell, and you didn't believe him. Bob declares, with a gallant upward turn, "I don't even hear a murmur of a prayer." You don't believe him, either.

MINNEAPOLIS, MINNESOTA. Dylan just played in Target Center, downtown. Toward midnight, walking away from the arena, I see a bus and a truck parked by a curb. A group of roadies are loading equipment. There is bright electric light from somewhere—the spotlight of a handheld TV camera, it turns out. People are standing around, smiling sheepishly, as they do in the presence of someone famous. My heart begins to beat a little faster. A man with thick, tangled hair is standing next to the bus, looking awkward as he signs autographs. It's Lyle Lovett, who has just finished playing on the stage around the corner. I walk back to my hotel.

This episode pointed up for me the embarrassment of fandom. I hadn't requested an interview with Dylan, but for a moment I thought I was about to see him up close. I felt the bubbling excitement of a fan. I'd been a fan, I suppose, since Dylan's music first hit me, a few years earlier, when I was staying in a friend's apartment in Berlin. *Highway 61 Revisited* was one of the few records my friend owned, and after a couple of days I'd fallen for it: the fiercely funny lyrics, the music that was both common and grand, the whole proud, angry, backward take on life. I later found that my belated conversion to Dylan corresponded all too well to an academic model of rock fandom: Daniel Cavicchi, in a book on Bruce Springsteen's audience, divides fans into categories out of William James's *The Varieties of Religious Experience*, noting that one kind of fan undergoes a sudden conversion, or "self-surrender," often in a state of isolation or in a foreign land.

Is fandom as foolish as it feels? Or is it the respect owed to the sort of person who used to be called "great"? Americans have always distrusted the concept of greatness, with its clammy Germanic air. Stardom, the cult of youth and wealth, long ago took its place. Dylan may be many things, but he is not a star: he can't control his image in the public eye. At the same time, he doesn't look, act, or sound like any great man that history records. He presents himself as a traveling musical salesman, like B.B. King or Ralph Stanley or Willie Nelson. He is generally unavailable to the media, but he is in no way a recluse, and reclusiveness is traditionally the zone in which American geniuses reside.

An "artist," by contemporary definition, is one who displays himself in art, who shares "felt" emotion and "lived" experience, who meets and greets the audience. Art becomes Method acting; art, in various senses, becomes pathetic. With Dylan, the emotion has certainly been felt, at one time or another, but it wells up spontaneously in the songs themselves, in the tangle of words and music. Even at his most confessional, he withdraws his personality from the scene—usually by becoming beautifully vague—and lets the music rise. The highest emotion hits late, in the wordless windups of his greatest songs—from "Sad-Eyed Lady" to "Not Dark Yet"—when the band plays through the verse one more time and language sinks into silence.

19

FERVOR

REMEMBERING LORRAINE HUNT LIEBERSON

On July 3, 2006, the mezzo-soprano Lorraine Hunt Lieberson died of complications from breast cancer. She was fifty-two years old. News of her passing aroused little interest outside the classical-music world: the singer was hardly a household name, lacking even the intermittent, Sunday-morning-television stardom achieved by the likes of Renée Fleming and Yo-Yo Ma. She recorded infrequently in later years; she was shy about being interviewed; she had no press agent. Her fame consisted of an ever-widening swath of ardor and awe that she left in her wake whenever she sang. Among those who had been strongly affected by her work, there was a peculiarly deep kind of grief.

I was one of those people. In her last years, I found it difficult to assume a pose of critical distance, even though I never got closer to her than Row H. In the days after she died, I tried to write about her and failed. It felt wrong to call her "great" and "extraordinary," or to throw around diva-worship words like "goddess" and "immortal," because those words placed her on a pedestal, whereas the warmth in her voice always brought her close. My attempts at chronicling her career—I saw her some twelve times—were an exercise in running out of words. When I first heard her sing, in Berlioz's *Beatrice and Benedict* at Boston Lyric Opera, in 1993, I described her as "brilliant" and "intense." When she appeared in *Xerxes* at New York City Opera, in 1997, I compared her to Maria Callas. In 2001, when she sang Bach cantatas at a Lincoln Center presentation, I reported that she had "sent the audience into a trance." In 2003, I claimed that her recording of the cantatas, on the Nonesuch label, was "beautiful enough to stop a war, if anyone thought to try." And, in 2005, I called her Handel disc, on Avie, "pull-down-the-blinds, unplug-the-telephone, can't-talk-right-now beautiful." To the extent that music can be captured in speech, she had gone beyond it. Nevertheless, empty superlatives will have to do. She was the most remarkable singer I ever heard.

I saw her for the last time in November 2005, when she came to Carnegie Hall with the Boston Symphony to perform *Neruda Songs*, composed by her husband, Peter Lieberson. She came onstage wearing a bright-red, free-flowing dress. Although her hair was shorter than in previous years and she looked a little thin, she appeared healthy. She sang that night with such undiminished power that it seemed as though she would be around forever. Then she was gone, leaving the apex vacant.

She was born Lorraine Hunt, in San Francisco, the daughter of two exacting Bay Area music teachers. She grew up studying piano, violin, and viola, settling on the viola as her instrument. She gave relatively few performances as a singer in her youth, but when she did she caught people's attention. At a concert by the Oakland Youth Orchestra, in 1972, she stepped forward to deliver an aria from Saint-Saëns's *Samson and Delilah*, and Charles Shere, in a perceptive review for the *Oakland Tribune*, described a now familiar spell being cast for perhaps the first time: "She simply stood there and sang, hardly even opening her mouth, with an even range, secure high notes, and marvelous control of dynamics in the swells."

By 1979, she was the principal violist of the Berkeley Symphony. When the orchestra decided to mount a production of *Hansel and Gretel* at San Quentin State Prison, she volunteered for the role of Hansel. Under these fittingly unconventional circumstances she made her operatic debut. She took up singing full-time while studying in Boston in the early eighties, drawing notice first for her precisely expressive accounts of Bach cantatas at Emmanuel Church, under the direction of Craig Smith. In an interview with Charles Michener, for a 2004 *New Yorker* profile, Smith related her singing to her playing: "A viola is a middle voice—it has to be alert to everything around it. There's something viola-like about the rich graininess of her singing, about her ability to sound a tone from nothing—there's no sudden switching on of the voice, no *click*. And, like most violists, she is also self-effacing: without vanity as a singer. When we first performed the Bach cantatas, she just disappeared as a person."

Her work at Emmanuel caught the attention of the young director Peter Sellars, who, in 1985, cast her as Sesto, Pompey's son, in a modern-dress production of Handel's *Giulio Cesare in Egitto*. The character of Sesto became a wild-eyed young radical, swearing vengeance with an Uzi in his hands. The singer was revealed not only as a supremely musical artist but also as a keenly dramatic one. "She started singing, and you were in the middle of this raging forest fire," Sellars recalled. "Certain things were a *little* out of control, but what you got was sheer power, sheer concentrated energy."

She went on to sing in a series of Handel performances and recordings with the Philharmonia Baroque, also of Berkeley, and appeared in Mark Morris's celebrated choreographic stagings of Handel's *L'Allegro, il Penseroso ed il Moderato* and Purcell's *Dido and Aeneas*. She decided to devote herself to singing full-time only after her viola was stolen. In the 1990s, she finally began to find wider fame, mainly on the strength of an instantly legendary performance in Sellars's production of Handel's *Theodora* at the Glyndebourne Festival, in 1996. She made a belated Metropolitan Opera debut in 1999, in John Harbison's *The Great Gatsby*. The ovations that greeted her Dido in *Les Troyens* at the Met, in 2003, signified her assumption of diva status.

Yet she fit uneasily into the classical mainstream. "Lorraine's a bit of a nut," people in the music business used to say. They were referring to her Northern California nature—her spiritual pursuits, her interest in astrology, her enthusiasm for alternative medicine. She sometimes rattled her colleagues with her raucous sense of humor and her braying laugh. She loved all kinds of music; in private settings, she'd give scorching renditions of jazz and blues standards, and she declared herself a fan of Joni Mitchell and Stevie Wonder, among others.

In retrospect, her extracurricular interests and supposed eccentricities were essential to the evolution of her art. She broke through the façade of cool professionalism that too often prevails in the classical world, showing the kind of unchecked fervor that is more often associated with the greatest pop, jazz, and gospel singers. I compared her to Callas, but she might have been closer to Mahalia Jackson. One of her favorite encores was the spiritual "Deep River," and there was something uncannily natural about her recitation of the text: "Deep river, my home is over Jordan / Deep river, Lord, I wanna cross over into camp ground."

The voice was rich in tone and true in pitch. There was something calming and consoling about the fact of the sound. "Time itself stopped to listen," Richard Dyer wrote in his obituary for *The Boston Globe*. Central to the singer's repertory was a group of arias that I think of as her benedictions, her laying on of hands: "Ombra mai fù," from *Xerxes*, a purely sensuous experience; "As with rosy steps the morn," from *Theodora*, which she made into an anthem of beatitude; Bach's "Schlummert ein, ihr matten Augen," which, in the uncomfortably haunting Sellars staging, she sang while attired in a hospital gown.

Such performances were the product not of intuition but of conscious craft. I asked the mezzo Rebecca Ringle, whom I met at Marlboro, to analyze how Lieberson's voice worked. "Her primary gift was for phrasing," Ringle told me. "It's a good instrument, but she has great technique, and superstar, beautiful-human-being phrasing." The vowels are very pure, Ringle observed, meaning that they sound much as they do in everyday speech, instead of being stretched out and distorted, as often happens in classical singing ("I am" becoming "ah ahm," and so on). "When I saw the Sellars Bach cantatas in Boston," Ringle said, "I was floored by one section that she sang quieter than I thought it would be humanly possible to understand, and yet I got every word."

Loveliness was just the point of departure. She could also communicate passion and pain and a fearsome kind of anger. At City Opera, her Xerxes, so bewitching at first appearance, whipped around to deliver an up-against-the-wall tirade in "You are spiteful, perverse, and insulting." There was a prophet-in-the-wilderness quality to her rendition of "La Anunciación," her centerpiece aria in John Adams's Christmas oratorio, *El Niño*. When she sang Benjamin Britten's cantata *Phaedra* at the New York Philharmonic, she froze listeners in their seats with her high monotone chant of the words "I stand alone." And as Irene, a leader of the martyrdom-bound Christians in *Theodora*, she made her voice into a kind of moral weapon. There is a DVD of the Glyndebourne *Theodora*, and the pivotal moment comes in the air "Bane of virtue, nurse of passions . . . Such is, prosperity, thy name." In other words, money kills the soul. The phrase "thy name" is sung eighteen times, and by the end the voice is seared around the edges, raised up like a flaming sword.

No modern singer rivaled her in Dido's Lament. On a recording with Nicholas McGegan and the Philharmonia Baroque, she begins in a mood of unearthly tranquility, joining notes in a liquid legato. The first iterations of the phrase "Remember me" are gentle, almost quiescent. But when the cry recurs, at the top of the range, her voice frays a bit, in a way that ratchets up the emotion of the scene. When the sequence is repeated, the first "Remember me" has a slightly weaker, more tremulous quality, while the last is suddenly bolder, more operatic. With utmost economy, she traces out the stages of Dido's grief, ending on tones of radiant defiance.

Having run the gamut from angelic serenity to angelic wrath, this most complete of singers concluded her career with a very human demonstration of love. She met Peter Lieberson in the summer of 1997, on the occasion of the premiere of his opera *Ashoka's Dream*, at the Santa Fe Opera. They fell in love and eventually married, and Lieberson began to write with his wife's voice in mind. By reputation an expert practitioner of twelve-tone technique, Lieberson had always had a secret yen for sensuous, late-Romantic harmony. I attended one of his classes in college, and I remember that at one session he spent an hour or more delving into the Adagietto movement of Mahler's Fifth Symphony, savoring each bittersweet suspension and enriched triad. When Lorraine Hunt entered his life, that pursuit of harmonic pleasure came to the forefront of his work, although the music remained scrupulous in method.

Neruda Songs contains some of the most unabashedly lyrical music that any American composer has produced since Gershwin. It is also courageously personal music, the choice of Neruda poems seeming to acknowledge the fragility of Lorraine's health. The final song, "Sonnet XCII," begins, heartbreakingly, with the words "My love, if I die and you don't—" The music is centered on a lullaby-like melody in G major, and it has the atmosphere of a motionless summer day. The vocal line ends on a B, and afterward the same note is held for two slow beats by the violas, as if they were holding the hand of the singer who came from their ranks. The composer is holding her hand, too. The last word is "Amor."

20

BLESSED ARE THE SAD

LATE BRAHMS

The composer Morton Feldman once told a story about music and meaning. "Two guys visit Haydn, two journalists from Cologne," Feldman said. "They ask him about literary, programmatic pieces and he says, 'Yes,' he says, 'oh, I wrote this piece which was a dialogue between God and a sinner.' Big theme, right? And they said, 'What's the name of that piece?' He said, 'I forget.'"

Feldman's joke—based on an episode from Haydn's biography—could have been told about Johannes Brahms. It could have been told *by* Brahms. This titan of German music, whom Hans von Bülow placed with Bach and Beethoven in the league of the "three B's," had a wily sense of humor, and he often did a variation on that little dance with meaning—a feint of disclosure, a quick step back.

In 1879, Brahms wrote a characteristically devious letter to the composer and conductor Vincenz Lachner, who had inquired about a passage in Brahms's Second Symphony. The work is ostensibly a pastoral scene in the summery key of D major, beginning with horn calls from afar and ending with an earthy dance for orchestra. But ominous shapes glide beneath the surface—low chords in the trombones and tuba, pungent dissonances in archaic cadences. Why such "gloomy lugubrious tones" at the outset of a light-filled piece, Lachner wished to know? Brahms replied:

> That first entrance of the trombones, that belongs to me—I can't get along without it, nor the trombones. Defending the passage would require me to be long-winded. I would have to confess, by the way, that I am a profoundly melancholy man, that black wings

incessantly flap above us, and that in my output this symphony is followed—perhaps not entirely by accident—by a little essay on the great "Warum?" [the motet *Why Is Light Given to Him That Is in Misery?*]. I will send it to you if you do not know it. It throws the necessary sharp shadows across the bright-spirited symphony and may explain those trombones and timpani.

At this point, Vincenz Lachner and all of us reading over his shoulder are thinking, "Aha! The Master is giving away secrets!" The Second Symphony has a subtext, and it is Job's despair, a blasphemous longing for death, quite literally a "dialogue between God and a sinner." Then Brahms laughs out loud: "Please don't take all this too seriously or too tragically, especially that one passage!" And he goes on to describe a passing dissonance in the closing bars of the movement as a "sensuously beautiful sound" that "comes about in the most logical way—entirely of its own accord."

In other words, it's all a question of technique. Such things as black wings and light in darkness and dialogues with God are sweets thrown to musical children. When we grow up, the music will be sufficient in itself. Brahms more or less repeated the joke in a letter to his publisher about the *Warum?* motet and its companion piece, *O Savior, Fling Open the Heavens*. He proposed, in the interest of saving space, the following advertisement: "Motets by Joh. Br. No. 1. *Why?* No. 2. *Oh!*"

Yet it is not so easy to forget those flapping black wings. They are like Dostoyevsky's polar bear, the one you are supposed to try not to think about. The message to Lachner is revealing because it mirrors a mechanism in the music itself. Not only does Brahms the letter-writer hint at, and then withdraw, meanings in his music; Brahms the composer does the same. The Second Symphony begins with a dipping-and-rising three-note figure, the thematic kernel of the entire piece. The opening paragraph—warm, deliberate, lushly scored—establishes the symphony's dominant mood. But the music soon loses momentum: the texture thins out, the strings wend their way downward, and that hooded Wagnerian quartet of trombones and tuba creeps onstage. The three-note figure sounds bleakly in the woodwinds, the timpani rumbling underneath. Thus Brahms breaks the conventional narrative rhythm of a symphonic movement. He has the tone of a storyteller who launches into his tale—"Once upon a time, in my youth . . ."—and then falls silent, overcome by some vague memory.

Just as remarkable is what happens next. Having shot a ray of darkness into a world of light, Brahms recovers light without struggle. He shrugs, and resumes. The main key of D major comes back, anchored more firmly in the bass, and the three-note pattern blossoms in a fluid, streaming violin line. It is a "fresh beginning," to quote Reinhold Brinkmann's book *Late Idyll: The Second Symphony of Johannes Brahms*. For Brinkmann, the music "conceals the unfathomable as the subterranean dimension of a seemingly secure composition." The tremor returns periodically, and in the coda of the movement it nearly takes over: the strings and a solo horn lose themselves in an aching chromatic extension of the first idea. Then the winds burst in with a new theme. It is a chipper, bouncing ditty, quoting Brahms's own song "Es liebt sich so lieblich im Lenze" ("Love is so lovely in springtime"). The music is as naïve as the words: the symphony might be trying to cheer itself up, cast off a nameless sadness. Perhaps this is what Brahms has been meaning to tell us all along. But it's closing time: the spring song whirls away in a fast diminuendo, like a group of revelers vanishing down an empty street. In the last bars, the horns come full circle, with the sad-happy opening chords.

Brahms is a complicated proposition. On the one hand, he may be the most purely classical of composers, the one who epitomizes the latter-day ethos of the art. He never wrote an opera; he disdained the Romantic fad for self-dramatization; he cultivated old forms of the Classical and the Baroque; he destroyed dozens of his own works in an apparent effort to leave an exquisite corpse for posterity. Richard Taruskin identifies Brahms as a pioneer of the historical mind-set—"the first major composer who grew up within, and learned to cope with, our modern conception of 'classical music.'" If you were in a prosecutorial frame of mind, you might argue that Brahms inaugurated the age of academic music—the practice of generating works that are designed more for scholarly dissection than for popular consumption.

At the same time, he is an intensely personal, even confessional artist. For those who love him, he is the most companionable of composers, the one who speaks to the essential condition of solitude in which we all find ourselves sooner or later. He addresses us not in the godlike voice of Bach, nor in some Mozartian or Schubertian trance, but on roughly equal foot-

ing, as one troubled mind commiserating with another. A work like the
Second seems to exhibit Brahms's own hour-by-hour struggle to stave off
paralyzing depression. I say seems, because an uncertainty remains. What
might be the composer's point of view in the street scene that I have suggested? Is he the mournful one who is left behind, tangled up in blue? Or
is he one of the laughing revelers who dance away? Are we the lonely ones,
we listeners in the dark?

Every great composer stays frozen in one readily reproducible image—
Bach grimacing under his wig, Mozart staring out with his tight little
smile, stormy-haired Beethoven clutching a pen. Brahms took the step of
manufacturing his own iconography: in 1878, at the age of forty-five, he
grew a shaggy beard and hid behind that apparatus until the end of his
life. With his silver mane and roly-poly belly, Brahms sometimes looked
like a grumpy Santa Claus, but more often he had the appearance of an
overbearing professor. The image went hand in hand with the stereotype
of Brahms as a ponderous composer, a captive of tradition. Gunther
Schuller, in his book *The Compleat Conductor*, writes, "The opinion held
in many quarters that Brahms's music is heavy and turgid, rather square,
and even 'academic,' exists primarily because most *performances* of his
music are 'heavy' and 'turgid,' emotionally overladen." Although Brahms is
firmly enshrined among the classics, you still find pockets of resistance—
echoes of the Francophile Boston critic Philip Hale, who once jested
that Boston's Symphony Hall should have signs reading EXIT IN CASE OF
BRAHMS.

Brahms came from a humble background, although, as with Verdi, the
extent of his deprivation has been exaggerated. Many biographies state
that Brahms grew up in a slum, and that his father, a working musician
who played in bands, forced him to make money for the family in various
unsavory ways, including playing the piano in sailors' taverns and brothels.
It has been said that Brahms was scarred by the squalor of his youth, to the
point of "shutting down," in the language of contemporary psychobabble.

Modern scholars have stressed that the Gängeviertel, where Brahms
grew up, became a crowded slum only in the later nineteenth century, and
that at the time of his birth, in 1833, it was a respectable working-class
neighborhood. It would seem that Brahms had a quiet, well-protected

childhood; that his parents, though far from wealthy, put all their resources into his musical training; and that the settings in which he first performed—businessmen's homes, local restaurants—were by no means unsavory. Styra Avins, who has painstakingly edited and annotated Brahms's letters, points out that the composer's early biographers "confused lack of money with lack of morals," spinning tales of sleaze and degradation.

Where did these tales come from, though? It's possible that Brahms himself told some version of them, elaborating on a situation that he had observed in passing. He may have looked in a window on his way to a lesson and later fantasized himself on the other side of it. The young Brahms had a fertile imagination: like his older colleague Robert Schumann, he steeped himself in the tales of E.T.A. Hoffmann, using them to fashion alternate artistic personalities. Tellingly, Brahms emulated Hoffmann's solitary, half-mad Kapellmeister Kreisler, signing letters and compositions with the name "Kreisler Junior." Even if the stories of playing piano in sailors' dives and being fondled by prostitutes are the invention of others, they remain interesting. They remind us how much speculation Brahms initially inspired—this lovely young man with the flowing blond hair.

Brahms's exit from the Gängeviertel was almost surreally easy. Through the Hungarian violinist Eduard Reményi he met Joseph Joachim, who, as violinist and composer, was on his way to becoming a major figure in nineteenth-century music. Joachim sent Brahms to see Liszt—a meeting that went sour when the young man dozed off during Liszt's B-Minor Sonata—and also encouraged a visit to Schumann. In August 1853, Brahms set off on a walking tour of the Rhine, ambled into Schumann's home in Düsseldorf some weeks later, and presented several of his piano works. Shortly after Brahms had begun playing, Schumann summoned his wife, the pianist Clara Schumann, and both of them listened transfixed. Robert promptly submitted a brief article, titled "New Paths," to his old magazine, the *Neue Zeitschrift für Musik*, hailing Brahms in terms not unlike those he had bestowed on Chopin more than two decades earlier ("Hats off, gentlemen, a genius!"). After extolling various of Brahms's youthful works, Robert wrote, "It seemed as though, roaring along like a river, he united them all as in a waterfall, bearing aloft a peaceful rainbow above the plunging waters below." Clara, for her part, found herself the object of an infatuation that she reciprocated in emotional terms, although the relationship probably remained platonic.

One of the works that Brahms played for the Schumanns was the Piano Sonata No. 1 in C Major, and while it exhibits the obvious borrowings of a novice composer—the keyboard-jumping opening chords of Beethoven's "Hammerklavier" are echoed at the outset—it is a work of startling finesse. The movement that most clearly telegraphs the Brahms to come is the Andante, which takes the form of variations on a folkish melody called "Stealthily Rises the Moon." (The tune comes from the 1838–40 anthology *Deutsche Volkslieder*; it resembles the hurdy-gurdy song that ends Schubert's *Winterreise*.) After giving the theme the full Romantic treatment, Brahms adds an epilogue in which he transforms its opening phrases into a translucent Bachian meditation, with a chromatic pattern woven into the inner voices and the single note C droning in the bass. At once learned and tender, this music has the voice of someone considerably more mature. Brahms possessed an old soul from the start.

Schumann's panegyric put Brahms on the map; the sonata and a set of songs were published before the year was out, with other works quickly following. Inevitably, the sudden ascent of this unknown youth stirred up a certain amount of skepticism, envy, and hostility. Brahms had his failures early on, notably when the First Piano Concerto flopped in Leipzig in 1859. In a letter to Joachim, Brahms gave a blackly humorous description of that event—"At the end, three hands attempted to fall slowly into one another, whereupon, however, a quite distinct hissing from all sides forbade such demonstrations"—and then struck a tone of equanimity: "I believe this is the best thing that can happen to one; it forces one to collect one's thoughts appropriately and raises one's courage. I am plainly experimenting and still groping." Schumann's praise gave Brahms the confidence to proceed at his own pace. It made possible the sensational refinement of Brahms's mature output. It bought him time.

Schumann soon departed from the scene, in a hauntingly gruesome way. In February 1854, he attempted suicide by jumping into the Rhine; he died two years later, in an asylum. The cause of his insanity, a doctor's diary suggests, was syphilis. Brahms may have been aware of the nature of his mentor's illness, and taken it into account. In January 1857, less than six months after Schumann's death, Brahms wrote to Joachim in praise of a book called *Self-Preservation, a Medical Treatise on the Secret*

Infirmities and Disorders of the Generative Organs Resulting from Solitary Habits, Youthful Excess, or Infection, and a little later he wrote to Clara Schumann with the advice that passions are "exceptions or excesses" that "must be driven off." (No doubt he was speaking more to himself than to her.) He returned to the theme in 1873: "*The memory of Schumann is holy to me.* The noble, pure artist ever endures as my ideal and I will probably never be allowed to love a better person—and will also, I hope, never witness the progress of such a dreadful fate from such ghastly proximity—nor have to share so in enduring it."

"Proximity" is the crucial word: Schumann came very close and then was torn away. Not long after the suicide attempt, Brahms began sketching a sonata for two pianos, which was to have become a symphony in D minor. The first movement of that work evolved into the first movement of the First Piano Concerto. Joachim once intimated that the concerto's brutal opening—a throbbing low D followed by a slashing B-flat-major figure—is a depiction of Schumann's plunge into the Rhine. Jan Swafford, the most probing of recent biographers, explains in musical terms why this picture is convincing: the ear expects D to be the tonic note of a D-minor triad, and when it turns out to be the middle note of a B-flat-major triad the effect is jarring, disorienting, vertiginous. In technical terms, the chord is an inversion; in programmatic terms, it is tumbling head over heels.

Another clue to the meaning of this fairly shocking prologue is buried in the bass. After the dread D, which is held for ten bars, the jagged opening theme is repeated, this time over a bass C-sharp, one semitone lower. Then elements of the theme's final phrases—shivering trills, plunging intervals—reappear over consecutively lower notes (C-natural, B-natural, B-flat), before the crisis subsides on a calming A. The notes make up a chromatic descending line, a *basso lamento.* And they belong to the same tragic-minded D-minor key to which the lamento has historically gravitated, notably in the overture to *Don Giovanni* and the first movement of Beethoven's Ninth. The motif returns at the beginning of the development, and again in the recapitulation, broken but still colossal. In the coda, it moves into the treble, flickering spectrally in the winds. In the sublime Adagio that follows, the droning D resurfaces, but it stays in place instead of stepping down. Toward the end, the low note rolls for six slow bars while the piano part, momentarily suggesting a Bach chorus, is filigreed with falling chromatic patterns. The tension of the first movement is gone, replaced by that tone of late-night consolation which may be Brahms's chief gift to the human race.

These charged motifs—drone, lamento, Bachian chorus—recur in the *German Requiem*, Brahms's vocal-orchestral masterpiece of 1868. He wrote it in memory of his mother, with Schumann still on his mind; the second movement, a setting of the biblical text "All flesh is as grass," is also derived from the two-piano sonata that took shape after Schumann's suicide attempt. In religious matters, Brahms remained agnostic; although he certainly intended to write a sacred piece that would please the God-fearing German public, he confined himself to an idiosyncratic mélange of passages from the Old and New Testaments, neglecting to mention Jesus Christ by name. The first movement conflates the second line of the Sermon on the Mount—"Blessed are they that mourn: for they shall be comforted"—with part of Psalm 126: "They that sow in tears shall reap in joy . . ." The movement begins with the note F, pulsing in the cellos and basses and sounding in the horns. Then some of the cellos trace a chromatic descent. The weeping figure is carefully woven through the movement that follows, recurring in a ritualistic, neo-Baroque manner.

All the while, Brahms had been worrying about the burden of the past, mulling over his unavoidable confrontation with the ghost of Beethoven. "I shall never compose a symphony!" he said a couple of years after finishing the *German Requiem*. "You have no idea how someone like me feels when he keeps hearing such a giant marching behind him." Nevertheless, a symphony did emerge, in 1876. It begins in an atmosphere of stupefying gloom, with a single note once more planted in the bass and lines diverging on either side of it: violins meander upward while violas go down the same staircase that the cellos take at the start of the Requiem. The sequence harks back to the opening chorus of Bach's *St. Matthew Passion*— "Come, daughters, help me mourn"—where a musical wedge shape surrounds a monotone. Bach places a tangy dissonance in his second bar; Brahms goes one better, letting an out-of-nowhere chord of F-sharp minor gnash against the fundamental C. Add to this an upper melody that sways unsteadily, almost drunkenly, outside the bar lines, and you have a scene no less disturbing than the opening of the First Piano Concerto.

From here on, Brahms's First Symphony sticks to a fairly conventional heroic-Romantic plot. Like Beethoven's Ninth, it goes through stages of struggle and reflection to attain a final victory. There is even a hummable hymnal theme in the closing movement. (When the resemblance to the "Ode to Joy" was pointed out, Brahms replied, "Any ass can hear that.") The symphony is a towering achievement, yet its emulation of Beethoven somehow rings a little hollow. The trouble isn't that Brahms cannot rejoice; his output has many sun-kissed pages. It's that the onward-and-upward, *per aspera ad astra* narrative goes against the grain of his personality, where happiness and sadness alternate unpredictably and the emotional reality lies somewhere in between. The Second Symphony, with its dances and shadows, is truer to his nature. When, in the finale of the First, Brahms comes around at last to the triumph that Beethoven's template demands, gears keep grinding the wrong way. The unadulterated C-major joy lasts about a minute.

Having produced the landmark works expected of him, Brahms abandoned the monumental mode. Significantly, in the years immediately following the Leipzig fiasco of 1859, he concentrated on chamber music—the first two piano quartets and the First String Sextet—and also wrote numerous songs, duets, vocal quartets, four-hand piano pieces, and other pieces suitable for the intelligent middle-class home. His chief model may have been not Beethoven but Schubert, whose music he studied intently. (The chromatic opening of Schubert's Quartet in G reappears in the fourth movement of Brahms's Serenade No. 2.) Or perhaps he aimed to fuse Schubert's effortless lyricism with Beethoven's laborious development of relatively short motives. The entire first movement of the Piano Quartet in G Minor stems from the simple four-note figure with which it begins (rising minor sixth, falling major third, rising minor second). Such works are no longer "veiled symphonies," as Schumann said of the First Piano Sonata; they are complete in themselves, worlds narrow yet deep.

Brahms's secret weapon is rhythm. Nineteenth-century classical music is generally not prized for its rhythmic invention—composers would generally put a 4/4 time signature at the outset of a piece, set a pulse in motion, and attempt to sustain large structures through harmonic means—but Brahms paid close attention to the science of the beat. He steeped himself in the elemental rhythms of folk music, filling up hundreds of pages of manuscript paper with arrangements of German folk songs. More important, in the 1860s he set about fashioning Hungarian dances for piano duet, opening himself to a Gypsy strain (and gaining a large popular audience in the process). His mature music is rife with syncopating accents, themes that hang back a beat or jump ahead, jaunty polyrhythms of three against two or three against four. The G-Minor Piano Quartet ends with a Rondo alla Zingarese that precisely evokes the exuberance of a Gypsy wedding band. "What Brahms was after was to create a tension, a tug of war, as it were, between the actual heard rhythm and phrase, and the underlying metric pulse," Gunther Schuller writes. Alas, rhythmic study is routinely neglected in the modern classical conservatory. As Schuller demonstrates in painful detail, Brahms's games around the beat are routinely smudged in performance and on recordings.

There was an ideological strain to Brahms's self-presentation in the 1860s and '70s. With his chamber-music obsession, his studied classicism, his punchy rhythms, and his scarcely hidden pessimism (all flesh is as grass, indeed), he was separating himself from the "New German School" of Liszt, Wagner, and their allies, who talked of the "music of the future" and insisted on the need for new forms. The appearance of that professorial beard, two years after the First Symphony, seemed to confirm Brahms's caretaker role. Yet it is easy to make too much of the difference between the young Brahms and the older one. If anything, his music grew more dream-besotted, more "youthful," as the years went by. His early works are the most academic, his later works the most fantastic. A fine epigraph to his career may be found in an aphorism by Novalis that Brahms entered in his notebooks: "Our life is no dream, but ought to be and perhaps will become one."

Brahms did not conform to social type, either the conservative or the bohemian. He believed in the German nation and in the wisdom of the middle class, but he had a tendency toward vagrancy, a sympathy for outcasts (at one dinner he toasted Sitting Bull's victory at Little Bighorn), a firm adherence to Viennese liberal views, and an outspoken scorn for anti-Semites. "Anti-Semitism is insanity!" he exploded when it became evident that Karl Lueger was going to be mayor of Vienna. In musical politics, he proclaimed, it is true, the supremacy of the past, but he was responding to a musical market that had already turned in favor of the "classical" canon. Aware of his audience's love of tradition, he composed with its literacy in mind. His music follows canonical models while also subverting them, asserting a skeptical modern self.

Brahms's relationship with Wagner was deliciously complex. By the 1870s, the two composers represented opposite poles of German music, the classicist and the futurist. Everyone had to answer the question *"Brahmsianer oder Wagnerianer?"* Brahms's chief critical ally, Eduard Hanslick, published reams of anti-Wagnerism in the *Neue Freie Presse* of Vienna; Wagner responded by laying into an unnamed but easily recognizable composer who dressed up "tomorrow in Handel's Hallelujah wig, another time as a Jewish czardas player." Still, Brahms made a point of praising his rival. For some years he had the original manuscript of the Paris version of the Venusberg scene from *Tannhäuser*, and when Wagner asked for it back Brahms agreed to return it if he could have another score as a replacement. *Das Rheingold*, the prologue to the *Ring*, arrived in the mail, and Brahms wrote back as follows: "I give the best and most appropriate thanks daily to the work itself—it does not lie here without being utilized. Maybe this section is not, at first, such a great inducement to the thorough study which your entire great work demands; this Rheingold did pass through your hands in a very special way, however, and so let the Walkyre [*sic*] radiate her beauty brightly, so as to outshine its accidental advantage." The tone is friendly, although one can imagine Wagner puzzling over the particulars of the phrases. One possible translation: the *Ring* turns out to be magnificent, though one would never guess as much from seeing nothing but E-flat-major chords on the first page.

What's striking about this letter is that Brahms is simply being candid about his mixed reactions to Wagner's music. His honesty in such moments was both endearing and infuriating. Very often he passed up the chance for the easy, problem-solving phrase; his offhand letters caused countless misunderstandings and strained several friendships. His closest relationships were fraught with tensions and breaks. He could be callous, unthinking, unfeeling. It is painful to read him berating Joachim for failing to fulfill his promise as a composer, as if such words could have helped matters. It is horrible to read him offhandedly lecturing Clara Schumann—one of the leading pianists of the age, and a composer of considerable gifts—on the direction and pace of her career. Yet he surely intended no gratuitous pain. Power trips were not his style. The British composer Ethel Smyth said: "[Brahms] knew his own worth—what great creator does not?—but in his heart he was one of the most profoundly modest men I ever met." In an age of Wagnerian megalomania, Brahms took a democratic view of the artist's role. "Art is a republic," he wrote to Clara. "Do not confer a higher rank upon any artist, and do not expect the minor ones to look up to him as something higher, as consul."

Out of many passages in the letters that give a sense of Brahms's down-to-earth nature, my favorite is a note that the composer sent to his father in 1867, supplying lovingly pedantic instructions on travel from Hamburg to Vienna (with a change in Berlin): "If you continue on right away in Berlin you must take a hackney to the other station. A policeman hands out the voucher at the exit. Before you travel the night through, as is practical in the heat, drink a glass of grog so you sleep well. But take along very little . . . No cigars, nothing new, nothing that is taxable. You'll find every conceivable thing here with me." There, basically, is the Life of Brahms.

Composers often gain strength as they get older. While other art forms thrive on youthful passion, the technique of composition—a hard, cumulative labor, a solitary process of trial and error—generally sharpens over time. In old age, certain composers reach a state of terminal grace in which even throwaway ideas give off a glow of inevitability, like wisps of cloud illumined at dusk. It's hard to think of another art form where so many peak achievements—Bach's *The Art of Fugue*, Beethoven's late quartets, Messiaen's *Saint Francis of Assisi*—arrive at, or near, the close of day. The youth-mad logic of the popular marketplace makes it considerably harder for nonclassical figures to pull off the same kind of late-career transfiguration, although Duke Ellington, Johnny Cash, Sarah Vaughan, and Bob Dylan, among others, have shown that age can find its voice.

Every so often, a music theorist tries to determine what late works have in common, with interesting but murky results. In 1937, Theodor W. Adorno wrote an essay titled "Late Style in Beethoven," in which he hazarded the idea that late works are "furrowed, even ravaged. Devoid of sweetness, bitter and spiny, they do not surrender themselves to mere delectation." This is apt enough for Shostakovich's spectral final string quartets, or for Stravinsky's *Requiem Canticles*, or for the densest thickets of *Parsifal*, but it hardly accounts for the sexual charge of Monteverdi's *Coronation of Poppea*, or the spacious rapture of Handel's *Theodora*, or the radiance of Richard Strauss's *Four Last Songs*. Some late works con-

solidate early gains; others spin off in fresh directions. Liszt, around the
age of seventy, began writing something like atonal music, to the conster-
nation of Wagner, who thought his friend had gone senile.

Verdi is perhaps the most astonishing case of all. In *Falstaff*, he took command of a genre—comic opera—that once had frustrated him, and in the
process he gave it new psychological depth. When, in the last act, Falstaff
arrives in Windsor Park, about to be tricked and merrily humbled, he counts
off the strokes of midnight—"*Una . . . due . . . tre . . . quattro . . .*"—and
there is a musical foreshadowing of the dejection that takes hold of Falstaff
at the end of Shakespeare's *Henry IV, Part 2* ("We have heard the chimes
at midnight"). The old man sings on one note while a weird mist of chords
revolves around him. The moment passes quickly, as such moments do in
late Verdi, but it gives the sense of a chasm opening.

The difficulty in describing the late style of Brahms—the composer
died of liver cancer in 1897, a month shy of his sixty-fourth birthday—is
that even in his youth he was a master of the twilight tone. In a way, all
Brahms is late Brahms. In *Late Idyll*, Reinhold Brinkmann devotes many
pages to Brahms's pervasive melancholy, which seems at once personal
and philosophical. It is rooted in the solitude that the composer chose for
himself, or that was forced upon him by his shyness and his fear of unpredictable social situations. Only in isolation, in bouts of endless labor, could
he obtain the purity that he sought. In a wider sense, he was marking the
passing of a golden age. As Brinkmann says, Brahms was haunted by the
sense of being a "latecomer," a straggler in the musical succession that
stretched from Bach to Mozart and on to Beethoven and Schubert. Like
little Hanno in Thomas Mann's *Buddenbrooks*, Brahms effectively drew a
line at the bottom of the musical family tree: after him there would be
nothing more.

He was, of course, entirely wrong. He met his match when he went out
walking one day with Gustav Mahler, the fiery young Austrian modernist.
Brahms launched into a diatribe against all that was new and futuristic in
music, saying that the last truly beautiful works had already been composed. As he said this, the two men were standing on a bridge over a
stream. Mahler, feeling puckish, pointed to a random ripple in the water
and exclaimed, "Look, *Herr Doktor*! Look!" Brahms asked, "What?"
Mahler replied, "There goes the last wave." Brahms rewarded him with a
gruff smile. Music, he admitted, no more has an end than it has a begin-

ning. All the same, Brahms did mark the end of a certain line; after him, Viennese classicism gently died away, and the language of music fractured into a Babel of competing dialects.

If there is a Brahmsian late style, it seems to emerge in the Third Symphony, which was sketched in the summer of 1883. Wagner had passed away several months earlier, and in the symphony Brahms nods several times to the wizard of Bayreuth: the Venusberg music floats in before the second theme of the first movement; questing, *Tristan*-esque chords sound in the winds about a dozen bars before the end of the first movement; and one scholar hears *Götterdämmerung* near the end of the Andante. But the real story may be that Brahms is again confronting Beethoven's ghost, now on his own terms. When Beethoven reached the number three, he unleashed the *Eroica*, the mightiest symphony yet written. Brahms, in his Third, disavows the hero role. The symphony begins with a sweeping, almost flamboyant violin theme that surges over the audience like ocean waves. At the end of the finale, the theme returns, but it is given a pianissimo halo, as if it were representing the obliteration of will. Like Wagner, Brahms had read Schopenhauer on the renunciation of self, but where Wagner's gestures of self-abnegation always seem a bit of a put-on—you are aware of the power being held in check—Brahms's come as second nature.

This is not to say that Brahms grew passive. Two minor-key chamber pieces conceived in the summer of 1886—the Third Piano Trio and the Third Violin Sonata—recall the heaven-storming works of decades past. More often, though, Brahms tended toward understatement. Various movements of the late chamber pieces have titles containing the word "*grazioso*," or gracefully—not always a prized value in the industrialized later nineteenth century. In slow movements, especially, Brahms backed away from the gigantism of the era. In these years, Anton Bruckner was writing adagio slow movements that went on for twenty minutes or more, and were often marked "*feierlich*," or solemn. Brahms, too, produced a string of adagios in his last years, but he avoided the rapt, ecstatic mode, which, as the musicologist Margaret Notley observes, was often associated with notions of peculiarly German soulfulness. Instead, in the G-Major String Quintet and the Clarinet Quintet, Brahms pointedly incorporated an aspect of Gyspy performance—the practice of "allowing a soloist to emerge from the band and play an elaborate improvisation," in Notley's

words. Gypsy impressions were common in rousing fast movements, less
so in adagios, where the composer was assumed to be speaking from the
heart.

Even more intimate are the four sets of short compositions for piano:
the Fantasias Opus 116, the Intermezzos Opus 117, and the Piano Pieces
Opus 118 and Opus 119. The title Intermezzo is attached to no fewer than
fourteen of the twenty pieces in this series. Brahms was no doubt aware
of the long history of the term; he may have been thinking back to the
Renaissance, when theatrical productions at the courts of Florence and
Ferrara were interspersed with *intermedi*, musical interludes that grew
ever more elaborate and led to the art of opera. Brahms's Intermezzos are
hardly operatic, but they are, in a sense, miniature dramas, too harmonically involuted and emotionally elusive to be considered occasional pieces.
They tilt toward dark keys with many flats or sharps—E-flat minor, B-flat
minor, C-sharp minor. The harmony often has an untethered quality,
theoretically justifying Arnold Schoenberg's claim, in his essay "Brahms
the Progressive," that the later Brahms anticipated the advent of an "unrestricted musical language," namely Schoenberg's own. The Intermezzo in
B-flat Minor, Opus 117, No. 2, almost neurotically evades the home triad
in root position. Schoenberg played similar games in the works he wrote
just before his leap into atonality.

Yet the greatest of the Intermezzos, Opus 117, No. 1, is outwardly the
simplest. The writing is straightforward enough that even a bad pianist
can get through the piece without incident. In one of his characteristic
confessional jokes, Brahms said the Intermezzos might be labeled "'Sing
Lullabies of My Sorrow' Nos. 1, 2, and 3," and at the top of No. 1 he placed
a quotation from Herder's folk-song collection: "Sleep softly, my child,
sleep softly and well." (The poem is a translation of the old Scottish song
"Lady Anne Bothwell's Lament": "Balow, my babe, lye still and sleipe / It
grieves me sair to see thee weipe.") The German text fits the rise and fall
of the opening melody, as Max Kalbeck, Brahms's devoted biographer,
noticed. Still, the black wings of depression hover overheard, opening
to their full span in the middle of the piece, when the music veers into
E-flat minor. Slow arpeggios in the left hand reach treacherously low in
the bass, at one point touching the bottom C on the keyboard. That note
tolls like a bell from whatever unknown church Brahms chose for his
doubting faith. Then the major-key material returns, wistfully garlanded

with sixteenth-note figures, its closing phrases broken by palpable sighs. For Mitsuko Uchida, Schubert is the music that you will hear when you die; for me, it is this.

The pensive tone that hangs over so much of the late Brahms is mainly absent from the Fourth Symphony, in which the composer bade farewell to the form that caused him such trouble. It would not be wrong to detect a streak of irony in Brahms's valediction. The symphony begins coolly, without fanfare. The first theme, a violin figure arranged around descending thirds, is so casual as to seem pedestrian: it's as if Brahms pulled back the curtain on a symphony already in progress. Here is another of his anti-Beethoven effects, the reverse of the abrupt, attention-getting gestures that begin the *Eroica* and the Fifth Symphony—although, as Raymond Knapp notes, the falling thirds distantly and strangely echo the Fifth's famous four-note opening.

The deliberately plain material in the Brahms Fourth—one wit wrote under the first theme, *"Es fiel . . . ihm wie . . . der mal . . . nichts ein"* ("Once more he had not one idea")—becomes a foil for the usual bouts of variation. Brahms also transforms his material by altering the context. The first movement follows the hallowed sonata-form structure of Viennese Classical tradition: exposition, in which first and second themes unfold in neighboring keys; development, in which principal themes are worked over; and recapitulation, where the themes recur, their keys now aligned. Here, though, when the theme in thirds makes its expected return, we hear it first in muffled, slowed-down, "frozen" form (to quote the scholar Walter Frisch); and between each halting phrase is a drawn-out shudder in the strings, like wind through a ruin. Then the first theme resumes, at the original ambling tempo, in the original laid-back scoring, and in the middle of the phrase. It is a cinematic coup, a jump cut. And it is an effect nearly impossible to bring off in performance. Brahms is using phrases in the literary sense: strands of speech are broken off and picked up again, with unspeakable emotions implied in the pauses.

In the slow movement, the harmony takes a turn to the ancient, with the E-major scale altered to resemble medieval and Renaissance modes. As Notley observes, such archaisms, which crop up fairly often in Brahms's final period, are characteristic of late style as Adorno defined it: they suggest an alienation from the present or a position outside the flow of time. Yet, in line with his mature practice, Brahms refrains from a somber, heavy-going adagio atmosphere. The movement is marked Andante moderato—a moderate walking tempo. (Alas, many modern conductors drag it out for twelve minutes or more, evidently under the impression that Brahms must have had something enormously weighty to say in the slow movement of his final symphony.) In the same spirit, the Scherzo, marked Allegro gio-coso, barrels along in merry fashion, as if it were purposefully forgetting the enigmas of the first movement and averting its eyes from the draco-nian finale that is imminent.

The final movement is the crux of the work, maybe of Brahms's entire career. Frisch, in his book on the Brahms symphonies, calls it "perhaps the most extraordinary symphonic movement written in the post-Beethoven and pre-Mahler era." It is marked Allegro energico e passionato: fast, en-ergetic, passionate. It begins with a furious statement in the winds and brass: blaring chords built around an eight-note theme that climbs up step by step and then plunges down. For the remainder of the movement this theme repeats in ostinato style, through thirty variations and a coda. Brahms has let go of time's arrow and returned to the cyclical Baroque. Indeed, the movement is a chaconne in all but name: the chaconne finale of Bach's Cantata No. 150, "Meine Tage in den Leiden / endet Gott den-noch in Freuden" ("My days that pass in sadness / God will end in joy"), is known to have inspired Brahms directly. Knapp also argues that Buxte-hude's Ciacona in E Minor served as a model. And there can be little doubt that the grimly driving mood of the movement owes much to Bach's Ciaccona in D minor for solo violin, which Brahms had arranged for piano left hand. "On a single staff, for a small instrument, the man writes a whole world of the deepest thoughts and the most powerful feelings," Brahms wrote to Clara Schumann, when he sent her that arrangement. "If I were to imagine how *I* might have made, conceived the piece, I know for certain that the overwhelming excitement and awe would have driven me mad."

Entering the zone of madness, Brahms deconstructs his models even as he copies them. He tends to keep the theme out of the bass, so that you sometimes have to strain to hear it. And, as Frisch demonstrates, the cha-conne form is overlaid with a traditional sonata form. Form upon form, layer upon layer: the music gives the impression not of a ranting individual but of a ranting architecture. Brahms is certainly musing on the musical past, but he may also be speaking to his contemporaries—donning the garb of the ancients to deliver a sermon on the music of the present. The movement could have carried the scathing inscription that Mahler placed on one manuscript of the Rondo-Burleske, the Scherzo of his Ninth Symphony: "To my brothers in Apollo."

At the center comes a respite: a halting, lamenting solo for flute, and, a little later, a funereal procession for choirs of wind and brass. This is also, in Frisch's analysis, the second theme of the sonata form. The brass sequence—led by another trio of trombones—smacks of *Tannhäuser*, the work over which Brahms and Wagner had their epistolary squabble. But the solemnity is soon disrupted by a blistering restatement of the main theme—echoing and amplifying that traumatic moment in Bach's Ciaccona when major darkens to minor. As events speed toward their conclusion, Brahms begins to treat the motif with a certain perversity. Its ceaseless upward motion stirs memories of Mozart's diabolically jumping figures in the hell scene of *Don Giovanni*. Only in the final bars does Brahms let us hear what we subliminally crave: a grand, contrary, descending motion, a kind of lamento fortissimo in the bass.

Reinhold Brinkmann sees the finale of the Fourth as an exercise in philosophical negation. He quotes the conductor Felix Weingartner: "I cannot get away from the impression of an inexorable fate implacably driving some great creation, whether it be an individual or a whole race, toward its downfall . . . This movement is seared by shattering tragedy, the close being a veritable orgy of destruction, a terrible counterpart to the paroxysm of joy at the end of Beethoven's last symphony." Brinkmann thinks at once of Thomas Mann's *Doctor Faustus*, in which the fictional composer Adrian Leverkühn is said to have "taken back" Beethoven's "Ode to Joy." But this may be going too far. Brahms was no iconoclast: his respect for tradition was absolute. His scary fury at the end of the Fourth may have to do with his determination to keep tradition alive. The music of the future, he implies, must be filtered through the inherited language. Premonitions of the spectral scoring of Schoenberg, Berg, and Webern—the atomization of the orchestra into floating timbres—show the need for a negotiation between past and future. And the tone is not quite tragic. There is a joy in darkness here, an animal pleasure in violence. In the first variation, the brass, timpani, and strings make a curious noise—*rrrrrRUH! rrrrrRUH!*—like the growl of a sleepy dog.

What does the movement evoke, if not the triumph of darkness? I wonder whether it is in some way a final answer to the question posed in the years after Schumann's death. Job asked: Why is light given? Why go on? What do we have that is better than death? In all the late works, Brahms may be contemplating that problem. In the Intermezzos, he extols solitude. In the chamber works for clarinet—two sonatas, a trio, the Gypsy-flavored quintet—he values companionship, long conversations into the night. In the *Four Serious Songs*, based on biblical texts, he sees that "all is vanity" and gives himself over to "faith, hope, and charity." In the Fourth Symphony, however, Brahms speaks in tones of rationalized thunder, as if he were reading aloud from the text of God's own contemptuous answer to Job: "Where is the way where light dwelleth? and as for darkness, where is the place thereof? . . . Hast thou entered into the treasures of the snow? or hast thou seen the treasures of the hail . . . ?"

The radiant terror of God's works finds an analogue in a tour de force of styles past and present. Around they go, chaconne and lament, Bach and Wagner, chorale and folk tune, village band and proto-modernist orchestration. The finale of Brahms's Fourth is a *Götterdämmerung* in nine minutes, an apocalypse in strict time, musical history stripped to the bone. At the center is nothing, the gray void that the first movement revealed in two or three shivery glimpses. The whole of it seems a convincing demonstration of Nietzsche's dictum that without music life would be a mistake.

NOTES

SUGGESTED LISTENING

ACKNOWLEDGMENTS

INDEX

NOTES

PREFACE

xiii *"Writing about music is like dancing about architecture"*: Alan P. Scott explores the provenance of this quotation at www.pacifier.com/~ascott/they/tamildaa.htm (accessed Dec. 7, 2009).

xv *"a specific variant"*: Bruno Nettl, "Music," in *The New Grove Dictionary of Music and Musicians*, 2nd ed., ed. Stanley Sadie (Macmillan, 2001), vol. 17, p. 427.

1. LISTEN TO THIS

This chapter is an expanded version of an article that appeared in *The New Yorker* on February 16, 2004.

4 *"Fewer classical records"*: James Goodfriend, "Losing Touch," *Stereo Review* 23:6 (Dec. 1969), pp. 54, 56.

4 *"The economic crisis"*: Alfred Wallenstein, "Plan for Self-Help; A Conductor Gives His Idea of How Orchestras Might Solve Problems," *The New York Times*, Dec. 10, 1950.

4 *"Concerts are poorly attended"*: Hans Heinz Stuckenschmidt, "Mechanical Music," in *The Weimar Republic Sourcebook*, ed. Anton Kaes, Martin Jay, and Edward Dimendberg (University of California Press, 1994), p. 598.

4 *"The death of classical music"*: Charles Rosen, *Critical Entertainments: Music Old and New* (Harvard University Press, 2000), p. 295.

6 *"melancholy, sometimes progressing"*: Charles O'Connell, notes to Jascha Heifetz's recording of the Tchaikovsky Violin Concerto with Fritz Reiner and the Chicago Symphony (RCA Victor LM 2129).

6 *"There has been a stab"*: Leonard Bernstein, *The Infinite Variety of Music* (Simon and Schuster, 1966), pp. 198–99.

7 *"I love the vast surface"*: Carl Nielsen, *Living Music*, trans. Reginald Spink (Hutchinson, 1953), p. 40.

10 dismissal proceedings: John Butt, *Music Education and the Art of Performance in the German Baroque* (Cambridge University Press, 1994), p. 17.

11 *"the former style of music"*: Hans T. David, Arthur Mendel, and Christoph Wolff, eds., *The New Bach Reader: A Life of Johann Sebastian Bach in Letters and Documents* (Norton, 1998), p. 149.

11 *"Right in the middle"*: Robert Spaethling, trans. and ed., *Mozart's Letters, Mozart's Life: Selected Letters* (Norton, 2000), p. 160.

11 *"While most were"*: James H. Johnson, *Listening in Paris: A Cultural History* (University of California Press, 1995), p. 9.

11 *Walt Whitman mobilized opera*: See section 26 of "Song of Myself."

12 *"the first classic that"*: Johann Nikolaus Forkel, *On Johann Sebastian Bach's Life, Genius, and Works*, in David, Mendel, and Wolff, *The New Bach Reader*, p. 420.

12 *"If the art"*: Ibid., p. 420.

12 *"patriotic admirers"*: Ibid., p. 418.

12 *"After the first act"*: Cosima Wagner, *Cosima Wagner's Diaries*, vol. 2, ed. Martin Gregor-Dellin and Dietrich Mack, trans. Geoffrey Skelton (Harcourt Brace Jovanovich, 1980), pp. 894, 898.

13 *"monumental character"*: Richard Wagner, *Selected Letters of Richard Wagner*, trans. and ed. Stewart Spencer and Barry Millington (Norton, 1988), p. 210.

13 "Kinder! macht Neues!": Richard Wagner and Franz Liszt, *Briefwechsel zwischen Wagner und Liszt*, vol. 1, ed. Erich Kloss (Breitkopf & Härtel, 1910), p. 179.

13 *"New works do not"*: Jan Swafford, *Johannes Brahms: A Biography* (Knopf, 1997), p. 190.

13 *"get upset when"*: William Weber, *The Great Transformation of Musical Taste: Concert Programming from Haydn to Brahms* (Cambridge University Press, 2008), p. 259. For statistics on concerts in Leipzig, see p. 171.

13 *"Music could quickly come"*: Wayne M. Senner, Robin Wallace, and William Meredith, eds., *The Critical Reception of Beethoven's Compositions by His German Contemporaries*, vol. 2 (University of Nebraska Press, 2001), p. 16.

13 *"the great works of the great composers"*: Lawrence Levine, *Highbrow/Lowbrow: The Emergence of Cultural Hierarchy in America* (Harvard University Press, 1990), p. 118.

14 *twenty-five cents*: Jessica C. E. Gienow-Hecht, *Sound Diplomacy: Music and Emotions in Transatlantic Relations, 1850–1920* (University of Chicago Press, 2009), p. 132.

14 *"America is saddled"*: Arthur Farwell, "The Incubus of Musical Culture," *The International* 6 (July 1912), pp. 31–32.

14 *"prestige-hypnotized"*: Daniel Gregory Mason, *Tune In, America: A Study of Our Coming Musical Independence* (Knopf, 1931), p. 44.

14 *"We would respectfully request"*: Ibid., p. 59.

14 *"After the Funeral March"*: Ibid., p. 52. For more on Stokowski and applause, see Oliver Daniel, *Stokowski: A Counterpoint of View* (Dodd, Mead, 1982), pp. 288–89; and Herbert Kupferberg, *Those Fabulous Philadelphians: The Life and Times of a Great Orchestra* (Scribner's, 1969), p. 78.

15 *Ellin Mackay*: "Why We Go to Cabarets: A Post-Debutante Explains," *The New Yorker*, Nov. 28, 1925, pp. 7–8. See also Mackay, "The Declining Function: A Post-Debutante Rejoices," *The New Yorker*, Dec. 12, 1925, pp. 15–16.

15 *"'Alexander's Ragtime Band,'" "the circus can be"*: Gilbert Seldes, *The Seven Lively Arts* (Sagamore Press, 1957), pp. 264, 309.

16 *"sick moment in the progress"*: Mason, *Tune In, America*, p. 164.

16 *"It is the Palais Royalists"*: Quoted in Henry Osborne Osgood, *So This Is Jazz* (Da Capo, 1978), p. 146.

17 $6.93: Howard Pollack, *Aaron Copland: The Life and Work of an Uncommon Man* (Henry Holt, 1999), p. 90.

17 *eighteen million copies*: Norman Lebrecht, *The Life and Death of Classical Music* (Anchor, 2007), p. 136.

17 *According to one report*: Goodfriend, "Losing Touch," p. 54.

18 *"I intentionally won't use"*: Alex Abramovich, "Curator Rock," *Slate*, Jan. 19, 2004, www.slate.com/id/2094027 (accessed Jan. 15, 2010).

18 *"No computers were used"*: David Hajdu, *Heroes and Villains: Essays on Music, Movies, Comics, and Culture* (Da Capo, 2009), p. 117.

19 *music is music*: Edward Jablonski, *Gershwin* (Doubleday, 1987), p. 167.

19 *"culturally aware non-attenders"*: Rebecca Winzenried, "Stalking the Culturally Aware Non-Attender," *Symphony*, Jan.–Feb. 2004, pp. 26–32.

2. CHACONA, LAMENTO, WALKING BLUES

22 *"given by the devil"*: Maurice Esses, *Dance and Instrumental Diferencias in Spain During the 17th and Early 18th Centuries*, vol. 3 (Pendragon, 1994), p. 131.

23 *"riding in to Seville"*: Thomas Walker, "Ciaccona and Passacaglia: Remarks on Their Origin and Early History," *Journal of the American Musicological Society* 21:3 (Autumn 1968), p. 302.

23 *"So come in, all you nymph girls"*: Miguel de Cervantes, *Obra completa*, vol. 2, ed. Florencio Sevilla Arroyo and Antonio Rey Hazas (Centro de Estudios Cervantinos, 1994), p. 771.

23 *"Vida bona"*: Richard Hudson, *Passacaglia and Ciaccona: From Guitar Music to Italian Keyboard Variations in the 17th Century* (UMI, 1981), pp. 6–8.

23 *"Un sarao de la chacona"*: Text from *Villancicos y Danzas Criollas*, recording by Jordi Savall's Hespèrion XXI and La Capella Reial de Catalunya (Alia Vox 9834).

24 *religious authorities had warned him*: Jodi Campbell, *Monarchy, Political Culture, and Drama in Seventeenth-Century Madrid: Theater of Negotiation* (Ashgate, 2006), pp. 50–51.

24 *"lascivious, dishonest"*: Louise K. Stein, "Eros, Erato, Terpsíchore and the Hearing of Music in Early Modern Spain," *Musical Quarterly* 82:3/4 (Autumn–Winter 1998), p. 661.

25 *"I consider music"*: Igor Stravinsky, *Chroniques de ma vie* (Denoël/Gonthier, 1962), p. 63.

25 *Psychologists have found*: Aniruddh D. Patel, *Music, Language, and the Brain* (Oxford University Press, 2008), p. 314.

25 *Mafa people of Cameroon*: Thomas Fritz et al., "Universal Recognition of Three Basic Emotions in Music," *Current Biology* 19:7 (April 2009), pp. 573–76.

26 *"A vision of the grave"*: Robert Müller-Hartmann, "A Musical Symbol of Death," *Journal of the Warburg and Courtauld Institutes* 8 (1945), p. 201.

26 *"Change me to a rainbow"*: Béla Bartók, *Rumanian Folk Music*, vol. 2, ed. Benjamin Suchoff (Martinus Nijhoff, 1967), p. 647; translation is in vol. 3, p. 561.

26 *"Woe is me"*: Lajos Vargyas, *Folk Music of the Hungarians*, trans. Judit Pokoly (Akadémiai Kiadó, 2005), pp. 504–505, 706.

26 *"killing the bride"*: Margarita Mazo, "Stravinsky's *Les Noces* and Russian Village Wedding Ritual," *Journal of the American Musicological Society* 43:1 (Spring 1990), pp. 99–142. See esp. example 8.

26 *Comparable laments*: See János Sipos, Dávid Somfai Kara, and Éva Csáki, *Kazakh Folksongs from the Two Ends of the Steppe*, trans. Judit Pokoly (Akadémiai Kiadó,

2001), p. 43; Elizabeth Tolbert, "The Musical Means of Sorrow: The Karelian Lament Tradition" (PhD diss., University of California, Los Angeles, 1988), p. 174; "Funeral Music" on the recording *Indian Music of the Upper Amazon* (Smithsonian Folkways FW04458); and Steven Feld, *Sound and Sentiment: Birds, Weeping, Poetics, and Song in Kaluli Expression*, 2nd ed. (University of Pennsylvania Press, 1990), pp. 86–111.

27   *"It comes from the first sob"*: Federico García Lorca, *Deep Song and Other Prose*, trans. and ed. Christopher Maurer (New Directions, 1975), p. 30.

27   *"Hey, the wind's blowing"*: Vargyas, *Folk Music of the Hungarians*, pp. 407, 669.

27   *Peter Kivy . . . argues*: Peter Kivy, *Sound Sentiment: An Essay on the Musical Emotions* (Temple University Press, 1989), pp. 71–83.

28   *"not mere signs"*: John Stevens, *Words and Music in the Middle Ages: Song, Narrative, Dance and Drama, 1050–1350* (Cambridge University Press, 1986), p. 303.

28   *"the intentions and passions"*: Oliver Strunk and Leo Treitler, eds., *Source Readings in Music History*, rev. ed. (Norton, 1998), p. 387.

30   *"cheerful harmonies and fast rhythms"*: Gioseffo Zarlino, *On the Modes*, trans. Vered Cohen (Yale University Press, 1983), p. 95.

31   *"If [the subject] be lamentable"*: Thomas Morley, *A Plain and Easy Introduction to Practical Music* (Randall, 1771), p. 202.

32   *"Speaking without a mouth," "pleasing melancholy"*: Robert Burton, *The Anatomy of Melancholy*, vol. 2 (Dent, 1932), pp. 116, 118.

32   *"No doubt pleasant are the tears"*: Peter Holman, *Dowland, "Lachrimae" (1604)* (Cambridge University Press, 1999), p. 52.

32   *"musical sounds can evoke"*: Patel, *Music, Language, and the Brain*, p. 319.

32   *"The world has become sad"*: Oscar Wilde, "The Decay of Lying," in *Complete Works of Oscar Wilde* (Perennial Library, 1989), p. 983.

32   *arsenic poisoning*: Francesco Mari, Aldo Polettini, Donatella Lippi, and Elisabetta Bertol, "The Mysterious Death of Francesco I de' Medici and Bianca Cappello: An Arsenic Murder?" *BMJ* 333 (Dec. 23–30, 2006), pp. 1299–1301.

32   *"stun the beholder with their grandeur"*: Skip Sempé, "La Pellegrina," essay accompanying his recording of *La Pellegrina* with the Capriccio Stravagante Renaissance Orchestra and Collegium Vocale Gent (Paradizo 0004).

33   *"new manner of song"*: Strunk and Treitler, *Source Readings in Music History*, pp. 659–62.

34   *"great submerged iceberg"*: Richard Taruskin, *The Oxford History of Western Music*, vol. 1, *The Earliest Notations to the Sixteenth Century* (Oxford University Press, 2005), p. 619.

34   *"a narrative of the flow"*: Alexander Silbiger, "On Frescobaldi's Re-creation of the Chaconne and the Passacaglia," in *The Keyboard in Baroque Europe: Musical Performance and Reception*, ed. Christopher Hogwood (Cambridge University Press, 2003), p. 18.

34   *"Zephyr returns and blesses the air"*: Translation by Alan Curtis, in notes to his recording of Monteverdi's Complete Duets, vol. 1, with Il Complesso Barocco (Virgin Classics 45293).

35   *"emblem of lament"*: Ellen Rosand, "The Descending Tetrachord: An Emblem of Lament," *Musical Quarterly* 65:3 (July 1979), p. 349.

36   *"opera as we know it"*: Ellen Rosand, *Opera in Seventeenth-Century Venice: The Creation of a Genre* (University of California Press, 1991), p. 1.

38 *"a display designed by men"*: Susan McClary, *Feminine Endings: Music, Gender, and Sexuality* (University of Minnesota Press, 1991), p. 89. See also Suzanne G. Cusick, "Re-Voicing Arianna (and Laments): Two Women Respond," *Early Music* 27:3 (Aug. 1999), pp. 437–49.

38 *"a sense of the supernatural"*: Wendy Heller, *Emblems of Eloquence: Opera and Women's Voices in Seventeenth-Century Venice* (University of California Press, 2003), p. 101.

39 *Rose Pruiksma notes*: Rose A. Pruiksma, "Music, Sex, and Ethnicity: Signification in Lully's Theatrical Chaconnes," in *Gender, Sexuality, and Early Music*, ed. Todd M. Borgerding (Routledge, 2002), pp. 227–48.

39 *"One dreads the arms"*: Ibid., p. 233.

40 *"proceed with relentless power"*: Wilfrid Mellers, *François Couperin and the French Classical Tradition* (Dover, 1968), p. 202.

43 *"of such a nature"*: Hans T. David, Arthur Mendel, and Christoph Wolff, eds., *The New Bach Reader: A Life of Johann Sebastian Bach in Letters and Documents* (Norton, 1998), p. 105.

43 *"presence of grace"*: Ibid., p. 161.

44 *"the lone violinist"*: Susan McClary, *Reading Music: Selected Essays* (Ashgate, 2007), p. 334.

44 *"repeated strumming"*: Alexander Silbiger, "Bach and the Chaconne," *The Journal of Musicology* 17:3 (Summer 1999), p. 375.

44 *"Some of these ventures"*: Ibid., p. 384. See also Raymond Erickson, "Secret Codes, Dance, and Bach's Great 'Ciaccona,'" *Early Music America* 8:2 (2002), pp. 34–43.

45 *Martin Luther vilified*: See Martin Luther's "Sermon von der Betrachtung des heiligen Leidens Christi" of 1519. Eric Chafe, in *Tonal Allegory in the Vocal Music of J. S. Bach* (University of California Press, 1991), pp. 134–40, argues that "Weinen, Klagen" is modeled on that sermon.

46 *"Time's cycle had been straightened"*: Karol Berger, *Bach's Cycle, Mozart's Arrow: An Essay on the Origins of Musical Modernity* (University of California Press, 2007), p. 176.

46 *"Orpheus's lyre opened the gates"*: E.T.A. Hoffmann, "Review of Beethoven's Fifth Symphony," in *E. T. A. Hoffmann's Musical Writings: "Kreisleriana," "The Poet and the Composer," Music Criticism*, ed. David Charlton, trans. Martyn Clarke (Cambridge University Press, 1989), p. 236.

46 *"that has the following Crucifixus"*: Lewis Lockwood, *Beethoven: The Music and the Life* (Norton, 2003), p. 406.

48 *Alexander Poznansky has established*: See Alexander Poznansky, *Tchaikovsky's Last Days: A Documentary Study* (Clarendon, 1996).

48 *So argued Stefan Wolpe*: See Martin Zenck, "Reinterpreting Bach in the Nineteenth and Twentieth Centuries," in *The Cambridge Companion to Bach*, ed. John Butt (Cambridge University Press, 1997), pp. 240–50.

49 *"I was very much impressed"*: György Ligeti, remarks at Theory and Musicology Symposium, New England Conservatory, March 9, 1993.

49 *Richard Steinitz . . . defines*: Richard Steinitz, *György Ligeti: Music of the Imagination* (Northeastern University Press, 2003), p. 294. See also Steinitz, "Weeping and Wailing," *Musical Times* 137:1842 (Aug. 1996), pp. 17–22; and David Metzer, *Musical Modernism at the Turn of the Twenty-first Century* (Cambridge University Press, 2009), pp. 144–62.

50 *"fast, exuberant, passionate"*: Steinitz, *Ligeti*, p. 340.

50 *"the weirdest music I had ever heard"*: W. C. Handy, *Father of the Blues: An Autobiography* (Da Capo, 1991), p. 74.

51 *chants of the Ewe and Yoruba peoples*: Gilbert Rouget, "Un Chromatisme africain," *L'Homme* 1:3 (1961), pp. 32–46.

52 *as Peter Williams points out*: Peter Williams, *The Chromatic Fourth During Four Centuries of Music* (Clarendon, 1997), pp. 237–38.

53 *As Everett notes*: Walter Everett, "Pitch Down the Middle," in *Expression in Pop-Rock Music: Critical and Analytical Essays*, 2nd ed., ed. Walter Everett (Routledge, 2008), p. 150. See also Everett, *Foundations of Rock: From "Blue Suede Shoes" to "Suite: Judy Blue Eyes"* (Oxford University Press, 2009), pp. 275–76.

53 *"absolutely stone, raving mad"*: Will Shade, "Dazed and Confused: The Incredibly Strange Saga of Jake Holmes," *Perfect Sound Forever*, Sept. 2001, www.furious.com/perfect/jakeholmes.html (accessed Aug. 21, 2009). Holmes went on to apply his talents to advertising, writing or co-writing such well-known commercial jingles as "Be All That You Can Be," "Be a Pepper," and "Raise Your Hand If You're Sure."

3. INFERNAL MACHINES

This chapter incorporates portions of two *New Yorker* articles: "The Record Effect," June 6, 2005, and "The Well-Tempered Web," October 22, 2007. In addition to the works cited below, I consulted Michael Chanan, *Musica Practica: The Social Practice of Western Music from Gregorian Chant to Postmodernism* (Verso, 1994); Timothy Day, *A Century of Recorded Music: Listening to Musical History* (Yale University Press, 2000); Evan Eisenberg, *The Recording Angel: Music, Records, and Culture from Aristotle to Zappa*, 2nd ed. (Yale University Press, 2005); Simon Frith, *Performing Rites: On the Value of Popular Music* (Harvard University Press, 1996); Roland Gelatt, *The Fabulous Phonograph: From Edison to Stereo* (Appleton-Century, 1965); David Suisman, *Selling Sounds: The Commercial Revolution in American Music* (Harvard University Press, 2009); and Emily Thompson, *The Soundscape of Modernity: Architectural Acoustics and the Culture of Listening in America, 1900–1933* (MIT Press, 2002).

55 *"These talking machines"*: "Statement of John Philip Sousa," *Arguments Before the Committee on Patents of the House of Representatives on H.R. 19853, to Amend and Consolidate the Acts Respecting Copyright* (Government Printing Office, 1906), p. 24.

55 *"The time is coming"*: Emily Thompson, "Machines, Music, and the Quest for Fidelity: Marketing the Edison Phonograph in America, 1877–1925," *Musical Quarterly* 79:1 (Spring 1995), p. 139.

55 *"The nightingale's song"*: John Philip Sousa, "The Menace of Mechanical Music," *Appleton's Magazine* 8 (Sept. 1906), p. 279.

56 *Glenn Gould . . . predicted*: Glenn Gould, "The Prospects of Recording," in *The Glenn Gould Reader*, ed. Tim Page (Vintage, 1990), p. 331.

57 *"annihilate time and space"*: Thomas A. Edison, "The Phonograph and Its Future," *The North American Review* 262 (May–June 1878), p. 536.

57 *"A friend may in a morning-call"*: Ibid., p. 533.

57 *"piano-finished"*: William Howland Kenney, *Recorded Music in American Life: The Phonograph and Popular Memory, 1890–1945* (Oxford University Press, 1999), p. 51.

58 *"The difference between what we usually hear"*: Greg Milner, *Perfecting Sound Forever: An Aural History of Recorded Music* (Faber and Faber, 2009), p. 67.

58 *"The orchestra's tone is so lifelike"*: Howard Taubman, "Records: Kubelik Leads Modern Selections on Mercury Label," *The New York Times*, Nov. 25, 1951.

58 *"audience distraction"*: Colin Symes, *Setting the Record Straight: A Material History of Classical Recording* (Wesleyan University Press, 2004), p. 74.

58 *"I wonder if pure tone"*: Milner, *Perfecting Sound Forever*, p. 54.

59 *Jack Mullin*: Ibid., p. 114.

59 *Clinton Heylin points out*: Clinton Heylin, *Bob Dylan: The Recording Sessions, 1960–1994* (St. Martin's, 1995), p. xi.

60 *"Listening to a CD"*: Milner, *Perfecting Sound Forever*, p. 195.

60 *As Jeff Chang recounts*: Jeff Chang, *Can't Stop Won't Stop: A History of the Hip-Hop Generation* (St. Martin's, 2005), pp. 7–85.

61 *Benjamin's discussion of the loss*: Walter Benjamin, "The Work of Art in the Age of Its Technological Reproducibility," second and third versions, in *Walter Benjamin: Selected Writings, Volume 3, 1935–1938*, ed. Howard Eiland and Michael W. Jennings, trans. Edmund Jephcott, Howard Eiland, and others (Harvard University Press, 2002), p. 119; and *Walter Benjamin: Selected Writings, Volume 4, 1938–1940*, ed. Howard Eiland and Michael W. Jennings, trans. Edmund Jephcott and others (Harvard University Press, 2003), p. 268.

62 *"a more effective unity"*: Gould, *The Glenn Gould Reader*, pp. 334–35.

62 *"phonograph effects"*: Mark Katz, *Capturing Sound: How Technology Has Changed Music* (University of California Press, 2004), pp. 3–7, 146.

62 *Katz proposes*: Ibid., pp. 85–98. For more on the vibrato issue, see Styra Avins, "Performing Brahms's Music: Clues from His Letters," and Clive Brown, "Joachim's Violin Playing and the Performance of Brahms's String Music," in *Performing Brahms: Early Evidence of Performance Style*, ed. Michael Musgrave and Bernard D. Sherman (Cambridge University Press, 2003), pp. 11–47, 48–98.

63 *"Musicians who first heard"*: Robert Philip, *Performing Music in the Age of Recording* (Yale University Press, 2004), p. 25.

63 *"Freedom from disaster"*: Ibid., p. 17.

63 *"sways either side of the beat"*: Ibid., p. 110.

64 *"death-of-tradition"*: Will Crutchfield, "What Is Tradition?" in *Fashions and Legacies in Nineteenth-Century Italian Opera*, ed. Roberta Montemorra Marvin and Hilary Poriss (Cambridge University Press, 2010), p. 248.

67 *"The machine is neither"*: Katz, *Capturing Sound*, pp. vii, 190.

67 *"Members of the musical public"*: David Hajdu, *Heroes and Villains: Essays on Music, Movies, Comics, and Culture* (Da Capo, 2009), p. 166.

67 *"In music, as in everything"*: Benjamin Boretz, "Interface Part II: Thoughts in Reply to Boulez/Foucault: 'Contemporary Music and the Public,'" in *Perspectives on Musical Aesthetics*, ed. John Rahn (Norton, 1994), p. 123.

68 *"We could not know"*: Hans Fantel, "Sound: Poignance Measured in Digits," *The New York Times*, July 16, 1989.

4. THE STORM OF STYLE

This essay appeared in *The New Yorker* on July 24, 2006.

71 *"As touchy as gunpowder"*: Michael Kelly, *Reminiscences of Michael Kelly, of the King's Theatre, and Theatre Royal Drury Lane, Including a Period of Nearly Half a Century;*

With Original Anecdotes of Many Distinguished Persons, Political, Literary, and Musical, vol. 1 (Henry Colburn, 1826), p. 257.

71 *"so rare a genius"*: Derek Beales, "Joseph II, Joseph(in)ism," in *The Cambridge Mozart Encyclopedia*, ed. Cliff Eisen and Simon P. Keefe (Cambridge University Press, 2006), p. 239.

72 *"the Viennese gentry"*: Emily Anderson, trans. and ed., *The Letters of Mozart and His Family*, 3rd ed. (Norton, 1985), p. 814.

72 *"the most extraordinary Prodigy"*: Stanley Sadie, *Mozart: The Early Years, 1756–1781* (Oxford University Press, 2006), p. 62.

72 *"the miracle whom God allowed"*: Ibid., p. 140.

72 *"Such people only come into the world"*: Anderson, *The Letters of Mozart and His Family*, p. 814.

72 *"as proud as a peacock," "dreadfully conceited"*: Ibid., p. 739.

72 *"I think that something is going on"*: Ibid., p. 532.

72 *John Rice's biography*: John A. Rice, *Antonio Salieri and Viennese Opera* (University of Chicago Press, 1998).

72 *"Salieri, that very gifted Kapellmeister"*: Anderson, *The Letters of Mozart and His Family*, pp. 938–39.

72 *"black thoughts"*: Ibid., p. 917. For sensations of coldness and emptiness, see pp. 943, 963–64.

72 *"true goal of our existence"*: Ibid., p. 907.

73 *"Two opposing elements"*: Ibid., p. 816.

73 *"Other great composers have expressed"*: Nicholas Kenyon, *The Pegasus Pocket Guide to Mozart* (Pegasus, 2006), p. 283.

73 *"sound of the loss of innocence"*: Scott Burnham, "On the Beautiful in Mozart," in *Music and the Aesthetics of Modernity: Essays*, ed. Karol Berger and Anthony Newcomb (Harvard University Press, 2005), p. 49.

74 *"Mozart as a Working Stiff"*: Neal Zaslaw, "Mozart as a Working Stiff," in *On Mozart*, ed. James M. Morris (Cambridge University Press, 1994), pp. 102–12.

74 *"erotically tinged drive"*: Maynard Solomon, *Mozart: A Life* (HarperCollins, 1995), p. 11.

74 *"Your whole intent"*: Robert Spaethling, trans. and ed., *Mozart's Letters, Mozart's Life: Selected Letters* (Norton, 2000), p. 192.

74 *Ruth Halliwell*: Ruth Halliwell, *The Mozart Family: Four Lives in Social Context* (Clarendon, 1998).

74 *"Where money is plentiful"*: Anderson, *The Letters of Mozart and His Family*, p. 545.

74 *"The best way to make"*: Ibid., p. 676.

75 *"love, joy, physical and spiritual contentment"*: David Cairns, *Mozart and His Operas* (University of California Press, 2006), p. 68.

75 *"moving, terrifying, and altogether unusual"*: Anderson, *The Letters of Mozart and His Family*, pp. 666, 700.

75 *"These concertos are a happy medium"*: Ibid., p. 833.

76 *"departure points"*: Ulrich Konrad, "Compositional Method," in Eisen and Keefe, *The Cambridge Mozart Encyclopedia*, p. 107.

77 *"evolved along sound lines"*: Hermann Abert, *W. A. Mozart*, ed. Cliff Eisen, trans. Stewart Spencer (Yale University Press, 2007), p. 45.

78 *"There is no real reason"*: Sadie, *Mozart*, p. 479.

79 *Scott Burnham notes*: Burnham, "On the Beautiful in Mozart," p. 44.

79   *"you see the trembling"*: Anderson, *The Letters of Mozart and His Family*, p. 769.

80   *"four completely different kinds"*: Charles Rosen, *The Classical Style: Haydn, Mozart, Beethoven*, rev. ed. (Norton, 1998), p. 286.

80   *"feelings of impending doom"*: Julian Rushton, *Mozart* (Oxford University Press, 2006), p. 220.

81   *"sensuous genius"*: Daniel Herwitz, "Kierkegaard Writes His Opera," in *The Don Giovanni Moment: Essays on the Legacy of an Opera*, ed. Lydia Goehr and Daniel Herwitz (Columbia University Press, 2006), p. 134.

82   *"a bon vivant who loves wine"*: E.T.A. Hoffmann, "Don Juan: A Fabulous Happening Which Befell a Traveling Enthusiast," trans. Julian Rushton, in Rushton, *W. A. Mozart, "Don Giovanni"* (Cambridge University Press, 1981), p. 128.

82   *"conflict between godly"*: Ibid., p. 128.

82   as Michael Noiray observes: Michael Noiray, "Don Giovanni," in Eisen and Keefe, *The Cambridge Mozart Encyclopedia*, pp. 145–47.

82   *"fate being underlined"*: Peter Williams, *The Chromatic Fourth During Four Centuries of Music* (Clarendon, 1997), p. 141.

83   *"change from ignorance to knowledge"*: Jessica Waldoff, *Recognition in Mozart's Operas* (Oxford University Press, 2006), p. 55.

83   *"unflinching, unreflecting"*: Ibid., p. 178.

83   *"life without awe"*: Philip Kitcher and Richard Schacht, "Authority and Judgment in Mozart's *Don Giovanni* and Wagner's *Ring*," in Goehr and Herwitz, *The Don Giovanni Moment*, p. 179.

5. ORBITING

This profile appeared in *The New Yorker* on August 20, 2001, under the title "The Searchers." In the course of researching the article, I attended the following Radiohead shows: Vista Alegre, Bilbao, May 26, 2001; Théâtre antique, Vaison-la-Romaine, May 28; Arena di Verona, May 30; Red Rocks, Denver, June 20; The Gorge, George, Washington, June 23; and South Park, Oxford, July 7. I consulted Mac Randall, *Exit Music: The Radiohead Story* (Delta, 2000) and Jonathan Hale, *Radiohead: From a Great Height* (ECW Press, 1999).

6. THE ANTI-MAESTRO

The original version of this profile appeared in *The New Yorker* on April 30, 2007.

105   *"culture of performance"*: Joseph Horowitz, *Classical Music in America: A History of Its Rise and Fall* (Norton, 2005), pp. 383–88.

106   *"The gravitational center"*: Alex Ross, "A Parade of the Maverick Modernists, Joined by the Dead," *The New York Times*, June 19, 1996.

107   *"We don't want a temple"*: Bernard Holland, "Los Angeles Plans New Concert Hall," *The New York Times*, June 1, 1988.

112   *"Somehow I've ruled out"*: Mark Swed, "Conductor in a Candy Store," *Los Angeles Times*, Oct. 20, 1996.

7. GREAT SOUL

The original version of this chapter appeared in *The New Yorker* on February 3, 1997. In addition to the works cited below, I consulted Peter Clive, *Schubert and His World: A*

Biographical Dictionary (Clarendon, 1997); Walter Frisch, ed., *Schubert: Critical and Analytical Studies* (University of Nebraska Press, 1986); Christopher Gibbs, ed., *The Cambridge Companion to Schubert* (Cambridge University Press, 1997); David Gramit, "The Intellectual and Aesthetic Tenets of Franz Schubert's Circle" (PhD diss., Duke University, 1987); Ernst Hilmar, *Franz Schubert in His Time*, trans. Reinhard G. Pauly (Amadeus, 1988); and Richard Kramer, *Distant Cycles: Schubert and the Conceiving of Song* (University of Chicago Press, 1994). More recent publications of interest include Charles Fisk, *Returning Cycles: Contexts for the Interpretation of Schubert's Impromptus and Last Sonatas* (University of California Press, 2001); Christopher Gibbs, *The Life of Schubert* (Cambridge University Press, 2000); Lawrence Kramer, *Franz Schubert: Sexuality, Subjectivity, Song* (Cambridge University Press, 1998); Scott Messing, *Schubert in the European Imagination*, 2 vols. (University of Rochester Press, 2006–2007); and Susan Youens, *Schubert's Late Lieder: Beyond the Song-Cycles* (Cambridge University Press, 2002).

124 *"You consider yourselves artists?"*: Friedrich Dieckmann, *Franz Schubert: Eine Annäherung* (Insel, 1996), p. 286.

125 *"I am Schubert"*: Franz Grillparzer, *Sämmtliche Werke*, vol. 1 (Cotta, 1887), p. 175.

125 *"Their world-system is human"*: Otto Erich Deutsch, ed., *Schubert: Die Dokumente seines Lebens* (Breitkopf & Härtel, 1996), p. 110.

125 *"pure, powerful being"*: Ibid., p. 193.

125 *"Enviable Nero"*: Ibid., p. 233.

125 *"guileless child"*: Robert Schumann, *Schumann on Music: A Selection from the Writings*, trans. and ed. Henry Pleasants (Dover, 1988), p. 142.

128 *Newbould has discovered*: Brian Newbould, *Schubert: The Music and the Man* (Gollancz, 1997), p. 13.

128 *"inner, unfathomable turmoil"*: Johann Wolfgang von Goethe, *The Sorrows of Young Werther and Selected Writings*, trans. Catherine Hutter (Signet, 1962), p. 107.

129 *John Reed suggests*: John Reed, *Schubert* (Schirmer, 1997), p. 143.

129 *"Beethoven does not lie here"*: Newbould, *Schubert*, p. 277.

129 *"disorder of experience"*: Charles Rosen, *The Romantic Generation* (Harvard University Press, 1995), p. 95.

131 *as Youens observes*: Susan Youens, *Schubert's Poets and the Making of Lieder* (Cambridge University Press, 1996), p. 189.

131 *"loving pair"*: Graham Johnson, "Schubert and the Classics," notes to vol. 14 of the Hyperion Schubert Edition (Hyperion CDJ33014), p. 28.

132 *"Schubert [is] half-sick"*: Maynard Solomon, "Franz Schubert and the Peacocks of Benvenuto Cellini," *19th-Century Music* 12:3 (Spring 1989), p. 201. For more on Schubert's sexuality, see Rita Steblin, "The Peacock's Tale: Schubert's Sexuality Reconsidered," *19th-Century Music* 17:1 (Summer 1993), pp. 5–33; Maynard Solomon, "Schubert: Some Consequences of Nostalgia," *19th-Century Music* 17:1 (Summer 1993), pp. 34–46; Kristina Muxfeldt, "Political Crimes and Liberty, or Why Would Schubert Eat a Peacock?" *19th-Century Music* 17:1 (Summer 1993), pp. 47–64; and contributions by Kogi Agawu, Susan McClary, James Webster, and Robert Winter in the same issue of *19th-Century Music*.

132 *"dominating aversion," "indifferent to the charms"*: Solomon, "Franz Schubert and the Peacocks of Benvenuto Cellini," p. 196.

133 *"fashionable political ideologies"*: Rita Steblin, letter to the editors, *The New York Review of Books*, Oct. 20, 1994.

133 *"open, flexible sense of self"*: Susan McClary, "Constructions of Subjectivity in Schubert's Music," in *Queering the Pitch: The New Gay and Lesbian Musicology*, ed. Philip Brett, Elizabeth Wood, and Gary C. Thomas (Routledge, 1994), p. 223.

133 *"If Schubert fell"*: Elizabeth Norman McKay, *Franz Schubert: A Biography* (Clarendon, 1996), p. 219.

133 *"Schubert is much praised"*: Karl-Heinz Köhler and Dagmar Beck, eds., *Ludwig van Beethovens Konversationshefte*, vol. 3 (VEB, 1983), p. 330.

133 *"Kill it, kill me"*: Deutsch, *Schubert: Dokumente*, p. 193.

134 *"history of my feelings"*: August von Platen, *Die Tagebücher des Grafen August von Platen*, ed. Georg von Laubmann and Ludwig von Scheffler (Cotta, 1896), p. 487.

135 *"It's sigh, it's nostalgia"*: György Ligeti, coaching the Borromeo String Quartet in Schubert's Quartet No. 15, New England Conservatory, March 10, 1993.

8. EMOTIONAL LANDSCAPES

This profile appeared in *The New Yorker* on August 23, 2004, under the title "Björk's Saga." I interviewed Björk in Reykjavík in January 2004; in Salvador, Brazil, in February; in London in April; and in New York that summer.

140 *"an earth sprite"*: Teresa Stratas, "Stratas, Lenya, and the Two Annas," notes to Lotte Lenya's recording of *The Seven Deadly Sins* (Sony Classical MHK 63222).

144 *"the tyranny of mankind"*: Halldór Laxness, *Independent People: An Epic*, trans. J. A. Thompson (Vintage, 1997), p. 211.

145 *"degenerate"*: Árni Heimir Ingólfsson, "'This Music Belongs to Us': Scandinavian Music and 'Nordic' Ideology in the Third Reich," paper delivered at the American Musicological Society New England Chapter meeting, March 23, 2002.

147 *"obsessed with the marriage"*: "Björk Meets Karlheinz Stockhausen: Compose Yourself," *Dazed & Confused* 23 (Aug. 1996).

147 *"all this retro"*: Ibid.

148 *"Bad Taste will use"*: Mark Pytlik, *Björk: Wow and Flutter* (ECW, 2003), p. 27.

153 *"Invisible and free!"*: Mikhail Bulgakov, *The Master and Margarita*, trans. Richard Pevear and Larissa Volokhonsky (Penguin, 1997), p. 235.

153 *"The album represented"*: Conversation between Björk and Ásmundur Jónsson, notes to *Live Box* (One Little Indian 355).

153 *"cyborg/nature dichotomy"*: Greg Hainge, Call for Papers, www.h-net.org/announce/show.cgi?ID=129595 (accessed Dec. 7, 2009).

9. SYMPHONY OF MILLIONS

This article appeared in *The New Yorker* on July 7, 2008. I visited Beijing in March 2008. My principal source for the history of classical music in China was Sheila Melvin and Jindong Cai, *Rhapsody in Red: How Western Classical Music Became Chinese* (Algora, 2004). I also consulted Yayoi Uno Everett and Frederick Lau, eds., *Locating East Asia in Western Art Music* (Wesleyan University Press, 2004); Hao Jiang Tian with Lois B. Morris, *Along the Roaring River: My Wild Ride from Mao to the Met* (Wiley, 2008); and Mari Yoshihara, *Musicians from a Different Shore: Asians and Asian Americans in Classical Music* (Temple University Press, 2007).

160 *"Facing dwindling popularity"*: "U.S. Conductor: China's Large Population Can Help Keep Classical Music Alive," Associated Press, Feb. 23, 2008.

161 *"concrete example"*: Joseph Kahn, "Chinese Unveil Mammoth Arts Center," *The New York Times*, Dec. 24, 2007.

164 *"By 1992, the Party"*: Richard Kraus, *The Party and the Arty in China: The New Politics of Culture* (Rowman & Littlefield, 2004), p. 171.

166 *"apply appropriate foreign principles"*: Melvin and Cai, *Rhapsody in Red*, p. 207.

166 *peculiar stylistic boundaries*: Ibid., pp. 252–54.

166 *When Henry Kissinger first visited*: Ibid., pp. 265–70.

10. SONG OF THE EARTH

This profile appeared in *The New Yorker* on May 12, 2008. I interviewed John Luther Adams in Alaska the previous month. The composer has published two collections of writings: *Winter Music: Composing the North* (Wesleyan University Press, 2004); and *The Place Where You Go to Listen: In Search of an Ecology of Music* (Wesleyan University Press, 2009). The quotation "Much of Alaska is still filled with silence" comes from p. 9 of *Winter Music*. John Haines's poem "Listening in October" can be found in his collection *The Owl in the Mask of the Dreamer: Collected Poems* (Graywolf Press, 1996); "Return to Richardson, Spring 1981" appears in Haines's *Of Your Passage, O Summer: Uncollected Poems from the 1960s* (Limberlost Press, 2004). Also worth reading are Haines's memoir *The Stars, the Snows, the Fire: Twenty-five Years in the Alaskan Wilderness* (Graywolf Press, 2000) and Barry Lopez's *Arctic Dreams: Imagination and Desire in an Arctic Landscape* (Scribner, 1986).

11. VERDI'S GRIP

This chapter is an expanded version of an article that appeared in *The New Yorker* on September 24, 2001.

189 *"Nobody comes to Verdi"*: Mark Lamos, quoted in Matthew Gurewitsch, "Poking Holes in Verdi to Let Audiences In," *The New York Times*, March 4, 2001.

190 *"What if it is entirely your fault"*: E.T.A. Hoffmann, "Beethoven's Instrumental Music," in *E. T. A. Hoffmann's Musical Writings: "Kreisleriana," "The Poet and the Composer," Music Criticism*, ed. David Charlton, trans. Martyn Clarke (Cambridge University Press, 1989), p. 98.

190 *"The box office is the proper"*: John Rosselli, *The Life of Verdi* (Cambridge University Press, 2000), p. 2.

190 *"You have to be wall-eyed"*: Giuseppe Verdi and Arrigo Boito, *The Verdi-Boito Correspondence*, ed. Marcello Conati and Mario Medici, trans. William Weaver (University of Chicago Press, 1994), p. xxi.

190 *"in your work you think"*: Robert Spaethling, trans. and ed., *Mozart's Letters, Mozart's Life: Selected Letters* (Norton, 2000), p. 221.

191 *As Mary Jane Phillips-Matz recounts*: Mary Jane Phillips-Matz, *Verdi: A Biography* (Oxford University Press, 1993), pp. 54–73.

191 *"The dominant mood"*: Rosselli, *The Life of Verdi*, p. 41.

192 *he was, in fact, criticized*: Roger Parker, *Leonora's Last Act: Essays in Verdian Discourse* (Princeton University Press, 1997), pp. 35–36.

193 *"that cheap, low, sentimental melodrama"*: Leonard Bernstein, *The Unanswered Question: Six Talks at Harvard* (Harvard University Press, 1976), pp. 411–17.

194 *"A fine civilization we have"*: Marcello Conati, ed., *Encounters with Verdi*, trans. Richard Stokes (Cornell University Press, 1986), p. 351.

195 *"USE FEW WORDS"*: Phillips-Matz, *Verdi*, p. 195.

195 *vocal babbling*: Julian Budden, *The Operas of Verdi*, vol. 2, *From "Il trovatore" to "La forza del destino,"* rev. ed. (Clarendon, 1992), p. 147.

195 *"Tadolini is a fine figure"*: Rosselli, *The Life of Verdi*, p. 51.

197 *"a dark-haired, impeccably gowned"*: Peter G. Davis, "Brangelina Sings!" *New York*, March 6, 2006, p. 70.

198 *"If I have to think" and other quotations*: Gurewitsch, "Poking Holes in Verdi to Let Audiences In."

199 *A 2008 staging in Erfurt*: Harry de Quetteville, "German Staging of Verdi's A Masked Ball on 9/11 with Naked Cast in Mickey Mouse Masks," *The Daily Telegraph*, April 11, 2008.

200 *as the staging manual explains*: David Rosen, "On Staging That Matters," in *Verdi in Performance*, ed. Alison Latham and Roger Parker (Oxford University Press, 2001), pp. 30–31.

200 *Philip Gossett . . . notes*: Philip Gossett, *Divas and Scholars: Performing Italian Opera* (University of Chicago Press, 2006), pp. 477–79.

200 *"Copying the truth"*: Rosselli, *The Life of Verdi*, p. 6.

200 *Gossett further points out*: Gossett, *Divas and Scholars*, pp. 473–74.

202 *"one needs to be totally pragmatic"*: Andrew Porter, "In Praise of the Pragmatic," in Latham and Parker, *Verdi in Performance*, p. 26.

203 *the scholar Roger Parker has found*: Roger Parker, *"Arpa d'or dei fatidici vati": The Verdian Patriotic Chorus in the 1840s* (Istituto Nazionale di Studi Verdiani, 1997), esp. pp. 83–84.

203 *"inappropriate reaction"*: Philip Gossett, "Becoming a Citizen: The Chorus in Risorgimento Opera," *Cambridge Opera Journal* 2:1 (1990), p. 55. See also Gossett, "'Edizioni distrutte' and the Significance of Operatic Choruses During the Risorgimento," in *Opera and Society in Italy and France from Monteverdi to Bourdieu*, ed. Victoria Johnson, Jane F. Fulcher, and Thomas Ertman (Cambridge University Press, 2007), pp. 181–242.

203 *The greatness of Verdi is a simple thing*: The final paragraph of this article was written on Sept. 12, 2001. When I wrote of "the spiritual magnificence of a dying man," I had in mind Father Mychal Judge, the chaplain of the New York City Fire Department, who died during the destruction of the World Trade Center the previous day. I once heard him speak, and I think of him often.

12. ALMOST FAMOUS

This article appeared in *The New Yorker* on May 21, 2001. More information about the St. Lawrence Quartet can be found at its website, www.slsq.com.

13. EDGES OF POP

This chapter incorporates four *New Yorker* articles: "Grand Illusions," May 19, 2003; "The Art of Noise," July 13, 1998; "Eighty-two Very Good Years," May 25, 1998; and "Generation Exit," April 25, 1994.

221 *"Vicenzo, how's your little girl?"*: Gay Talese, "Frank Sinatra Has a Cold," in *The Frank Sinatra Reader*, ed. Steven Petkov and Leonard Mustazza (Oxford University Press, 1995), p. 128.

223 *As Michael Azerrad points out*: Michael Azerrad, *Come As You Are: The Story of Nirvana* (Doubleday, 1993), p. 228.

224 *"jock numbskulls"*: Ibid., pp. 199–200.

224 *"I wanted to fool people"*: Ibid., p. 215.

225 *"Rock Death in the 1970s"*: Greil Marcus, *In the Fascist Bathroom: Punk in Pop Music, 1977–1992* (Harvard University Press, 1999), pp. 57–78.

225 *"No detestation nor dehortation"*: John Donne, *Biathanatos*, ed. Michael Rudick and M. Pabst Battin (Garland, 1982), p. 46.

14. LEARNING THE SCORE
This article appeared in *The New Yorker* on September 4, 2006.

229 *In California, between 1999 and 2004*: Music for All Foundation, 2004, *The Sound of Silence: The Unprecedented Decline of Music Education in California Public Schools: A Statistical Review*, available at www.musicforall.org/resources/advocacy/sos.aspx (accessed Dec. 17, 2009), p. 12.

229 *In 1993, researchers claimed*: Frances H. Rauscher, Gordon L. Shaw, and Katherine N. Ky, "Music and Spatial Task Performance," *Nature* 365 (Oct. 14, 1993), p. 611. For challenges to the original study, see Christopher Chabris and Kenneth Steele et al., "Prelude or Requiem for the Mozart Effect," *Nature* 400 (Aug. 26, 1999), pp. 826–27.

230 *"represented single"*: Music for All, *The Sound of Silence*, p. 18.

230 *"In the true spirit"*: Richard Deasy and Mike Huckabee, "Putting the Arts Front and Center on the Education Agenda," www.ecs.org/html/projectsPartners/chair2005/ArtsPubs.asp (accessed Jan. 16, 2010).

236 *"remote pedestal"*: John Dewey, *Art as Experience* (Penguin, 2005), p. 4.

236 *"When an art product"*: Ibid., p. 1.

236 *"In my own experience"*: Paul Woodford, *Democracy and Music Education: Liberalism, Ethics, and the Politics of Practice* (Indiana University Press, 2005), p. 74.

236 *"To tap into imagination"*: Maxine Greene, *Releasing the Imagination: Essays on Education, the Arts, and Social Change* (Jossey-Bass, 2000), p. 19.

15. VOICE OF THE CENTURY
The original version of this chapter appeared in *The New Yorker* on April 13, 2009.

239 *"In this great auditorium"*: Allan Keiler, *Marian Anderson: A Singer's Journey* (University of Illinois Press, 2002), p. 212.

239 *once every hundred years*: Ibid., p. 156.

239 *"My roof is too low"*: Marian Anderson, *My Lord, What a Morning: An Autobiography* (University of Illinois Press, 2002), p. 149.

240 *"She sang as never before"*: Martin Luther King, Jr., *The Papers of Martin Luther King, Jr.*, vol. 1, *Called to Serve, January 1929–June 1951*, ed. Clayborne Carson, Ralph E. Luker, and Penny A. Russell (University of California Press, 1992), p. 110.

240 *"Genius, like justice"*: Keiler, *Marian Anderson*, p. 212.

240 *"a nation that, for a few measures"*: Richard Powers, *The Time of Our Singing* (Picador, 2004), p. 48.

241 *"We don't take colored"*: Anderson, *My Lord, What a Morning*, p. 38.

241 *"a voice of unusual compass"*: "Miss Anderson Sings," *The New York Times*, Aug. 27, 1925.

241 *"mistress of all she surveyed"*: Howard Taubman, "Marian Anderson in Concert Here," *The New York Times*, Dec. 31, 1935.

242 *"spirit of pragmatism"*: Raymond Arsenault, *The Sound of Freedom: Marian Anderson, the Lincoln Memorial, and the Concert That Awakened America* (Bloomsbury, 2009), pp. 105–106.

242 *"I always bear in mind"*: Anderson, *My Lord, What a Morning*, p. 244.

242 train-station waiting room: Franz Rupp related this story in the documentary *Marian Anderson*, produced by WETA-TV and aired in May 1991.

243 *"My music was dedicated"*: Nina Simone with Stephen Cleary, *I Put a Spell on You: The Autobiography of Nina Simone* (Da Capo, 2003), p. 91.

243 *"No white symphony orchestra"*: Miles Davis with Quincy Troupe, *Miles: The Autobiography* (Simon and Schuster, 2005), p. 59. For "ghetto mentality," see p. 61.

244 *"Bach made me dedicate"*: Simone, *I Put a Spell on You*, p. 23.

244 *"looked on with intense suspicion"*: William Eddins, "Soul Food for Thought," Sticks and Drones, www.insidethearts.com/sticksanddrones/2009/01/16/bill-eddins/1091 (accessed Dec. 10, 2009).

16. THE MUSIC MOUNTAIN

This article appeared in *The New Yorker* on July 29, 2009. I visited Marlboro Music on three occasions during the summer of 2008. I interviewed, among others, Emanuel Ax, Jonathan Biss, Anthony Checchia, Sasha Cooke, Charlotte Dobbs, Richard Goode, Romie de Guise-Langlois, Soovin Kim, Yo-Yo Ma, Philipp Naegele, Nicholas Phan, Rebecca Ringle, Frank Salomon, James Austin Smith, Joshua Smith, the late David Soyer, Arnold Steinhardt, and Mitsuko Uchida.

246 *"create a community, almost utopian"*: Rudolf Serkin interviewed on the *Bell Telephone Hour*, 1967, as quoted in notes to the Music from Marlboro recording of Schubert's "Trout" Quintet (Columbia MS 7067, LP).

251 *"It's all wrong"*: Stephen Lehmann and Marion Faber, *Rudolf Serkin: A Life* (Oxford University Press, 2003), p. 17.

252 *"covering everything and just getting the notes"*: Karen Campbell, "Republic of Equals," *Symphony*, May–June 2000, p. 18.

17. THE END OF SILENCE

This chapter appeared in *The New Yorker* on October 4, 2010.

265 *"There's no such thing"*: Richard Kostelanetz, *Conversing with Cage*, 2nd ed. (Routledge, 2003), p. 65.

265 *"Good people of Woodstock"*: David Revill, *The Roaring Silence—John Cage: A Life* (Arcade, 1992), p. 166.

265 *"Now, Earle"*: Kyle Gann, *No Such Thing as Silence: John Cage's 4'33"* (Yale University Press, 2010), p. 191.

266 *"an act of framing"*: Ibid., p. 11.

266 *"let sounds be just sounds"*: John Cage, *Silence: Lectures and Writings by John Cage* (Wesleyan University Press, 1973), p. 70.

266 *"It begged for a new approach"*: Gann, *No Such Thing as Silence*, p. 11.

266 *"Art is a sort of experimental station"*: Cage, *Silence*, p. 139.

266 *"absolutely ridiculous"*: Gann, *No Such Thing as Silence*, p. 15.

267 *"John Cage was the first composer"*: *Morton Feldman Says: Selected Interviews and Lectures, 1964–1987*, ed. Chris Villars (Hyphen, 2006), p. 183.

267 *"John, I dearly love you"*: Cage, *Silence*, p. ix.

267 *"Noted for: being radical"*: Thomas S. Hines, "'Then Not Yet "Cage"'": The Los Angeles Years, 1912–1938," in *John Cage: Composed in America*, ed. Marjorie Perloff and Charles Junkerman (University of Chicago Press, 1994), p. 78.

268 *"Much of our of boredom"*: John Cage, *I–VI* (Wesleyan University Press, 1997), p. 9.

268 *"not much different from not being"*: Kostelanetz, *Conversing with Cage*, p. 280.

268 *"He was open, frank"*: Carolyn Brown, *Chance and Circumstance: Twenty Years with Cage and Cunningham* (Random House, 2007), p. 81.

268 *"Don't you ever parrot"*: Ibid., p. 104.

268 *"cheerful existentialist"*: *John Cage: An Anthology*, ed. Richard Kostelanetz (Da Capo, 1991), p. 146.

269 *"One of the greatest blessings"*: Ibid., p. 48.

269 *"People would lie in wait"*: Hines, "'Then Not Yet "Cage,"'" p. 74.

269 *Cage seems to have been the only American pupil*: "String Quartet Plays at Composer's Party," *Los Angeles Times*, Jan. 6, 1937.

270 *"I believe that the use of noise"*: Cage, *Silence*, pp. 3–4.

270 *"I decided to use only quiet sounds"*: Ibid., p. 117.

270 *"to sober and quiet the mind"*: James Pritchett, *The Music of John Cage* (Cambridge University Press, 1993), p. 37.

270 *"art imitates nature"*: Gann, *No Such Thing as Silence*, p. 93.

270 *"haunting and lovely"*: Ross Parmenter, "Ajemian Plays Work by Cage, 69 Minutes," *The New York Times*, Jan. 13, 1949.

271 *"Well, they're just playing my piece"*: John Cage and Morton Feldman, *Radio Happenings I–V*, recorded at WBAI, New York City, July 1966–January 1967, available at www.archive.org/details/CageFeldmanConversation1 (accessed Dec. 9, 2010).

271 *Silverman…rightly emphasizes*: Kenneth Silverman, *Begin Again: A Biography of John Cage* (Knopf, 2010), pp. 267–74.

272 *"improperly"*: Brown, *Chance and Circumstance*, p. 266.

272 *"It is because of his specifications"*: Lydia Goehr, *The Imaginary Museum of Musical Works: An Essay in the Philosophy of Music* (Oxford University Press, 1992), p. 264.

272 *"to its purest, scariest peak"*: Richard Taruskin, *The Danger of Music and Other Anti-Utopian Essays* (University of California Press, 2009), p. 272.

272 *"Listening to or merely thinking"*: Gann, *No Such Thing as Silence*, p. 198.

272 *John Adams…describes*: John Adams, *Hallelujah Junction: Composing an American Life* (Farrar, Straus and Giroux, 2008), pp. 56–61.

273 *"You mean he got paid for that?"*: Gann, *No Such Thing as Silence*, p. 12.

273 *$24.15 a month in rent*: Ibid., p. 14.

273 *"I wanted to make poverty elegant"*: Kostelanetz, *Conversing with Cage*, p. 212.

274 *"the twenty-four kinds"*: Silverman, *Begin Again*, p. 168.

274 *"I consider laughter preferable to tears"*: The video can be viewed at www.youtube.com/watch?v=SSulycqZH-U (accessed Dec. 9, 2010).

274 *"[A] monk was walking along"*: John Cage, *A Year from Monday* (Wesleyan University Press, 1967), p. 135.

275 *"For two hundred years the Europeans"*: Revill, *The Roaring Silence*, p. 283.

276 *"We would do well to give up the notion"*: Typescript reproduced in the exhibition catalogue *The Anarchy of Silence: John Cage and Experimental Art*, ed. Julia Robinson (MACBA, 2009), p. 268.

277 *Cagemusicircus*: See Alex Ross, "John Cage Tributes," *The New York Times*, Nov. 7, 1992.

278 *"When one dies with this world"*: Pages of Merce Cunningham's diary supplied by Laura Kuhn, John Cage Trust.

278 *"I couldn't be happier"*: From Elliot Caplan's 1991 film *Cage/Cunningham*.

18. I SAW THE LIGHT

The original version of this chapter appeared in *The New Yorker* on May 10, 1999, under the title "The Wanderer." In the course of researching the article, I attended the following Dylan shows in 1998: Puyallup, Washington, Sept. 22; Portland, Oregon, Sept. 23; Eugene, Oregon, Sept. 24; Concord, California, Sept. 25; Mountain View, California, Sept. 26; Reno, Nevada, Sept. 27; Duluth, Minnesota, Oct. 22; Minneapolis, Minnesota, Oct. 23; Chicago, Illinois, Oct. 25; and New York, New York, Nov. 1.

In addition to the works cited below, I consulted John Bauldie, ed., *Wanted Man: In Search of Bob Dylan* (Citadel, 1991); Glen Dundas, *Tangled Up in Tapes: The Recordings of Bob Dylan* (SMA Services, 1994); Michael Gray, *Song and Dance Man III: The Art of Bob Dylan* (Continuum, 2000); Clinton Heylin, *Bob Dylan: The Recording Sessions, 1960–1994* (St. Martin's, 1995); C. P. Lee, *Like the Night: Bob Dylan and the Road to the Manchester Free Trade Hall* (Helter Skelter, 1998); Wilfrid Mellers, *A Darker Shade of Pale: A Backdrop to Bob Dylan* (Oxford University Press, 1985); Robert Shelton, *No Direction Home: The Life and Music of Bob Dylan* (Da Capo, 1997); Bob Spitz, *Dylan: A Biography* (Norton, 1989); Paul Williams, *Bob Dylan: Performing Artist: 1974–1986* (Omnibus, 1994); and Paul Williams, *Bob Dylan: Watching the River Flow—Observations on His Art-in-Progress, 1966–1995* (Omnibus, 1996).

Since the article was published, several significant books on Dylan have appeared: David Hajdu, *Positively 4th Street: The Lives and Times of Joan Baez, Bob Dylan, Mimi Baez Fariña, and Richard Fariña* (Farrar, Straus and Giroux, 2001); Benjamin Hedin, ed., *Studio A: The Bob Dylan Reader* (Norton, 2004); Greil Marcus, *Like a Rolling Stone: Bob Dylan at the Crossroads* (PublicAffairs, 2005); Mike Marqusee, *Chimes of Freedom: The Politics of Bob Dylan's Art* (New Press, 2003; republished in paperback as *Wicked Messenger*); Christopher Ricks, *Dylan's Visions of Sin* (HarperCollins, 2003); and Bob Dylan, *Chronicles: Volume 1* (Simon and Schuster, 2004), which, perhaps inevitably, turns out to be the best book ever written on the subject.

281 *"I wish Bob Dylan died"*: Marc Jacobson, "Tangled Up in Gray," *The Village Voice*, Jan. 30, 1978.

281 *"My God, he sounds"*: James Wolcott, "Bob Dylan Beyond Thunderdome," in *The Dylan Companion*, ed. Elizabeth Thomson and David Gutman (Da Capo, 2001), p. 278.

281 *"Bob Dylan, who helped transform"*: Anthony Scaduto, "The Dylan Infection," *Newsday*, May 29, 1997.

281 *"Bob Dylan, whose bittersweet"*: Bruce Weber, "Dylan in Hospital with Chest Pains; Europe Tour Is Off," *The New York Times*, May 29, 1997.

284 *"one of the least talented"*: Carl Benson, ed., *The Bob Dylan Companion: Four Decades of Commentary* (Schirmer, 1998), p. x.

284 *"Even if half-mad"*: Don DeLillo, *Great Jones Street* (Penguin, 1994), p. 1.

285 *"Tarantula has six main themes"*: Robin Witting, *The Cracked Bells: A Guide to Tarantula*, rev. ed. (Exploding Rooster Books, 1995), pp. 13, 34.

286 *"a reduction of form"*: Aidan Day, *Jokerman: Reading the Lyrics of Bob Dylan* (Blackwell, 1988), p. 116.

286 *"Late April. Dylan attends"*: Clinton Heylin, *Bob Dylan: A Life in Stolen Moments—Day by Day, 1941–1995* (Schirmer, 1996), p. 149.

286 *"Between January and June 1972"*: Clinton Heylin, *Bob Dylan: Behind the Shades Revisited* (William Morrow, 2001), p. 334.

286 *"Friends describe"*: Ellen Willis, *Beginning to See the Light: Sex, Hope, and Rock-and-Roll*, 2nd ed. (Wesleyan University Press, 1992), p. 5.

287 *"There's enough of everything"*: Paul Zollo, *Songwriters on Songwriting* (Da Capo, 2003), p. 74.

287 *Joan Didion wrote of Joan Baez*: Joan Didion, *Slouching Towards Bethlehem* (Farrar, Straus and Giroux, 1968), p. 47.

288 *"Bob Dylan has walked"*: Ad reproduced in Patrick Humphries and John Bauldie, *Oh No! Not Another Bob Dylan Book* (Square One, 1991), p. 175.

288 *"I wrote that when I didn't figure"*: Anthony Scaduto, *Bob Dylan*, rev. ed. (Helter Skelter, 1996), p. 127.

289 *"Look what they did"*: Greil Marcus, *Invisible Republic: Bob Dylan's Basement Tapes* (Henry Holt, 1997; republished in paperback as *The Old, Weird America*), p. 17.

289 *"As if he had been waiting"*: Marcus, *Invisible Republic*, pp. 35–36.

290 *"I was very disappointed"*: Andy Gill, "Judas!" *The Independent*, Jan. 23, 1999. The identity of the "Judas!" shouter is contested; Andy Kershaw, in "Bob Dylan: How I Found the Man Who Shouted 'Judas,'" *The Independent*, Sept. 23, 2005, proposed that one John Cordwell should hold the title instead.

291 *"certain bedrock strains"*: Marcus, *Invisible Republic*, p. xiii.

291 *"What is this shit?"*: Greil Marcus, "Self Portrait No. 25," in Hedin, *Studio A*, p. 74.

291 *"more Dock Boggs"*: Greil Marcus, "Comeback Time Again," *The Village Voice*, Aug. 13, 1985.

291 *"If people are going to dismiss"*: Lester Bangs, "Love or Confusion?" in Hedin, *Studio A*, p. 156.

293 *"cause-chasing liberals"*: Paul Williams: *Bob Dylan: Performing Artist, 1960–1973* (Omnibus, 1994), p. 94.

293 *"Genius is a terrible word"*: Jules Siegel, "Well, What Have We Here?" *The Saturday Evening Post*, July 30, 1966, reprinted in *Bob Dylan: The Early Years—A Retrospective*, ed. Craig McGregor (Da Capo, 1990), p. 159.

298 *"I believe in Hank Williams"*: Jon Pareles, "A Wiser Voice Blowin' in the Autumn Wind," *The New York Times*, Sept. 28, 1997.

301 *"self-surrender"*: Daniel Cavicchi, *Tramps Like Us: Music and Meaning Among Springsteen Fans* (Oxford University Press, 1998), p. 43.

19. FERVOR

This chapter is an expanded version of a column that appeared in *The New Yorker* on September 25, 2006.

303 *"She simply stood there"*: Charles Shere, review in the *Oakland Tribune*, April 17, 1972, reprinted by Barbara Stack in *"In Memoriam* Lorraine Hunt Lieberson (1954–2006)," July 11, 2006, www.sfcv.org/arts_revs/lorrainehuntliebersontribute_7_11_06 .php (accessed Dec. 7, 2009).

303 *"A viola is a middle voice"*: Charles Michener, "The Soul Singer," *The New Yorker*, Jan. 5, 2004, pp. 42–43.

304 *"She started singing"*: Ibid., p. 44.

305 *"Time itself stopped"*: Richard Dyer, "Lorraine Hunt Lieberson: Her Luminous Voice Transported Listener," *The Boston Globe*, July 5, 2006.

20. BLESSED ARE THE SAD

This chapter incorporates portions of an article that appeared in *The New Republic* on March 23, 1998, under the title "Why Is Light Given?"

307 *"Two guys visit Haydn"*: Morton Feldman, *Give My Regards to Eighth Street: Collected Writings of Morton Feldman*, ed. B. H. Friedman (Exact Change, 2000), p. 166. For the original Haydn story, see Richard Will, "When God Met the Sinner and Other Dramatic Confrontations in Eighteenth-Century Instrumental Music," *Music and Letters* 78:2 (May 1997), p. 175.

307 *"That first entrance of the trombones"*: Brahms's letter to Lachner is transcribed in Reinhold Brinkmann, "Die 'heitre Sinfonie' und der 'schwer melancholische Mensch': Johannes Brahms antwortet Vincenz Lachner," *Archiv für Musikwissenschaft* 46:4 (1989), pp. 301–302.

308 *"Motets by Joh. Br."*: Styra Avins, ed., *Johannes Brahms: Life and Letters*, trans. Avins and Josef Eisinger (Oxford University Press, 1997), p. 553.

309 *"fresh beginning"*: Reinhold Brinkmann, *Late Idyll: The Second Symphony of Johannes Brahms* (Harvard University Press, 1995), pp. 88, 84.

309 *"the first major composer"*: Richard Taruskin, *The Oxford History of Western Music*, vol. 3, *The Nineteenth Century* (Oxford University Press, 2005), p. 683.

310 *"The opinion held in many quarters"*: Gunther Schuller, *The Compleat Conductor* (Oxford University Press, 1997), p. 279.

311 *"confused lack of money"*: Avins, *Johannes Brahms*, p. 4.

311 *"It seemed as though"*: Oliver Strunk and Leo Treitler, eds., *Source Readings in Music History*, rev. ed. (Norton, 1998), pp. 1157–58.

312 *"At the end, three hands"*: Avins, *Johannes Brahms*, p. 189.

313 *"exceptions or excesses"*: Ibid., pp. 150–51, 157.

313 "The memory of Schumann": Ibid., p. 449.

313 *Joachim once intimated*: Max Kalbeck, *Johannes Brahms*, vol. 1 (Wiener Verlag), p. 173.

313 *Jan Swafford . . . explains*: Jan Swafford, *Johannes Brahms: A Biography* (Knopf, 1997), p. 169.

314 *"I shall never compose"*: Brinkman, *Late Idyll*, p. 138.

315 *"Any ass can hear that"*: Max Kalbeck, *Johannes Brahms*, vol. 3 (Deutsche Brahms-Gesellschaft, 1910), p. 109.

315 *"veiled symphonies"*: Strunk and Treitler, *Source Readings in Music History*, p. 1157.

316 *"What Brahms was after"*: Schuller, *The Compleat Conductor*, p. 293.

316 *"Our life is no dream"*: Swafford, *Johannes Brahms*, p. 41.

316 *"Anti-Semitism is insanity!"*: Margaret Notley, *Lateness and Brahms: Music and*

Culture in the Twilight of Viennese Liberalism (Oxford University Press, 2006), p. 211. For Little Bighorn, see Swafford, *Brahms*, p. 530.

317 *"tomorrow in Handel's Hallelujah wig"*: Robert W. Gutman, *Richard Wagner: The Man, His Mind, and His Music* (Harcourt Brace, 1968), p. 397.

317 *"I give the best and most appropriate thanks"*: Avins, *Johannes Brahms*, p. 479.

317 *"[Brahms] knew his own worth"*: Ethel Smyth, *Impressions That Remained: Memoirs* (Knopf, 1946), p. 238.

318 *"Art is a republic"*: Swafford, *Johannes Brahms*, p. 180.

318 *"If you continue on right away"*: Avins, *Johannes Brahms*, pp. 347–48.

318 *"furrowed, even ravaged"*: Theodor W. Adorno, *Essays on Music*, ed. Richard Leppert, trans. Susan H. Gillespie (University of California Press, 2002), p. 564.

319 *Brinkmann devotes*: Brinkmann, *Late Idyll*, pp. 125–44.

319 *"Look, Herr Doktor!"*: Ernst Decsey, "Stunden mit Mahler," *Die Musik* 10:21 (1910/1911), p. 146.

320 *Brahms nods several times*: On Wagner allusions in Brahms, see David Brodbeck, "Brahms, the Third Symphony, and the New German School," in *Brahms and His World*, ed. Walter Frisch (Princeton University Press, 1990), pp. 65–80; and Robert Bailey, "Musical Language and Structure in the Third Symphony," in *Brahms Studies: Analytical and Historical Perspectives*, ed. George S. Bozarth (Clarendon, 1990), pp. 408–409.

320 *"allowing a soloist to emerge"*: Margaret Notley, "Late-Nineteenth-Century Chamber Music and the Cult of the Classical Adagio," *19th-Century Music* 23:1 (Summer 1999), p. 59.

321 *"unrestricted musical language"*: Arnold Schoenberg, *Style and Idea: Selected Writings of Arnold Schoenberg*, ed. Leonard Stein, trans. Leo Black (University of California Press, 1984), p. 441.

321 *"'Sing Lullabies of My Sorrow'"*: Max Kalbeck, *Johannes Brahms*, vol. 4 (Deutsche Brahms-Gesellschaft, 1914), p. 281. For the matching of words to the melody of Opus 117 No. 1, see p. 279.

322 *as Raymond Knapp notes*: Raymond Knapp, "The Finale of Brahms's Fourth Symphony: The Tale of the Subject," *19th-Century Music* 13:1 (Summer 1989), p. 10.

322 *"Es fiel . . . ihm wie"*: Swafford, *Johannes Brahms*, p. 4.

322 *"frozen"*: Walter Frisch, *Brahms: The Four Symphonies* (Yale University Press, 2003), p. 125.

322 *As Notley observes*: Margaret Notley, "Plagal Harmony as Other: Asymmetrical Dualism and Instrumental Music by Brahms," *The Journal of Musicology* 22:1 (Winter 2005), pp. 128–29.

323 *modern conductors drag*: On slowing tempos in modern Brahms performance, see Frisch, *Brahms: The Four Symphonies*, pp. 163–88; and Walter Frisch, "Whose Brahms Is It Anyway?: Observations on the Recorded Legacy of the B-flat Piano Concerto, Op. 83," in *Musical Meaning and Human Values*, ed. Keith Chapin and Lawrence Kramer (Fordham University Press, 2009), pp. 102–15.

323 *"perhaps the most extraordinary"*: Frisch, *Brahms: The Four Symphonies*, p. 130.

323 *Knapp also argues*: Knapp, "The Finale of Brahms's Fourth Symphony," pp. 6–8.

323 *"On a single staff"*: Avins, *Johannes Brahms*, p. 515.

324 *"I cannot get away"*: Brinkmann, *Late Idyll*, p. 221. For Mann, see pp. 222–25.

SUGGESTED LISTENING

These recommendations reflect one listener's taste; prospective buyers can compare audio samples online before making any purchases. All recordings are available as this book goes to press, although some will inevitably go out of print as record companies reduce their catalogues. Most are also available as MP3 downloads.

LISTEN TO THIS

A secondhand LP of Leonard Bernstein conducting Beethoven's *Eroica* Symphony ignited my love of classical music. Although kids today might just as easily fall under the spell of Stravinsky's *Rite of Spring* or Steve Reich's *Music for 18 Musicians*, Beethoven's indestructible masterwork remains a logical place to start. According to an online discography maintained by Eric Grunin, more than five hundred recordings of the *Eroica* have entered circulation since the invention of the phonograph: they range from the sinewy Arturo Toscanini (a 1939 live version with the NBC Symphony captures the maestro at white heat) to the compellingly neurotic Wilhelm Furtwängler (his grittiest reading comes from December 1944, with the Vienna Philharmonic) to the granitic Otto Klemperer (a 1959 EMI recording with the Philharmonia Orchestra is the most commanding of various efforts). Bernstein's vigorous *Eroica* with the New York Philharmonic is currently available on a Sony disc that also includes the conductor's *Eroica* lecture ("There has been a stab of intrusive otherness"). If you're looking for a complete set of the Beethoven nine, Herbert von Karajan's 1961–62 survey with the Berliners (DG) is consistently satisfying, though a little lacking in fire. Osmo Vänskä's cycle with the Minnesota Orchestra (BIS) is a formidable modern rival.

CHACONA, LAMENTO, WALKING BLUES

Juan Arañés's "Un sarao de la chacona," a joyous example of the original chacona dance, springs to life on the collection *Villancicos y Danzas Criollas*, with Jordi Savall leading Hespèrion XXI and La Capella Reial de Catalunya (Alia Vox). Johannes Ockeghem's somber *Missa Fors seulement* is resonantly sung by the Schola Discantus on a Lyrichord disc. Savall and company have also produced the most bewitching of all recordings of John Dowland's *Lachrimae*, although at the moment it is available only as an MP3 download (Alia Vox). Andreas Scholl lends his pure-toned, emotionally charged countertenor to Dowland songs on the albums *A Musicall Banquet* (Decca) and *Crystal Tears* (Harmonia Mundi).

Various classic arias of lament, including Hecuba's apocalyptic threnody from Cavalli's *Didone*, appear on the disc *Lamenti*, with Emmanuelle Haïm conducting Le Concert d'Astrée and assorted star singers (Virgin Classics). The Concerto Vocale's recording of Monteverdi's *Madrigali guerrieri ed amorosi* (Harmonia Mundi) has a strikingly sensuous *Lamento della ninfa*. There have been many lovely versions of Purcell's *Dido and Aeneas*; I cherish a 1994 Harmonia Mundi CD with Lorraine Hunt Lieberson as Dido and Nicholas McGegan conducting the Philharmonia Baroque. The discography of Bach's cycle of Sonatas and Partitas, which includes the Ciaccona in D Minor, is intimidatingly large, embracing most of the major violinists of the past hundred years; among latter-day recordings, I'd choose the idiosyncratic, questing Gidon Kremer on ECM. In the awesome realm of Bach's B-Minor Mass, no conductor has gone deeper than Philippe Herreweghe, the leader of the Collegium Vocale Gent; his second account of the work, for Harmonia Mundi, sets the modern standard.

INFERNAL MACHINES

Exploring the early archives of recording requires a tolerance for hiss, pop, crackle, and other artifacts of premagnetic technology. One obvious starting point is Enrico Caruso, whose golden tenor was first captured in 1902; the Nimbus label provides a robust-sounding Caruso anthology in its Prima

Voce series, although the tenor's recordings have now entered public domain and have proliferated on the Internet (see www.archive.org/details/Caruso _part1 or search YouTube). Edward Elgar's startlingly brash, freewheeling performances of his own works have appeared on various labels; in a volume of EMI's Great Recordings of the Century series, he guides the teenage Yehudi Menuhin through his Violin Concerto. EMI also offers Bruno Walter's haunting interpretation of the Mahler Ninth Symphony, recorded live with the Vienna Philharmonic on the eve of the Anschluss; the British audio wizard Michael Dutton has released an even better remastering on his Dutton Laboratories label.

THE STORM OF STYLE

Mozart playing has changed drastically over the past century: a lush Romantic style has given way to crisper attacks and leaner textures. A paragon of the old school is Carlo Maria Giulini's towering 1959 recording of *Don Giovanni*, which boasts one of those lustrous casts that the British producer Walter Legge assembled so effortlessly for EMI in the postwar era: Eberhard Wächter as the Don, Joan Sutherland as Donna Anna, Elisabeth Schwarzkopf as Donna Elvira, Giuseppe Taddei as Leporello, and Gottlob Frick emitting pitch-black sounds as the Commendatore. Yet, as the countertenor-turned-conductor René Jacobs has proved in a slew of original-instrument Mozart recordings for Harmonia Mundi, the golden age of the LP has no monopoly on this composer. Jacobs's *Marriage of Figaro*, with Lorenzo Regazzo as Figaro, Patrizia Ciofi as Susanna, and Simon Keenlyside as the Count, is wonderfully nimble and raucous, as if the story were being told from Figaro's point of view rather than from the Count's. Four other Mozart opera favorites: Erich Kleiber's *Figaro* (Decca), Otto Klemperer's *The Magic Flute* (EMI), Karl Böhm's *Così fan tutte* (EMI), and Charles Mackerras's *Idomeneo* (EMI).

A long procession of major pianists—Walter Gieseking, Rudolf Serkin, Clifford Curzon, Sviatoslav Richter, Alfred Brendel, Alicia de Larrocha, and Mitsuko Uchida, among others—has graced the Mozart piano concertos. No player is more direct, more devoid of artifice, and more warmly human than Richard Goode, who has recorded eight of the major concertos with the Orpheus Chamber Orchestra (Nonesuch). Mackerras's set of the Symphonies Nos. 38–41 with the Scottish Chamber Orchestra (Linn) is bracingly clear and brisk. In the chamber music, I recommend as a point of departure a three-CD set of the magnificently varied String Quintets with the Grumiaux Trio and allied players (Philips). Every year brings new recordings of the Requiem, Mozart's tragically unfinished farewell; the one led by Peter Schreier, which appears both on a single disc and as part of the Philips Mozart edition, achieves rugged authenticity from the start.

ORBITING

The brainy blokes of Radiohead have generated eight studio albums to date, with another in the works as of this writing. If you like your rock and roll with clear-cut tunes, you will probably be happiest with the band's second and third efforts, *The Bends* (1995) and *OK Computer* (1997). If you have an ear for off-kilter harmonies and twitchy electronic textures, you may prefer *Kid A* (2000), *Amnesiac* (2001), and *Hail to the Thief* (2003). Radiohead's most recent albums, the self-released *In Rainbows* (2007) and *The King of Limbs* (2011), hold melody and texture in even balance; they contain the band's subtlest, mellowest work. The best of Radiohead's various EPs and singles is *Airbag/How Am I Driving?*, which has the sinuous instrumental "Meeting in the Aisle" and the postmodern anthem "Palo Alto."

THE ANTI-MAESTRO

The composer-conductor Esa-Pekka Salonen has a knack for making necessary recordings. A twentieth-century specialist, he combines a modernist yen for complexity with a Nordic feeling for landscape. One of his first projects with the Los Angeles Philharmonic was to record Witold Lutosławski's Third Symphony, which applies an avant-garde vocabulary to a sprawling symphonic structure; that pioneering effort is still available on Sony, paired with Lutosławski's Fourth. For the same label, Salonen and the L.A. Phil surveyed the film music of Bernard Herrmann, focusing on the famous Alfred Hitchcock scores (*Vertigo*, *Psycho*). Moving to the DG label, Salonen fashioned one of the tautest modern interpretations of Stravinsky's *Rite of Spring* (with Bartók's *Miraculous Mandarin* Suite and Mussorgsky's *Night on Bald Mountain*). He has also produced definitive readings of Magnus Lindberg's *Kraft*, with the Finnish Radio Symphony (Ondine); John Adams's *Naïve and Sentimental Music*, with the L.A. Phil (Nonesuch);

and Kaija Saariaho's opera *L'Amour de loin*, with Gerald Finley, Dawn Upshaw, and forces from the Finnish National Opera (DG DVD). There are
four discs of Salonen's own music, showing a progression from antic avant-
gardism to enlightened eclecticism. Begin with the DG collection *Wing on
Wing*: the high-tech textures of the title work shimmer like the wings of
Disney Hall.

GREAT SOUL

In Schubert, absolute precision of execution matters less than unerring
identification with the composer's mercurial moods. In this respect, older
recordings often win out over newer ones, where too often the notes glitter
in place but the emotions are held in check. Almost all modern accounts
of the String Quintet in C fade next to a 1952 recording from Pablo
Casals's Prades Festival, with Isaac Stern, Alexander Schneider, Milton
Katims, Paul Tortelier, and Casals himself (Sony). Intonation wobbles,
notes are dropped here and there, and someone keeps grunting, but the
sustained legato in the slow movement is like light pouring in from another
world. For an extraordinary compendium of pre–Second World War Schubert playing, search the Internet for a four-CD set of the chamber music
on the now dormant Andante label. Again, the lyrical intensity of the performances, featuring such legendary musicians as Casals, Alfred Cortot,
Jacques Thibaud, Adolf Busch, Rudolf Serkin, Artur Schnabel, Sergei
Rachmaninov, and Fritz Kreisler, makes most modern renditions of this
music sound coldly clinical.

Still, many first-rate Schubert discs have emerged from the digital age.
Klaus Tennstedt's 1983 recording of the Ninth Symphony with the Berlin
Philharmonic (EMI) has a fine dancing energy, appropriate to Schubert's
brawniest work. Leonard Bernstein's reading of the Ninth with the New
York Philharmonic (Sony) shows a similar vitality, and is paired with a handsomely brooding "Unfinished." In the song cycle *Winterreise*, the singer
must convey existential solitude and more than a trace of madness; to my
taste, a high-lying tenor voice communicates that desperation better than
a baritone, and so, in place of classic recordings by Hans Hotter and Dietrich
Fischer-Dieskau, I recommend an acutely expressive Decca CD with Peter Schreier and András Schiff. Hyperion's epochal survey of Schubert
songs—thirty-seven volumes in all—is neatly distilled on a disc of high-

lights, titled "Voyage of Discovery." Pianists on the order of Schnabel, Clifford Curzon, and Sviatoslav Richter have made their mark on Schubert's august Sonata in B-flat; the young players Paul Lewis and Inon Barnatan (on Harmonia Mundi and Bridge) prove that the poetic sensibility of the prewar era has by no means died away.

EMOTIONAL LANDSCAPES

As with Radiohead, Björk's records fall roughly into two phases, one tending toward pop and the other toward the electronic and classical avant-garde. Her first mature solo albums, *Debut* (1993) and *Post* (1995), are stocked with manically singable anthems ("Venus as a Boy," "Isobel," "Hyper-ballad"). *Homogenic* (1997) inaugurated her "avant" period, which culminated in *Vespertine* (2001) and *Medúlla* (2004). *Vespertine* is the most magically Björkian work of the lot—an organic song cycle comparable to Radiohead's *Kid A*, from the previous year. *Selmasongs* is a hybrid 2000 album derived from Björk's semi-symphonic soundtrack to the Lars von Trier film *Dancer in the Dark*. Björk has also sent forth various live records, box sets, and videos; the collection *Family Tree* contains, among other quirky treasures, her Messiaen-infused version of "Cover Me." Since my profile appeared, in 2004, Björk has released another soundtrack, the densely orchestrated *Drawing Restraint 9* (for a film by Matthew Barney), and another full-length album, *Volta* ("Declare Independence" is a new Björk classic). Her 1996 performance of Schoenberg's *Pierrot lunaire*, with Kent Nagano conducting, has yet to materialize on recording, although samizdat excerpts have surfaced on the Internet.

SYMPHONY OF MILLIONS

Tan Dun is the most often recorded of contemporary Chinese composers, although he may not prove to be the most significant. His operas *Marco Polo, Tea,* and *The First Emperor* are all currently available on DVD, along with such multimedia works as *Paper Concerto, Water Concerto,* and *The Map.* Only the last-named piece—a cello concerto interspersed with video portraits of traditional Chinese musicians—succeeds fully in uniting East and West. Chen Yi and Zhou Long, two other members of Tan Dun's generation, have long been resident in America; the Beijing New Music Ensemble, under the leadership of Eli Marshall, has recorded several of their works on a Naxos disc titled *Wild Grass*. Guo Wenjing, who stayed behind in China, has been almost entirely ignored in the West, although samples of his music float around YouTube.

SONG OF THE EARTH

The Alaskan composer John Luther Adams may not be a household name, but almost a dozen recordings devoted to his sub-Arctic soundscapes have appeared. The 1993 disc *The Far Country* (New Albion) shows Adams working in a more traditional orchestral mode, at times brushing against the *Fanfare for the Common Man* style of Aaron Copland, although the glacial unfolding of events hints at the composer's mature voice. His real break-through occurred in the immensely spacious chamber-orchestra pieces *Clouds of Forgetting, Clouds of Unknowing* and *In the White Silence*, both of which have discs to themselves on New World. Adams's violently inventive writing for percussion can be heard on *Strange and Sacred Noise* (Mode CD/DVD) and *The Mathematics of Resonant Bodies* (Cantaloupe). The Cold Blue disc *Red Arc/Blue Veil* contains the two-piano version of *Dark Waves*, one of Adams's most gripping recent works. To hear *The Place Where You Go to Listen*, you must book a flight to Fairbanks, Alaska, and drop by the Museum of the North at the University of Alaska.

VERDI'S GRIP

You might begin at the zenith, with *Otello*. It battles *Don Giovanni* and *Tristan und Isolde* for the title of the greatest opera ever written, and on many nights it wins. Having witnessed Plácido Domingo's wrenching embodiment of the lead role at the Met in 1994, I'm tempted to pick the *Otello* recording that the tenor made the previous year, under Myung-Whun Chung's direction (DG), but Cheryl Studer's Desdemona is a bit eccentric. Instead, I'd choose Domingo's earlier, scarcely less gripping effort, which has Renata Scotto as Desdemona, Sherrill Milnes as Iago, and James Levine on the podium (RCA). Then it is necessary to have something by Maria Callas. Her volcanic 1955 live performance of *La traviata* at La Scala is preserved on EMI; Giuseppe di Stefano sings incisively as Alfredo, and Carlo Maria Giulini conducts. It is also advisable to have one of Leontyne Price's regal Verdi interpretations—perhaps her 1961 *Aida*, with Jon Vickers as Radamès and Georg Solti conducting (Decca); or her 1962 *Trovatore*, with Franco Corelli as Manrico, Giulietta Simionato as

Azucena, and Herbert von Karajan in the pit (DG). I'd balance those diva-driven tours-de-force with Claudio Abbado's rich-hued take on *Simon Boccanegra*, featuring Piero Cappuccilli, Mirella Freni, and José Carreras (DG); and Karajan's crackling *Falstaff*, in which Tito Gobbi is alive to every nuance of the title role (EMI). For early Verdi, a good first choice is Giuseppe Sinopoli's *Nabucco*, with Cappuccilli, Domingo, and a smoldering Ghena Dimitrova (DG).

ALMOST FAMOUS

The St. Lawrence Quartet has so far put out six discs on the EMI label and one on Naxos. The most distinctive of the series is *Yiddishbbuk*, devoted to the Argentinian-born composer Osvaldo Golijov, whose extroverted, folk-inflected music matches the quartet's spirit; in the clarinet quintet *The Dreams and Prayers of Isaac the Blind*, they provide a vibrant background for the klezmer stylings of the clarinetist Todd Palmer. Two other outstanding releases are a trio of Shostakovich quartets—Nos. 3, 7, and 8—and a pairing of Tchaikovsky's First and Third Quartets.

EDGES OF POP

This chapter glances at artists from all over the popular map: the cabaret duo Kiki and Herb, the free-jazz master Cecil Taylor, the avant-rock band Sonic Youth, the incomparable crooner Frank Sinatra, and the anguished rock star Kurt Cobain. If I had to choose representative discs for each, I'd pick Taylor's 1978 album 3 *Phasis*, with Jimmy Lyons, Raphé Malik, Ramsey Ameen, Sirone, and Ronald Shannon Jackson (New World); Sonic Youth's 1988 album *Daydream Nation* (Geffen); Sinatra's *Only the Lonely*, with ravishing arrangements by Nelson Riddle (Capitol); and Nirvana's enduring hit *Nevermind* (Geffen). As for Kiki and Herb, who went on indefinite hiatus in 2008, they have left behind a suitably demented document of their Carnegie Hall debut, a live album titled *Kiki and Herb Will Die for You*.

VOICE OF THE CENTURY

On a VAI disc titled *Marian Anderson: Rare and Unpublished Recordings, 1936–1952*, the iconic contralto basks in the lamenting glow of Purcell's

"When I am laid in earth" and delivers chilling renditions of Schubert's "Der Doppelgänger" and "Der Erlkönig." On a similarly varied Pearl disc, she applies her cavernous lower register to Brahms's *Alto Rhapsody* and lavishes care on songs of Sibelius. Alas, most commercial releases from the 1950s show Anderson in steadily declining voice. No recording captures the luminous aura that so many listeners ascribed to the singer in her prime; we can only imagine what she must have been like. Nina Simone's searing rewrite of "Strange Fruit" appears on the double CD *Anthology* (RCA).

THE MUSIC MOUNTAIN

Rudolf Serkin and Adolf Busch, the presiding spirits of Marlboro Music in Vermont, made many recordings together and with members of their extended family. Busch and Serkin play together on the Andante Schubert set mentioned above; on an EMI disc, you can hear the Busch Quartet's furiously committed readings of the final two Schubert quartets. ArkivMusic.com offers an out-of-print Sony disc containing two adamantine Serkin performances from Marlboro: Beethoven's Piano Concerto No. 4 and his *Choral Fantasy*, with Alexander Schneider conducting. Still in print is a much-loved 1967 rendition of Schubert's "Trout" Quintet by Serkin and various Marlboro collaborators; it's paired with Mozart's Clarinet Quintet. The current co-directors of Marlboro, Mitsuko Uchida and Richard Goode, have both released dozens of discs. Goode's Mozart concertos are praised above; the pianist has also applied his uncommonly lyrical touch to the five Beethoven concertos (Nonesuch). Important Uchida recordings include her impeccable cycle of Mozart concertos, her "Hammerklavier" Sonata, her Debussy Études, and her Schoenberg Piano Concerto, all on Philips.

THE END OF SILENCE

As of this writing, Mode Records' monumental Cage Edition runs to forty-two volumes. Two excellent points of departure are Philipp Vandré's CD of the *Sonatas and Interludes,* Cage's most ambitious work for prepared piano; and the Arditti Quartet's recording of *String Quartet in Four Parts* and *Four*—austerely beautiful pieces from earlier and later stages of

Cage's career. Almost everything in the Mode series is done with careful attention to the composer's intention and spirit. An ECM CD titled *The Seasons* supplies a superb single-disc survey, setting the attenuated lyricism of the prepared-piano music against later experiments in chance. Wergo's reissue of *The 25-Year Retrospective Concert of the Music of John Cage*—a celebratory concert at Town Hall, New York, on May 15, 1958—gives you a sense of the controversy that swirled around Cage in the 1950s and '60s; boos compete with applause after the presentation of the tape collage *Williams Mix*.

I SAW THE LIGHT

Bob Dylan has put out nearly fifty studio and live albums since he joined the Columbia label in 1961. *The Freewheelin' Bob Dylan* is the strongest record of his early, folk-oriented period; *Highway 61 Revisited* and *Blonde on Blonde* are the twin peaks of his electric mid-sixties phase; *Blood on the Tracks* is the prize of the seventies; and *Time Out of Mind*, from 1997, ushered in a darkly searching late period, which has continued with *"Love and Theft,"* *Modern Times*, and *Together Through Life*. Dylan's famous 1966 live show in Manchester, England ("Judas!") is available as Volume 4 of Columbia's *Bootleg Series*. The true Dylan obsessive must go beyond official releases into the murky realm of bootlegs, where some of the Maestro's most remarkable achievements still lie hidden. My playlist of favorite bootlegs includes "Freeze Out," the first draft of "Visions of Johanna"; "Million Dollar Bash" and "Sign on the Cross," from the complete Basement Tapes; "Abandoned Love," live at the Other End in 1975; "The Groom's Still Waiting at the Altar," live in San Francisco in 1980, with Mike Bloomfield on guitar; "The Lonesome Death of Hattie Carroll," live at the El Rey in 1997; and the initial version of *Blood on the Tracks*, a more intimate and harrowing creation than the commercial release, and the most transfixing work of Dylan's career.

FERVOR

The mezzo-soprano Lorraine Hunt Lieberson, like Marian Anderson before her, exerted in person a quasi-spiritual force that recordings never fully captured. Perhaps the best evidence of her uncanny art is a Kultur DVD of Handel's *Theodora*, from the Glyndebourne Festival, with Peter Sellars directing, William Christie conducting the Orchestra of the Age of Enlightenment, and Dawn Upshaw, David Daniels, and Richard Croft assuming other lead roles. Two other essential documents of her animating way with Baroque repertory are a disc of Bach's Cantatas Nos. 82 and 199, with Craig Smith conducting the Emmanuel Music Orchestra (Nonesuch), and a collection of Handel arias, with Harry Bicket leading the Orchestra of the Age of Enlightenment (Avie). A Wigmore Hall Live release, preserving a 1998 recital with Roger Vignoles at the piano, shows her sympathy not only for Handel but also for Brahms and Mahler. It's difficult to speak objectively about her account of Peter Lieberson's *Neruda Songs*, with James Levine conducting the Boston Symphony (Nonesuch); the recording was made less than eight months before her death, and it burns with private passion.

BLESSED ARE THE SAD

Behind Brahms's professorial façade was a well of deep feeling. The challenge in interpreting his music is to reconcile that feeling with the orderly forms that contain it. The First Piano Concerto is Brahms at his darkest and boldest; with regretful glances at recordings by Emil Gilels and Leon Fleisher, I'll stay with a longtime companion, Clifford Curzon's monumental rendition with George Szell and the London Symphony (Decca). No set of the four symphonies is perfect, although a Music & Arts compilation of live Furtwängler performances is riveting throughout, and Charles Mackerras's cycle with the Scottish Chamber Orchestra (Telarc) delivers exceptionally lucid rhythms. For the First Symphony alone, I'd suggest either Klemperer and the Philharmonia (EMI) or Toscanini and the NBC Symphony (live in 1940, available at pristineclassical.com); for the Second, Mackerras; for the Third, Bruno Walter and the Columbia Symphony (Sony); and for the Fourth, Carlos Kleiber and the Vienna Philharmonic (DG)—one of the most potent symphonic recordings ever made. Klemperer's *German Requiem*, with Elisabeth Schwarzkopf and Dietrich Fischer-Dieskau as the soloists (EMI), is ponderous in the best sense: slow, grave, grandly moving. For an introduction to Brahms's chamber music, try a warmly idiomatic collection of quartets, quintets, and sextets by the Amadeus Quartet and various colleagues (DG). Radu Lupu's disc of the late Intermezzos and Piano Pieces, Opp. 117–119 (Decca), contains playing of such unmannered beauty that you seem to meet the elusive soul of Brahms face-to-face.

ACKNOWLEDGMENTS

During my time at *The New Yorker*, I have been under the benign control of two great editors, both of whom contributed decisively to my development as a writer. Charles Michener read passionately, broadened my musical sympathies, and proved to be an improbably convivial supervisor, to the point where the laughter emanating from his office drew puzzled stares. When Charles left, I was fortunate to fall into the hands of Daniel Zalewski, who is younger than I, and wiser. I am profoundly indebted to Daniel's panoptic vision, pinpoint editing, fervent advocacy, and uncommonly generous spirit. David Remnick, the editor of *The New Yorker*, is a model boss and a model colleague; I consider myself lucky to be living in his golden age.

Tina Brown, during her tenure at the magazine, hired me and let me roam free. Pam McCarthy, Henry Finder, and Dorothy Wickenden, in the editorial offices, and David Denby, Nancy Franklin, Joan Acocella, Sasha Frere-Jones, David Grann, and Luke Menand, in the writers' warrens, have been intensely supportive over the years. *The New Yorker*'s copy editors, led by the wizardly Ann Goldstein, have deepened my love of language. The fact-checker for most of these pieces was Martin Baron, who has since retired; in my previous book, I called him "the greatest fact-checker that ever was or ever will be," and I stand by the claim. I'm also grateful to Nana Asfour, Jake Goldstein, Nandi Rodrigo, Jennifer Stahl, and Greg Villepique for their excellent checking work. Peter Canby, Leo Carey, Will Cohen, Bruce Diones, Kate Julian, Daniel Kile, Russell Platt, Lauren Porcaro, Aaron Retica, and Rhonda Sherman helped out at one time or another.

Many people contributed to the making of these essays. I'd especially like to thank Radiohead (most of all Colin Greenwood), Courtyard Management, Steve Martin of Nasty Little Man, Esa-Pekka Salonen, Deborah Borda, Adam Crane, Björk, Scott Rodger, Valgeir Sigurðsson, Árni Heimir Ingólfsson, Ken Smith and Joanna Lee, Nick Frisch (an invaluable guide in Beijing), John Luther Adams, Hassan Ralph Williams, Joe Horowitz, Sebastian Ruth, Frank Salomon, Mitsuko Uchida, Leon Wieseltier, and Alex Abramovich, my Dylan road companion. I received scholarly counsel from Will Crutchfield, Drew Davies, Walter Everett, Walter Frisch, Luis Gago (who noticed the resemblance between Nina Simone's "Strange Fruit" and "Der Doppelgänger"), Christopher Gibbs, Philip Gossett, Wendy Heller, Andrew Patner, Ellen Rosand, Alexander Silbiger, and Richard Taruskin. Alex Star, Paula Puhak, Jason Shure, and Mike Vazquez, ex-WHRB DJs, converted me to punk rock, and Steven Johnson alerted me to Radiohead. The Goldstines—Josh, Stephanie, Eli, Theo, Danny, and Hilary—make trips west a joy. Ellen Pfeifer of the New England Conservatory and Jane Gottlieb of the Juilliard Library assisted with research inquiries. Jake Holmes, Peter Bartók, Sigríður Þorgrímsdóttir, and Jeff Rosen of Special Rider Music were most generous with permissions.

Eric Chinski is again the book editor of my dreams; I am still reeling from the magnanimity that he showed in the making of *The Rest Is Noise*. Jonathan Galassi, Laurel Cook, and Jeff Seroy provided yet more vital support at FSG; Eugenie Cha elegantly disposed of nagging details; John McGhee was a quick, incisive copy editor; Charlotte Strick made another brilliant cover; Chris Peterson, the production editor, guided the book smartly to the end. Tina Bennett, my agent, continues to work magic on my behalf, as does Dorothy Vincent. William Robin, my assistant and fellow blogger, was hugely helpful in researching, checking, and fine-tuning the manuscript. Maulina, Bea, and Minnie brightened my days; Penelope is ever so missed. My parents; my brother, Christopher; and my beautiful husband, Jonathan, surrounded me with love.

INDEX

ILLUSTRATION CREDITS

22 Detail of "Misero Apollo" from Francesco Cavalli's *Gli amori d'Apollo e di Dafne*. Reproduced by kind permission of the Biblioteca Nazionale Marciana, Venice.

26 A *bocet*, or Romanian lament, as recorded by Béla Bartók in the village of Mânerău in 1917. Reproduced by kind permission of Peter Bartók and the Columbia University Rare Book and Manuscript Library.

29 Johannes Ockeghem's "Fors seulement," from the late-fifteenth-century Wolfenbütteler Chansonnier. Reproduced by kind permission of the Herzog August Bibliothek Wolfenbüttel.

37 "Misero Apollo" from Francesco Cavalli's *Gli amori d'Apollo e di Dafne*. Reproduced by kind permission of the Biblioteca Nazionale Marciana, Venice.

38 Hecuba's lament from Cavalli's *Didone*. Reproduced by kind permission of the Biblioteca Nazionale Marciana, Venice.

41 "When I am laid in earth" from Purcell's *Dido and Aeneas*, in an eighteenth-century copy. Reproduced by kind permission of the Juilliard Manuscript Collection.

43 The Ciaccona of Bach's Partita No. 2 for solo violin, in an anonymous copy made in the mid- or late-eighteenth century. Reproduced from volume 44 of the Bach-Gesellschaft Ausgabe, published in 1895.

45 The "Crucifixus" of Bach's B-Minor Mass, in Bach's hand. Reproduced from volume 44 of the Bach-Gesellschaft Ausgabe.

47 From the coda of the first movement of Beethoven's Ninth Symphony, in the working copy prepared for the first publication. Reproduced by kind permission of the Juilliard Manuscript Collection.

53 The initial bass line of Jake Holmes's "Dazed and Confused." Reproduced by kind permission of Jake Holmes.

PERMISSIONS ACKNOWLEDGMENTS

Grateful acknowledgment is made for permission to reprint excerpts from the following previously published material:

"Listening in October" from *Winter News*, copyright © 1966 by John Haines. Reprinted by permission of Wesleyan University Press.

"Return to Richardson, Spring 1981" from *Of Your Passage, O Summer*, copyright © 2004 by John Haines. Reprinted by permission of Limberlost Press.

"Vökuró" from *Kvæði*, copyright © 1960 by Jakobína Sigurðardóttir. Reprinted by permission of Mál og menning.

Grateful acknowledgment is made for permission to reprint lyrics from the following:

BJÖRK
"Hidden Place," words and music by Björk Guðmundsdóttir, Guy Sigsworth, and Mark Bell, copyright © 2002 by Universal Music Corp., EMI Virgin Music, Inc., and Warp Music Ltd. All rights for Warp Music Ltd. controlled and administered by EMI Virgin Music, Inc. All rights reserved. Used by permission. Reprinted by permission of Hal Leonard Corporation.